Writers on Writing

Epictetus	If you wish to be a good writer, write.
George Meredith	The art of the pen is to rouse the inward vision.
Elizabeth Janeway	Great writers leave us not just their works, but a way of looking at things.
Rachel Carson	The discipline of the writer is to learn to be still and listen to what his subject has to tell him.
Joanne Greenburg	Your writing is trying to tell you something. Just lend an ear.
W. H. Auden	Language is the mother, not the handmaiden, of thought: words will tell you things you never thought or felt before.
Rudyard Kipling	Words are, of course, the most powerful drug used by mankind.
Mark Twain	A powerful agent is the right word.
Ralph Waldo Emerson	Good writing is a kind of skating which carries off the performer where he would not go.
Gabriel Fielding	Writing to me is a voyage, an odyssey, a discovery, because I'm never certain of precisely what I will find.
Henry Miller	Writing, like life itself, is a voyage of discovery.
John Updike	Writing and rewriting are a constant search for what one is saying.
Robert Hayden	As you continue writing and rewriting, you begin to see possibilities you hadn't seen before.
William Stafford	I don't see writing as a communication of something already discovered, as "truths" already known. Rather, I see writing as a job of experiment. It's like any discovery job; you don't know what's going to happen until you try it.

WRITING:
Discovering Form
and Meaning

Writing:

Discovering Form and Meaning

Charles W. Bridges
New Mexico State University

Ronald F. Lunsford
Clemson University

Wadsworth Publishing Company
Belmont, California
A Division of Wadsworth, Inc.

English Editor: Kevin J. Howat
Production Editor: Sally Schuman
Interior and Cover Design: MaryEllen Podgorski
Copy Editor: Jonas Weisel
Illustrator: Blakeley Graphics
Signing Representatives: Jane Moulton, Nancy Tandberg

Printed in the United States of America

2 3 4 5 6 7 8 9 10—88 87 86 85 84

ISBN 0-534-02998-1

Library of Congress Cataloging in Publication Data

Bridges, Charles W.
    Writing—discovering form and meaning.

    Includes index.
    1. English language—Rhetoric.   I. Lunsford, Ronald F.
II. Title.
PE1408.B693   1984   808'.042   83-14789
ISBN 0-534-02998-1

Preface

What does it mean to write? This is the question we attempt to answer in this book. We see writing as a creative act steeped in discovery—as the writer moves the pen across the page, she creates, discovers, and shapes meaning. Our purpose in writing this text is to help student writers find ways into this creating, discovering, and shaping process.

Our basic assumptions are these:

1. that writing is a powerful means of learning. Through writing, the writer refines his thinking. He toys with ideas; ideas toy with him.

2. that writing is a recursive act that most often proceeds not smoothly but in fits and starts as the writer struggles to find meaning.

3. that writing must be marked by significance. Thus, the writer's task is to reveal her insight into a particular topic to a reader.

4. that form is a function of meaning.

In structuring this book, we have moved from the self of the writer outward, from the writer on a personal level to a more public level. But even on the public level, we have stressed the necessity of the writer's interpreting his topic so that he uses writing first to settle his own mind about the topic and then to report this "settling" to the reader. To shape this movement, we have chosen James Britton's division of expressive, transactional, and poetic writing, though we have, out of necessity, not discussed poetic writing at any length.

In Part One—Discovering Meaning—we focus on *expressive writing* to help the writer see that she does have things to say and that she must find her own stance on a topic. The best way to do these initially is to ground the writer in her own experience. From this point, we move outward in Part Two—Shaping Meaning—to *transactional writing*, stressing the writer's need to shape her meaning for wider audiences and to go beyond herself to find that meaning.

In Part Three—Refining Writing—we focus on the effect of words, sentences, and paragraphs on a potential reader, while in Part Four—Editing—we focus on various aspects of grammar and mechanics. These last two sections constitute a brief handbook for writing. We have chosen, however, not to present them under the label of "handbook" because we want to emphasize that revising is something the writer may do at any point in his writing; it is more than just a final stage of writing in which the writer tidies an essay. In integrating Parts Three and Four into our rhetoric, we intend to stress the important role revision plays in the writing process.

To help the student move through the writing process, we present a seven-step model of writing. Although this model is certainly not the only model of the writing process, it is a model our own students have found helpful, especially in the early stages of a writing course. The process we present began as a description of what we do when we write; at its core is the need to revise extensively and continuously.

Part of this seven-step model is a set of questions, titled "Questions for Analysis," which is designed to help students discover information about their topics. We derived this discovery model from Kenneth Burke's essay, "The Philosophy of Literary Form." In this important work, Burke outlines three questions for analyzing a piece of literature. These questions form the basis of our discovery model, and we wish to acknowledge here our indebtedness to him.

Throughout the text, we provide exercises and writing assignments. With only a few exceptions, the exercises are open-ended; that is, there are no preconceived answers—we ask the student to consider pieces of writing, some of which he or she has written, and to make value judgments about them. Throughout, our intent has been to provide exercises that reinforce the points we wish to make about writing. The writing assignments derive from the various topics under consideration in each chapter. Early in the text, the assignments call primarily for expressive writing; later, when the student may feel more at ease with writing, the assignments call for transactional writing. Thus, our assignments initially are grounded in the student's experience and then move outward toward more global concerns.

Here we need to say a word about our use of pronouns. We support the use of nonsexist language and have chosen to show this support by alternating use of third-person singular feminine and masculine pronouns. We think that using only one pronoun instead of two (*she* vs. *she or he, his* vs. *his or her*) makes for less awkward writing and that using singular instead of plural pronouns makes for a more direct approach to the reader. In most cases, we have used singular pronouns in our remarks about what *the writer* or *a writer* may do. These remarks we intend as examples of the kinds of activities in which the student writer might engage. Not all writers are so inclined; thus, we have avoided plural pronouns in these cases as appropriate.

As in any undertaking like this text, there are a number of people who have worked to help make it possible, and we wish to thank all those who have helped us shape this book. We have received invaluable advice from these writing teachers as they reviewed our text's manuscript in its various forms: Lucien L. Agosta, Kansas State University; Don Richard Cox, University of Tennessee; Kirby L. Duncan, Stephen F. Austin State University; Eileen B. Evans, Western Michigan University; George D. Haich, Georgia State University; Mary Hayes, Miami University; George F. Hayhoe, Virginia Polytechnic & State University; Eileen T. Lundy, University of Texas at San Antonio; Celest A. Martin, University of Rhode Island; George Miller, University of Delaware; Jeannette Morgan, University of Houston; Mark Reynolds, Jefferson Davis State Junior College; Kenneth C. Risdon, University of Minnesota at Duluth; Jeanne Simpson, Eastern Illinois University; Eugene Smith, University of Washington; and Fred D. White, University of Santa Clara. We would also like to acknowledge the assistance of Professor Margaret Marks, Lauder College, who contributed to the chapters on sentences, mechanics, and grammar and usage review. We thank all our students who labored with us as we worked to revise the materials in this text, and we especially wish to thank the following student writers for permission to use their essays and writings: Cecilia L. Cano, Mickey Carter, Carla Collins, Barbara Hall, Laurie Logsdon, Tim Meiers, Carolyn Miller, Karen Pinckley, Elizabeth Ann Sandry, Amy Smith, Stephanie Weikert, and Arlene Yusnukis.

We also thank the staff of Wadsworth Publishing Company for their patience and assistance: Kevin Howat, English editor, Sally Schuman, production editor, and MaryEllen Podgorski, designer.

Finally, we wish to thank Professor James M. McCrimmon who, while we were students at Florida State University, taught us far more than rhetoric.

Charles W. Bridges
Ronald F. Lunsford

Brief Contents

Detailed Contents

Part One

Discovering Meaning

Writing is a process of discovering and shaping meaning. Implicit in this definition is that writing requires communicating that meaning to someone, whether this audience consists solely of the writer or is a group of "someones" beyond the writer. The need to communicate is one of humankind's dominant traits, and writing well is one of the best ways we can communicate with one another.

But writing can serve a greater purpose than being only a means, however good or effective, of transmitting ideas from one person to another. Writing is a powerful means of *learning*, one of the most important means we have available to us. Through writing, we can come to know what we think and then refine that thinking. In this text, one of the major coordinates is that you must discover something you think to be of importance, something you think to be worth knowing, as you work through a writing assignment. Whether you communicate what you learn to someone else will depend on the context of the writing. If, for example, you are at work on an assignment calling for persuasive writing, then your task is to communicate what you have learned to an audience beyond yourself.

Whether you are writing for yourself or an outside audience, the best writing you do will carry your viewpoint of your topic. Good writing, then, is marked by the writer's interpretation of a topic so that the piece of writing reveals what the writer thinks to be significant in the topic. Your job initially is to probe your topic to discover what it means for you. To do this, you should first write from a personal perspective before moving to a more public perspective.

Part One—Discovering Meaning—reflects these concerns. In the four chapters constituting this section, we outline how you may decide which topics may hold significance for you, how you may invent or generate information about a particular topic, and then how you may work that information into a piece of expressive writing.

Writing well is not always an easy task, but it is a manageable one. To help you manage your writing, we outline a seven-step model of the writing process, and we encourage you to try it. It is a model that focuses the writer on the necessity of discovering significance in his or her topic and on the necessity of revising so as to present that significance to a reader as effectively as possible. It is a model our students have used successfully, as the student writing examples attest. Our purpose in presenting it is not to suggest that it is the only way a piece of writing should be written. In fact, the best use you can make of it is to work through it a time or two and then adapt those aspects of it you find useful as you develop or refine your own process. We see our model as a description of a successful process, and we present it as a means of helping you effectively manage your writing.

Chapter One

Good Writing

We believe that the subject matter in a writing course should be writing—your writing as well as that of other students and professional writers—and that the goal of such a course should be to help you develop your ability to write well, to produce good writing. Essential to our discussion of writing is a definition of good writing; so before you read the rest of this chapter, respond to the following writing assignment.

WRITING ASSIGNMENT

What is good writing? In a paragraph of about 250 words, outline the traits that you believe characterize good writing. If you get stuck early on for ideas, think about pieces of writing that you have read that you thought were good. Then, in a paragraph, describe the things that made them good. When you have finished your paragraph, read the rest of this chapter, and then share your paragraph with your classmates and teacher.

Our definition of good writing follows in this chapter; in fact, it follows throughout the rest of this book. Your definition may differ from ours somewhat, because each of us may emphasize different aspects of good writing. Absolute agreement is not necessary, but establishing a common understanding of good writing must precede our attempt to provide instruction or to give advice on how to write well.

Many students think that professional writers sit down at the typewriter to compose a piece of writing, grasp an idea, and dash off a poem, play, essay, or novel without stopping or without making a mistake. These students see the writing process as a series of steps consisting of outline, rough draft, and finished draft. Seldom, however, is this the case. Instead, the writer moves back and forth from outline (or prewriting) to first draft, back to the outline, back to the draft, and so forth. The writing process involves considerable trial and error as the writer tries to place a message on the page as clearly and as effectively as possible. The writer weaves in and out of thoughts on the way to producing a piece of good writing. In doing so, the writer encounters both frustration and exhilaration.

Elusive Ideas

Part of the frustration you, as a writer, may encounter probably stems from the tyranny of the blank page: How will you ever fill that page? How will you ever find ideas to use in your writing? Other student writers have faced this problem. Here, for example, Carolyn Miller, a student writer, describes the problem of finding an idea.

> Memories run around in my mind like little gremlins in a huge multi-roomed house. Late at night, when I'm desperate for sleep, they clamor for attention, laughing from down a hall or loudly whispering from distant rooms. They tease me as I wash my hair, taunt me while I read a book, and torture me every time there is a very dull but very necessary lecture. At the most inopportune times they call, "Come play awhile, you know we're fun." Oh, how they laugh, chatter, whisper, or sob until I come looking for them. Then the gremlins scramble away and quite rudely slam doors in my face. I plod the long, dark, quiet halls, lucklessly knocking at the closed doors. I softly curse the silence of their game, only to hear a giggle, too low and too brief to pinpoint. Those cautious and stubborn memories don't come out. They haven't been touched by the pen; possibly they fear it. I sit chewing on my pencil and stare at an almost blank piece of paper. Thoughts are so elusive when I'm writing for a class.

Laurie Logsdon, another student writer, describes her experience.

> . . . sometimes it's so hard to make the words say what I feel when I attempt to write something subjective. Perhaps the hitch is that in trying to please a hoped-for audience, I tend to suppress those things that come naturally and try to substitute something "better" or "more suitable"—with far worse results! It seems to be a matter of being honest with myself—writing what I really feel and see, and not what I think others want me to feel and say. Despite these instances of frustration, I still find writing a joy. Those occasions on which I *do* produce something really worthwhile make up for those times when I am discouraged.

As Laurie points out, writing can be worthwhile. In finding out what she wants to say, the writer may see writing as exhilarating, as a joy. Writing can also be extremely rewarding. Communicating is one of humankind's most characteristic acts, and writing is one of the most widespread and potentially one of the most effective (and thus rewarding) means of communication. Despite the fact that telecommunications (television, telephone, and so forth) seem at times to threaten writing's position as a means of communication, writing continues to be important. The very properties that seem to be weaknesses of writing are, in fact, its strengths. For example, the physical nature of the act renders writing a slow process when we compare it with delivering a message over the telephone. Often, producing a piece of good writing takes time and, as we have already implied, much effort. But that effort can be rewarding. The writer may, if she chooses, take time to consider her words carefully as she writes and then to reconsider her words after she has written. This process is likely to help her discover what she really means.

Another of writing's special properties is that the reader has before him a manuscript he may read and consider, and then reread and reconsider, so that he may come to understand more fully the writer's message. Think for a minute about your own reading. When you reread something—whether book, poem, letter, or essay—you probably notice different details than you noticed on previous readings. These details may help you understand the writer's point of view more clearly than you had before, and they may even cause you to change the opinion you held after previous readings. By reconsidering your writing, a reader may see details he has not seen before, thereby gaining a fuller understanding of your writing.

The Recursiveness of Writing

As we said earlier, in this text we will take a process view of writing; that is, we will view writing as a recursive series of activities. These are activities that loop backward while moving forward, so this involves considerable trial and error on the part of the writer. The writer experiments with words, trying them out until she feels they are right. She moves backward as well as forward. The writer begins, perhaps by attempting an introduction, jumps ahead to list points for consideration at later points in the paper, then returns to the introduction, and so forth. At any stage of the process, the writer may generate ideas which must be incorporated into her paper, ideas which had not occurred to her before she began writing. Sometimes those ideas demand that an entirely new structure be given the paper; at other times, they require only a minor change. But whatever the demands, they must be met if the essay is to be as fully developed as the topic requires. To submit a paper in which those demands have not been met is to submit an incomplete, unfinished paper.

A piece of writing frequently assumes a life of its own; one idea fosters another, then another, and then another, until the writer exhausts his topic. But how does the writer establish this flow of ideas? At times, the ideas and the words just will not come. This "writer's block" is a common phenomenon. When you encounter a block, how can you overcome it and continue the writing process? First, it may help to examine the various stages of that process. Second, it may help to examine how you write. Here you can identify your "stuck points" and consider how to remedy them. In this way, you may begin to recognize and refine your own process. Third, it may help to consider such aspects of good writing as purpose, significance, topics, audience, and language.

STAGES IN THE WRITING PROCESS

Even though we cannot neatly divide the writing process into separate units, it is useful and convenient to talk about three stages—prewriting, writing, and rewriting—as if they were discrete units. This separation allows us to deal with smaller entities than the whole of the writing process.

Prewriting

Prewriting, which occurs before the writer produces the first rough draft, is a planning and preparation stage. In prewriting, the writer selects a subject and begins to discover what she wants to say about it and how best to present her thoughts to her intended audience. The prewriting stage provides the foundation for any discoveries made in the writing process; it is the germination or gestation period for the paper, the stage in which ideas begin to take shape.

To discover and begin to develop these ideas, you may do any number of things. You may read pertinent books or articles, taking notes as appropriate; you may write in a journal; you may take a field trip; you may sit and stare out a window; you may freewrite; you may outline, doodle, talk to a friend, go to a movie. Any or all of these may be necessary for you to get started. Often writers are stymied by the starkness of a blank page. If that happens to you, the best thing to do is simply to begin, to write something on the page—a sentence, an idea, a working title. What you write at this point may not appear at all in the final draft. The idea is to put on paper something you can work with.

Freewriting is an excellent way to get started. To freewrite, just write down what comes to mind about your topic for a specified period, say, ten minutes. If you cannot think of anything to say, that is what you write—"I can't think of anything to say. I can't think of anything to say"—until something to say occurs to you. Usually it will. When you have finished freewriting, look back over the passage. Are there any ideas beginning to emerge or take shape? Mark them. Are there any sentences or phrases that sound interesting or promising? Mark them. These ideas, sentences, and phrases may not find their way into your finished essay; then again, they may. But the point is this: You have started; you have begun your prewriting, and you have something to work with and from.

Writing

Writing is the stage in which the writer produces a rough draft of the paper. Here the writer should concentrate on actually writing his ideas; he should not be concerned with such matters as finding exactly the right word, restructuring sentences or paragraphs, or correcting errors in spelling or punctuation. Too much attention to these matters may constrict or stop the flow of ideas. But the free flow of ideas is essential during this writing stage.

Sometimes, no matter how hard you try not to stop, you stop. If you find that you are thoroughly derailed—perhaps the right word or idea seems to hang in the air right before you, and you think you can grab it with just a little more time—use freewriting to get back on track. Spend ten minutes writing about the "stuck point." Ask questions; try to identify the problem; write whatever comes to mind about the topic. Or back up a paragraph or two and read what you have written; then freewrite with this rereading still fresh in your mind.

Rewriting

Rewriting, that part of the process in which the writer revises the draft produced in the writing stage, is an important part of writing that is at times neglected by many student writers. This stage requires the writer to make decisions that determine the final shape and effectiveness of her writing; thus, rewriting is fundamental. It involves both editing for grammatical and mechanical correctness and recreating. On the one hand, rewriting is a "nuts and bolts" stage. Here the writer corrects spelling and punctuation errors. On the other hand, rewriting is just as creative as the other two stages. It may require that the writer change only a few things in the draft. Or it may require an entirely new draft, and perhaps another new draft after that one, and so on until the writer gets her words right. If a writer is to produce a piece of good writing, she must "work" the paper—deleting what is not wanted in the final draft, making what remains stronger, leaving alone what is satisfactory, or culling everything and starting again. Whatever the changes at this stage, they must come in light of decisions already made in the other stages of the process. The writer is not bound, however, by these previous decisions. Changes made at this stage reflect the writer's ability to see the previous stages of the writing process from a new vantage point. To revise is to see again and to change the paper as the "seeing again" dictates. Thus, revising is creating anew.

There are any number of strategies you may use to revise. The best way to begin revision is to set the draft to be reworked aside for at least a few hours while you do other things so that you can return to the essay with more objectivity. A good practice, once you return to the draft, is to read without marking anything, then to reread, this time making notes about such things as what should stay, what should go, what should be reworked completely, what should be reworded, what material needs to be added, what should be reordered or restructured.

Another good revision practice is to find someone else to read your paper and comment on its strengths and weaknesses. This outside reader may either read the essay silently, marking it as appropriate, or he may read it aloud to you, so that you hear your words in someone else's voice. Or you can read your own writing aloud, listening for where it sounds right, and where it does not. As you read, you may find that you need to move a sentence or paragraph to a different place in the paper. Since you are working with a rough draft, cut and tape—cut the paper apart, move the sentence or paragraph to a new place in the paper, and then tape it in place.

Whatever you do by way of revising, you must become ruthless, ready to cut out and throw away what must be cut and thrown. It may be hard for you to eliminate words you have struggled to find and whole paragraphs you have labored to write, but if those words or paragraphs do not fit, they must not appear in the finished paper—you must give them up. Such an approach to revision may seem painful, but it is the approach many successful writers have taken.

Examination of the rough drafts of professional writers supports this idea that revising often requires the writer to consider whole passages as well as individual words. For example, in one part of a manuscript he was working on, Aldous Huxley (author of *Brave New World*) scratched out an entire passage three paragraphs long and began a revision of it in the margin, but scratched that out too. Huxley may not have wanted to give up this section, but he thought it necessary to do so.

James Jones (author of *From Here to Eternity*) had a different revision problem than Huxley did. An original passage from one of Jones' novels reads this way: "Solid and dense, sweeping away to the foothills in the distance, it might have been an ancient avalanche of green lava which had rolled down from some volcano to form this flat-topped plateau a hundred feet high . . . ." The revised version reads this way: "Solid and dense, sweeping away to the foothills in the distance, it might have been an ancient green lava flow laid down by some volcano centuries ago to form this flat-topped plateau a hundred feet high. . . ." Jones made but few revisions in this sentence, but those he made strengthened the sentence and so the passage in which it appears. Consider the change in the verb *rolled*. Jones listed four choices in the margin before he decided to change *rolled* to *laid*. By choosing *laid*, he attributed an active role to the volcano—the lava did not merely flow from it; instead, the volcano assumed a life of its own and laid the lava down to form the plateau. It is important to note that Jones did not bother with this word choice while he was drafting. He did not stop while writing to find exactly the right term but returned to the draft to work it only after he had gotten his thoughts down on the page.

No matter what the writer is working on, revision plays an important role, if the writer is to make his writing as effective as possible. A dramatic example of effective revision is this draft of President Franklin D. Roosevelt's speech to Congress following Japan's attack on Pearl Harbor (Figure 1.1).

Roosevelt's original draft probably would have effectively carried his request— that Congress declare a state of war between the United States and Japan—but he wanted the speech to convey as accurately as possible the outrage and shock

Good Writing

DRAFT No. 1   December 7, 1941.

PROPOSED MESSAGE TO THE CONGRESS

Yesterday, December 7, 1941, a date which will live in ~~world history~~ infamy

the United States of America was ~~simultaneously~~ suddenly and deliberately attacked

by naval and air forces of the Empire of Japan.

The United States was at the moment at peace with that nation and was

still in ~~continuing the~~ conversation with its Government and its Emperor looking

toward the maintenance of peace in the Pacific. Indeed, one hour after

Japanese air squadrons had commenced bombing in Oahu ~~the Philippines~~

the Japanese Ambassador to the United States and his colleague delivered

to the Secretary of State a formal reply to a ~~recent~~ recent American message. ~~from the~~

~~Secretary.~~ While This reply ~~contained a statement~~ stated that diplomatic negotiations it seemed useless

~~must be considered at an end, it~~ it contained no threat ~~and no~~ or hint of war or

armed attack.

It will be recorded that the distance ~~of Hawaii, and especially~~ of

Hawaii, from Japan makes it obvious that the attack was deliberately

planned many days or even weeks ago. During the intervening time the Japanese Govern-

ment has deliberately sought to deceive the United States by false

statements and expressions of hope for continued peace.

DRAFT NO. 1

The attack yesterday on ~~Manila and on the Island of Oahu have~~ *the Hawaiian Islands has*

caused severe damage to American naval and military forces. Very

many American lives have been lost. In addition American ships

have been torpedoed on the high seas between San Francisco and

Honolulu.

Yesterday the Japanese Government also launched an attack

against Malaya.

Last night Japanese forces attacked ~~Japan has, "therefore," undertaken a "surprise offensive extending~~ *the Philippine Islands*

throughout the Pacific area. The facts of yesterday speak for

themselves. The people of the United States have already formed

their opinions and well understand the implications ~~to the very~~

to the safety of our nation.

As Commander-in-Chief of the Army and Navy I have

directed that all measures be taken for our defense.

Long will we remember the character of the onslaught against

us.

(A) *No matter how long it may take us to overcome this premeditated invasion, the American people will in their righteous might win through to absolute victory.*

I speak the will of the Congress and of the people ~~of this~~

~~country~~ when I assert that we will not only defend ourselves to

the uttermost but will see to it that this form of treachery shall

never endanger us again. Hostilities exist. There is no mincing

the fact that our people, our territory and our interests are in

grave danger.

I, therefore, ask that the Congress declare that since the

unprovoked and dastardly attack by Japan on Sunday, December

seventh, a state of war ~~exists~~ _has existed_ between the United States and the

Japanese Empire.

＊＊＊＊＊＊＊＊＊＊＊＊＊＊＊＊＊＊＊＊＊＊＊

he felt. Thus, Roosevelt revised the speech to make it an even more effective statement than the original draft. He changed individual words so as to find exactly the right word. In the first line (page 1 of the draft), note the difference in emotional impact of *world history* and *infamy*. *World history* is a neutral term; *infamy* is not. Roosevelt also added some material, as is shown at the bottom of the draft's second page. There he added, "No matter how long it may take us to overcome this premeditated invasion the American people will in their righteous might win through to absolute victory." With these words Roosevelt stressed the viciousness of the attack—it was not accidental; like a murder, it was premeditated. Moreover, he stressed the will of the American people and what he saw as the rightness of the American cause. With these two revisions Roosevelt improved his speech, making it far more dramatic and more truly representative of his feelings; thus, he made it more effective.

Writing Is Rewriting

About revision, Donald M. Murray says:

> All effective writers know writing is rewriting. The inexperienced writer feels a revision is a failure. The amateur believes the writer is the person who can sit down and rip off an essay or a report. The professional writer knows better. Rewriting is what you do when you are a writer, for it is an essential part of the process of writing. It is the way in which you fit ideas into language.*

Writing *is* rewriting. Your goal as a writer should be to produce a piece of writing that is the best it can be. Because you are not likely to reach that goal in your first draft, revision must become an integral part of your writing process.

As we stated earlier, it is not easy to make neat distinctions or separations among the three stages of the writing process. Sometimes they come together. Think about your own writing. When you have been writing a rough draft or answering an essay examination, how many times have you combined writing and rewriting by scratching out a word, sentence, or paragraph and substituting a more appropriate choice? You have probably done so many times. You have probably also written sentences or paragraphs (*writing*) in your exploration of a subject (*prewriting*) and revised them on the spot (*rewriting*) before incorporating them into a paper. The fact that these stages frequently occur simultaneously reinforces our statements that writing is a recursive creative process that involves considerable trial and error as the piece of writing unfolds and takes shape.

DESCRIBING YOUR WRITING PROCESS

What do you do when you are faced with a writing assignment? How do you proceed? The following essay by Barbara Hall, a student writer, answers these two questions. Read through it; then answer the questions that follow it.

---

*Donald M. Murray, *A Writer Teaches Writing* (Boston: Houghton Mifflin, 1968), p. 11.

Good Writing

MY ~~WRITING~~ PROCESS
~~ACCORDING TO HALL~~

THE WAY IT IS   ~~MY WAY~~

(HOW DO I WRITE?)

WRITING MY WAY

Why is this such a difficult assignment? After all, it's my writing process I'm supposed to describe, so no one else can read this and say I'm wrong. So what's the problem? Oh, ho. Wait a minute. I think I may have discovered a clue. That word, "wrong." There's always something wrong with what I write, so I guess there's something wrong with my process, too. And how can any process which produces nothing any better than mine does, possibly be worth describing? Obviously, if I had amassed great fame and fortune through my writing, I would feel justified in exploring my process for the benefit of mankind, but—

Okay, okay—Sometimes when I'm stuck about how to begin, I just start writing—anything—whatever I think of. Often this gets thrown out, usually altered, and only rarely does it get to stay, but at least it gets me started.

This preliminary agonizing is part of the necessary prewriting process, and I believe the more I write, the more time I spend on this stage. I used to think writing meant taking pen in hand and putting words on paper, but this describes only the physical act, not the creative process involved in deciding *what* to write, and describing thought processes is a rather difficult task. Fragments of ideas, snatches of thoughts rise, sink, and rise again like bubbles in a viscous liquid. Many times a day, while driving or waiting in line somewhere, I shake the assignment container and watch the bubbles form again, hoping to discover a pattern, a solution to the problem of what or how to write about a particular subject.

Sometimes, after hours or days of agitation, it suddenly becomes clear. I know what I want to say and rush to put it down on paper before I forget. Of course, I have learned that the brilliant, perfect solution which appears at the end of a long day may, when exposed to scrutiny in the next morning's light, have changed into something dull and totally worthless. But when it's that bad, I don't mind throwing it out. Occasionally when I have something I really want to say, the words seem to rush to get through pen to paper. This happens rarely, but it is exciting and satisfying when it does.

Seldom does a whole paper flow smoothly. There are always spots which are rough, sentences so awkward I finally disown them, and paragraphs which refuse to fit together smoothly.
Sometimes most of a paper is satisfactory, but I have trouble with the conclusion. Or I find that the introduction just doesn't work because the paper I thought it was introducing isn't the paper I wrote. Trouble spots like these I smooth out in revision.

After I have completed the basic structure of the paper, I begin to revise. Writing, like jelly, needs to set for a while before you can tell what it is really like. I must put it away for a few hours or overnight now and then so that I can take a fresh look and see what needs changing or is worth keeping. I have awakened at 5 a.m. knowing how I should change something, so ideas must percolate even in my subconscious. This may go on for days, a few changes here one time and more somewhere else the next day.

With all these changes, my rough draft usually becomes such a messy conglomeration of insertions and deletions (with alternative words and phrases in parentheses) that I can't even read it. At this point, I recopy, or even better, type a draft. Sometimes seeing sentences typed makes their faults more apparent or helps highlight awkward patterns.

Finally, because I can't think of a better way to say anything, or because I have run out of time, I type a final draft, heave a fatalistic sigh, and go on to something else. It seems that my writing process involves tossing ideas about, finally managing to get something on paper, and then revising and revising it. This seems to be a fairly standard procedure for many writers, so maybe I have something in common with the rich and famous after all.

Questions for Discussion

1. How would you characterize Barbara's writing process? How recursive is it?

2. What insights into writing does this paper help you to see?

3. What specific advice does this paper contain about the various stages of the writing process (prewriting, writing, rewriting)?

4. How does Barbara's process compare and/or contrast to your own process?

WRITING ASSIGNMENT

In an essay, describe your writing process. How do you write a paper? How do you proceed? What are the various steps in your process? What do you do to prewrite, write, and rewrite? What spots create problems for you? What problems do you encounter? How do you overcome them? What about your process do you see as being strong? Weak? Why?

So far, we have taken a fairly broad overview of the writing process and have found it to be a complex process requiring the writer to make numerous decisions. Many of those decisions focus on such elements of writing as purpose, significance or meaning, topics, audience, and language. We will consider these elements in the rest of this chapter as we complete our definition of good writing.

GOOD WRITING—PURPOSE

You write for a number of reasons, many of them utilitarian. You write in response to assignments such as tests, essays, research papers, and laboratory reports. You also write to fulfill personal needs in letters, journal or diary entries,

Good Writing

and notes jotted to help you remember important information. Perhaps you think the ability to write well can help you on the job market. Nevertheless, good writing and the ability to write well hold far more for the writer than these utilitarian ends.

So far we have made a number of statements about writing as a process. To these, we must add that writing is a process of discovery. As such, it allows for personal growth. There is an old adage, attributed to the English novelist E.M. Forster, that has been phrased in the following ways: How do I know what I mean till I see what I say? Or, how do I know what I think till I say what I mean? Either version implies that, while engaged actively in the writing process, the writer may discover that one of her previously unexamined opinions must be modified in some way. In making such discoveries, the writer may come to know herself better. Martha Minnehan, a student writer, sees her writing as a means of knowing herself: "I've always saved the papers I've written because they have a lot to say about my feelings toward life at that particular time. They express my attitudes and let me know how my attitudes have changed since." Unlike talk, writing allows the writer to fix her ideas on the page, thereby enabling her to return to those ideas later to see what they are and then to reconsider or revise them. Thus, as a process of discovery that may help the writer come to realize things about herself, writing is one of the most humanizing and therefore one of the most important activities in which anyone can engage.

Because writing enables you to examine your thoughts, learning to write well can help you not only to clarify your ideas but also to strengthen your ability to think critically. This is especially true when you analyze the ideas of others—whether they be your classmates, your teacher, or professional writers. Clear writing and clear thinking both flow from a control of language. In turn, clear writing and clear thinking allow the writer to order and, thus, to control his world.

All these ingredients—language, writing, thinking, and control of one's world—come together in the concept of defining or, more simply, naming. In order to control her world, a writer must use language to order things. This process is defining. If, for example, an individual were on a camp-out and heard strange noises in the night, what would be the effect of saying, "Oh, that's just raccoons after bacon"? The mere naming of the noise in the night makes familiar the unfamiliar; it shrinks the two-headed beastie with twelve-inch claws and razor-sharp fangs to something much smaller and much friendlier—a raccoon after bacon. Although this example of our use of language to order reality is rather simplistic, it does suggest how writing can help you obtain control over your world. Writing well can help you define your stance on more than concrete questions that can be answered with a quick yes or no; it can help you examine abstract questions, those questions beginning with *why*.

Thus far, our discussion of purpose in writing has centered primarily on what writing can do for you, the writer, in fairly broad terms. It is true that writing can help you discover things you did not know so that you may gain insight into your world and, indeed, into yourself in the process. It is also true that by writing you may strengthen your critical reading and thinking skills. Of course, your writing is not always intended only for yourself; it may provide information for readers and it may influence readers to change their opinions as a result of the information you provide them. These broad purposes may be subdivided into three more specific purposes: Your writing will have an expressive, a transactional, or a poetic purpose.*

Expressive Writing

Expressive writing invites the reader to consider the writer's feelings on a particular topic. The writer expresses thoughts for the reader so that he may come to see what the writer sensed about the topic; expressive writing remains close to the level of sensory impressions. Examples of this kind of writing include freewrites, journal and diary entries, notes, transcribed conversation, and letters to close friends and family. In such writing as this, the writer attempts to get thoughts out so as to air feelings and ideas about the topic. Expressive writing also includes that writing in which the writer addresses on a personal level a more public audience than friends or family members. Thus, a primary goal of a writer using the expressive purpose is to give the reader insight into the writer.

Transactional Writing

Transactional writing conveys factual information to the reader and/or attempts to persuade the reader to take some action. The writer's goal is to select pertinent pieces of information so as not to burden the reader with material she already knows. At the same time, the writer must be sure that the reader is sufficiently familiar with the information (and the language it is delivered in) to understand what is said. The writer's goal might also be to move the reader to take some action, whether that action is physical (for example, writing a letter to a congressional representative or buying a product) or nonphysical (for example, understanding the basis of the writer's point of view, whether the reader agrees or not). Examples of transactional writing include news stories, laboratory reports, exposition, editorials, political speeches, informational and propagandistic pamphlets, and sales pitches of all kinds. Thus, we may say the primary goals of transactional writing are to give the reader insight into a topic and/or to incite her to action.

Poetic Writing

Poetic writing is a generic term; that is, it is a label for fiction (short stories, novellas, novels), drama, and poetry. The writer's emphasis is on the topic and the language of the piece of poetic writing so that the writer captures and reveals her view of universal truths as those truths are embodied in the topic of the writing. The language of poetic writing is frequently more stylized than that of either expressive or transactional writing as the writer attempts to present ideals

---

*James Britton, Tony Burgess, Nancy Martin, Alex McLeod, and Harold Rosen, *The Development of Writing Abilities, 11–18* (London: MacMillan Education Ltd., 1975), pp. 88–91.

Good Writing

in her writing. Often, the writer chooses poetic writing solely for the pleasure of playing with language.

Purpose is an important concept for the writer; without an understanding of purpose, the writer may proceed without a sense of direction. That sense of direction is, however, crucial if the writer is to produce good writing. The writer's realization of purpose, which may come at any time during her writing, determines the audience, the kinds of detail she will use, the language she will use, and the structure of the writing. As the writer's purpose shifts, the nature of the writing changes, so that a piece of expressive writing will carry a different emphasis on a given topic than a piece of transactional or poetic writing on that same topic.

EXERCISE

Find examples of expressive, transactional, and poetic writing on the same topic. (For example, Patrick Turnbull's *Dunkirk: Anatomy of a Disaster*, Winston Churchill's speech "Dunkirk" in *Into Battle: Speeches by the Right Honorble Winston S. Churchhill, C.H.M.P.*, and Paul Gallico's *The Snow Goose* take the battle at Dunkirk as their topic.) After you have considered each, answer the following questions.*

1. Which example is expressive? Transactional? Poetic? On what do you base your assessment of the aim of each example?

2. How would you characterize the language of each?

3. How does the detail presented differ among the three pieces of writing? How do you account for these differences?

4. How would you characterize the distance between the writer and the topic in each? On what do you base your assessment?

5. How would you characterize the distance between the writer and reader in each? On what do you base your assessment?

6. How well does each piece of writing achieve its aim or purpose?

GOOD WRITING—SIGNIFICANCE

As we will see beginning in Chapter Two, none of us interprets experience, including facts, in exactly the same way, and the writer should work to present his interpretation of experience, whether choosing expressive, transactional, or poetic writing. A piece of good writing carries its author's point of view, revealing the writer's particular thoughts about the topic and his attitude toward both topic and audience through details, structure, and language. A piece of good

---

*This exercise was suggested by James L. Kinneavy in *A Theory of Discourse* (New York: W.W. Norton & Company, 1971), p. 68.

writing has a personal quality about it, because it is the product of someone's mind actively at work; that writing reveals the writer's emotions, attitudes, and even prejudices as it presents the order the author creates in the writing situation. These characteristics lend to good writing its distinguishing trait—significance.

Significance is a bothersome term for some student writers, because they often think they have nothing of importance to write about. If you have felt this way, perhaps it is because you think that in every paper you must capture and reveal deep insight into a topic. But such insight is not what we mean by significance. Although it is true that you may find such insight in writing, sometimes you will not, and certainly you will not find such insight every time you write. The significance we speak of in good writing arises from the writer's interpretation of what she has written about; the message is an honest representation of what the writer thinks important about her subject. What is significant, then, is the writer's point of view, carefully considered and revealed.

As an individual, you have a unique perspective from which to view events, and it is that perspective, or point of view, that we would expect to find in your writing. In his journal Henry David Thoreau tells us that "observation, to be interesting, *i.e.* to be significant, must be *subjective*." Whether journal entry, essay, novel, lab report, letter, drama, or poem—good writing is subjective. It does not merely report about a topic; it interprets that topic. You will know when you have created a paper carrying this significance when you have fulfilled one of the purposes listed earlier—to give the reader insight into the writer (expressive), to convey information to the reader or to incite the reader to action (transactional), or to "live" in an event through poetic language (poetic). Each of these purposes requires the writer to present his interpretation of a topic.

GOOD WRITING—TOPICS

Oftentimes, the writing you do will have a well-defined topic—an assigned essay topic or an essay exam. On other occasions you may choose your own topic to explore. At such times you may already have a topic you want to write about; then again, you may not. You may, in fact, think you have absolutely nothing purposeful to write about. But we think you actually do, because you are an individual who has experienced many interesting events. To help you focus on them so that you may discover events you can and want to write about, we offer this assignment.

WRITING ASSIGNMENT

Answer as fully as you can the questions under at least five of the following six topic headings. After you have written your responses, make a second copy so that both you and your teacher may have a copy to keep for the entire semester's work. (Photocopy this set, if you wish.) This assignment is designed to help you select meaningful topics for your writing. There are no right or wrong answers, only *your* answers.

1. Community
   a. Where do you live?
   b. What type of community is your hometown or neighborhood?
   c. What especially interests or disturbs you about your community? Why?
   d. What particular places or events in your community do you enjoy? Why?
   e. What things about your community would you like to see changed? Why?

2. Family/Friends/Acquaintances
   a. What about your family is unique?
   b. Which of your relatives are especially interesting to you? Why?
   c. What special customs does your family have? (For example, is there anything special about the way in which your family celebrates such events as birthdays, Christmas, Easter, or Thanksgiving?)
   d. What type(s) of pet(s) do you have? Have you had? Would you like to have?
   e. Which of your friends are especially interesting to you? Why?
   f. Do you know any unusual people? What makes them unusual?
   g. Which of your neighbors are especially interesting to you? Why?

3. Education
   a. What type of educational background do you have? (Consider kindergarten, elementary school, and so on. Think about size, what you learned, and teachers who impressed you.)
   b. What types of courses have you taken? Are you taking? Which are your favorites? Which do you dislike? Why?
   c. If you could change anything about any of the schools you've attended, what would you change? Why?
   d. What informal (not strictly related to school) educational experiences have you had? How were they educational?

4. Jobs
   a. What type(s) of job(s) have you had? What aspects of them interested you? Disturbed you? Why?
   b. What career do you hope to have? Why have you chosen this particular field?

5. Leisure
   a. What hobbies do you enjoy? What makes each enjoyable?
   b. What kinds of movies, music, and reading material do you like? Why?
   c. What types of vacations or travel do you enjoy? If you could travel anywhere you'd like, where would you go? Why?
   d. What types of extracurricular activities do you engage in? Why?

6. Attitudes and Issues
   a. Have you experienced a change in your attitude toward such things as politics, religion, school, family, or friends? If so, what was that change, and what caused it?
   b. What event(s) in the past year or so has (have) interested you most? Disturbed you most? Why?
   c. What types of issues (for example, political, ecological) interest you? Why?
   d. Have the technological advances or changes you've seen been for the best? Why or why not? What technological developments would you like to see take place? Why?
   e. Have the societal changes or advances you've seen been for the best? Why or why not? What changes in society would you like to see take place? Why?
   f. What particular social customs interest or disturb you? Why?

WRITING ASSIGNMENT

Pick two of the answers you gave in the Interest Inventory and freewrite about them for fifteen minutes each. (If you are keeping a journal, use this as a journal assignment.) How much and what kinds of information did you generate about each answer? Did you discover anything about the topic of the freewrite that you did not know you knew? If so, what? What kind(s) of essays do you think could be based on each freewrite? On what do you base your assessment?

GOOD WRITING—AUDIENCE

In our discussion of purpose, we imply that the writer must consider the audience when producing a piece of good writing. In any writing situation there is an audience of at least one—the writer himself. Thus, if the writer does not become involved with his topic and, therefore, produces a message not worth a reader's time and effort, the writer will waste some reader's time, even if he is that reader. But a given situation demanding good writing usually involves someone beyond the writer as reader, and the writer is obligated to produce writing that other readers will consider significant and therefore worth the time and effort it requires. The writer's knowledge of the intended audience for each piece of writing is extremely important, because any audience has needs that the writer must fulfill, needs that vary from audience to audience.

Discussing good writing, the English novelist and essayist Virginia Woolf says this of the essay: "Vague as all definitions are, a good essay must have this permanent quality about it; it must draw its curtain around us, but it must be a curtain that shuts us in, not out."* In placing heavy responsibility on the writer,

---

*Virginia Woolf, "The Modern Essay," *Collected Essays*, Vol. II, ed. Leonard Woolf (London: Chatto and Windus, 1966), p. 50.

Good Writing

Woolf supports our view that the reader's needs—in Woolf's terms, those things the reader must know to be shut inside the essay's curtain—are of utmost importance in the writing process. Your perception of your audience helps you to determine what must be said and how it must be said. The next two writing assignments will help to illustrate this point.

Respond to one of the following assignments. After you have finished, share your response with your classmates and teacher. Then answer the questions that follow.

1. Pick an event in which you participated during your first week at your college or university and write two letters about that event—one to your best friend, the other to a prominent person (for example, a businessperson, teacher, minister) in your hometown. Write these letters as if you intended to mail them.

2. Choose a news event. Write one letter explaining it to one of your professors and then a second letter explaining it to a child. Write these letters as if you intended to mail them.

3. Slip into the role of a high school sophomore. On the morning following one of the wildest parties you ever attended, you decide to write brief thank-you letters to the host or hostess, who happens to be your best friend, and to your friend's parents, who knew of the party but were out of town and so did not attend. Write these letters as if you intended to mail them.

Questions for Discussion

1. Did the details you selected to report change from one letter to the next? If so, why did you decide to make these changes? How and why did the content of the letters change as the audience changed?

2. Did the language you used change from one letter to the next? Which letter is the more formal? Why?

3. What do you notice about such matters as sentence and paragraph structure in each letter? Is there a difference in the length and complexity of the sentences and paragraphs from one letter to the next? If so, why?

We may not legitimately ask which letter is the better of the two. If we asked this question, we would be asking you to make a value judgment without considering the context of either letter, and we cannot consider appropriateness of any piece of writing apart from context. Each letter may well be entirely appropriate for its intended audience; neither, we suspect, would be appropriate for the other's audience. The context of a piece of writing is the setting of the writing, including the writer, the reader, and the writer's purpose or intent.

In the letter to your best friend, you may well have used slang or colloquial language, contractions, or sentence fragments; you may have spelled *through* as *thru* or used "&" for *and*, and so forth. Given the context of such a letter, your choices would be entirely appropriate. We would, however, question such usage in your letter to your friend's parents or to a prominent adult in your community. A recipient of this second letter could be surprised at what she thinks to be a piece of nonstandard writing. If so, your chances of getting your message across are greatly reduced, because your letter will not have met the reader's needs; it will not be effective. A good writer, then, must anticipate the reader's needs. In later chapters, we will discuss in more detail both the importance of such anticipation and how to fit your writing to those anticipations. We think this concept so important, however, that we include here another writing assignment requiring you to consider the needs of an audience in the overall context of purpose.

Pick a topic that is fairly controversial in nature—for example, a local environmental issue or a campus issue. Write two paragraphs about this issue—one paragraph with an expressive purpose and one paragraph with a transactional purpose. (If you wish, write a third paragraph with a poetic purpose.) Although the topic remained the same, how did each shift in purpose change the shape of the paragraph? How did the details change? How did the audience change? How did the language change? How did the structure of the writing change? How do you account for whatever changes you found?

GOOD WRITING—LANGUAGE

The language of good writing is vivid, concrete, and specific in the context of the writing. It enables the writer to fulfill his purpose—to have the reader experience, however vicariously, what the writer experienced. It allows the reader to feel, think, and see with the writer so as to come to understand the writer's point of view. To return to Virginia Woolf's definition of the essay, we can say that it is the language of good writing that shuts us in.

One of the most important tasks you will have as a writer is choosing the words that most clearly reveal your point of view toward your subject and, thus, that best carry your meaning. The following two paragraphs represent two very different points of view on the same topic, alcohol-induced hangover. After you read them, answer the questions that follow.

WRITING SAMPLES

Dixon was alive again. Consciousness was upon him before he could get out of the way; not for him the slow, gracious wandering from the halls of sleep, but a summary, forcible ejection. He lay sprawled, too wicked to move, spewed up like a broken spider-crab on the tarry shingle of the morning. The light did him harm, but not as much as looking at things did; he resolved, having done it once, never to move his eyeballs again. A dusty thudding in his head made the scene before him beat like a pulse. His mouth had been used as a latrine by some small creature of the night, and then as its mausoleum. During the night, too, he'd somehow been on a cross-country run and then been expertly beaten up by secret police. He felt bad.

Kingsley Amis, *Lucky Jim*

Simple acute alcohol intoxication is a benign process, assuming no traumatic mishaps. The alcohol may induce sleep, and the subject usually will be sober on awakening. If the drinking has been severe, then a minor acute withdrawal syndrome may lead to medical management. Left to their own devices, however, millions of persons routinely recover from acute alcohol intoxication without complications. A variety of interesting remedies and prophylactics are prescribed to avoid discomfort from "hangover" or to hasten the detoxification process. Most of these have no objective support for their supposed efficacy.

Nada J. Estes and M. Edith Heinemann,
*Alcoholism: Development, Consequences,
and Interventions*

Questions for Discussion

1. Who is likely to be the audience for each paragraph? Is each paragraph appropriate for the audience you have identified for each? Why or why not?

2. What is the purpose of each paragraph? Does each fulfill its purpose? Why or why not?

3. Identify the words and phrases you think most important in conveying the writer's or writers' attitudes in each paragraph. Are these words and phrases sufficiently vivid, concrete, and specific for each paragraph's context? Why or why not?

EXERCISE

In the paragraph by Kingsley Amis describing the hangover of his novel's protagonist, Jim Dixon, it is easy to see just how bad Dixon feels. In fact, if Amis omitted the last sentence of the passage, we could infer it. That is, we could make the generalization that Dixon felt bad just from looking at the detail Amis has given. Sometimes, student writers write such a generalization as "he felt bad" without offering any detailed support for it. But if a reader is to see the truth or rightness of the generalization, if she is to be shut in by the writing, she must be convinced by supporting detail.

Choose one of the following sentences and write a paragraph based on it to illustrate the sentence's general meaning.* Do not use the sentence in the par-

---

*This exercise was suggested by Rebekah Caplan and Catherine Keech in *Showing-Writing: A Training Program to Help Students Be Specific* (Berkeley, CA: Bay Area Writing Project, 1980).

agraph; do not write it on the page at all—use it only as a starter. Your goal is to write the paragraph so that a reader could infer the sentence from the detail you provide. When you have finished, exchange paragraphs with one of your classmates and answer the questions following the sentences.

1. He (or she) is a weird person.

2. He (or she) has a great personality.

3. It was the best (worst) experience I've ever had.

4. Dating is a real hassle (joy).

5. The party was fun.

6. I was embarrassed.

7. The trip was boring.

8. The teacher is a good instructor.

9. My friends seemed angry.

10. He (or she) was overdressed.

11. School is exciting (dull, boring).

12. Devise your own sentence, one similar in nature to these.

Questions for Discussion

1. What is the general statement the paragraph is based on? How easy was it for you to infer this statement? How could the writer have made it easier for you to infer the statement.

2. How well does the paragraph shut you in? What suggestions can you offer the writer to strengthen the paragraph?

3. How vivid, concrete, and specific is the language the writer used? Underline the images you think to be particularly good. What revisions can you suggest the writer make to sharpen the language of the paragraph so that it does a better job of shutting you, the reader, in?

GOOD WRITING—EXAMPLES

The following two papers were written by Ceci Cano, a freshman; the second of the two is a revision of the first. We present them at the end of this chapter because we think they illustrate particular points about good writing. After you read them, respond to the questions that follow them and share your responses with your classmates and your teacher.

Good Writing

Only a Reflection

First draft

1   Infectious sounds reached our ears as we stepped into the dim passage. My friend and I strolled towards the chattering voices and tinkling laughter coming from a larger room in which we could see small tables and chairs. As we approached the entrance, the music rose and surrounded us, deafening my ears to any other sound, and we entered into a wonderland of lights and sounds.

2   My attention was immediately focused on the brilliant dance floor in the center, an oasis of bright color in the otherwise unilluminated room. I was drawn to it and became one of the many swaying, swinging bodies caught in the pulsating rhythm of the disco hit. The floor throbbed with radiant yellows, reds, greens, and blues. Overhead, reflecting hues bounced off the ceiling in equal excitement. Stardust sprinkled from a sparkling globe suspended over our heads, creating an aura of make-believe. The tempo quickened, vibrant and wildly electrifying, rising until suddenly only the turbulent percussion was left, beating like the heart of a huge creature, and strobe lights began to flash, catching seconds and holding them for a fleeting moment before they whisked away to become minutes. Just as I couldn't stand it for any longer the music became fluid and smooth once more, coaxing my body to glide along with it.

3   As I made a quick turn, my hand slid against a smooth, cold surface. Startled, I looked to see what it was. Staring back at me was someone who looked very familiar, and I realized it was my reflection. The whole wall was mirrored. What I thought was the other half of this fantasy world was actually only a reflection. I turned back, shocked and a little disillusioned. The blinking lights didn't seem as alive anymore. The rocking music was noise pounding in my head. The swaying bodies were no longer in unison with mine. Instead they jostled and bumped into me, stepping on my feet and irritating my nerves. "Where had the dreamland gone?" I wondered, and as I slowly pivoted, I saw it in the reflection on the wall.

Only a Reflection

Second draft

1   Infectious sounds reached our ears as we stepped into the dim passage. My friend and I strolled towards the chattering voices and tinkling laughter coming from a larger room in which we could see small tables and chairs. As we approached the entrance, the music rose and surrounded us, deafening my ears to any other sound, and we entered a wonderland of lights, sounds, and action.

    My attention was immediately focused on the brilliant dance floor in the center, an oasis of bright color in the dim, candle-lit room. I was drawn to it and became one of the many swaying, swinging bodies caught in the pulsating rhythm of the disco hit. The floor throbbed with radiant yellows, reds, greens, and blues. Overhead, reflecting hues bounced off the ceiling in answering frenzy. Stardust sprinkled from a sparkling globe

2   suspended over our heads, creating an aura of make-believe. The tempo
quickened, vibrant and wildly electrifying, rising until suddenly only
the turbulent percussion was left, beating like the heart of a huge creature,
and strobe lights began to flash, catching seconds and holding them for
a fleeting moment before they whisked away to become minutes. Just as I
couldn't stand it any longer, the music became fluid and smooth once
more, coaxing my body to glide along with it.

Other dancers were caught in the turbulence of the floor, their masklike
faces floating around me. Not to be outdone by the lights around them,
most of the dancers wore exceptional outfits; some girls were dressed
in swirling dresses of light chiffon, some in clinging straight-leg pantsuits
with three-inch heels on their feet, others in satin blouses which reflected

3   the brilliancy of the floor. The guys wore dark suits with bright colored
shirts underneath, or slacks which emphasized long muscular legs topped
with striped shirts and thin neckties. Everyone was transformed into an
ideal character, dressed in costumes they would not dream of wearing
in any real world. Here in this disco fantasy everyone was beautiful, sexy,
and desirable.

I watched as some of the dancers became tired and drifted off the floor.
They walked around tables until they came to a short flight of stairs
leading to a smoky, crowded loft. As they reached the top of the stairs, the

4   crowd separated and I glimpsed small pool tables illuminated by a single
tassled lamp swaying above each. This area was dominated by guys
holding cue sticks, chain-smoking, and drinking from glasses close at
hand. When they weren't shooting, they could overlook the dance floor
and the tables surrounding it.

I suddenly wondered who or what was controlling all the swinging
bodies caught up in the wonderland of flashing lights and throbbing
sounds. I looked over a sea of heads to a tiny enclosed corner of the floor.
Standing on a slightly elevated platform was a young man surrounded
by knobs, switches, and two turntables. He held an earphone to his ear
with one hand and placed the needle on a record with the other hand,

5   preparing for the next song. When the record being played ended, the
dancers stopped for a minute, only to be called back to the dance when
this young man beckoned. He started the next record, twisted a few knobs,
flipped a few switches, and transformed the disco from yellow to blue to
green. Completely absorbed in what he was doing, the young man seemed
almost to be a puppeteer, controlling the life of the disco with music and
lights as his strings.

Quickly, I turned away. My hand slid against a smooth, cool surface.
Startled, I looked to see what it was. Staring back at me was someone who
looked familiar, and I realized it was my reflection. The whole wall was
mirrored. What I thought was the other half of this fantasy world was
only a reflection. I turned back, shocked and a little disillusioned. The

6   blinking lights didn't seem as alive anymore. The rocking music was noise
pounding in my head. The swaying bodies were no longer in unison
with mine. Instead, they jostled and bumped into me, stepping on my feet
and irritating my nerves. Where had the dreamland gone? As I slowly
pivoted, I saw it in the reflection on the wall.

1. Of the purposes we identified earlier, which does this paper fulfill—expressive, transactional, or poetic? How well does it fulfill that purpose?

2. Do both papers reveal the significance of the scene for the writer? What is that significance; that is, what is the writer saying in these essays? Are you adequately prepared for the revelation of significance in both papers? If not, does one paper better prepare you for this revelation? If so, which one, and how?

3. Which of the two papers does the better job of shutting you as reader in? Why? How descriptive is the language of both papers? How vivid, specific, and concrete is the language of both? What effect does this language have on you as reader?

4. What do you think made the revision of the original paper necessary? Do you think the revision was a success? Why or why not?

The revision is the better of the two papers because it reveals more fully Ceci's meaning than the original does. The revision is an example of good writing, although it is not a perfect essay. For example, the term *exceptional outfits* in paragraph 3 is vague, and the examples that are supposed to define *exceptional* do not fully do so. Further, paragraph 4, which describes the area of the disco given to pool tables, should be tied more clearly to the rest of the paper. Ceci's essay shows how she came to realize that the world of the disco was a sham, only a reflection of reality, and then it shows the effect that realization had on her. But paragraph 4 does not develop this idea that the disco lets people slip out of their real selves to become someone else, although it could do so by talking about how the pool shooters, like the dancers, have tried to slip out of an everyday personality and into something else. Ceci's paper, therefore, is not a perfect paper, but it is a very good one.

The revision fulfills Ceci's purpose well; it is an expressive essay, revealing very well her feelings and impressions about the experience of the disco and then her interpretation of the experience. Although both papers reveal the event's significance, the revision does so better than the original. When Ceci presented the original to her classmates, they spoke favorably of the language and of the images the paper evoked. But then one person asked, "Why did you make a quick turn?" Look again at both essays. In the original, Ceci reports that the tempo became intense and turbulent, but that soon "the music became fluid once more, coaxing my body to glide along with it." The question her classmate raised is a logical one. If Ceci was lulled by the music, why the quick turn? Obviously, there was a gap between paragraphs 2 and 3 of the original; a revision was necessary if Ceci was to fulfill her expressive purpose for her audience, her classmates. Ceci's audience called for more details to prepare them for the revelation of the significance; those details form paragraphs 3, 4, and 5 of the revision. Ceci doubled the length of her paper, but doing so was essential.

The language Ceci uses is vivid, concrete, and specific; it takes the reader into the disco and directs the reader's attention so that he sees the disco from Ceci's point of view. In the paper Ceci emphasizes the illusory quality of the disco as she perceives it. She focuses on this quality throughout the paper, from the title through the last sentence. In any piece of good writing a reader will find important words and phrases that may be grouped together because they are alike in some way or they help convey much the same meaning. We may label these words and phrases *key terms*; to group them is to index them. Here is an index of the key terms found in Ceci's paper.

> Reflection (title)
> wonderland (paragraph 1)
> reflecting (paragraph 2)
> aura of make-believe (paragraph 2)
> masklike faces (paragraph 3)
> everyone . . . transformed into an ideal character (paragraph 3)
> costumes . . . not . . . in any real world (paragraph 3)
> disco fantasy (paragraph 3)
> wonderland (paragraph 5)
> young man (paragraph 5)
> transformed (paragraph 5)
> puppeteer (paragraph 5)
> reflection (paragraph 6)
> fantasy world (paragraph 6)
> mirrored (paragraph 6)
> dreamland (paragraph 6)

This index reveals at least three things about Ceci's paper.

1. Paragraph 4 does not fit very tightly into the paper; it has none of the key terms that develop or reveal the paper's significance.

2. Except for paragraph 4, the paper is unified; that is, each paragraph develops some aspect of the paper's significance.

3. Ceci's point of view is consistent. In the language with which she describes the scene before her, she consistently stresses the fantasy or make-believe quality of the disco, so that the reader is well-prepared for the essay's conclusion.

In short, Ceci's paper shuts us into her view of the disco's escapism. As readers, we feel what she felt, hear what she heard, see what she saw; we are well-prepared for her realization that the world of the disco is false.

WRITING ASSIGNMENT

1. In an essay of 500 to 1,000 words, describe an event from which you learned something. (If you are stuck for an event, review your Interest Inventory for a possible topic.) Your task is to recreate, through your language, your impressions of the event so that the reader, insofar as possible, can experience what you experienced. After reading your essay, the reader should feel that he has been at least an observer of the event, if not a participant in it.

2. Choose one of the following laws and describe a situation in which it was or is at work in your experience. Or invent your own law (one similar in nature to these), give it your name, and describe a situation in which it was or is at work in your experience. After reading your essay, the reader should feel that he has been at least an observer of the event, if not a participant in it.

Murphy's Law: Nothing is as easy as it looks; everything takes longer than you expect; and if anything can go wrong, it will and at the worst possible time.

Gumperson's Law: The probability of anything happening is in inverse proportion to its desirability. (That is, the chance of the buttered side of a piece of toast dropping on a carpet increases geometrically with the price of the carpet.)

Wickert's Law: Any situation is in the hands of its enemy.

Pogo's Observation: We have met the enemy, and he is us.

Farber's Law: We're all going down the same road in different directions.

Chapter Two

Discovering Order

In Chapter One, we said that good writing results from discovery and is characterized by significance. Your task as a writer is to engage in this discovery process and to find that significance. Although you may occasionally begin a writing assignment—for example, an essay examination—knowing what you want to say, discovering significance is not always easy. In many cases you may not know how you want to respond, and you probably will feel some frustration. Such feelings are normal. But there are things you can do to discover significance in a topic, whether that topic is assigned to you or is one you select yourself.

OBSERVING

Visual Perception

Discovering significance is tied very closely to observation, because what you think to be significant in a topic depends on what you see in that topic. Each of us perceives things differently; thus, the same event holds different things for each of us. To begin our illustration of this particular point, we offer some optical illusions. What do you see in Figures 2.1 and 2.2?

Obviously, both images listed for this drawing are, in a sense, present in it; what we see at any one time is determined by our perspective on the drawing.

The next three illusions (Figures 2.3, 2.4, and 2.5) are slightly different in nature from the preceding ones, because they require you to make judgments within a particular context.

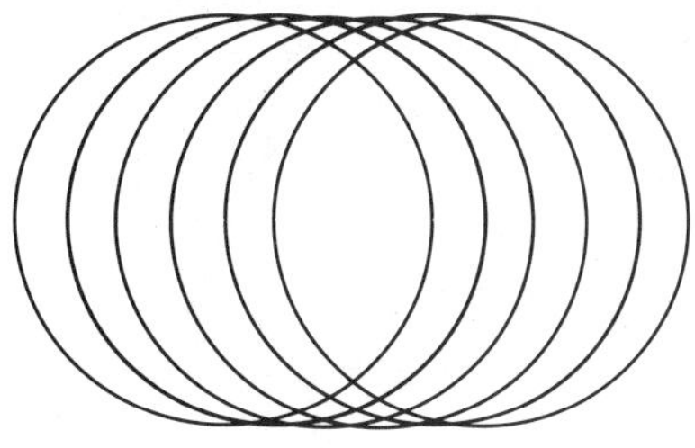

Figure 2.1 / Does the tube run from left to right or from right to left?

The answer to the questions about the circles and the boxes is that the circles are identical in size and so are the boxes. However, the context of each drawing controls what we perceive. When the middle circle is in a context of larger circles, it appears to be small; when the distance between the converging lines is great, the box appears to be small. As the context changes—that is, as our vantage point on each figure changes—we see different things; we see figures that are larger or smaller than those to which we compare them. The vase-or-profiles drawing is slightly different because it requires us to construct the context; either the white portion dominates (thus showing the vase) or the dark portion dominates (thus showing the profiles). In either case, what we see depends on what we are looking for.

Perspectives on Experience

We look at other experiences in much the same way as we looked at the optical illusions. The context of a situation controls how and even what we see in that situation. We cannot see all that there is to see because various elements of a

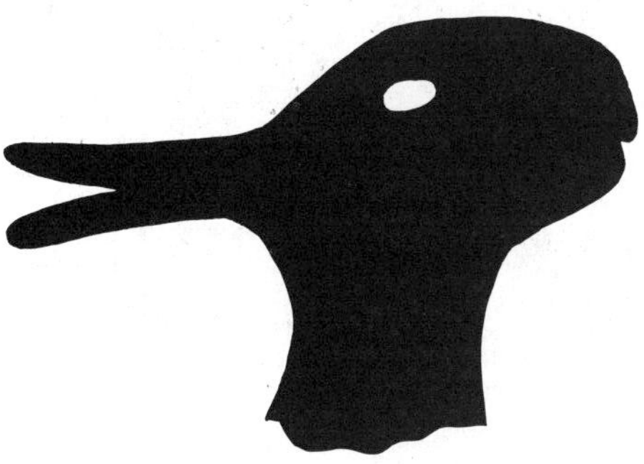

Figure 2.2 / Is this a duck or a rabbit?

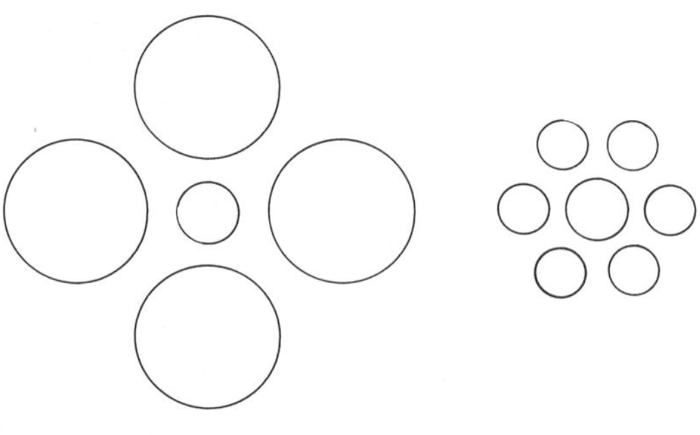

Figure 2.3 / Which of the two circles in the center is the larger?

given event clamor for our attention more than others do, and we pay attention to those elements. They stand out against the context of the event, and they stand out later in our minds because they are the elements of the event on which we focused our attention.

As our perspective on our experience changes, we may well find different meaning in it. Just as shifting our perspective or point of view on the optical

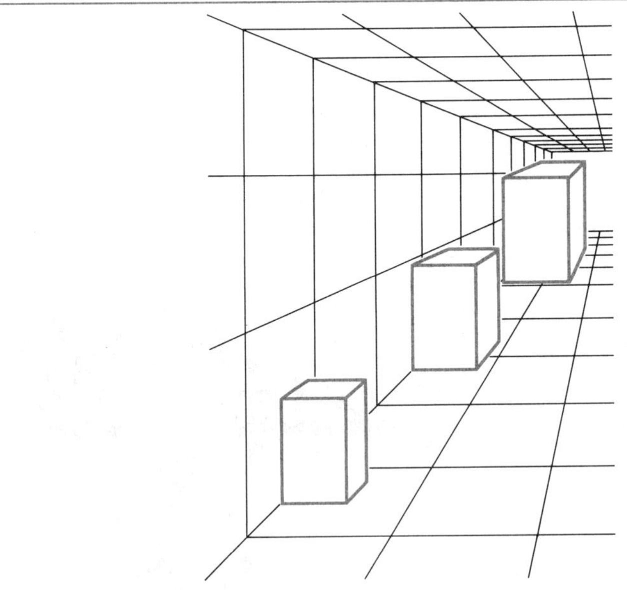

Figure 2.4 / Which box is the largest of the three?

Discovering Order

illusions resulted in a change in what we saw in them, so a shift in perspective on our own experience can result in a change in what we may see in it. Consider this excerpt from Mark Twain's *Life on the Mississippi*.

WRITING
SAMPLE

Now when I had mastered the language of this water, and had come to know every trifling feature that bordered the great river as familiarly as I knew the letters of the alphabet, I had made a valuable acquisition. But I had lost something, too. I had lost something which could never be restored to me while I lived. All the grace, the beauty, the poetry, had gone out of the majestic river! I still kept in mind a certain wonderful sunset which I witnessed when steamboating was new to me. A broad expanse of the river was turned to blood; in the middle distance the red hue brightened into gold, through which a solitary log came floating, black and conspicuous; in one place a long, slanting mark lay sparkling upon the water; in another the surface was broken by boiling, tumbling rings, that were as many-tinted as an opal; where the ruddy flush was faintest, was a smooth spot that was covered with graceful circles and radiating lines, ever so delicately traced; the shore on our left was densely wooded, and the somber shadow that fell from this forest was broken in one place by a long, ruffled trail that shone like silver, and high above the forest wall a clean-stemmed dead tree waved a single leafy bough that glowed like a flame in the unobstructed splendor that was flowing from the sun. There were graceful curves, reflected images, woody heights, soft distances; and over the whole scene, far and near, the dissolving lights drifted steadily, enriching it every passing moment with new marvels of coloring.

I stood like one bewitched. I drank it in, in a speechless rapture. The world was new to me, and I had never seen anything like this at home. But as I have said, a day came when I began to cease from noting the glories and the charms which the moon and the sun and the twilight wrought upon the river's face; another day came when I ceased altogether to note them. Then, if that sunset scene had been repeated, I should have looked upon it without rapture, and should have commented upon it, inwardly, after this fashion: "This sun means that we are going to have wind to-morrow; that floating log means that the river is rising, small thanks to it; that slanting mark on the water refers to a bluff reef which is going to kill somebody's steamboat one of these nights, if it keeps on stretching out like that; those tumbling 'boils' show a dissolving bar and a changing channel there; the lines and circles in the slick water over yonder are a warning that that troublesome place is shoaling up dangerously; that silver streak in the shadow of the forest is the 'break' from a new snag, and he has located himself in the very best place he could have found to fish for steamboats; that tall dead tree, with a single living branch, is not going to last long, and then how is a body ever going to get through this blind place at night without the friendly old landmark?"

No, the romance and beauty were all gone from the river. All the value any feature of it had for me now was the amount of usefulness it could furnish toward compassing the safe piloting of a steamboat. Since those days, I have pitied doctors from my heart. What does the lovely flush in a beauty's cheek mean to a doctor but a "break" that ripples above some deadly disease? Are not all her visible charms sown thick with what are to him the signs and symbols of hidden decay? Does he ever see her beauty at all, or doesn't he simply view her professionally, and comment upon her unwholesome condition all to himself? And doesn't he sometimes wonder whether he has gained most or lost most by learning his trade?

As his knowledge of the river and its signs grew, Mark Twain gained new insights into the river, and although he seemingly deplores these insights for taking away the river's magic for him, gaining them was essential for him to become a successful river pilot. As his perspective on the river shifted—that is, as he learned to "read" the river's signs—Twain's understanding of the river became more and more comprehensive.

<table>
<tr><td>EXERCISES</td><td>1.</td><td>Observe the same physical object (for example, a tree, a statue) or one of your favorite locales from the same spot at different times during the day. Spend an hour observing in the morning and another hour later in the day, perhaps in mid-afternoon or at dusk. Take notes on what you see during each observation period. How are the two sets of notes similar? Different? What did you note during the second hour that you did not note during the first? If it was in the scene all along, why did you not notice it during the first hour? How significant are the differences? Overall, how do you account for the differences?</td></tr>
<tr><td></td><td>2.</td><td>Observe the same physical object or one of your favorite locales from different spots. Spend fifteen to thirty minutes in close observation at one place, taking notes, then move to another place and spend fifteen to thirty minutes in close observation, again, taking notes. How are the sets of notes similar? Different? How significant are the differences?</td></tr>
</table>

The preceding example and exercises were primarily concerned with how our perception of physical objects may change as we shift our point of view. However, perception is not limited to physical objects, and shifts in perspective

Discovering Order

can also change the way we perceive situations and relationships. We may gain insight into the way in which these shifts influence our perceptions of relationships from the following paper by Tim Meiers, a student writer.

Remains to Be Heard

Grandmother told adventure stories. She would brisk about her kitchen, poking quickly into immaculate cabinets where everything was arranged just so, and sift together the makings of banana bread while also sifting together the ingredients of a story. It was seemingly effortless for her to both concentrate on a recipe and recount the "old days." Occasionally, though, with her hands in the mixing bowl, she would encounter a stiffening batter and quiver her voice as she struggled to thoroughly mix the dessert. At times, but not often, my head bobbed in response to her high and low pitch levels because I was completely hooked by tales of lawmen, outlaws, prairie fires, blizzards, mountain caves, mesa flatlands, and the odd array of ranching tools. Mostly, however, I was off somewhere mentally playing baseball, or fishing, or when I did sweep back to the kitchen, fidgeting quite impatiently for the banana bread cake in the oven.

After the kitchen had been tidied, but before the cake ever came out of the oven, Grandmother would lead the way into the living room. There, in her favorite rocking chair, she would pick up her always-in-progress embroidery and resume her deft stitching. The stories she told while sewing were usually less action charged. The living room seemed a lot calmer place than the kitchen, the sewing more tranquil than the clank, clank of cooking. Sometimes her voice became so quiet that the ticking of the wind-up clock, the one Grandmother had had forever, hung on my ears like crystal ringing earrings. The brassy bongs that foretold the hours frequently allowed me to comment that time marched on, and perhaps I should be marching home—or, given that certain situation, march into the kitchen to see if the cake was done. Whatever form my marching took, it usually moved away from one of Grandmother's stories.

Grandmother died in her sleep. It was totally unexpected. One day she said, "I'll see you tomorrow," and the next day, the very next morning, tomorrow became forever. I stood there in Grandmother's house, after the ambulance left, and waited for something. I didn't know for what, exactly. There was no cake in the oven to drool over, no embroidery picture to spring to life on a cuptowel; even the old wind-up clock had run down completely—first time I ever recalled that the ticking had stopped. Grandmother the cook, Grandmother the seamstress, was gone. There was something else, though. The lump in my throat, choking my voice, reminded me. Grandmother the storyteller was gone, also.

Many times I try to recall the historical details from Grandmother's stories. Who was the outlaw that Grandmother's brother, an Arizona ranger, tracked clear into Mexico and brought back for trial? What happened to the ranch hands who were trapped in an arroyo full of burning tumbleweeds? When was the blizzard that took over half of the Shattuck's herd of cattle? Where is the cave that Grandfather descended into and almost never found his way out of? Why did the cattle raisers so dislike herds of sheep on the mesas? How did the traces attach to the singletree?

My questions stay unanswered. A living part of history had been available to me, but I made no records.

My parents tell good stories. I listen this time. No distractions from baseball, or fishing, or cakes in the oven. I listen and write down, tape, preserve. Because someday, if for no other reason than curiosity, I might want to know how cows are milked, horses are shod, mattresses used to be stuffed, or wood-burning stoves were constructed. And though I listen and record, I often think of other tales, older tales. Those memories are but skeletal remains of once full-bodied events. Grandmother told adventure stories.

Questions for Discussion

What changes does Tim report in this essay? What was the cause of those changes? What results from those changes? How has Tim's view of his Grandmother changed? What meanings does he assign to her and her stories today that he did not as a young teenager? How valuable to Tim is the realization of what he has lost?

WRITING ASSIGNMENT

Write a paragraph in response to one of the following assignments.

1. Have you changed your mind about something that means a great deal to you? About what did you change your mind? What caused the change? What have you realized from the change? How do your views of the subject before the change compare to or contrast with your views today? Is there a significant difference? If so, how do you account for this difference? If not, has the change really been a significant or a profound one?

2. Since having come to college, have you been home? How has your hometown changed? How have your friends changed? How significant is the difference? How do you account for this difference?

3. Look again at the two letters you wrote to different audiences in response to an assignment in Chapter One (see p. 21). How were those letters similiar? How were they different? How do you account for the similarities and the differences? From what vantage points or perspectives did you write? How did these points or perspectives affect the letters you wrote?

QUESTIONING

Writing and Puzzling

In order to explore the topic of your writing fully, you will often need to shift your perspective on that topic; that is, you will need to consider more than a single facet of it to discover what in it you think to be significant. In your search for significance, you will probably engage in considerable trial and error before

Discovering Order

discovering what you want to say. It may help if you think of this search as being in some ways like solving a jigsaw puzzle. When you work a puzzle, you are confronted by a jumble of pieces from which you must create order. More than likely, you do so by grouping like pieces with like (for example, matching border pieces, those with at least one straight side, with other border pieces, or by matching color to color), by separating pieces or groups of pieces that are not alike, and then by building increasingly larger units of pieces until the puzzle takes shape.

These same activities may be useful in writing. You may see the writing assignment as a hodgepodge, a jumble of pieces of information, for you to piece together in some meaningful way. In prewriting, you create many of the various pieces you will be working with; in writing and rewriting, as you see how the pieces relate to each other, you fit them together until you begin to see meaning in the emerging patterns.

Before you can begin fitting these various pieces together, however, you must have some type of information—a text—to work with. To help create this text and to discover meaning in it, you may ask a series of questions, like those listed under the following heading, Questions for Analysis.* The questions can help you explore a topic by helping you shift perspectives on it, and your answers or responses can help you see relationships between and among the various elements of the topic.

These questions are derived from the basic processes by which we think; that is, they are based on the principles of association, dissociation, and sequence. The various questions are grouped in sets; the lead question in each set represents the principle of thought from which the other questions are derived. Because these questions are derived from principles of thought, they can provide a means of exploring a topic from several perspectives. As we have discussed, considering a topic from more than one perspective may help you discover meaning you could not have found from only one viewpoint.

By no means are these questions inclusive; instead, we intend them to illustrate the kinds of questions you may ask as you explore a given topic. When you understand the principles on which these questions are based, you can go beyond them to devise your own questions as you think necessary. Here, then, is the group of questions. In them, X represents whatever is being explored.

<table>
<tr><td>QUESTIONS FOR ANALYSIS</td><td>

What goes with X? (Association)

    What is X?

    What physical entities go with X?

    What do you associate with X?

    What has been written or said in favor of X?

    In what context is X set?

</td></tr>
</table>

---

*These questions are based on three questions outlined by Kenneth Burke in *The Philosophy of Literary Form*, 2nd ed. (Baton Rouge: Louisiana State University Press, 1967), pp. 20, 69, 71.

How is *X* like other things?

In what class do you place *X*?

What opposes *X*? (Dissociation)

What physical entities oppose *X*?

What theoretical or philosophical opposition is there to *X*?

What has been written or said against *X*?

How does *X* stand out against its context?

How is *X* unlike other similar things?

What about *X* is odd, incongruous, or unusual?

What follows or follows from *X*? (Sequence)

What follows *X* chronologically? Spatially?

How did *X* come to be?

What are the causes of *X*?

What results from *X*?

What problems does *X* pose? What are their solutions?

What opportunities does *X* offer?

What are the implications of *X*?

Is *X* good? Bad? Desirable? Undesirable? Necessary?

To give you some experience in working with the Questions for Analysis, we outline here the meanings of the three key terms: association, dissociation, and sequence.

Association

Defining **Association** enables us to attribute traits or characteristics to things. For example, an economy car and a sports car have certain traits or characteristics. The two cars hold in common some of these traits—for example, size (both are small) and comfort (neither has luxurious appointments). They do not share other traits—for example, gas mileage, engine size, and performance. By listing such traits, we define the thing to which we attribute those characteristics. Consider the following definition of *democracy* by the American writer E.B. White.*

WRITING
SAMPLE

Democracy

July 3, 1943

We received a letter from the Writer's War Board the other day asking for a statement on "The Meaning of Democracy." It presumably is our duty to comply with such a request, and it is certainly our pleasure.

---

*From *The Wild Flag* (Houghton Mifflin) ©1943, 1971 E.B. White. Originally in *The New Yorker*. Reprinted with permission.

Discovering Order

Surely the Board knows what democracy is. It is the line that forms on the right. It is the don't in don't shove. It is the hole in the stuffed shirt through which the sawdust slowly trickles; it is the dent in the high hat. Democracy is the recurrent suspicion that more than half of the people are right more than half of the time. It is the feeling of privacy in the voting booths, the feeling of communion in the libraries, the feeling of vitality everywhere. Democracy is a letter to the editor. Democracy is the score at the beginning of the ninth. It is an idea which hasn't been disproved yet, a song the words of which have not gone bad. It's the mustard on the hot dog and the cream in the rationed coffee. Democracy is a request from a War Board, in the middle of a morning in the middle of a war, wanting to know what democracy is.

White defines *democracy* without making a single direct statement about the system of government a democracy would have. Instead, White defines this term by example, listing those things that best illustrate what he sees as exemplifying democracy's primary trait: respect for the individual's freedom and rights.

Sorting Association also helps us sort or classify things; that is, with association we see how things are of a particular type or how they may be grouped with similar things. Think, for example, how college students are sorted or grouped into various classes—as freshmen, sophomores, juniors, or seniors; as women or men; as undergraduate or graduate students; as students living on campus or off; as residents (in-state) or nonresidents (out-of-state); as pursuers of particular academic majors; and so forth.

Comparing Association also leads to comparisons. At times, we compare essential attributes of physical objects. When, for example, we shop for the best food buys or for the best car for our needs, we compare the attributes (in terms of price and quality) of one product with the attributes of another product. At other times, we use association to help make the unfamiliar more familiar by transferring the attributes of something familiar to something unfamiliar to us. When speaking of the relative ease with which a task may be done, we might say, "It's as easy as falling off a log." To emphasize the starkness of a particular place, should we be describing it to a friend who has never been there, we might say, "The land there is as desolate as the surface of the moon." In the following passage, the science writer Isaac Asimov uses association, comparing thinking with breathing, to help illustrate his abstract idea that thinking may be voluntary or involuntary.

It is my belief . . . that thinking is a double phenomenon like breathing. You can control breathing by deliberate voluntary action: you can breathe deeply and quickly, or you can hold your breath altogether, regardless of the body's needs at the time. This, however, doesn't work well for very long. Your chest muscles grow tired, your body clamors for more oxygen, or less, and you relax. The automatic involuntary control of breathing takes over, adjusts it to the body's needs and unless you have some respiratory disorder, you can forget about the whole thing.

Well, you can think by deliberate voluntary action, too, and I don't think it is much more efficient on the whole than voluntary breath control is. You can deliberately force your mind through channels of deductions and associations in search of a solution to some problem and before long you have dug mental furrows for yourself and find yourself circling round and round the same limited pathways. If those pathways yield no solution, no amount of further conscious thought will help.

On the other hand, if you let go, then the thinking process comes under automatic involuntary control and is more apt to take new pathways and make erratic associations you would not think of consciously. The solution will then come while you *think* you are *not* thinking.*

Asimov associates or attributes the characteristics of breathing to thinking, so as to make a difficult concept—a description of thinking—less difficult by comparing it to a phenomenon—breathing—that is very familiar.

The following questions may help you discover what you associate with a given topic. X represents the topic.

What is *X*?
What physical entities go with *X*?
What do you associate with *X*?
What has been written or said in favor of *X*?
In what context is *X* set?
How is *X* like other things?
In what class do you place *X*?

<table>
<tr><td>EXERCISE</td><td>Pick one of the following terms and apply the questions of association to it, substituting the term you have chosen for X. What kinds of information do the questions help you generate?</td></tr>
</table>

democracy	feminist
pro-life	male chauvinist pig
politics	moral majority
education	immoral minority

Dissociation

Dissociation implies physical confrontation, and certainly we often think about what confronts us in such terms. Two teams oppose each other in this sense; protestors oppose the object of their disaffection in this sense. But opposition is more than this. Have you ever made a decision after listing both "pros" and "cons" about the situation? If so, you used the principle of opposition by establishing what you saw as both the positive and negative aspects of the situation.

---

*From Isaac Asimov's "The Eureka Phenomenon." Reprinted with permission of the author.

Further, as we demonstrated in our discussion of optical illusions, things have meaning in context, and we may use opposition to see how a given thing contrasts with or stands out against its context. Look again at the figure of the boxes in the converging lines. In each instance, a box is defined by how it stands out against a smaller and then still smaller context—as the lines converge, each box increasingly dominates the context or background against which it is seen.

With opposition, we may also consider odd, incongruous, or unusual aspects of a situation. Consider this sentence: For a 300-lb. tackle, he certainly is slow. Normally, we would expect a different adjective to follow the verb. Rather than *slow*, we would expect something like *agile, quick, fast,* or *a good dancer.* Thus, *slow* stands in opposition to our notions about what should complete the sentence; *slow* provides an incongruous ending for the sentence.

In *Writing with a Word Processor,* William Zinsser uses incongruity to underscore his scoffing at the quietness and neatness that word processors have brought to the newsroom.

> I knew how a newspaper office should look and sound and smell—I worked in one for thirteen years. The paper was the *New York Herald Tribune,* and its city room . . . was dirty and disheveled. Reporters wrote on ancient typewriters that filled the air with clatter; copy editors labored on coffee-stained desks over what the reporters had written. Crumpled balls of paper littered the floor and filled the wastebaskets—failed efforts to write a good lead or a decent sentence. The walls were grimy—every few years they were painted over in a less restful shade of eye-rest green— and the atmosphere was hazy with the smoke of cigarettes and cigars. At the very center the city editor . . . bellowed his displeasure with the day's work, his voice a rumbling volcano in our lives. I thought it was the most beautiful place in the world.*

Zinsser provides a counterpoint to the bleakness of the *Herald Tribune*'s newsroom; his last sentence reveals just how fondly he remembers all the noise and activity, things lost with the advent of word processors.

Opposition also provides a useful means of defining. Often we imply what a thing is by telling what it is not. In the following passage, historian Carl Becker first defines democracy by stating its chief attribute as a system of government— "government by the people as opposed to government by a tyrant, a dictator, or an absolute monarch"—and then clarifies the definition by giving examples of governments that were not democracies, though they may have been labeled as such.

> In this antithesis there are, however, certain implications, always tacitly understood, which give a more precise meaning to the term. Peisistratus, for example, was supported by a majority of the people, but his government was never regarded as a democracy for all that. Caesar's

---

*William Zinsser, *Writing with a Word Processor* (New York: Harper and Row, 1983), pp. 1–2.

power derived from a popular mandate, conveyed through established republican forms, but that did not make his government any the less a dictatorship. Napoleon called his government a democratic empire, but no one, least of all Napoleon himself, doubted that he had destroyed the last vestiges of the democratic republic. Since the Greeks first used the term, the essential test of democratic government has always been this: the source of political authority must be and remain in the people and not in the ruler.*

The following questions will help to reveal opposing elements in a given topic. *X* represents the topic.

> What physical entities oppose *X*?
> What theoretical or philosophical opposition is there to *X*?
> What has been written or said against *X*?
> How does *X* stand out against its context?
> How is *X* unlike other similar things?
> What about *X* is odd, incongruous, or unusual?

<table>
<tr><td>EXERCISE</td><td>

Pick one of the following terms and apply the questions of opposition to it, substituting the term you have chosen for *X*. What kinds of information do the questions help you generate?

</td></tr>
</table>

> nuclear energy   a specific environmental issue
> energy crisis   a specific political issue
> education   feminist movement

Sequence

Finally, *sequence* helps us establish the order of things and their causes. Here we need to consider the principles of *proximity* and *causation.*

Proximity *Proximity* involves the questions of what surrounds a particular thing in terms of time and/or space. This principle enables us to narrate a story— first this happened, then this, then this, and so forth—as we relate the order or sequence of events. If, for example, you attended a football game and wished to tell what happened, you could use any of the following orders, all of which are based on chronology, or movement in time.

1. From pregame to half-time to postgame activities of the crowd or of the band.

2. From the first through the fourth quarters, should you wish to focus on the team's play or on the crowd's mood.

---

*Carl Becker, *Modern Democracy* (New Haven: Yale University Press, 1941), pp. 6–7.

Discovering Order

3. From one play to the next, should you wish to focus on a particular series of plays—for example, a series that resulted in a score.

These are only three possible foci you could choose; each illustrates how you may use chronology as an ordering principle. Chronology is also the basis of giving instructions; in this case each step in completing a given task follows in turn. Think for a moment about brushing your teeth. Before you put toothpaste on your brush, you must remove the cap from the toothpaste tube. Steps in a process, then, proceed chronologically.

The principle of proximity also enables us to fix or describe the spatial order of things. In the football example, if you wished to describe the stadium or the crowd, you could order that description spatially by beginning at your seat and moving in any of several ways.

1. From left to right (or from right to left) around the stadium till you return to your seat, describing in turn, say, the home team's student body, then the next group (the band, perhaps), and so forth.

2. From one point of interest to another, then another, and another till you cover all the points of interest you wish. Here the order would not be as straightforward as that detailed in the previous example, but it would still be ordered by space because you would be shifting your focus from one area to another, moving, therefore, in space.

Causation Causation or *cause and effect* enables us to order experience by speculating about why something happened or what may happen if something else happens. For example, if your car will not start in the morning, what do you do? Once past an initial reaction of anger, disgust, or frustration, you probably think about why the motor will not turn over. Is the battery dead? Are the battery cables loose? Are the cable connections greasy? Any of the three could be the reason (the cause) for the car's not starting (the effect). For another example, if the bread you are baking does not rise (the effect), you may think that you failed to stir in the yeast (a possible cause), that you dissolved the yeast in water that was too hot, thereby killing the yeast (another possible cause), or that the yeast was just too old to do the job it was supposed to (a third possible cause).

Although we may not think of dead batteries and flat bread as problems of great significance, these examples illustrate how we think about or order experience using cause and effect. Situations of far greater significance than batteries and bread lend themselves to this causal thinking. What will happen if the pollution of one of your favorite places is not stopped? What will happen if too much coal is burned to produce electricity? What will happen if the construction of nuclear power plants is discontinued? What will happen if you change your major, or if you do not change your major? Obviously, these are questions of potential significance, and considering the causes and effects inherent in them can be a powerful way of exploring them.

The following questions are based on the principles of proximity and causation. *X* represents a given topic.

What follows *X* chronologically? Spatially?
How did *X* come to be?
What are the causes of *X*?
What results from *X*?
What sort of problem does *X* pose? What are its solutions?
What opportunities does *X* offer?
What are the implications of *X*?
Is *X* good? Bad? Desirable? Undesirable? Necessary?

Pick one of the following terms and apply the questions of proximity and/or causation to it, substituting the term you have chosen for *X*. What kinds of information do the questions help you generate?

nuclear energy	a specific political issue
energy crisis	a specific campus issue
a specific environmental issue	

So far, we have talked about each set of questions in isolation. To help you see how the various sets work together in the exploration of a particular topic, we provide the following three applications. The first two involve only prewriting. The first is for a "physical" topic—a hypothetical refining or smelting company's plant. The second is for a cartoon. The third application involves a student essay, "Forest Fire" by Mickey Carter. Remember that as we go through these applications we need not respond to every question, because particular questions may not be readily applicable.

APPLICATION 1
THE XYZ REFINING COMPANY (XYZRC)

Have you ever seen a refining or smelting company in operation? In all likelihood you have, and what probably stands out in your memory are its smokestacks. Such stacks are large and, due to the smoke they emit, highly visible. Try to visualize the plant or plants you have seen as we proceed with our application of the Questions for Analysis to the XYZRC. In the application, the *X* in each question is replaced by the subject, XYZRC.

What Goes with What?

1. What goes with the XYZRC? (Association)

a. What is the XYZRC? It is a refining corporation that refines such metals as copper from raw ores.

b. What physical entities go with the XYZRC? The actual physical plant covers a number of acres, mostly devoid of plant life. It's a bleak place, grimy, with a large parking lot, usually full of the cars of commuting workers. It has several smokestacks, all in use twenty-four hours a day, the smaller ones up to 750 feet high, the largest one a 1200-foot-high giant. At times these stacks belch a thick, black, sooty smoke that hangs over the countryside like a pall. What's the particulate composition of that smoke? What kinds of chemicals are those stacks putting into the air? We don't know these things right now, but we'll try to find out.

c. What do you associate with the XYZRC? Last year there was a big flap about the plant's smoke emissions. At the request of a concerned group of citizens, a team from the Environmental Protection Agency (EPA) inspected the plant and found that it was emitting at least twice the amount of pollution allowed by EPA standards. Nearly every local newspaper covered the story, all of them praising the EPA's attempts to restrict this pollution. But nothing was done, thanks to court action brought by XYZRC attorneys. XYZRC seems to have little, if any, concern for the public's or the environment's well-being. Other things—the plant has a big payroll and pays a lot of local and state taxes. It employs 847 people in all.

d. What has been said or written in favor of the XYZRC? Company officials ran a big ad campaign not too long ago—TV, newspapers, radio, billboards. The general message was that the XYZRC was the county's friend because it employs a lot of people, pays a lot of taxes, and produces materials vital to national security. All this put the company in a very positive light, presenting only the company's point of view. We need to find these and look at them again.

e. In what context is the XYZRC set? The context is a broad one. First is the immediate context, the countryside surrounding this plant. It is set in a rural area with cultivated fields surrounding it on three sides. Within four or five miles of the plant are several small towns, each having a population under 5000. Within thirty miles is a large city with a population of close to 1,000,000. Nearly all the workers at this plant commute from the city; only a small part of the workforce comes from the smaller nearby towns. A larger context involves the economical setting; that is, the XYZRC is set in a context of industrialism and big business.

f. How is the XYZRC like other similar things? It is like other businesses that emit smoke and pollutants. In this sense, it is like chemical plants that release toxic wastes into rivers as well as into the air. It is also like power plants fueled by oil and coal.

g. In what class do you place the XYZRC? The class is refining companies. (Because the XYZRC is a typical refining company, this question will not produce much new information.)

2. What opposes the XYZRC? (Dissociation)

a. How does the XYZRC stand out against its context? The plant provides a stark contrast with the countryside immediately surrounding it. That countryside is lush and green and is characterized by cultivated fields seemingly carved out of forest. As far as standing out against the larger context of industrialism or big business, this particular plant does not; rather, it blends right in and is actually indistinguishable from other plants and similar businesses.

b. What physical opposition is there to the XYZRC? Within the last two or three years, a group of concerned citizens formed a special-interest group and became a "watchdog" on this plant. It was this group that called in the EPA inspection team, and since that team's visit, this group has filed suit in the federal courts to force strict compliance by the XYZRC with EPA guidelines. In addition, three local newspapers have begun writing about the plant's continued pollution and so have begun exposing the XYZRC to public scrutiny. The group's and the papers' goal is to see the plant stop its pollution entirely or shut down.

c. What theoretical or philosophical opposition is there to the XYZRC? This question may seem at first not to apply, until we consider the possible long-term effects of the plant's pollution. Lately, there has been much concern over the acid rains afflicting much of the northern United States, and great debate between environmentalists and businesspeople has ensued. Environmentalists offer much opposition, though not just to this plant.

d. What has been said or written in opposition to the XYZRC? All the local newspapers ran negative stories about the pollution. These stories discussed plants dying, greater incidence of respiratory illnesses the closer you got to the plant, and so on. Several investigative reporters really took company officials apart. We need to find copies of these articles. Then there are the articles on acid rain published by *National Geographic* and other environmentally oriented magazines. Because the XYZRC has been accused of contributing to this problem, these articles might set the company's problems in a broader context. We'll need to locate these articles also.

e. How is the XYZRC unlike other similar things? This question does not seem to apply readily, unless we can find a refining plant that does not pollute the environment.

f. What about the XYZRC is odd, incongruous, or unusual? This question does not readily apply.

What Follows or Follows from What?

3. What follows or follows from the XYZRC? (Sequence)

a. What follows the XYZRC chronologically? Spatially? This pair of questions does not readily apply.

b. How did the XYZRC come to be? It grew up in an era when there was little concern for pollution standards, because the American public seemed simply to want more and more material goods. It is about thirty years old now, and it has quadrupled in size since it was first built. It is a very profitable plant for its owners, hence the dynamic growth.

c. What are the causes of XYZRC? This question does not readily apply.

d. What results from the XYZRC? Two primary products: the refined copper, which is beneficial, and the pollution, which is not.

e. What problem does the XYZRC pose? What are its solutions? Obviously, the problem this plant poses is pollution of the countryside. Given the way tall stacks disperse pollutants into the atmosphere, the XYZRC may well pose an environmental problem to areas many miles away as well. The solutions are complex. Either the plant should clean up its emission or shut down. To clean up the emissions will require expensive scrubbers for the smokestacks; to shut down will result in the loss of 847 jobs at the plant, as well as the loss of business to those businesses (for example, a railroad, chemical suppliers, equipment suppliers, and companies subcontracted to perform maintenance at the plant) that support the plant.

f. What opportunities does the XYZRC offer? Another expansion is planned; so there will be more jobs, ranging from jobs for construction workers during the building of the expansion to jobs for more XYZRC workers to staff and run the expansion.

g. What are the implications of the XYZRC? Continued emissions at the present level will do the environment no good whatsoever. Continued operation of the plant will do the local and, by extension, the national economy much good.

h. Is the XYZRC good? Bad? Desirable? Undesirable? Necessary? These last questions call on us to make a value judgment. That judgment is: The XYZRC plant is necessary, but at present not at all desirable. From this could come a proposal that the plant be required to install the scrubbers necessary to clean up its emissions and that antipollution devices and procedures be required in the new expansion, so that the expansion will not aggravate the problem. We would not want the plant to shut down because of its importance to the local economy, but neither would we want the plant to continue polluting the environment.

In examining the XYZRC as the subject for a paper, we uncovered a great deal of material a writer could use in an essay. We also discovered aspects of this topic that called for more investigation. Were we to investigate them, we would generate still more information. Obviously, a writer could not use all this information, nor would he wish to. Instead, he would have to take a stance on the subject and then use only that information supportive of this position. If, for example, the writer agreed with our value judgment, he could mention the benefits of the XYZRC plant, but he would emphasize how much the plant pollutes and the effect of that pollution on the environment.

Pick a subject similar to that of our first application—the XYZ Refining Co.—and prewrite a paper for that topic. Use the Questions for Analysis, applying each one in turn so that you gain a familiarity with them. What kinds of information did the questions help you generate? How much information were you able to generate? What insights into the subject did the questions help you to discover that you did not realize before you began your exploration?

APPLICATION 2 CARTOON ANALYSIS

This second application will be to a cartoon with an environmental topic. While we will generate some fairly obvious information about the cartoon, we do so to illustrate how you may apply the Questions for Analysis to discover meaning in such potential writing topics as works of art (drawings, paintings, sculptures), literature (short stories, novels, dramas, poems), news items, essays, cartoons, and photographs.

This cartoon, drawn by Herb Brammeier, makes a humorous but serious statement about corporate thinking. Look at the cartoon carefully, and hold it in mind as we apply several of the Questions for Analysis to it.

1. What goes with the cartoon? Of the questions listed under "Association," only three are really applicable to this cartoon:

    a. What is the cartoon? It is a political/environmental statement about corporations. We have what we assume is a big energy company, Icarus Oil, Gas & Nuclear Corporation, considering a name change to Icarus Earth Science Facilities, Inc.

    b. What do you associate with the cartoon? The cartoon's figures—there are two men shown in the drawing, one seated at a modernistic desk, the other standing. The one seated we can assume is the company president, or at least some big wheel in the corporation—his desk and office furnishing (plush chairs, impressive desk top with all kinds of buttons and pens, the tall, wide window behind his chair) show him to be a man of substance within the company. He seems to be older than the man standing and is probably the standing man's superior—he is older (more seniority in the company); he is seated; the man standing is showing him something (the new name) for approval. He also has less hair than the man standing, and we associate increasing baldness with older men. He is also heftier (thicker, chunkier, less trim) than the man standing, more tied to his desk, less active. The seated man's response to the new name is "I like it!"

    The two company names—the names are significant because they represent the company to the public. *Icarus Oil, Gas & Nuclear Corporation* implies big business, especially big energy business, which many of us do not look on very favorably. *Icarus* is a terrific term for this company—Icarus

"I like it!"
(Herb Brammeier, Jr., Audubon Magazine. Reprinted with permission.)

being the character from Greek mythology who joined feathers with wax to form wings and flew too near the sun. He fell to his death in the sea below. The name suggests something of a blindness or lack of consideration on the part of the company, since Icarus created his own destruction. The new name is more positive because it hides the big energy business, or at least it masks it with a new orientation. The new name, still incorporating the *Icarus,* speaks of concern for the earth and works at presenting a positive image to represent the company.

c. In what context is the cartoon set? There are actually two contexts at work. The first is the immediate context—the cartoon came from a section of the March 1980 issue of *Audubon* called "Econotes." This section carries various opinions and reports concerning ecological triumphs and disasters; so the cartoon forms a comment on a potential disaster—the fooling of the public with a simple name change, or at least it seems simple, on the surface. *Audubon* is known for its concern with the environment and isn't likely to print anything that will approve of or contribute to environmental or ecological destruction.

The broader context is the whole concern with our environment; in this context, the cartoon could fit with our discussion of the XYZ Refining Corporation. There is concern on the parts of citizens' groups, special interest groups (e.g., the Sierra Club), and various individuals about the seeming lack of concern for the environment.

Part of this broader context is that of big energy, with major oil, coal, and nuclear companies coming to mind. Three Mile Island, oil spills, big government contracts for coal leases on public lands, especially in the West, groups like the Clamshell Alliance (nuke protest group)—all these are elements of this context. We have seen advertising campaigns this cartoon reminds us of—one oil company's touting its conservation record or its concern for the environment, another stressing the applications of its petrochemical research in such fields as medicine.

There is a lot of distrust of such companies and of government, especially given the controversy surrounding James Watt (Secretary of the Interior in Ronald Reagan's administration) and the Environmental Protection Agency (EPA) in 1983. This distrust often makes us think that many companies and the government are less concerned with protecting the environment than with making a buck.

2. What opposes the cartoon? There will not be a great deal of opposition to this cartoon, though some big energy companies could take at least some offense. But they would not be directly or immediately threatened by the cartoon and would probably see it as a harmless piece of sarcasm or satire. However, the cartoon recognizes a tension in expressing many people's attitude toward these companies. It affirms the stance toward big energy companies taken by environmentalists and so maintains whatever opposition to these companies environmentalists may have.

Of the questions under the heading "Dissociation," only two are truly applicable: the lead question (what opposes what?) enables us to consider opposition at work within the cartoon, while the question about incongruity enables us to consider the quality of the name change.

a. What opposes what within the cartoon? The two names—there is tension at work in the cartoon itself, as the two names of the company may be seen in adversary roles. The first name is directly opposite the second. It suggests big money, lack of concern for the environment (which we associate with much of big business), corporate welfare over all else. This original name also suggests pollution, which we also associate with big energy—drilling for oil is not clean; burning oil and gas produces pollution via emissions; creating energy through nuclear fuels produces pollution because there is no place to dispose of spent fuels safely. The new name hides the big energy aspect of the company, suggesting that the company is actually concerned with environmental concerns. It does not exploit the earth's resources; instead, it facilitates our use of them. And it looks on its work as science, not as business.

b. Odd or incongruous things: The new name does not fit our perception of the company very well. We assume that the company's business is to exploit the earth's resources; the new name implies conservation. So the new name will be odd or incongruous.

3. What follows or follows from the cartoon? Of the "Sequence" questions, those of time and space are not very relevant in this instance. Instead, the questions calling for value judgments are more important.

What are the implications of the cartoon? This question we can use to consider whether the possible causes of the name change and whether that change is good, bad, desirable, and/or necessary. The corporate biggies obviously feel the name change is important and good, else they would not be considering it. Somewhere down the line, they have decided to present a new image to the public, and they have chosen to make that image a much more positive one than the old name suggests. From the corporation's point of view, the change is at once good, necessary, and desirable. From the public's or environmentalist's point of view, the name change is somewhat sinister. It seems a deliberate attempt to hide the true nature of the company and to focus the public's attention on something other than what the company really does. From the environmentalist's perspective, the name change is bad and undesirable. Given the cartoon's immediate context (*Audubon*), we can say that the cartoonist is making a negative value judgment on such corporations as the Icarus Oil, Gas & Nuclear Corporation. There is a lack of concern for the public welfare implicit in the name change; the company's only concern is for its own well being. And that concern is what most of us associate with big business.

Those of us concerned with the environment would see this cartoon as making an appropriate statement about the energy business, because the cartoon neatly captures the attitude toward big business that many people have. Given the cartoon's context, we can say that it is a very effective work; it addresses concerns held by most of its viewers, and it expresses well the lack of trust most of them would have of big energy companies.

This analysis has been a simple one, but it has generated a good bit of information about the cartoon, some of which we did not realize before we started. For example, we had not fully considered the appropriateness of *Icarus* as the name for an energy company. Remembering the Icarus myth enhanced the cartoon's meaning for us, so that we now see the cartoon in a different light than when we began. The examination has also raised new points for us to consider, maybe not now but later, and in the context of other assignments. As we will see in Chapter Three, the language we use directs our attention, that is, it manipulates us by causing us to see some things but not others in certain events. How is the name change more than just a change in words? What does the new name imply that the old name does not? How can this new name manipulate or create the company's image?

---

  1. Find a cartoon about a controversial topic. (One place to look is the editorial page of your local newspaper.) Analyze the cartoon's message. What point does the artist wish to make? Most often, a cartoon consists of a drawing and a caption. Describe these elements, and apply the Questions for Analysis to them, either using each question in turn or applying only those questions you think pertinent to the cartoon you have chosen. What kinds of information did the questions help you generate? How much information were you able to generate?

2. Prewrite an analysis of either of the following advertisements (Figures 2.6 and 2.7). Your task is to interpret the ad you select, much as we interpreted the cartoon, so that you find the basis of the ad's sales appeal and then decide how effective that appeal is. Either apply the Questions for Analysis completely, taking each one in turn, or apply only those questions you think to be pertinent to the ad you have chosen. What kinds of information did the questions help you generate? How much information were you able to generate? What insights into the ad did the questions help you to discover?

APPLICATION 3
"FOREST FIRE"

The third application of the Questions for Analysis involves an essay written by Mickey Carter, a student writer, in response to number one of the description assignment given at the end of Chapter One (see p. 28). Mickey's paper could have been occasioned by at least two of the entries from the Interest Inventory, 4.a. and 6.b. Under the first of those entries, Mickey listed that his jobs included work as a forest fire fighter. Under the second of those entries he listed people's carelessness and thoughtlessness with the environment as being disturbing, and he cited as examples several forest fires. Mickey had an opinion to express about forest fires that are caused by people, and it was that opinion he saw as being significant. His job, once he decided to express that opinion, was to find and to order the details necessary for the reader to share or to recognize the validity of the opinion. Mickey chose to write about one particular fire, that in the Modoc National Forest in 1977, because it affected him deeply.

Forest Fire

I cautiously weaved my way down through the thick, scratchy, deathly-dry brush until I finally reached the boulder I had spotted from the top of the ridge. I stepped out on it, hoping for a better vantage point of the once densely forested plateau below. I took the stance of a hiker who had just reached a high mountain summit and paused to rest on his walking stick. I imagined how he would study the beautiful country around him and smile as he felt the fresh, cool breeze sweep through his hair. I was not this hiker, though. I was a Forest Service fire-fighter, as my luminous yellow shirt, olive-drab peg-leg pants, and silver hard hat showed. The stick I rested on was my shovel, the breeze that would have

1   been more than welcome didn't come, and I was not here to sightsee. I was somewhere in the Modoc National Forest in Northern California, looking for spot fires that might start from sparks blown across the control lines when the fire was raging two days ago. Now, though, all there was to see was a huge, irregularly shaped pool of black poles and black ground

Figure 2.6 / Advertisement used by permission of Volvo.

Figure 2.7 / Courtesy of the Advertising Council.

that occasionally spewed billows of grey smoke. As my eyes crept through the deadness, I lost all interest in my duty and sat down to rest my feet, hot and smothered in their casing of tight, leather logger's boots. Sitting there on that piece of mountain gave me the first solitary feeling I had had in three days. My mind relaxed, and I began to remember the series of events that brought me to this forest.

I remembered the plane that stole ninety-six of us from seeing the New Mexico sunrise on the first day of August, 1977. It was a surprisingly plush, but cold, DC-6 turbo-prop. The emergency in California prompted quick decisions, so the plane was slightly overloaded, with a rough take-off

Discovering Order

2   the result. We bounced twice, but nobody showed even a twitch of concern. Our tight brows could get no tighter, and the lines around our sunken eyes could get no darker. All of us were preoccupied with thoughts of gloomy uncertainty, trying to anticipate the dangers we would shortly be facing on the fireline. A little of my worry was transformed into anger as our crew was given the facts about the fire. One cigarette butt, flipped out of a vehicle window, was the cause of all this anguish in the people around me, and of who knows how many people already on the fire.

3   I remember landing smoothly in Klamath Falls, Oregon, where we were transported by school buses across the stateline to our fire camp. While the squad bosses of our crew went to orientation, the rest of us had lunch. We were served under the sun by a group of prison convicts on a minimum security work detail. They loaded our plates with food, and I ate every bit, even though my stomach was tight with anxiety, because I knew I would need all the energy it would provide when I was put to work on the fire. The bosses were still in orientation when I finished eating, so I decided to walk around the camp and learn about the fire's condition for myself. I found out all I needed to know without speaking a word to anyone. I saw the bright red tarps, strung up between the barely branched red cedar trees, where surplus army cots and sooty fireshirts gave evidence of the existence of at least nine hundred other persons like me. I saw the parking area, where ten bulldozers and about one hundred other heavy vehicles, probably water tank trucks, rested at one time. I saw the helicopter pad that seven different ships leaped on to and off, as they rushed supplies toward the haze of smoke twenty miles away. And I saw the quartermaster's tent where crates and crates of new shovels, axes, chainsaws, canteens, and K-rations were being opened, probably for us. "The cost of one cigarette." I walked away.

The freezing weather that miraculously struck the morning we arrived enabled the night crew to stop the fire's spread long enough for the dozer teams to construct a triple-wide control line around its head. Our job, for the next two days, was to mop up the fire's edge, to extinguish all smokes two hundred feet inward. I trudged through that land of white ash and charcoal trying, at first, not to imagine the beauty that once existed there, but as the hours crawled by, my defense broke down. I imagined seeing the tall, proud pine trees waving their green branches as the brisk wind flew past, and I imagined birds frolicking on the larger limbs. I saw a few deer bedded down in the nearby shade, with the buck keeping alert, but browsing, occasionally, on a sprig of oak. I even saw a gopher pop his head out of a hole to get his bearings. It *was* beautiful!

4   But then I saw the fire, thick black clouds followed by flame, that pulled its way through the dry grass at a murderous rate. The deer bounded off and the birds screamed warnings as they scattered. The gopher vanished into a hole, but I'm sure he died there, as wisps of smoke soon curled out the entrance. And the trees. The collection of past years' needles below them kindled the blaze just enough to attack their lowest branches. From there, a laddering effect occurred. The flames sizzled upward, from branch to branch, until the area resembled a giant torch, tossing sparks and embers to the wind, which placed them where it pleased. And to think, all this killing when someone decided to retire a cigarette, one

roll of ignited, cancerous tobacco, that was not ready to cease its destructive ways.

A breeze finally came to me as I lifted myself off that cold rock, a chilling breeze. My mind drifted back to the present and tightened around a bit of newly attained knowledge. I could now realize the magnitude of the harm a large forest fire creates. I had experienced first hand the intense human suffering, the death, and the economic and environmental cost. I bent for my shovel, looked at my watch, and then wandered away, down the hill.

Although the term *forest fire* appears as the essay's title and may seem to be the subject Mickey explored, the actual subject of this paper is *1977 Modoc fire,* a more specific subject than *forest fire.* Whether he was fully aware of doing so, Mickey found a specific subject, one he could handle within the prescribed limits of the paper. Rather than writing generalities about someone's carelessness and stupidity, Mickey wrote about such carelessness and stupidity by giving a specific instance illustrating them. And because the instance was one Mickey was intensely and directly involved with, the paper holds much significance for him.

Mickey's job was to derive a paper from the subject *1977 Modoc fire,* a term rich in associations for him. He began by jotting down impressions of the Modoc fire—that is, what he associated with this fire. Those impressions found their way into the paper. Here is an index of the terms Mickey generated using the first set of questions listed in the Questions for Analysis.

Indexing Key Terms

Paragraph 1
  Modoc National Forest
  fire . . . raging
Paragraph 2
  emergency
  gloomy uncertainty
  danger
  worry transformed into anger
  cigarette butt
  anguish
Paragraph 3
  fire camp
  fire's condition
  catalog of equipment—red tarps, ten bulldozers, one hundred heavy
    vehicles, seven helicopters, crates and crates of new shovels, axes,
    chainsaws, canteens, and K-rations
  at least nine hundred other fire fighters
Paragraph 4
  white ash and charcoal

murderous
killing
cigarette
destructive
Paragraph 5
harm

Each of these terms expresses either the horror Mickey and his fellow fire fighters felt or the enormity of the entire scene of the fire.

To help him make his point about the fire's destructiveness, Mickey decided a before-and-after description might work, and he included this description in paragraph 4. We can look at the two descriptions (before and after) as standing opposite each other. Because the destruction of the fire is contrasted with or opposed by the beauty of the forest, we can look at the two descriptions as having been generated by the second set of questions. The following list is an index of terms standing opposite the fire, terms Mickey generated by using the second set of questions.

beauty that once existed
tall, proud pine trees
green branches
birds frolicking
deer bedded down
buck
gopher
beautiful

Although these terms almost cause Mickey to lapse into a fairly sentimental view of the forest, they are essential to the essay because they enable him to detail very closely the extent of the destruction and the suffering that wildfire can bring to the forest and its wildlife.

Finally, Mickey looked back over the terms and realized that it was during his experience with the Modoc fire that he fully understood the awesomeness of this and other fires. In paragraph 5 he writes, "I could now realize the magnitude of the harm a large forest fire creates. I had experienced first hand the intense human suffering, the death, and the economic and environmental cost." These two sentences show that Mickey examined the terms he had generated up to that point in prewriting and speculated about what those terms implied for him, trying to discover how best to articulate the significance of those terms for him. The paper is the result of this discovery.

Exploration Procedure

In summary, Mickey's exploration of the key term *1977 Modoc fire* followed this order.

1. He settled on the fire at Modoc as the probable topic for his paper. We say "probable" because he could have found it necessary to switch to another topic if the Modoc topic were not to develop well.

2. He applied the Questions for Analysis, writing down first those things he associated with the fire, then those things opposing the fire, and finally the implications of the terms he had generated.

3. He decided on some ordering principle that seemed inherent in the material he had generated. Rather than writing an essay with a trite, weighty thesis such as "Forest fires are one of the worst catastrophes on earth," Mickey chose to let the details tell this and show, at the same time, the fire's effect on him. The order that seemed most appropriate was chronological. Basically, the paper traces Mickey's involvement with the fire in the order of that involvement. He boarded the plane, arrived at the fire camp, wandered around the camp, and then fought the fire. Then he chose to present this order as the heart of a reminiscence about the fire. This reminiscence framework works well because it shows clearly that Mickey's realization of theextent of the fire's damage came only as he surveyed the whole scene and then thought back over the past few days.

4. He produced a rough draft that was read by his peer group, a group of four other students in his freshman composition class.

5. Using his group's comments, Mickey revised his essay and then submitted it.

Mickey progressed from one term, *1977 Modoc fire*, to a paper of just over 1000 words, producing a piece of good writing by exploring the meanings of terms. Using the Questions for Analysis, he expanded the meaning for him of *1977 Modoc fire* until he discovered what he specifically wanted to say. In finding this significance, Mickey generated enough information to use in writing the essay.

WRITING ASSIGNMENT

Respond to one of the following topics in an essay.

1. In working through the three applications of the Questions for Analysis, we asked you to prewrite two essays, one on a topic similar to that of the XYZRC exercise and another on a topic similar to that of the "Icarus" cartoon. Use either of these prewritings as the basis of an essay. Submit your prewriting along with your finished draft.

2. From your responses to the Interest Inventory, pick a subject similar to that of Mickey Carter's essay and use it as the basis for a narrative account of some event that had a significant effect on you. Use the Questions for Analysis to guide your prewriting, and submit the prewriting along with your finished draft.

3. Revise the essay you wrote in response to the description assignment at the end of Chapter One. As you look again at this essay, apply the Questions for

Analysis to those parts of the essay your instructor marked as being in need of revision. Do you need to add more detail? Do you need to discover and/or reveal the event's significance more clearly? Submit your application of the Questions for Analysis along with your revised draft.

Chapter Three

Creating Order

In Chapter Two we focused our attention on finding material to write about. In doing so, however, we could not ignore relationships—order. We found that when we confront a new experience, we understand, or give meaning to, that experience by comparing it with our previous experience. Ordering depends on establishing relationships, a point we can illustrate in Figure 3.1.

The circles in the middle of each set are identical, but they are made to appear to be of differing sizes by the contexts in which they appear—the middle circle on the left appears to be larger than the middle circle on the right. However, divorced from context, the circles are obviously identical (Figure 3.2).

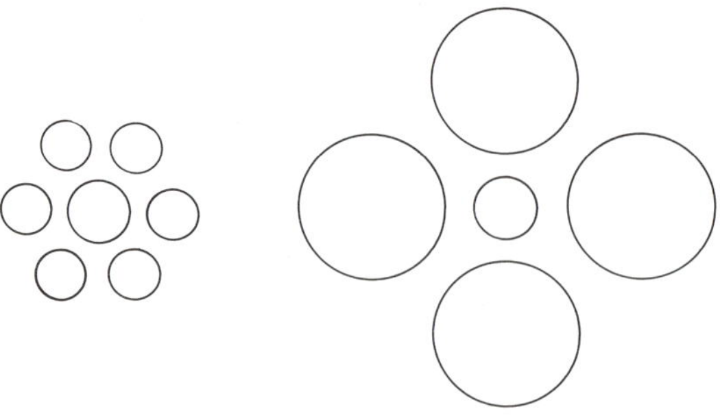

Figure 3.1

Figure 3.2

Even in Figure 3.2, we establish meaning by comparing the two circles to each other. But what if we are given only one circle (Figure 3.3) and asked whether it is a large circle?

Now what can we say? The only truthful statement we can make is that we do not know. Surely some people would attempt to answer the question, but in doing so, they would be comparing this circle with some "standard" or "average" circle existing only in their minds. Their decision concerning the size of this circle would be the meaning they find in this situation, and, as we have seen, that meaning would be entirely dependent upon the concept of the "standard" or "average" circle they bring to the situation.

Meaning, then, derives from relationships. In these drawings we derive meaning—our judgment regarding the circles' sizes—from the contexts in which the circles are placed or the contexts in which our mind's eye places them.

In this chapter we will examine the ways in which we create meaning through relationships—first from the perspective of individual words and then from the perspective of larger units. In all sections we will view order as deriving from a web of relationships, so that we see order as dependent upon context.

RELATIONSHIPS BETWEEN WORDS

Just as the "meaning" we find in these circles derives, in part, from the associations we make with other circles, words in sentences derive meaning from associations with other words. For example, when we see or hear the word *bank*, what meaning do we give it? If we associate it with other words such as *draft, deposit, money,* or *John Dillinger,* we will arrive at a meaning such as this: "A business establishment authorized to perform one or more of the following services: receive and safeguard money and other valuables; lend money at interest; execute bills of exchange . . . purchase and exchange foreign currency; and issue notes of circulation or currency" (*The American Heritage Dictionary of the English Language*). If, however, we relate the word to other words such as *river,*

Figure 3.3

alluvial, *current*, and *water*, we will arrive at a meaning such as this: "The slope of land adjoining a body of water, especially adjoining a lake, river or sea" (*The American Heritage Dictionary of the English Language*).

Isolated from any context, *bank* may have either of the preceding meanings as well as several others—snowbank, bank shot, cloud bank, banking to the left, and so forth. However, in a given context we have no difficulty assigning a meaning to the word because of its relation with other words. Consider the following two sentences.

John just came back from the bank with the money he needs.
John spent the afternoon on the bank with his line in the water.

These examples help us see that the words in a sentence often make it impossible for the reader to have difficulty assigning a meaning to a potentially ambiguous word such as *bank*. Indeed, the cues we find in sentences are so effective in causing us to perceive the meanings of individual words in these sentences that we often fail to recognize how much the meaning depends on these cues. We come to feel that such a word as *bank* contains its meaning entirely in itself and that we would know what the word means in any context, or even isolated from any context. And in a sense we would. No doubt if we were presented with this word in isolation, we would immediately assign it a meaning without even thinking about other possible meanings that exist. But even this assigned meaning would be dependent upon implicit relationships. If we immediately assign the meaning of "business establishment" to *bank*, we do so because we associate words such as *draft* and *deposit* with this word. In such a situation we are much like the person who sees a circle and immediately thinks of it as "small" by comparing it to some concept of "standard-sized circle" in her subconscious.

As these examples illustrate, the words we select to represent things and ideas actually do more than simply "represent." They direct our attention to the various associations we have with them. Thus, a word may have one "meaning" to one person, but an entirely different "meaning" for someone else, depending upon the associations these individuals bring to that word. In "The War Prayer" Mark Twain illustrates how the associations of a word control its meaning. Read the story and then answer the questions that follow it.

The War Prayer

Mark Twain

It was a time of great and exalting excitement. The country was up in arms, the war was on, in every breast burned the holy fire of patriotism; the drums were beating, the bands playing, the toy pistols popping, the bunched firecrackers hissing and spluttering; on every hand and far down the receding and fading spread of roofs and balconies a fluttering wilderness of flags flashed in the sun; daily the young volunteers marched down the wide avenue gay and fine in their new uniforms, the proud fathers and mothers and sisters and sweethearts cheering them with voices choked with happy emotion as they swung by; nightly the packed mass meetings listened, panting, to patriot oratory which stirred the deepest deeps of their hearts, and which they interrupted at briefest intervals with cyclones of applause, the tears running down their cheeks the while; in the churches the pastors preached devotion to flag and country, and invoked the God of Battles, beseeching His aid in our good cause in outpouring of fervid eloquence which moved every listener. It was indeed a glad and gracious time, and the half dozen rash spirits that ventured to disapprove of the war and cast a doubt upon its righteousness got such a stern and angry warning that for their personal safety's sake they quickly shrank out of sight and offended no more in that way.

Sunday morning came—next day the battalions would leave for the front; the church was filled; the volunteers were there, their young faces alight with martial dreams—visions of the stern advance, the gathering momentum, the rushing charge, the flashing sabers, the flight of the foe, the tumult, the enveloping smoke, the fierce pursuit, the surrender!—then home from the war, bronzed heroes, welcomed, adored, submerged in golden seas of glory! With the volunteers sat their dear ones, proud, happy, envied by the neighbors and friends who had no sons and brothers to send forth to the field of honor, there to win for the flag, or, failing, die the noblest of noble deaths. The service proceeded; a war chapter from the Old Testament was read; the first prayer was said; it was followed by an organ burst that shook the building, and with one impulse the house rose, with glowing eyes and beating hearts, and poured out that tremendous invocation—

"God the all-terrible! Thou who ordainest,
Thunder thy clarion and lightning thy sword!"

Then came the "long" prayer. None could remember the like of it for passionate pleading and moving and beautiful language. The burden of its supplication was, that an ever-merciful and benignant Father of us all would watch over our noble young soldiers, and aid, comfort, and encourage them in their patriotic work; bless them, shield them in the day of battle and the hour of peril, bear them in His mighty hand, make them strong and confident, invincible in the bloody onset; help them to crush the foe, grant to them and to their flag and country imperishable honor and glory—

An aged stranger entered and moved with slow and noiseless step up the main aisle, his eye fixed upon the minister, his long body clothed in a robe that reached to his feet, his head bare, his white hair descending in a frothy cataract to his shoulders, his seamy face unnaturally pale, pale even to ghastliness. With all eyes following him and wondering, he made his silent way; without pausing, he ascended to the preacher's side and stood there, waiting. With shut lids the preacher, unconscious of his presence, continued his moving prayer, and at last finished it with the words, uttered in fervent appeal, "Bless our arms, grant us the victory, O Lord our God, Father and Protector of our land and flag!"

The stranger touched his arm, motioned him to step aside—which the startled minister did—and took his place. During some moments he surveyed the spellbound audience with solemn eyes, in which burned an uncanny light; then in a deep voice he said:

"I come from the Throne—bearing a message from Almighty God!" The words smote the house with a shock; if the stranger perceived it he gave no attention. "He has heard the prayer of His servant your shepherd, and will grant it if such shall be your desire after I, His messenger, shall have explained to you its import—that is to say, its full import. For it is like unto many of the prayers of men, in that it asks for more than he who utters it is aware of—except he pause and think.

"God's servant and yours has prayed his prayer. Has he paused and taken thought? Is it one prayer? No, it is two—one uttered, the other not. Both have reached the ear of Him Who heareth all supplications, the spoken and the unspoken. Ponder this—keep it in mind. If you would beseech a blessing upon yourself, beware! lest without intent you invoke a curse upon a neighbor at the same time. If you pray for the blessing of rain upon your crop which needs it, by that act you are possibly praying for a curse upon some neighbor's crop which may not need rain and can be injured by it.

"You have heard your servant's prayer—the uttered part of it. I am commissioned of God to put into words the other part of it—that part which the pastor—and also you in your hearts—fervently prayed silently. And ignorantly and unthinkingly? God grant that it was so! You heard these words: 'Grant us the victory, O Lord our God!' That is sufficient. The *whole* of the uttered prayer is compact into those pregnant words. Elaborations were not necessary. When you have prayed for victory you have prayed for many unmentioned results which follow victory—*must* follow it, cannot help but follow it. Upon the listening spirit of God the Father fell also the unspoken part of the prayer. He commandeth me to put it into words. Listen!

"O Lord our Father, our young patriots, idols of our hearts, go forth to battle—be Thou near them! With them—in spirit—we also go forth from the sweet peace of our beloved firesides to smite the foe. O Lord our God, help us to tear their soldiers to bloody shreds with our shells; help us to cover their smiling fields with the pale forms of their patriot dead; help us to drown the thunder of the guns with the shrieks of their wounded, writhing in pain; help us to lay waste their humble homes with a hurricane of fire; help us to wring the hearts of their unoffending widows with unavailing grief; help us to turn them out roofless with their little children to wander unfriended the wastes of their desolated land in rags and hunger and thirst, sports of the sun flames of summer and the icy winds of winter, broken in spirit, worn with travail, imploring Thee for the refuge of the grave and denied it—for our sakes who adore Thee, Lord, blast their hopes, blight their lives, protract their bitter pilgrimage, make heavy their steps, water their way with their tears, stain the white snow with the blood of their wounded feet! We ask it, in the spirit of love, of Him Who is the source of all Love, and Who is the ever-faithful refuge and friend of all that are sore beset and seek His aid with humble and contrite hearts. Amen."

(*After a pause.*) "Ye have prayed it; if ye still desire it, speak! The messenger of the Most High waits."

It was believed afterward that the man was a lunatic, because there was no sense in what he said.*

EXERCISES

1. Describe briefly the various views of the coming war. How does the minister perceive it? The congregation? The angel?

2. Each spokesman (the minister and the angel) describes the same event. How do you account for the vast dissimilarities in these descriptions? How successfully does each spokesman use language to direct the audience's attention?

3. What are the key terms of the minister's prayer? The angel's? What associations do you have with those key terms? Which are positive? Negative? What do they reveal about how each spokesman depends upon associations to make meaning?

RELATIONSHIPS BETWEEN LARGER UNITS: SENTENCES AND PARAGRAPHS

As we deal with words, the meaning we create for ourselves and our readers is the result of a web of contexts in which the various words interrelate in meaningful ways, much as the "meaning" of a puzzle is the result of the relationships among its pieces. No one piece of the puzzle has meaning in itself; but when it is placed alongside other pieces, the combined pieces become meaningful.

The Web of Relationships

This puzzle analogy works well to help us gain insight into the role of relationships between larger units in writing. As we begin to work with a puzzle, we focus our attention on individual pieces, spreading them out onto a table to find ways of combining them. In a very simple puzzle we may be able to continue operating within this perspective. If one piece of the puzzle is blue and one piece is brown, we may place them side by side (that is, relate them) and thus see that the blue is an ocean and the brown is its shore. Such a simple puzzle illustrates our assertion that no individual thing has meaning in itself. In this case the blue piece and the brown piece do not become meaningful (that is, become an ocean and a shore) until they are related to each other.

The analogy between puzzle solving and writing works well when we move from simple to more complex puzzles requiring the puzzle worker to build

---

*From *Europe and Elsewhere* by Mark Twain. Copyright 1923, 1951 by The Mark Twain Company. Reprinted with permission of Harper & Row, Publishers, Inc.

larger and larger pieces so that the individual piece is no longer the basic unit. In this more complicated puzzle the solver is likely to find several blue pieces and several brown pieces. As he separates the pieces into piles, the solver no longer thinks of these individual pieces as the units, or building blocks. Rather, all the blue pieces come to be a unit, the blue section, and all of the brown pieces come to be a unit, the brown section. From this perspective, neither the blue section nor the brown section is meaningful in itself. But when the solver relates these two units, they become meaningful: the blue section, an ocean; the brown section, its shore.

Just as the puzzle solver cannot always consider the individual pieces of the puzzle the basic units, the writer cannot always consider words her basic units. As words link together—as they "associate" with one another—they produce increasingly larger contexts and so increasingly more comprehensive meanings. So too with sentences and paragraphs. The writer must consider the web of relationships that sentences establish in creating paragraphs and that paragraphs establish in creating an entire essay. In this way she comes to understand that these sentences and paragraphs are fully meaningful only in their contexts.

Relationships Between Sentences

What does the sentence "But it is very warm in here" mean? At first, the meaning of this sentence may seem exceedingly clear. But suppose this sentence is one of the units constituting the following paragraph.

> **I am so relieved to be in this office. The heat has been turned off in my office, and I have been freezing all morning. But it is very warm in here.**

Then consider this same sentence in the following context.

> **I thought this office would be more comfortable than it is. Usually, this is the coolest spot on campus. But it is very warm in here.**

In the first context the sample sentence is a means by which the writer expresses approval of the room; in the second, it is the means by which he expresses disapproval. We could, of course, argue that the same basic assertion is being made in both sentences, but in order to do so we would have to look at the sentence as a group of units (words) that have a meaning in relation to one another; in other words, we would view the sentence as a whole. But when we look at the sentence as a unit in the larger whole of a paragraph, we see that its meaning is dependent upon its relationship with other units (sentences) in that paragraph.

EXERCISE

We have seen that if we are to deal with the meaning that a sentence has in a context, we cannot limit ourselves to the point of view in which the sentence is a whole composed of units (words). From this broader perspective the meaning of the sentence "Frank often speaks out in class" can vary greatly from one context to the next.

Creating Order

Write one paragraph in which this sentence seems to compliment Frank. Then write another paragraph in which it seems a criticism of Frank. After you have done so, consider the following questions.

1. What words in the first paragraph are crucial in causing the sentence to be seen as a compliment? (Remember our earlier discussion in which we showed that such words as *draft* and *deposit* control our interpretation of the word *bank*.)

2. What words in the second paragraph are crucial in causing the sentence to be seen as a criticism?

3. How could you paraphrase the words *speaks out* in the first paragraph?

4. How could you paraphrase the words *speaks out* in the second paragraph?

5. If a person were using only this sentence as a description of Frank's behavior and wanted to make sure that the sentence would cause the hearer to have a favorable opinion of Frank, what words might he change? Write this new sentence.

To this point we have talked about relationships in rather general terms. We will now turn our attention to an actual student essay and discuss the role of relationships in creating the order and meaning of that essay. The following essay was written by Stephanie Weikert, a student at Clemson University. As you read it, note how each paragraph relates to those around it.

Franklin Elementary School

1   On a chilly fall morning, Franklin Elementary School awaited the beginning of another day. Its ugly, ancient frame solemnly rose from the ground and met the morning sun. Classroom lights shone through the dirty windows and illuminated the hard ground below. The wind blew through the swings on the empty playground, making them squeak and creak like a door turning on rusty hinges. Three tall maple trees vainly attempted to hide the eyesore. A steel fence enclosed the school property, separating it from the rest of the neighborhood. Surrounding Franklin were the small, grim ghetto shanties filled with youngsters preparing for the school day.

2   As I viewed these surroundings, I felt a sense of disappointment. Of the five elementary schools in Wadsworth, I had to be dumped at Franklin to work as a teacher's aide. I had hoped to work at Overlook Elementary or Valley View School. Unlike Franklin, they were both beautiful new schools in the better section of town. Because of its ghetto location and age, most people considered Franklin the "scum" of the school district.

  When I entered the school, I expected to see nothing but filth and poverty. I prepared for the shock of unsanitary conditions, graffiti on the walls, and scurrying rats. Instead, clean brick walls and the fresh scent of disinfectant mingling with the aroma of breakfast greeted me. Much to my surprise, there was no sign of uncleanliness. In the middle of the lobby, an old door mat covered the floor and provided a place for muddy little feet to clean themselves. To my left, there was a simple "lost and found" corner that contained a coat rack and a cardboard box. The box contained forgotten remnants of clothing. The moth-eaten sweaters and thin homemade mittens with no mates patiently waited for their owners to retrieve them. A staircase on the right ascended to the classrooms. The classroom where I would work for nine months was at the top of these stairs.

As I exited the lobby and mounted the dimly lit stone staircase, I glanced around at my surroundings. The wall was plastered with photographs of animals and posters warning youngsters to "cover your mouth when you sneeze." On two large bulletin boards, brightly colored artwork was displayed. This part of the school was still quite clean although its age was evidenced by the cracked ceiling and peeling paint. I walked past the other rooms until I finally came to the door of the kindergarten classroom. Here I was to work.

Immediately after entering the room, I felt as though I was Gulliver walking into the land of the Lilliputians. Everything was made to fit the small bodies of kindergarteners. In the front of the room, seven small tables were neatly arranged and 28 petite chairs waited for their owners. One large teacher's desk stood out of place. The back of the room was a child's paradise. There were rows of shelves filled with toys. A red fire engine waited for a young lad to arrive and extinguish a pretend fire. Dollies with brown and black yarn hair and brightly painted eyes watched for little girls who would be their mommies. For the youngsters who wanted to be "grown-ups," there were many boxes filled with ancient hats, shoes, and dresses. A Lilliputian kitchen took up a whole corner. The orange stove, refrigerator, and sink were "just like mommy's." As I took in this classroom environment, my attitude toward Franklin School began to change. I started to see an interesting and well-kept school.

Time passed as I observed my new surroundings. Suddenly, I realized that the bell was about to ring and my new students would soon begin to flood into the room. At first, I was apprehensive as to how the children would act. Because they came from the ghetto, I expected them to be juvenile delinquents who wanted nothing to do with school. I also thought they would be poorly dressed and underfed. As the bell signaled the beginning of school, I anxiously watched the youngsters bounce in like excited roly-poly puppies. Much to my surprise, they appeared healthy and happy. The morning progressed and I also found that the kindergarteners were actually very intelligent and obedient.

By the end of the school day, I realized that I was totally wrong about Franklin School. I had thought it would be a dirty, miserable place to work, but it was actually a clean and enjoyable building. I was foolish to listen to other people's views and let my first impression of the exterior of the school form my opinion. In the end, I learned a valuable lesson and found a comfortable place to work.

Stephanie's is obviously a good essay, one that developed as she worked her way through several revisions. In the following section we will examine the structure by which she develops the meaning of her final draft.

Aristotle gave us one of the most general statements about the order of a composition when he said that it must have a beginning, a middle, and an end. Although we hope to provide more specific insights into order, Aristotle's pronouncement is a good starting place for our discussion.

We may refer to Aristotle's three divisions in more conventional terms—introduction, body, and conclusion. Of course, we know that all complete compositions have these three parts, but we may be uncertain about just how these parts are shaped. Do we simply write an introduction in the first paragraph and a conclusion in the last paragraph? Although many compositions may fit this rather exacting mold, many do not.

We began this chapter by noting the strong ties between organizing (putting the parts of the essay together) and inventing (finding those parts). Because these concerns are so intertwined, we may learn something about the structure of essays by examining the ways in which the content of those essays develops. In order to do that, we reintroduce a device we used in Chapter Two, the Questions for Analysis. At the same time that they help us find materials, these three basic questions—What goes with what?, What opposes what?, and What follows (from) what?—represent the principles by which we order, and thus give meaning to, experience—association, dissociation, and sequence. Using these principles, we can outline the order of Stephanie's essay in the following fashion.

Section	*Paragraph*	*Subject Summary*
Introduction	One	Picture of Franklin Elementary School
	Two	Stephanie's preconceptions of the school
Body	Three	View of the school's lobby
	Four	Stephanie's trip to her classroom
	Five	View of her classroom
	Six	Arrival of the students
Conclusion	Seven	Stephanie's reflections on her experience

We sectioned this essay by examining the basic relations between the paragraphs within the essay. First we looked at the relation between the first two paragraphs. In paragraph 1, Stephanie presents an overall view of this school. Then in paragraph 2, she introduces the feelings she had about this school before working in it. Paragraphs 1 and 2 "go together" because both prepare the reader for Stephanie's experience in this school. Before entering the lobby with Stephanie (in paragraph 3), the reader has a picture of the school and knows something about Stephanie's attitude toward the school.

There is a marked change at paragraph 3 in Stephanie's essay. Paragraphs 3 through 6 cluster together, forming the body of the essay, because in each of them Stephanie tells us about some particular aspect of her first day at Franklin Elementary School.

Finally, we come to paragraph 7, the conclusion. Here Stephanie reflects upon what she learned in her time at Franklin Elementary: Specifically, she was wrong about Franklin Elementary, and generally, it is possible for first impressions to be quite misleading.

At the same time that the what-goes-with-what? question helps us to see how the various paragraphs cluster together, the what-opposes-what? question helps us to see how the paragraphs separate themselves into three sections. Paragraphs 3 through 6 oppose, or differ from, paragraphs 1 and 2. Each of the "body" paragraphs contains specific discussion of the things that happened during Stephanie's first day as an aide. These paragraphs cluster together because they report details of this first day. Paragraphs 1 and 2, however, do not contain actual details of this day. Even though the materials in paragraph 1 are different from the materials in paragraph 2, both paragraphs are general in nature and, thus, they may be grouped together because of the contrast between their generality and the detail in paragraphs 3 through 6. The same is true of paragraph 7. Here Stephanie talks "about" the experience in Franklin Elementary and what it meant to her, in contrast to the body paragraphs, which narrate the events of the first day.

Using the Questions for Analysis, we have sectioned this entire essay into three major parts. But we must remember that these three units have no meaning in themselves; their meaning depends on their relationship to one another. Look at any of these parts. Does it make sense without the others? Do you get a sense of completeness when you finish reading the introduction, paragraphs 1 and 2? Do you know what school Stephanie refers to in the opening sentence of paragraph 3 if you disregard the introduction and the title? Do you have any basis for judging the validity of the opening sentence of the conclusion, paragraph 7? The answer to each of these questions is no.

Paragraphs 1 and 2 (the introduction) and 7 (the conclusion) form a backdrop against which we see paragraphs 3 through 6 (the body). Together paragraphs 1 and 2 set up a problem—Stephanie's disappointment in being assigned to Franklin Elementary. Then, paragraphs 3 through 6 recount the initial experience Stephanie had in that school. Finally, paragraph 7 shows us the effect this experience had on Stephanie—that is, how the experience resolved a problem for her.

<table>
<tr><td>EXERCISE</td><td>Look at an essay you have written in response to an assignment in this course. Examine the overall organization—beginning, middle, and end—of that essay in the way in which we examined the overall structure of Stephanie's essay. After performing this analysis, answer the following questions.</td></tr>
</table>

1. Is there a clear beginning in the essay? If so, what principle of order helps you decide which sentences or paragraphs make up the beginning?

2. Is there a clear ending? If so, what principle of order helps you decide what sentences or paragraphs make up the ending?

Creating Order

3. How does each section—beginning, middle, end—relate to the other sections to create meaning? Have you established a strong web of relationships? If not, what could you do to strengthen this web?

THE RELATIONSHIP OF FORM AND MEANING

Just as the meaning of the various sections of an essay depends on the relations between those sections, the meaning of the units within those sections depends on relationships. In the Franklin Elementary essay, paragraphs 3 through 6 (the body) provide detail about Stephanie's first day in the school. In order to develop this day's meaning for her, Stephanie had to take the reader back to school with her as she recounted her first impressions. To help the reader sense the importance of those individual impressions, Stephanie had to show how the various parts of the school and her thoughts about each combined to create that day's meaning. These parts she described in separate paragraphs that join with one another to produce this meaning, as the following chart shows.

Section	Paragraph	Subject Summary
Body	Three	Stephanie enters school. She finds a clean orderly lobby, mat for muddy feet, and lost and found corner.
	Four	Stephanie walks up stairs. She finds photographs of animals and brightly colored artwork. The staircase is clean.
	Five	Stephanie walks into her classroom. She finds small chairs and many toys.
	Six	The children enter. They are excited, healthy, and happy.

In paragraph 3 Stephanie concentrates on the very first things she sees upon entering the school. This paragraph is organized around the lobby of the school. In the next paragraph Stephanie concerns herself with the stairway leading to her classroom. In paragraph 5, she focuses on the classroom itself. And finally, the focal point of paragraph 6 is the arrival of the children. At some point, then, Stephanie saw each of these paragraphs as a unit in itself and generated the material of that paragraph around some unifying concept. The essay is about Stephanie's first day at Franklin Elementary, and each of these "body" paragraphs is about some particular place or event related to this experience.

Our puzzle analogy, as we have applied it to Stephanie's essay, should make us aware of two important principles in the writing process. The first is that it is impossible to separate form from meaning. Just as the picture that develops through the puzzle process depends on the way the solver puts together the pieces, the meaning that results through the composing process depends on the way the writer puts together the basic units. The second is that the writer's ability to shift perspective is crucial in creating meaning. Like the puzzle solver, the writer cannot constantly focus on the essay as the basic unit of meaning. At the various stages of the writing process, she needs to change focus so that paragraphs, sentences, and even words become the basic units.

We can explain these principles rather simply by referring to Stephanie's essay. We begin with the second principle: A writer must learn to shift focus in the writing process. In order to compose her essay, Stephanie could not continue to deal with her topic as her first day at Franklin Elementary. At some point she had to think of the parts of this experience: her entrance into the school, her walk up the stairs to her classroom, and so forth. This analysis brings us to our first principle: It is impossible to separate form from meaning. Stephanie may not have known at first just what meaning she wished to convey in this essay. That is, she may have had a vague notion of what she intended to convey but no clear idea of what the actual content of the essay was to be.

However, as she began to decide what the parts of her experience were and how she might shape those parts into an essay, she began to discover the meaning of the essay. For example, when she decided to retrace her steps so that the reader would gradually realize, just as she had done, that Franklin School is a lively, vital place, Stephanie could generate material by examining, in her mind's eye, everything she could see while standing in different places in the school—the lobby, the stairs, the classroom.

<table>
<tr><td>EXERCISE</td><td>Look at the body of the descriptive or narrative essay you wrote in response to a previous assignment. Examine its order as we have examined the order in Stephanie's essay. What is each paragraph about? How does each paragraph join with those around it to produce meaning? Are there any paragraphs that do not contribute substantially to this meaning? If so, why not? What could you do to strengthen their contribution? Are there any missing pieces in this "puzzle"? If so, fill in those pieces.</td></tr>
</table>

When working to create meaning in a sentence, paragraph, or essay, the writer must be aware of two principles of order: unity and coherence.

Unity

Unity involves direction. A sentence, paragraph, or essay is unified if it develops the writer's meaning without any extraneous material interfering. At times when we talk with friends, we digress; that is, we begin talking about one topic, then move to another topic, then another, and perhaps, finally, back to the original topic. In a typical conversation about baseball, for example, we could begin by talking about a favorite American League team (say, the Texas Rangers), move to talking about Ricky Henderson's speed and base-stealing record in the 1982 season (Henderson set this record while playing for another American League team, the Oakland Athletics), move from there to talking about Tony Dorsett's speed (Dorsett is a running back for the Dallas Cowboys of the National Football League), and then back to the Rangers' doomed 1982 season. If we wrote all this in a paragraph, we would cover these topics: a favorite baseball team, a player on another baseball team, a player on a football team, and a favorite baseball team. Such a paragraph would lack in unity; it would jump all around professional sports. In conversation this lack of unity is easily overcome, because in the give-and-take of talking, the listener can raise questions to get the speaker back onto the original idea. But, in writing, such digressions can disrupt the chain of thought the writer should be working to establish.

Coherence

Coherence involves connection. In coherent writing the connections between parts of sentences, sentences, paragraphs, and even larger units will be clear to the reader. This is not to imply that writing that is not clear and coherent lacks connections. In such writing, the writer is making connections for himself; if he were not, his writing would not be meaningful to him. However, he is not making these connections available to his readers.

To illustrate the ways in which writers make connections available to readers, we return to Stephanie Weikert's essay, "Franklin Elementary School." In our discussion of Stephanie's essay, we said that the three key relationships—association, dissociation, and sequence—account for the connections between sentences of a coherent paragraph. In the following list we reproduce the third paragraph of Stephanie's essay and point out these connections.

1. When I entered the school, I expected to see nothing but filth and poverty.

Association

2. I prepared for the shock of unsanitary conditions, graffiti on the walls, and scurrying rats.

Dissociation (Opposition)

3. Instead, clean brick walls and the fresh scent of disinfectant mingling with the aroma of breakfast greeted me.

Association

4. Much to my surprise, there was no sign of uncleanliness.

Association

5. In the middle of the lobby, an old door mat covered the floor and provided a place for muddy little feet to clean themselves.

6. To my left, there was a simple "lost and found" corner that contained a coat rack and a cardboard box.

7. The box contained forgotten remnants of clothing.

8. The moth-eaten sweaters and thin homemade mittens with no mates patiently waited for their owners to retrieve them.

9. A staircase on the right ascended to the classrooms.

10. The classroom where I would work for nine months was at the top of these stairs.

We should preface our discussion of the preceding schema by saying that we do not offer it as a method of learning to organize. Rather, we intend it as a device to help illustrate what you already know intuitively about order.

Having made that point, we turn to the connections we have inserted between the sentences of the paragraph. The material in sentence 2 is associated with, or goes with, the material in sentence 1. That is, sentence 1 introduces the general concept of filth and poverty, and sentence 2 gives specific examples— graffiti and rats. As the transitional word *instead* indicates, the relation between sentences 2 and 3 is characterized by opposition. "Clean brick walls and the fresh scent of disinfectant" do not "go with" graffiti and rats. Stephanie expected one type of environment, but she found quite a different one. The relation between sentence 3 and sentence 4 is again associative. That is, sentence 3 gives specific examples of cleanliness, and sentence 4 makes a general statement about the cleanliness of the lobby. Sentence 5 continues this chain of associations. The old doormat, which catches the mud from the children's feet, "goes with" the general clean and orderly state of the lobby, just as does the "lost and found" corner, mentioned in sentence 6. Sentence 7 is obviously associated with sentence 6, because it continues to explain just what is in the box mentioned in that previous sentence. Sentence 8 is, of course, associated with sentences 6 and 7, because it continues to treat the contents of the lost and found corner. The transitional phrase *on the right* in sentence 9 signals a change in the pattern of relations. Stephanie turns her attention from the lost and found corner to the staircase that leads to her classroom. The only apparent relation between this sentence and the previous one is the physical relationship between the items mentioned in them—the lost and found corner and the staircase. As indicated by the phrase *at the top*, the relation between sentences 9 and 10 is also formed by sequence. By inserting these relation words—association, dissociation, and sequence—between the sentences of Stephanie's third paragraph, we intend to draw your attention once again to the inherent connection between organization and content, or form and meaning. No matter how badly you may want to insert a sentence, if it has no logical relationship to the other sentences in the paragraph, it does not belong in that paragraph.

Again we must emphasize that our purpose is not to suggest that you should consciously concern yourself with connections as you write. Rather, we have introduced these connections because they help us isolate three chief devices for achieving coherence: (1) transitional words and phrases, (2) repetition of key words and phrases, and (3) repetition of sentence structures. As you use any of these devices, you establish relationships and so create order.

Transitional Words and Phrases The first device should be fairly obvious; we all use such terms as *and, but, still, therefore*, and *because*. To help you see the principles underlying transitional words and phrases so that as you revise you may use the most appropriate transitions, we have listed the most frequently used transitional words and phrases under the headings of our Questions for Analysis.

Association (goes with)	*Dissociation* (opposes)	*Sequence* (follows)	*Sequence* (follows from)
and	but	next	because
also	contrary to	then	therefore
in addition to	yet	soon	thus
furthermore	still	afterwards	since
likewise	not	following	so
not only, but also	in opposition to	since	
both, and	however		
either, or	notwithstanding		
similarly	although		
moreover	neither, nor		

These words and many others like them are sure signs that the writer can use to let readers know how the parts of her writing are connected. They are not, however, sure signs of successful writing. The writer who depends too heavily upon them will tend to use these connectors to force relationships. The skillful writer will use the other two devices, which we will introduce next, to make relations seem so natural that she will need few signals; when the writer does use these signals, they will seem to reflect relationships that are already there.

Repetition of Key Words and Phrases The second device, repetition of key words and phrases, is not as familiar or as obvious as transitional signals. By means of key word repetitions, the writer shows readers that the parts of the essay are connected, as the following two sentences illustrate.

John left yesterday. The train he took was late.

In this sentence the repetition of the words *he* and *took* provides a connection. As this example illustrates, we are using the term *repetition* rather loosely. An exact repetition would be a second use of the words *John* and *left*. In some cases repetition of identical terms will occur, but in many cases the repetition will take the form of a paraphrase. In our example the word *he* obviously stands for *John*. There is also a sense in which the verb *took* is a restatement of *left*. That is, John *left* by *taking* the train. Thus, with the word *took* we have another view of his leaving.

Repetition of key words is perhaps the most important tool for coherent writing. At the same time, it may be the most difficult one to master because of the varied forms this repetition may take and because writers always make these connections, in their own minds, when they put two things together. The writer of such sentences as

John left yesterday. The train was late.

is connecting the two events in his own mind. The writer knows that the train mentioned in the second sentence is the train John left on; thus, he may have much difficulty in seeing how any reader could fail to make this connection.

Repetition of Sentence Structures   The third device for achieving coherence involves repetition of sentence structures. Our sentence structuring can go a long way toward helping readers see relationships we want them to see, as the following section of a paragraph by E. B. White illustrates.

> By rights New York should have destroyed itself long ago, from panic or fire or rioting or failure of some vital supply line in its circulatory system or from some deep labyrinthine short circuit. Long ago the city should have experienced an insoluble traffic snarl at some impossible bottleneck. It should have perished of hunger when food lines failed for a few days. It should have been wiped out by a plague starting in its slums or carried in by ships' rats. It should have been overwhelmed by the sea that licks at it on every side. The workers in its myriad cells should have succumbed to nerves, from the fearful pall of smoke-fog that drifts over every few days from Jersey, blotting out all light at noon and leaving the high offices suspended, men groping and depressed, and the sense of world's end.*

With one exception, sentence 6, the subject of every sentence in this paragraph is *New York*, or a semantic equivalent*—*city* or *it*. With few exceptions these subjects are at the beginning of their sentences, and every verb is preceded by the auxiliary phrase "should have." The effect of this structural repetition is to pile up a list of potential disasters that confront the city; the repetition reinforces and draws attention to the number of items in the list.

---

*E. B. White, "Here Is New York," *Holiday*, April 1949, p. 36.

                                                    Creating Order

There is, of course, repetition of key words and phrases in White's paragraph, but even with this repetition, the coherence of the paragraph, and its overall effect, would be diminished without the structural repetition.

EXERCISE

WRITING
SAMPLE

Nature writer Loren Eiseley wrote the following paragraph in "The Brown Wasps."

Some years ago the old elevated railway in Philadelphia was torn down and replaced by a subway system. This ancient El with its barnlike stations containing nut-vending machines and scattered food scraps had, for generations, been the favorite feeding ground of flocks of pigeons, generally one flock to a station along the route of the El. Hundreds of pigeons were dependent upon the system. They flapped in and out of its stanchions and steel work or gathered in watchful little audiences about the feet of anyone who rattled the peanut-vending machines. They even watched people who jingled change in their hands, and prospected for food under the feet of the crowds who gathered between trains. Probably very few among the waiting people who tossed a crumb to an eager pigeon realized that this El was like a food-bearing river, and that the life which haunted its banks was dependent upon the running of the trains with their human freight.*

Examine the coherence in this paragraph by circling transitional signals, underlining once examples of key word repetitions and underlining twice examples of structural repetitions. Which of these devices did Eiseley use most? Can you offer any suggestion as to why he used this device so frequently? Do you think his paragraph would have been more effective if he had used one of these devices more, or less, than he did?

EXERCISE

Analyze the unity and coherence of two paragraphs from an essay you wrote earlier in this course. How unified and coherent are those paragraphs? Which of the three devices for coherence did you tend to use more frequently? How could you improve the unity and coherence in these paragraphs? Rewrite them, paying particular attention to unity and coherence.

THE STRUCTURE OF ESSAYS

Closely related to the unity and coherence of paragraphs and essays is the overall shape of the essay. Discussing the form of essays, Gilbert Highet tells us how he learned that all essays must have a definite shape.

---

*Loren Eiseley, from "The Brown Wasps," *The Night Country*. Copyright © 1971 Loren Eiseley. Reprinted with permission of Charles Scribner's Sons.

The next thing is to devise a form for your essay. This, which ought to be obvious, is not. I learned it for the first time from an experienced newspaperman. When I was at college I earned extra pocket- and book-money by writing several weekly columns for a newspaper. They were usually topical, they were always carefully varied, they tried hard to be witty, and (an essential) they never missed a deadline. But once, when I brought in the product, a copy editor stopped me. He said, "Our readers seem to like your stuff all right; but we think it's a bit amateurish." With due humility I replied, "Well, I am an amateur. What should I do with it?" He said, "Your pieces are not coherent; they are only sentences and epigrams strung together; they look like a heap of clothespins in a basket. Every article ought to have a shape. Like this" (and he drew a big letter *S* on his pad) "or this" (he drew a descending line which turned abruptly upward again) "or this" (and he sketched a solid central core with five or six lines pushing outward from it) "or even this" (and he outlined two big arrows coming into collision).

I never saw the man again, but I have never ceased to be grateful to him for his wisdom and for his kindness. Every essay must have a shape. You can ask a question in the first paragraph, discussing several different answers to it till you reach one you think is convincing. You can give a curious fact and offer an explanation of it. You can take a topic that interests you and do a descriptive analysis of it: a man's character (as Hazlitt did with his fives champion), a building, a book, a striking adventure, a peculiar custom. There are many other shapes which essays can take; but the principle laid down by the copy editor was right.*

Highet's discussion of the shape of essays leads us into an examination of the overall structure of essays. Although every essay has a unique structure, there are certain common features that we can capture by offering structuring categories.

Modes

Depending upon our overall perspective in a writing situation, we may choose one of three basic forms, or modes: narration, description, or exposition. In a narrative the writer focuses upon a story or an event. Descriptive writing is very similar to narrative writing, but whereas the focal point of a narrative is a happening, at the center of a descriptive piece is a person, place, or thing. The writer looks at this topic as an image to be captured in the words of his essay. Exposition is probably the most familiar type of writing. The writer of an exposition sees his topic as a subject to be explained to his readers.

Once we know which of these structures we will employ in a given writing situation, we know quite a bit about the form of the essay we will compose. For example, once we decide to tell a story, we can structure our essay by means of time. We may not choose to relate the events in the chronological order in which they occurred, but we will use chronology as the connecting agent that puts the

---

*From *Explorations* by Gilbert Highet. Copyright © 1971 by Gilbert Highet. Reprinted with permission of Oxford University Press, Inc.

Creating Order

parts together. Similarly, the descriptive structure is based on spatial connections—literal or figurative. The connections in exposition are not quite so simple as those in narration and description. In expository essays the writer makes use of the connections we introduced in the Questions for Analysis. That is, she connects the parts by means of associations, dissociations, and causal relations.

We will discuss modes of discourse throughout this book. We introduce modes in this chapter, which concerns itself with the shape of essays, to suggest that your choice of mode will help determine the final shape of a given piece of writing.

Having introduced the basic structures that form the essays we will write, we are in the position to trace other implications of Highet's comments. His insistence, or rather, the copy editor's insistence, that every essay must have a definite shape is reminiscent of Aristotle's statement that every discourse must have a beginning, middle, and end. This principle can be explained in terms of our emphasis in this chapter on relationships. There is a sense in which the material in the body of an essay is what the essay is about. However, by itself this material is incomplete because it lacks the beginning and end that provide the perspective the reader needs to see the overall shape, and thus the overall meaning, of the essay. In the following sections we will have more to say about beginnings and endings.

Beginnings

The beginning, or introduction, of an essay is one of three main sections of an essay. It may be very short or rather lengthy, but it must fulfill its purpose of preparing the readers for the overall shape, or form, of the essay. To illustrate this point, we can return to the introduction to Stephanie Weikert's essay.

> On a chilly fall morning, Franklin Elementary School awaited the beginning of another day. Its ugly, ancient frame solemnly rose from the ground and met the morning sun. Classroom lights shone through the dirty windows and illuminated the hard ground below. The wind blew through the swings on the empty playground, making them squeak and creak like a door turning on rusty hinges. Three tall maple trees vainly attempted to hide the eyesore. A steel fence enclosed the school property, separating it from the rest of the neighborhood. Surrounding Franklin were the small, grim ghetto shanties filled with youngsters preparing for the school day.
>
> As I viewed these surroundings, I felt a sense of disappointment. Of the five elementary schools in Wadsworth, I had to be dumped at Franklin to work as a teacher's aide. I had hoped to work at Overlook Elementary or Valley View School. Unlike Franklin, they were both beautiful new schools in the better section of town. Because of its ghetto location and age, most people considered Franklin the "scum" of the school district.

Stephanie introduces the form of her entire essay in the first paragraph, in which she begins to describe Franklin Elementary as she saw it on her first day as an aide. The reader is, thus, prepared for the body of the essay in which

Stephanie will move from one room of the school to another, describing the things and people in the school. In the second paragraph, Stephanie further prepares her readers for the information in the body of her essay. Her description of Franklin Elementary is set in the context of her original distaste for the school. In this second paragraph Stephanie prepares the reader to experience Franklin as she experienced it. It would be one thing to find such a tidy, enticing atmosphere at Valley View School, but it is quite another to find it here. Stephanie helps her readers to see how her experience at Franklin caused her to recognize her tendency to prejudge.

WRITING ASSIGNMENT

Choose a person or thing with which you are reasonably familiar, and write a short description (350 to 450 words) of that person or thing. Then look back over your description and see whether it helped you to see your topic differently or to see anything about your topic that you had previously not been conscious of. If so, rewrite the introduction to your description so that it prepares your readers for this insight.

As we have said, Stephanie's essay is structured by description. The following excerpt is the introduction to a narrative essay.

WRITING SAMPLE

> One of my daughters is about to write a letter to a young lady she has never met, informing her that in a feckless mood she recently sold her younger brother a gold bracelet and regrets it so much that she wants to buy it back.
>
> It's a likely story, but it's the best my daughter could do on the spur of the moment, and, indeed, I know of no other way out of the predicament, which had been caused, in part at least, by her father's forgetfulness.
>
> I relate the story to you not in order to advertise the solution but as a warning against that forgetfulness. If you are a parent to a teen-age boy, do not forget how much he can be in love, how much that love demands attention and to what lengths he will go to gain it.
>
> I had forgotten until the other day when I came unexpectedly upon a piece of paper lying on the floor, picked it up preparatory to throwing it in the nearest wastepaper basket and then glanced at it to make sure that it was something to be thrown away.*

In this introduction to "The Gold Bracelet," Tom Braden sets the stage for the narrative to follow. At the end of the introduction, the reader knows that chronology will structure the essay; that is, the reader knows that Braden is going to continue telling what happened after he did not throw this note away.

---

*This and all other quotes from this source are from Tom Braden's "The Gold Bracelet." *The Washington Post*, September 2, 1978. Used with permission of *The Washington Post*.

    Creating Order

But, as is the case in Stephanie's introduction, Braden does more than prepare the reader for the structure of the essay; he also prepares the reader for its content. Braden has learned a lesson about teen love and about how not to react when it causes one's child to behave in unacceptable ways.

Next, we offer an introduction to an expository essay, "Learned Words and Popular Words," which is structured by contrast.

> In every cultivated language there are two great classes of words which, taken together, comprise the whole vocabulary. First there are those words with which we become acquainted in ordinary conversation, which we learn, that is to say, from the members of our own family and from our familiar associates, and which we should know and use even if we could not read or write. They concern the common things of life, and are the stock in trade of all who speak the language. Such words may be called "popular," since they belong to the people at large and are not the exclusive possession of a limited class.
>
> On the other hand, our language includes a multitude of words which are comparatively seldom used in ordinary conversation. Their meanings are known to every educated person, but there is little occasion to employ them at home or in the market-place. Our first acquaintance with them comes not from our mother's lips or from the talk of our schoolmates, but from books that we read, lectures that we hear, or the more formal conversation of highly educated speakers who are discussing some partic- ular topic in a style appropriately elevated above the habitual level of everyday life. Such words are called "learned," and the distinction between them and "popular" words is of great importance to a right understanding of linguistic process.*

Once again this introduction prepares the reader for the essay to follow. As these two introductory paragraphs indicate, the authors, J. B. Greenough and G. L. Kittredge, structure the essay by the contrast between the origins and characteristics of "popular" words and the origins and characteristics of "learned" words. The second of these paragraphs also prepares the reader for the overall impact of the essay, because its final sentence tells him just why this information should be of interest.

Finally, we offer the introduction to S. I. Hayakawa's essay "How Dictionaries Are Made."

> It is widely believed that every word has a correct meaning, that we learn these meanings principally from the teachers and grammarians (except that most of the time we don't bother to, so that we ordinarily speak "sloppy English"), and that dictionaries and grammars are the supreme authority in matters of meaning and usage. Few people ask by what authority the writers of dictionaries and grammars say what they say. I once got into a dispute with an English woman over the pronuncia-

---

*This and all other quotes from this source are from James B. Greenough and George L. Kittredge's *Words and Their Ways in English Speech* (New York: Macmillan, 1900).

tion of a word and offered to look it up in the dictionary. The English woman said firmly, "What for? I am English. I was born and brought up in England. The way I speak is English." Such self-assurance about one's own language is not uncommon among the English. In the United States, however, anyone who is willing to quarrel with the dictionary is regarded as either eccentric or mad.

Let us see how dictionaries are made and how the editors arrive at definitions. What follows applies, incidentally, only to those dictionary offices where first-hand, original research goes on—not those in which editors simply copy existing dictionaries.*

In his first paragraph Hayakawa raises the question of just how dictionaries are made. He then offers an anecdote, which attracts the attention of the readers, and relates this anecdote to the topic of the essay. However, the introduction is not completed in the first paragraph, for it does not give the reader any clue as to how the essay will be organized. Hayakawa does this in the first sentence of the second paragraph, where he shows that his essay will make use of process, one of the expository structures we will examine in Chapter Five. Each of the subsequent paragraphs in the body of Hayakawa's essay contains information about the process of dictionary making.

As our look at these four different introductions shows, a good introduction prepares the reader for the essay's form and content. Of course, a writer's ability to vary the ways in which she accomplishes these tasks is limited only by her imagination. For example, the writer may begin with a narrative or an anecdote, or cite revealing statistics. She may begin with an example or with a statement by a noted authority or famous person. Whatever method she chooses, she must provide insight into what the essay will say and how it will be structured.

Before we leave introductions, we should say a word about their place in the writing process. Some writers may prefer to begin writing their essays by composing the introduction. However, many, perhaps even most writers, will not do so, and for the very good reason that the successful introduction previews the information in the essay. In order to write an introduction first, the writer must have prewritten the essay; that is, he must know what he is going to say in the essay before actually composing it. Some writers find this possible, but most do not. Thus, in many cases the introduction will be one of the last sections the writer composes.

<table>
<tr><td>EXERCISE</td><td>Look again at the descriptive or narrative essay you wrote earlier. How effective is its introduction? What does that introduction do for the reader? How well does it establish a context for the essay it introduces? If you find that your introduction does not work, rewrite it.</td></tr>
</table>

---

*This and all other quotes from this source are from *Language in Thought And Action*, Fourth Edition, by S. I. Hayakawa. © 1978 by Harcourt Brace Jovanovich, Inc. Reprinted with permission of the publisher.

                                                          Creating Order

There is quite a difference between ending an essay and merely stopping it. The ending, or conclusion, of an essay is the final section, which completes the background against which the material in the body is to be placed and thus helps shape the overall meaning of the essay. It is more than a simple summary, though it may include a summary in certain situations, particularly when the essay is rather long and involved.

In this section we will offer two very general types of conclusions that often help writers provide the perspective readers need to interpret the material in an essay. The first type is illustrated by Stephanie Weikert's conclusion.

> **By the end of the school day, I realized that I was totally wrong about Franklin School. I had thought it would be a dirty, miserable place to work, but it was actually a clean and enjoyable building. I was foolish to listen to other people's views and let my first impression of the exterior of the school form my opinion. In the end, I learned a valuable lesson and found a comfortable place to work.**

In order to categorize Stephanie's conclusion, we need to refer to our earlier statement that Stephanie's conclusion "shows us the effect this experience had on Stephanie." What we were saying, in effect, is that the relation between the body of Stephanie's essay and its conclusion is sequence: What follows from what? Stephanie recounts an experience in the body of the essay and then examines the implications of that experience in her conclusion. This relation exists between the body and conclusion of many different types of essays as the following two examples help us illustrate. In the first example Tom Braden concludes his essay "The Gold Bracelet." You will remember his earlier introduction in which he tells of his daughter's attempt to get a bracelet back for her brother, who had stolen it from his mother and given it to his girlfriend. In the body of the essay, Braden narrated his discovery of the theft and his impulsive verdict that his son must get the bracelet back. Here he examines the possible implications of his decision. He begins by trying to think of the things his son might say to his girlfriend.

> **Imagine. "I sent you my mother's bracelet by mistake." Or, "I am not what you think I am. I am just a little boy who gets into his mother's bathroom and steals things off her dresser."**
>
> **How in the world was he supposed to get that bracelet back without suffering utter degradation in the eyes of her for whom all must be risked, including, even, the stealing of a bracelet?**
>
> **But I had said it. If I took it back, might he not suppose the theft unserious? Besides, wasn't utter degradation his due? I did not take it back.**
>
> **Wrong. You don't have to tell me. What's a cause for suicide against a silly bracelet?**
>
> **I had made the mistake of forgetfulness, and both the boy and I are lucky that he has an older sister.***

---

*Braden, 1978.

Next we look at the conclusion to S. I. Hayakawa's "How Dictionaries Are Made."

The writing of a dictionary, therefore, is not a task of setting up authoritative statements about the "true meanings" of words, but a task of recording, to the best of one's ability, what various words have meant to authors in the distant or immediate past. The writer of a dictionary is a historian, not a lawgiver. If, for example, we had been writing a dictionary in 1890, or even as late as 1919, we could have said that the word "broadcast" means "to scatter" (seed, for example), but we could not have decreed that from 1921 on, the most common meaning of the word should become "to disseminate audible messages, etc., by radio transmission." To regard the dictionary as an "authority," therefore, is to credit the dictionary writer with gifts of prophecy which neither he nor anyone else possesses. In choosing our words when we speak or write, we can be guided by the historical record afforded us by the dictionary, but we cannot be bound by it, because new situations, new experiences, new inventions, new feelings, are always compelling us to give new uses to old words. Looking under a "hood," we should ordinarily have found, five hundred years ago, a monk; today, we find a motorcar engine.*

Hayakawa's conclusion is a bit more complicated than our previous examples. He summarizes what he has said in the essay, both by way of restatement and examples of the changes that have occurred in the meanings of *broadcast* and *hood*. However, his conclusion is more than mere summary. Midway through the conclusion, Hayakawa offers one sentence in which he shows how a proper view of the dictionary will inform our use of words; that is, we can be "guided by the historical record afforded us by the dictionary, but we cannot be bound by it, because new situations, new experiences, new inventions, new feelings, are always compelling us to give new uses to old words."

The three previous conclusions share a basic similarity: Each of them traces the implications of what has been said in the body of the essay. As we said earlier, this is one of two primary devices for concluding an essay. The second device is illustrated by the conclusion to "Learned Words and Popular Words."

The terms "popular" and "learned," as applied to words, are not absolute definitions. No two persons have the same stock of words, and the same word may be "popular" in one man's vocabulary and "learned" in another's. There are also different grades of "popularity"; indeed there is in reality a continuous gradation from infantile words like "mama" and "papa" to such erudite derivatives as "concatenation" and "cataclysm." Still, the division into "learned" and "popular" is convenient and sound. Disputes may arise as to the classification of any particular word, but there can be no difference of opinion about the general principle. We must be careful, however, to avoid misconception. When we call a word "popular," we do not mean that it is a favorite word, but simply that it belongs to the people as a whole—that is, it is everybody's word, not the possession

---

*Hayakawa, 1978.

Creating Order

of a limited number. When we call a word "learned" we do not mean that it is used by scholars alone, but simply that its presence in the English vocabulary is due to books and the cultivation of literature rather than to the actual needs of ordinary conversation.*

Like Hayakawa, the authors of this essay, J. B. Greenough and G. L. Kittredge, summarize in their conclusion. However, they are led into this summary, not by an attempt to capture the implications of their essay's content, but by an attempt to qualify. They want to be sure that readers have not misread them and heard them to be saying something they were not intending. Thus, the relation between this conclusion and the essay's body could be characterized by the what-opposes-what? connection. The writers are contrasting what they have said to what readers could have heard them say.

EXERCISE — Look again at a descriptive or narrative essay you have written earlier in this course. Does it do more than summarize? Could it be more effective? If so, rewrite it.

WRITING ASSIGNMENT

Respond to one of the following assignments in a well-developed essay. After you have written this essay, examine its language and structure in light of our discussion of how we use language and structure to create order.

1. Choose an advertisement and break it into its components. How do these various parts form a web of relationships? How well do the parts work together? Which component is the featured part of the advertisement's sales pitch? How do individual words work to create a web of relationships; that is, how does the ad's language evoke associations? What are those associations? How effectively do they contribute to the sales pitch? How well does the language direct your attention?

2. How do we create stereotypes? Why? Pick a stereotype who represents a group you are familiar with. Describe the person—typical dress, actions, language, and so on. Do you know any people who fit this stereotype? How well do they fit it? What do you associate with this type? What language have you used to represent this type? How does that language influence your response to people of this stereotype when you meet them? What role does your language play in your consideration of this type? How does your language work to direct your attention? How well does that language represent this type?

3. In what situations have you heard sexist or racist language at work? Think about past experience—school, reading, political campaigns, radio, televi-

---

*Greenough and Kittredge, 1900.

sion, sports, church, and so on. Describe a situation and your response to it. How did you feel? What was the outcome? What was the language used? What did you associate with it? What did it imply? How did that language work to direct your attention? What was its effect on its target? How well did that language represent its target?

Chapter Four

Writing an Expressive Essay

In Chapter One, we introduced three aims or purposes of writing: expressive, transactional, and poetic. We found that expressive writing is closest to the self of the writer and that, in expressive situations, the writer's purpose is to give readers insight into herself. In this chapter we will look at expressive writing in greater detail.

THE ROLE OF EXPRESSIVE WRITING

Expressive writing is related to transactional and poetic writing as shown in Figure 4.1.* Note that there are two kinds of expressive writing in this diagram: One stands on a plane with transactional and poetic writing; the other "feeds" all three aims. In the latter sense, expressive writing is the "seedbed" for ideas, as the writer records his experience and attempts to make some sense of it. You have already done a good bit of this kind of writing. You have done freewriting, written in a journal, used the Questions for Analysis, taken notes, and jotted ideas and partial interpretations of them. In each instance you were writing expressively as you recorded and then began interpreting your experience.

---

*Adapted from Britton, et al. (1975), p. 83.

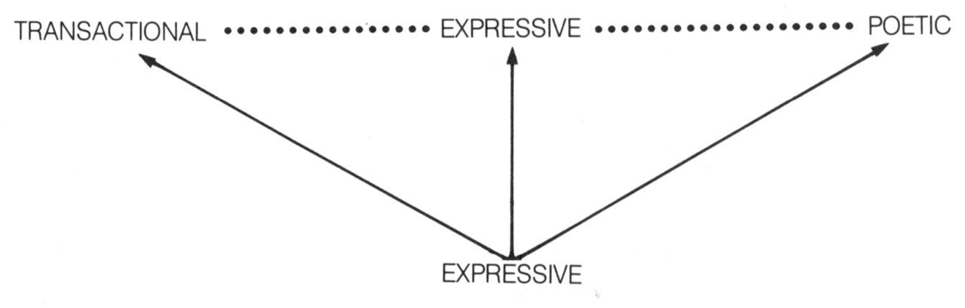

Figure 4.1

Expressive writing provides a foundation for all three aims of writing; it is the vehicle by which you try out ideas before shaping them for a wider audience than yourself. But you will usually want to shape those initial jottings into something that will be comprehensible to some audience. In this chapter we will look at the process by which your initial expressive writing may be shaped into a fully developed expressive essay.

EXPRESSIVE ESSAYS

Writing an expressive essay requires you to look beyond yourself as audience so that you write to give your reader some insight into your thinking about and ordering of some topic. Your goal, then, is to structure your thoughts so that your reader can experience, insofar as possible, what you experienced. Ceci Cano's "Only a Reflection" in Chapter One (pp. 24–26) is an expressive essay. In that paper Ceci attempted to bring her readers into the world she saw at the disco and then to bring those readers to the same realization she had had— that the disco was at best only a shadow of reality, at worst a sham. She began by freewriting and found a topic there.

Having settled on a topic, Ceci gave a more definite shape to that freewriting, structuring it according to what she wanted her readers to experience. If writing is to be meaningful to readers, it must offer them some structure; that is, the writer must create the order she wishes the reader to see. Ceci's job, then, was to shape the ideas her freewriting held.

Ceci began that shaping by using the Questions for Analysis to explore what the disco meant for her, looking into the associations, dissociations, and implications that evening held. Her intent was neither to write an explanatory analysis of the disco's popularity nor to frame an argument designed to expose the disco's falseness. Instead she wished to work back through the experience in order to understand it more fully and then to represent the understanding she gained to her readers.

     Writing an Expressive Essay

No one explained the disco's sham nature to Ceci; rather, she experienced it for herself. In her expressive essay she attempted to represent her experience so faithfully that her readers could gain insight into what it meant for her. Because she wanted to represent or recreate the experience, Ceci structured her essay using the narrative and descriptive modes, both of which are especially appropriate for the expressive aim.

Narrative Structures

How to structure a piece of writing is a consideration of overriding importance. If writing is to be more than a personal log—that is, if the writer envisions an audience other than himself—his writing must have a definite structure. Most of us find freewriting relatively easy and often quite enjoyable. But when it is time to consider an overall shape for the piece that is to be formed from our freewriting, composing may become more difficult.

At first it may seem strange that shaping a narrative could be difficult because chronology accounts for its overall structure. The difficulty arises, nevertheless, because chronology by itself is never sufficient to account for the meaning we find in an experience. To illustrate this point, we offer two versions of the conclusion to an expressive essay, "An Enlightening Experience in France," by Carla Collins. The first version is the real conclusion, which explains how a visit—to the grandmother of the French family she has been staying with—helped Carla overcome her homesickness. The second version was written by one of the authors of this book, Ron Lunsford.

<table>
<tr><td>

WRITING
SAMPLE

First version

</td><td>

When it was time to go I was sad. For some reason I felt drawn to this warm, sweet old grandmother—and then I realized that she was in many ways like my own grandmother. Mme. de Rango, like my own grandmother, loved her grandchildren, was proud of her cooking, and proudly shared her family with her friends. She was wonderfully human and caring, not at all a strange old French woman with odd customs and ways. From that point on, I felt more at ease in the de Rango family and the rest of my stay with them was a joy. While some of their customs were strange, I knew somehow despite these differences, we were very much alike.

</td></tr>
<tr><td>

Second version

</td><td>

For some reason I felt drawn to this warm, sweet, old grandmother. It was getting late, and the father suggested that we should go. The grandmother got our purses. She didn't know which purse was mine, so I had to pick it out for her. We said our good-byes. We walked to the car. It was getting slightly cold outside now, and it felt good when we got into the car. The motor would not crank on the first attempt, so the father had to pump the gas and try again. It started and we left. I was tired when we got to the de Rango home, so I went to bed.

</td></tr>
</table>

These two conclusions help us make an important point about narratives: They rely upon association, dissociation, and causal connections just as expository essays do. This is true because the writer who is shaping a narrative cannot possibly tell everything that happened in a given event. She must choose which things to include and which things to leave out.

In the second of the preceding two samples, Ron attempts to record the things that happened as the family prepared to leave Mme. de Rango's cottage. Of course, Ron's account cannot capture everything that transpired, but it does make the point that such a recording would not produce a narrative expressive essay. Carla's conclusion, which is a narrative, sounds quite different from Ron's because she is doing much more than providing a list of the things that happened as the family prepared to leave. Rather than attempting to tell in a mechanical fashion everything that happened, Carla chooses to narrate those things that have some significance for her. This significance is provided by association, dissociation, and causal connections.

Of course, Carla's overall structuring device for this paragraph, as well as for the entire essay, is chronology. However, the items in the narrative are connected in additional ways. Carla tells the reader that she was sad when it was time to leave Mme. de Rango's. In the next two sentences, Carla shares her feelings about this French grandmother. And in the last two sentences she relates the fact that she felt more at ease with her French family after this trip to their grandmother's cottage. The only obvious connection between Carla's realizations concerning this grandmother and her new attitude toward living with the de Rango's is chronology. However, perceptive readers will share a causal connection with Carla; they will know that this trip to Mme. de Rango's cottage *caused* a change in Carla's attitude.

This last sentence brings us back to our earlier statement that narratives and descriptions are particularly well suited to expressive writing. As we have said, the writer of an expressive essay is attempting to give readers insight into himself by allowing them to enter into an experience with him. Narratives and descriptions are well suited to this purpose because they allow the writer to show, or represent, rather than to tell. We can explain the difference between the two approaches by referring to Stephanie Weikert's essay, "Franklin Elementary School" (pp. 67–68). If Stephanie had wanted to explain what she learned by working at Franklin Elementary, she would have chosen an expository structure. For example, she could have compared what she found at Franklin Elementary with what she had expected to find. However, Stephanie did not want to tell; she wanted to show. That is, she wanted to describe her first day at Franklin so vividly that the reader could enter into the experience with her. If she has written a good description—and she has—the reader will feel the association, dissociation, and causal connections that she feels. However, because hers is an expressive essay, she will not make these connections explicit.

Descriptive Structures

You will note that we concluded our discussion of narrative structures with an example that is really a description. Or is it? "Franklin Elementary School" illustrates the fact that narration and description are often so intertwined as to be inseparable. There is, however, an important difference between the narrative process and the descriptive process. Whereas the overriding structuring agent in narration is chronology, descriptions are built upon spatial connections.

The following passage illustrates the role that space plays in descriptive writing.

> The face of the statue looked much the worse for its years of wear. The eyes which were no doubt once well defined against the cheeks were now barely discernible. The nose was obviously in the process of wearing completely away. The arms seemed to have fared better than the facial features; they were still clearly discernible against the chest. The feet of the statue were planted squarely on the ground, as if to assert that the elements might wear against them but not destroy them.

A spatial connection is implicit between each of the sentences in this paragraph. For example, the reader knows that the eyes, mentioned in sentence 2, are in the upper section of the face. The nose, mentioned in sentence 3, is just below the eyes, and so forth. Thus, the writer shapes this paragraph by moving in space from the top of the statue to its bottom.

The primary connector in physical description, then, is space. However, these spatial connections are not always literal. Often the writer asks readers to think of some nonphysical subject as if it were physical and, thus, could be described in terms of space. James Agee and Walker Evans, in *Let Us Now Praise Famous Men*, connect sentences by means of figurative space in describing the "odor or odors which are classical in every thoroughly poor white southern country house."

> It is compacted of many odors and made into one, which is very thin and light on the air, and more subtle than it can seem in analysis, yet very sharply and constantly noticeable. These are its ingredients. The odor of pine lumber, wide thin cards of it, heated in the sun, in no way doubled or insulated, in closed and darkened air. The odor of woodsmoke, the fuel being again mainly pine, but in part also, hickory, oak, and cedar. The odors of cooking. Among these, most strongly, the odors of salt pork and fried and boiled pork lard, and second, the odor of cooked corn. The odors of sweat in many stages of age and freshness, this sweat being a distillation of pork, lard, corn, woodsmoke, pine, and ammonia.*

Because the subject, an odor, is not visible, it does not lend itself to a literal movement from one of its parts to another. However, the writers treat the odor as if it were physical and could be divided into parts; the movement from one of these figurative parts to another provides the order for the description.

Space provides the overall structure for description. But as was the case with the chronological connections in narration, space cannot account for all of the order, or meaning, in a description; the "real" meaning of a description will derive from associations, oppositions, and implications, which arise as the writer

---

*James Agee and Walker Evans, *Let Us Now Praise Famous Men* (Boston: Houghton Mifflin, 1939), p. 154.

shapes the description. Our analysis of Stephanie Weikert's essay in Chapter Three (pp. 69–75) has already provided an illustration of this principle. In her third paragraph, we found association, dissociation, and spatial connections.

COMPOSING AN EXPRESSIVE ESSAY

In Chapter Three we used the Questions for Analysis to examine the structure of a finished product, Stephanie Weikert's "Franklin Elementary School." However, as we saw in Chapter Two, these questions are primarily a means of discovering. Because the order, or form, of a piece of writing is actually a part of its content, the questions should allow you to shape the content of your writing. This questioning process is not a device by which you can force a method of order onto a composition; such a composition is not likely to be significant for you or for your readers. It is rather a plan for exploration of a topic that does not take away your freedom to discover what you want to say.

To illustrate the mixture of freedom and control that this questioning process allows, we will lead you through a narrative assignment in a series of seven different steps. Our purpose in dividing the assignment into these steps is to help you see writing as a process composed of various activities, drafts, and revisions. As our discussion of revision in Chapter One implied, few professional writers produce a finished essay at one sitting—certainly, we do not. Thus, we do not expect you to produce a finished, significant paper without working your way through the various stages that constitute your writing process.

Note that in the preceding sentence we referred to "your" writing process, not "the" writing process. As we said in Chapter One, there is no magic formula everyone can follow to produce good writing; there are as many processes as there are individuals who write. All of us do different things while we prepare to write, while we write, and after we have written. We offer this model, not as a formula, but as something you can use as is or adapt to suit your needs.

Here, then, is our model.

Step 1: Freewrite
Step 2: Select and Examine Your Topic
Step 3: Devise a Planning Page
Step 4: Write a Discovery Draft
Step 5: Select and Analyze Your Audience
Step 6: Write a Second Draft
Step 7: Write a Final Draft

Steps in Composing the Essay

Step 1: Freewrite For at least fifteen minutes, you will jot down everything that comes to mind. If an assignment directs you to write about an event from which you learned something, you can freewrite about past events that seem important to you. When you find a single event that seems a good topic, or if you settle

Writing an Expressive Essay

immediately on such an event, you can freewrite about it. Organization, style, grammar, and mechanics are unimportant at this stage; what counts most is getting your initial thoughts about a topic on paper.

Step 2: Select and Examine Your Topic Once you select at least a tentative or potential topic, you will begin to explore it to see what meaning it may hold for you. Identify the topic with a descriptive term or label; then answer the Questions for Analysis to reveal what you already know and think about the topic. As you use the Questions, look for aspects of the topic that you may need more information about.

Step 3: Devise a Planning Page At this stage you will examine the materials you have generated in steps 1 and 2 and create a Planning Page, consisting of a Lead Sentence and several Topic Sentences, for the paper you will write. You must keep in mind that the focus you state here is tentative; as you write, you should be prepared to change your mind at any time. This Lead Sentence is designed to help you continue in your writing process, not to restrict your freedom. In almost all cases, the Lead Sentence will not appear in the final draft of your essay.

Step 4: Write a Discovery Draft With the focus statement as a guide, you will write a discovery draft. You should not be overly concerned with grammatical and mechanical matters, with always finding the exact word, or, indeed, with creating a perfectly structured essay. There will be time for these concerns later. What is important at this stage is that you write a draft that begins to give shape to the ideas you have generated about the topic.

Step 5: Select and Analyze Your Audience If the assignment specifies an audience, you can analyze that audience, using the Questions for Analysis as a guide. If no audience is assigned, you must select one, being sure to select an audience that will benefit from an essay of the type you envision. Your audience analysis will help you shape a thesis statement and then select details to support that thesis.

Step 6: Write a Second Draft Using the audience analysis as a technique for revision, you will write your second draft. In the first draft you were concerned only with shaping your own feelings about this topic. At this stage you will shape that draft so that it meets the needs of the audience you have chosen to write for. You should be mindful of your prerogative to change whatever you think necessary, including the essay's topic.

Step 7: Write a Final Draft The emphasis in this draft is on final revisions. You will strive to find the exact, rather than the approximate, word and to revise any awkward or troublesome sentence structures. You will also proofread thoroughly to ensure that there are no grammatical or mechanical errors.

Working through this process will take a good bit of time and effort. But, as we said earlier, you may adapt this process to suit your own needs. If, for example, you know what your specific topic will be, you may bypass step 1. And if you find that your first draft comes together in such a way as to fulfill the needs of the audience you select, you may bypass step 6. Unless your instructor allows more than one class period, you will not have time to work through this process for in-class papers. But your practice in out-of-class assignments will help you in those in-class situations; for example, in-class essay examination questions should be easier if you have worked through the Planning Page stage in out-of-class situations.

FREEWRITE

We are now ready to enter the writing process. The following is the assignment for the essay we will write.

WRITING ASSIGNMENT

Write an expressive essay about an event or place that affected you deeply. Your task is to express what this event or place meant to you.

As we explore the various stages of this assignment, we will present an essay—"Purple Mountains' Majesty" by Arlene Yusnukis, a student at New Mexico State University. Arlene wrote this essay by working through the seven-step model outlined here, and we present the steps exactly as Arlene submitted them. As you fulfill the various assignments in the following pages, you will want to examine Arlene's writing process, paying particular attention to changes in content, language, structure, grammar, and mechanics as the essay develops.

We begin by presenting Arlene's freewriting.

WRITING
SAMPLE

> I remember being sprayed in the face with a chemical fire extinguisher at 2:30 in the morning, backpacking in the pecos wilderness the rams eating crackers, waterskiing for the very first time, cliff jumping, the green station house with the card rack when mom and I got off the train, riding my tricycle in circles around a big red ant, my grandmother dying of cancer & being there for a month going to school in spokane, the hot lunch cart getting bronchitis and letters from dad c/o my aunt my cousins picking on my brother my grandfather and his horses. Flicka a horse bit my brothers hand. Meeting Kelli and Paul my boyfriend and the initiation into the band, going to Denver and freezing the huge Bronco football players, stepping on head phones. sleeping by the bathroom. Sneaking out to play frisbee in the middle of the night and getting caught cuz the frisbee was loud cuz we never caught it. trying to make poptarts quietly in the dark. My dog dying. Our toilet getting stuck flushing. Being in two accidents in less than a year seeing the front grill of the truck before it hit us. Physical therapy migraines, pills for schizophenics. The old age home and smell—

After Arlene had engaged in this totally unrestricted writing, she chose one particular event from it and produced the following focused freewriting.

Driving up there the road dirt for so long and our caddy not liking the drive but tolerating it. Trying to get everyones packs into the trucks and trunks. The storm clouds over the pecos mountains as we drove up. The quaint little town inside the canyon, Jack's creek. The beautiful campground at the top where we started from. Climbing up and up at a steep angle and looking down to my left at a vertical nearly drop. Switchbacks, losing my sleeping bag having to bring up the rear with Brad and Chip, fellow workers, up front slowpokers in back, Hard to get transportation. Chip not wanting to charge for gas. Rain in the late afternoon. The big high country meadow with posts to mark trail in snow. The smell, clear sky, critters heaviness of pack & Brad taking lighter stuff as trip goes on. Cold in rain. Finally stop near Pecos baldy lake. Small lake. Pecos baldy bald! Just flat rocks—shale? Wet, brad no warm clothes water cold to wash face in. Brad sick. Starting Svea stove quick! Finally getting all kids in tents in bed. Teresa & I talking for a long time. Boys growl whole camp awake. Sunny next morning. Better tempers cute people in morning messy hair, buffalo breath.

One ram one ewe big horn sheep come down embankment near camp. Ewe no hair on neck, radio collar rubbed off. Eat out of Ross hand knock over packs a camp away & eat crackers. Climbing saddle to leave PB area. Switchbacks tight-zipper. Relief on other side. Walk forever that day. Walking just behind storm. See hail everywhere but not on us. Worry that won't get out in time. Boys tell steve to eat skunk cabbage cabonions. Pest bad news hard to get in the swing of walking after them. Knives of pain on top of shoulder. hip strap much too big for me. Ross gets stuck between rock & log. Steve fell over one. Don't stop where we were supposed to. Have to go on Pretty golden meadow. Clumps of trees on mntn on either side. Narrow with stream in middle Horse Thief meadows. Finally stop to camp on top of flat hill base of mtn sparse trees no camp in meadow Steve sick. Cabbage poison could die. Gets dry heave scares us. We eat rest, massage shoulders me no hiking boots only tennies, no blisters yet. We eat wash up in red stream below. Notice old forbidden trails. Steve OK we sleep. Me with a stick in my middle. Go on. Next day.

See Stewart and Spirit lakes. Rain no fun my poncho-day glo-orange rips. We know where we want to camp—by Santa Fe baldy. Some want to climb. I do. send rest to camp spot. Climb steep hill above timber line. Takes longtime. Big rocks. On top see into eternity rest on rocks. Marmits whistle at us. We see SFB lake-glacier lake Finally leave. Run down jumble insides. cow almost charges us. Join group and play. Sleep Rain.

Chip & Brad too anxious to leave. They go ahead. I take poky ones like me later. We catch up go to rondevous and wait for 1 1/2 hrs. I told them no rush. rain. Mr Tatro watermelon yum. Ski basin pretty home. limp blisters cut open by bad surgeon. Relief bath. sleep.

Because Arlene did not know what event or place she would use as the topic for this paper, she began by freewriting about whatever events or places came to mind. The topic Arlene eventually selected is hinted at in the second entry in the initial freewrite—"backpacking in the pecos wilderness the rams eating crackers." In the second freewrite she focused on the backpacking trip, jotting everything she remembered about it without worrying about anything but getting as much down as she could. We have presented Arlene's freewriting in its uncorrected form to show just how "free" even her focused writing is. In many cases we do not know exactly what Arlene is referring to in this freewriting, but she does and that is all that matters.

Step 1: Freewrite for at least fifteen minutes about events and places that come to mind. After you have done so, choose one particular event or place and jot down every memory about it that comes to mind in the next fifteen minutes. Do not be concerned with grammatical or mechanical matters. Do not stop writing until the time has elapsed. If you cannot think of anything, simply copy the last line you wrote until something occurs to you.

SELECT AND EXAMINE YOUR TOPIC

After having completed her freewriting, Arlene decided that her topic would be "the backpacking trip to the Pecos." As we said in Chapter Three, the words we use to represent a subject to ourselves control our perspective of that subject and, thus, to a great degree the content we will generate in writing about that subject. In selecting "backpacking trip," Arlene was choosing a narrative view of her subject. Had she chosen "the Pecos Baldy Mountain," she would probably have employed a descriptive structure. If she had wanted to explain the benefits of backpacking in an expository essay, she might have chosen a topic such as "backpacking."

We do not mean to suggest that once one selects a topic, all decisions regarding structure have been made. At any point in her writing process, Arlene could have changed her view of her subject and, thus, the structure of her essay. However, at this point, she seems to prefer the narrative structure, and her selection of a topic reflects this preference.

Once she had made this decision, she was ready to examine that topic by asking the Questions for Analysis. In the following we present this stage of Arlene's writing process.

QUESTIONS
FOR
ANALYSIS

What goes with this backpacking trip?
What physical entities go with this trip?
mountain meadows
wall of pine—spruce, fir, varying colors
natural tiny lakes
rain

dizzying heights

steep hills

switchbacks endlessly up steep hills

rams, ewe, big horn sheep

marmots

sunshine through the trees

tinkling of mountain streams, runoff from high country snow

pain from backpack straps

smells

What do I associate with the trip?

freedom

escape

non routine

walking

exercise

How is this trip like other things?

I guess it could be like a trip on drugs—only a natural high

like reading a good book—relief from mundane pressures

What opposes this backpacking trip?

What physical entities oppose this trip?

cities

cars

the luxury of modern day camping trips

technology

commercialism

flush toilets

electricity

warm water tanks

What about this trip is odd, etc.?

The fact that we use all available modern technology and resources to make
our trips as full of modern comforts as possible

What follows (from) the trip?

an appreciation of the power and beauty of nature

a sense of peace

How did the trip come to be?

the desire of the kids at church to go backpacking

not knowing what the trip entails

What opportunities does the trip offer?

the chance to appreciate what we have

the chance to escape from society for a while

What problems does the trip pose?

blisters

sore everywhere

Is the trip good, bad, etc.?

The trip was great. Everyone who is fit to pack should try it at least once.

By referring to the Questions for Analysis in Chapter Two (pp. 37–38), we can see that Arlene did not answer all of the questions. Rather, she limited herself to those questions that immediately triggered a response, and in doing so, she generated quite a bit of material. Arlene repeats a good bit of the information in the freewriting, but this is as it should be for her purpose here is to write down whatever comes to mind, as it comes. Thus, if a question generates something already written in the freewriting stage, she writes it down with no fear of repetition.

WRITING ASSIGNMENT

Step 2: Select a topic from your freewriting and use the Questions for Analysis as a tool for examining this topic. Use only those questions that trigger an immediate response and do not be concerned if you repeat material already generated in your freewriting.

DEVISE A PLANNING PAGE

This is an extremely important stage in the writing process, for here we must introduce some order to the mass of materials we have generated. The freewriting stage and the questioning stage have been free of the restraints of order, but if our writing is to be meaningful at some point we must give it a shape.

On one level Arlene's essay will seem to organize itself. This is because, as her topic reveals, she is going to organize by means of the narrative mode. Because she is writing about a trip, it would seem that all she has to do to order the essay is to recount the various things that happened on that trip. But, as we said earlier, the narrative structure is not nearly so simple. Far too many things occurred on this trip for Arlene to relate them all; thus, she must choose to include certain details of the trip and to exclude many other details. She must, therefore, select some method of ordering the essay that will help her decide what to include and what to omit.

That order is provided by Arlene's statement of focus, which we shall refer to as her "Lead Sentence."

The hike to Santa Fe Baldy was an exciting, eventful trip.

We call this a Lead Sentence to emphasize the mixture of freedom and control Arlene needs at this stage. This sentence will offer some control in that it will lead her to those aspects of the trip that, in her estimation, show the excitement of this trip. However, the sentence is in no way a constraining device that commits her to doing any one specific thing in the essay.

Once Arlene has written her Lead Sentence, she can generate her Topic Sentences from it. Together the Lead Sentence and the Topic Sentences make up the Planning Page. The following is Arlene's Planning Page.

PLANNING PAGE

Lead Sentence

The hike to Santa Fe Baldy was an exciting, eventful trip.

Topic Sentences

(Points to cover in order: use of sequence of trip to structure essay)

packing up and leaving church parking lot

trip to Jack's Creek

1st day of hike—"wandering" sleeping bag, high country hiking, trailmark (deep snow), ill-fitting pack, rain, Brad's T-shirts, 1st campfire

2nd day of hike—bighorn sheep at breakfast, difficult trail, bad weather, skunk cabbage incident (Steve sick from it), Horsethief Meadows

3rd day of hike—view from Santa Fe Baldy, steep, tiring hike, very tired, but beautiful trip

4th day of hike—left behind with slower hikers, downhill hiking to Santa Fe ski basin, home, great trip

Perhaps we should make a few clarifying statements about Arlene's Planning Page at this point. The first is that in designating the supporting material as "Topic Sentences," we are using the word *sentence* in a very loose sense. Obviously, Arlene is not presenting the information in the form of sentences, though she could do so. When we examine the Planning Page for a piece of transactional writing in Chapter Six, we will see more formal sentences in the Topic Sentence designation. Our second clarifying statement is in response to a question we anticipate. Why have we chosen new names for the old standbys— *thesis sentence* and *outline*? That is, the Lead Sentence might be seen as a thesis sentence and the entire Planning Page as a sentence outline. To be sure, there are basic similarities here, but we have chosen new names because of a key difference between the two approaches. The thesis sentence-outline format seems to imply that a writer can know what her paper is going to say before writing it. We want to be clear that writing is a process and that the content of an essay will develop *as* the essay develops, not before.

Arlene's focus statement is rather general, though it does serve as a starting point. Its generality points to the fact that Arlene has not yet found a true focal point for her essay; she has not decided specifically how to express this trip's effect on her. She has decided, however, that the best structuring device for the first draft is chronology, so she sets down each day's events in order. From this tentative focus, she wrote the first draft of her essay.

Step 3: Compose a Planning Page for the essay you are to write.

WRITE A DISCOVERY DRAFT

The following is Arlene's discovery draft.

WRITING
SAMPLE

First Draft

Purple Mountains' Majesty

It sure was a good thing that the whole trip didn't turn out as hectic as it started. The difficulties getting twenty-five backpackers and gear for a four day trip into one church truck and two car trunks is amazing. Its even harder to get 14 kids together to leave. My spirits weren't lifted when, after driving nearly 90 miles, we hit a dirt road which was to last for fourteen miles before we reached our destination, Jack's Creek Campground. Intermitent showers added to the frustration as well as not being able to find the Forest Service Headquarters to pick up our permit.

Once at Jack's Creek, after passing a quaint little town nestled in a canyon whose walls rose steeply, the situation improved. The air was clear, the storm had rolled back farther into the high county—where we were headed. The view was breathtaking. After a quick energy boosting snack, my two other co-directors, Chip and Brad, headed up the trail that was to be our home for the next 4 days, leaving me to bring up the rear behind the slowpokes. I didn't grumble. I didn't even say anything when my sleeping bag decided to tour on its own and almost rolled down the mountain to the left of the path. Someone got the fearless leaders' attention and they waited for me. That got the stragglers caught up.

I sure was thankful for running at 6:00 in the morning or else I would have been as winded as the stragglers. Our initial elevation had been 9,000 feet above sea level and now we were almost 1,000 more. There was a huge sloped meadow which we came upon as we broke through the woods. A huge post stood sentinel by the trail. Answering my question, which I had asked aloud unintentionally, Teresa, the most experienced and jovial packer, said it was a trail mark when the snow fell. Must snow deep up here! Looking back I wish I could say that I didn't feel the heaviness of the misfitted pack until the second day at least. I'm not tough. When the first rest came, I enjoyed it fully. The smell of the crystal air, the chattering and scolding of bushy-tailed squirrels and bossy jays, the darkness of the rich soil, the vibrant colors springing out, my senses were barraged with mother nature's Sunday best dress. It had just turned spring up here after a late winter.

Toiling along later that afternoon a few splashes of rain filtered down through the trees. I put on my day-glo orange rain poncho and glanced up for the first time in what must have been quite a while. Thunder heads were meshing into one big thunder cloud. I hadn't noticed, bent under the weight of the pack whose hip strap slid easily over most of my body at its tightest. My shoulders were supporting the entire weight of the borrowed pack and its contents. I sure could miss a lot, bent like that!

Rain poured from then on and it wasn't until we'd almost reached our first night's destination that I discovered our fearless 21 year-old-leader had brought only T shirts to keep warm in. I was so disgusted I couldn't even sympathize even though hypothermia is a real danger with the high countrys cool dusk and evening hours. At last we reached Pecos Baldy Lake, a small deep lake, very cold. The damp of the rain, although it had stopped, sharpened the night chill and we retired early. Tired or not, Teresa and I discovered a unique ability to communicate and do so loudly until one of the boys growled and scared the whole camp awake. Having the whole camp upset with us shut us up.

The next day dawned clear as a bell and fresh as springtime. My impinding challenge was to light a Svea stove. Struggling to do so I felt a tap on my shoulder. Looking up I saw a big horn ram gracefully leap down the rocks into our campground. Intent on the wild creature, I almost fell over when the realization hit me. He is not intimidated by us at all. He ate a raw egg and cracker out of Ross's hand. An ewe joined him and they proceeded to the nearby camp to eat their crackers.

After climbing the saddle to get out of the valley below the baldy, we were all ready to stop for another night. Little did we realize that this was to be the longest day. The switchbacks, when viewed from a distance, were so tight and numerous upon the hill that the trail looked like a zipper placed at an angle. Everywhere we went that day fresh hail was piled in the protection offered by the tall pine shade. We weren't fifteen minutes behind the storm. They say storms bring out the worst in people. Well this one must have had a hex with it! Juniors and going-on-seniors in high school are not notorious for their common sense and our group was probably below average. We had entered a small valley covered with skunk cabbage. The young men this day were miniature Euell Gibbons. One of them suggested a taste of the cabbages as a main course to the dandelion and strawberry leaf hors d'oeuvres, and Steve jumped at the chance to show his true colors. He ate enough for fourteen of us.

The air was cool and fresh and excellent for any manual labor. It turned out to be the best break we had all day. Chip had decided we were not going to make it out in time and that we could not stop at Horsethief Meadows, but must push on. The meadows are hardly that but are unique among the ones we had seen. Actually they were the crotch of the two mountains, where one green tree-laden wall met another and a tiny stream had carved out a narrow thin flat area. It was as if God carved out a piece of golden grassy prarie plains and stuck it in the middle of the Rocky Mountains.

Pushing on mile after dreary mile, we finally reached a suitable camping spot where Steve promptly lost his entire days meals. Had I known how desperately sick he really was, it probably would have made me sick. Skunk cabbage can be fatal and vomiting is the only thing that saves the victim's life. Steve, and the rest of us, were lucky. I slept uneasily that night on top of a stick, with knives of pain spearing the tops of my shouders and the base of my neck.

Bright and early the next morning we set out. Our goal was Santa Fe Baldy. We passed by two lakes, small and dirty, thankful we did not stop here.

At last, its bald rock summit rising far above the saddle along side it,

Santa Fe Baldy projected itself 12,600 feet into the air. Our group split. The females, except myself, and two of the guys moved on to set up camp. Six of us decided to go for the gusto and climb the baldy. Easier said than done. An hour and a half for a two mile climb is a long time. The breathtaking view from the top was worth it. The whole trip was worth the incomparable panorama before my eyes as I reached the peak. I could see my home town, the whole pecos wilderness, all the burns and storms. From Albuquerque to Las Vegas to San Antonio. Mountains in Colorado lay seemingly at my feet.

Never wanting to leave and not wanting to get caught in an electrical storm well above the timberline, we rested, basking in the sun like the marmits whose whistles and curiosity were abundant. Rested, we ran back down 1300 feet in 20 minutes as, I think, my insides got confused and forgot what went where. I sure did sleep well that night.

The next morning Chip and Brad, anxious to hurry out and wait for rides, got disgusted with me and left me and the restless, but also unrushed, kids of the group to catch up. Which we did, but not soon. The hike out to Santa Fe basin was a joy. Downhill all the way, bathrooms at the end. We did end up waiting—for two hours. All of our rides home brought us some treats—watermelon and lemonade. After three and a half days without, we couldn't handle all the "with." Home at last, I bathed, shaved, and nursed my two open blisters, ready in five minutes to do it all over again.

In her discovery draft Arlene attempts to tell the whole story of her camping trip. At this point the approach was appropriate. It was sure to produce a paper much too long and unfocused, but, at the same time, it was likely to produce the raw materials that could be shaped into the paper she wanted to write. Although it is very long, this draft probably took relatively little time to write. Once Arlene had composed her Planning Page, she could have written about as fast as her handwriting or typing would allow.

Step 4: Compose a discovery draft of your essay. At this stage do not be overly concerned with grammatical or mechanical matters. If you cannot find the exact word you are looking for, settle for an approximate word or for a blank. Your task is to produce the raw material that you can eventually shape into the paper you want to write.

SELECT AND ANALYZE YOUR AUDIENCE

With this fifth step of the writing assignment we reintroduce a matter already discussed in some detail in Chapter One. There we said a writer is obligated to produce material that readers will consider significant and therefore worth the time and effort required to read it. In order to define what we meant by *signif-*

icant, we talked in Chapter One about the various purposes a writer may choose for his essay. There we said that a significant piece of writing will be designed to give the reader insight into the writer (expressive), to inform and/or persuade the reader (transactional), or to create an experience that conveys, in highly stylized language, the writer's view of truth (poetic).

We must add that just as is the case with modes, the purposes of writing are closely related. It is impossible to think of a piece of writing that dedicates itself entirely to self-expression with no concern for its effect upon a reader or its use of language. All three ingredients—writer, reader, and language—are present in all writing situations; nevertheless, various types of writing tend to emphasize one purpose more than others.

With these comments about significance and purpose in mind, let us re-examine the rough draft that Arlene wrote in response to the step 4 assignment. There is a great deal of material in this draft, but just how significant is that material? Another way of asking this question is this: Just who is Arlene writing this essay for and what does she hope the essay will do for (to) them? If her essay accomplishes any one of the three purposes just mentioned for any audience, it can be seen as a significant essay. But does it do so?

Which readers would be interested in the "information" Arlene gives them? When answering this question, we must remember that if the essay is informative, its information must be inherently interesting, not interesting for the insight it gives the reader into Arlene. Perhaps a person who is considering where to take a backpacking trip could be interested in some of the information in this paper, but she would not be interested in other things in this paper, such as the number of blisters on Arlene's feet.

At this stage in her writing process, it is important for Arlene to decide just who her audience is and what her purpose in writing for this audience is. Once she has analyzed the essay, she will no doubt discover that she is writing the essay in an attempt to express her feelings about this backpacking trip; thus hers will be an expressive essay.

Having determined that her aim is expressive, Arlene can choose an audience quite easily. If her purpose were transactional—either informative or persuasive—she would have to take more care in choosing an audience, but nearly any audience should be receptive to, and suitable for, an expressive essay.

We will have more to say about the audiences for transactional writing in Chapters Six and Eight, but for now we can offer a brief explanation. Because the writer of a transactional essay is either informing or persuading, he must take care to address an audience that needs and wants the information or that is suitable for persuading. A speaker does not tell a convention of medical doctors how to treat a first-degree burn—unless, of course, he is telling them of a new treatment that has been discovered since most of the doctors were in medical school. Likewise, a speaker does not try to persuade a convention of pro-lifers that abortion should not be legalized. It would also probably be unwise to address this appeal to a gathering of those ardently supporting free choice, because their decisions have already been made. Rather, the proper audience is a group of people who have not made their decisions or who are open to examining the decisions they have made.

We have made the preceding comments about audiences for transactional writing in order to contrast them with audiences for expressive writing. Arlene's primary purpose is to express exactly how she feels about this topic. To whom does she express herself? There is a sense in which she is addressing this essay to herself; but, of course, she is ultimately writing for an audience. However, the audience is not addressed in the direct manner that it would be if this were a transactional essay. Rather, it looks over the shoulder of the writer, as it were, and discovers things about the writer as she discovers things about herself. Nothing is asked of the audience, other than to be interested in human beings.

When we write in transactional situations, we will find it helpful to analyze our chosen audience, using the Questions for Analysis, much in the same fashion we have used them to find out what we think about the subject. However, a less complex statement of audience and purpose will suffice for an expressive essay. The following is Arlene's audience statement and a statement of her purpose in writing for this audience.

> My audience is this composition class. My purpose is to show my readers some of the beauty in and pleasure I derived from our four-day backpacking trip.

Step 5: Examine the first draft of your essay and select an audience for whom you would like to rewrite this draft. State what your purpose in writing this next draft will be.

WRITE A SECOND DRAFT

As we move into the second draft stage of Arlene's essay, we find a remarkable change in the quality of her language. Whereas she tended to bog down in rather boring, general language in the first draft, here she seems to be well on the way to finding the exact, vivid language to express the awe and beauty of this experience.

Before presenting Arlene's second draft, however, we need to make a few comments about the connection between Arlene's first and second drafts. Examining her first draft, Arlene discovered that she needed to focus on those aspects of the backpacking trip that were most influential in giving her a new appreciation for the beauty and grandeur of nature. Thus, she freed herself from the travelogue structure of the first narrative. She was then at liberty to describe in more detail and more vividly those things that so deeply affected her.

One key to Arlene's ability to find this new focus is her revised statement of focus. After analyzing her first draft, Arlene wrote a different kind of plan for her next draft. Her Planning Page (p. 99) had consisted of a focus statement (the Lead Sentence) and several Topic Sentences, which served to indicate what the various parts of the backpacking trip were. At that point, Arlene's Planning Page served her well. However, at this point, Arlene is beginning to get insight

Writing an Expressive Essay

into the real meaning of the trip to her. She reveals this meaning in a series of focusing sentences. These sentences are not intended as a guide to the actual structure of the essay; they will not appear in the final draft. Their only function is to help Arlene clarify in her own thinking just what it is that she wishes to express in this essay.

> During a backpacking trip in the mountains, I saw the beauty and majesty of nature relatively untouched by human hands.
> The beauty was not without a price—backpacking is painful, and one is subject to the whims of nature.
> The beauty of the mountains filled all of my senses with their presence.
> The trip made me realize how small the individual is when he or she is standing alone, especially compared with the enormousness of nature.
> The peace that permeates the wilderness is healthy and I was fortunate to take some of it back with me in the form of a change in attitude.

Arlene did not feel the need to write an outline of the type she wrote in the Planning Page of her first draft. She had made some definite decisions regarding changes in the structure of this next essay, but she felt that the parts of her essay were fitting together well. She was concerned at this stage that the details she chose to include were captured in expressive language. Thus, her focus statements were an attempt to review her feelings concerning this experience.

The following is her second draft of the essay.

Purple Mountains' Majesty

I stood by the pit outhouse patiently waiting my turn, surveying the new world unfolding before my eyes. At 9,000 feet up in the New Mexico Rockies my vision seemed sharper, probably due to the excitement and eagerness to begin the trip bubbling just beneath my calm exterior. This excitement and eagerness had heightened all my senses and honed my thinking process to a fine point. This is a Rocky Mountain high, I thought, one which lasted throughout the four day backpacking trip into the Pecos Wilderness. Those four days were crammed full of events, disasters, surprises, and beauty beyond compare. It was my duty to chaperone eleven high school kids as well as the other two directors of summer activities. These people, our trip up here, and the interactions of the kids with their temporary environment are three stories on their own. For me, the trip was a constant amazement, a continual demanding barrage on my senses. The winter had been a late one and it looked like early spring instead of early June. The smells attracted my attention first, or rather the absence of some of them. There was no obnoxious odor of exhaust, only the pungent perfume of the pines and field flowers, no dry desert sand to clog up the nostrils, only the ever present smell of loam, dark and spongy, underlying all the scents when dry and overiding them when rain threatened. When I stepped away from the outhouse the smell was sweeter still.

Anxious to be off, the whole motely crew started up the trail which would take us from Jack's Creek Campground, across several mountains, to Santa Fe Ski Basin. I brought up the rear, which was not so bad since it was quiet; those in the rear of the group were concentrating fiercely on walking gracefully with their packs and I could absorb all I wanted to.

The pines, ancient and gnarled, yet majestic, creaked and groaned in the slight wind they were receiving from the edge of a storm. Interspersed among the pines were white barked aspens, slender and flexible, as well as scrub oak. The brown earth was only visible on the trail where many feet had worn a scar in the mountainside. Elsewhere, it was covered by dirty dead leaves, needles, and occasionally fallen trees, too old and feeble to withstand the rough play of mother nature's summer storms and winter snows. Looking up through the tops of the trees to the now cloudy sky, I felt like I had somehow slipped backwards in time to when I was four. I could not remember having to crane my neck so much to see my daddy's head as I did to see the sky above the tops of the pines.

After a while we came to some meadows, a few of the many we were to see over the next days. At first glance, they seemed so green, so grassy. But walking over them the blanket of green dissolved into patches of green, and then to little tufts of wiry grass anchored firmly to the ground. On entering the set of meadows, the sky seemed brilliantly blue especially compared with the dusky shadows of the forest. Upon entering the trees again, I immediately became aware of the sounds. There were beetles clicking slowly, birds squawking, jays chattering, and bushy-tailed squirrels scolding and running from tree to tree to keep up and continue lecturing, only to realize they had forgotten what the lecture was about.

The air became heavier and heavier with the impending rain. I could even taste the rain. Looking up I saw the thunderheads, characteristic of the summer mountain storms tumbling and meshing until one solid sheet of rain cloud was formed. It poured. The damp of the rain sharpened the chill and it penetrated my day-glo orange rain poncho and wool jacket and raised my skin in gooseprickles.

By the time we reached Pecos Baldy Lake, the air had the feel of three hours past dark, but the air was fresh, washed clean by mother nature herself. The baldy rose like the rounded end of a loaf of French bread that has been in the oven too long. There were no trees on it even though the ridge connecting it with the rest of the range was dappled green from top to bottom. The trees stopped just at the seam of the ridge and baldy. The little lake which was at the bottom of the peak was as cold as if the glacier had deposited it yesterday instead of eons ago.

The connecting ridge, a saddle actually between two peaks was steep on the lake side, so steep that the switchbacks which were par for the course, were so small, numerous, and tight that the trail resembled a zipper sewn askance on the hillside.

Our campsite that night was like a boulder box, with us camped in the bottom and the two sides and top gone. The two remaining sides were like walls off some forgotten castle long since tumbled down, only the lower portions of two walls remaining, crumbled and overgrown with moss. The morning after the thunderstorm dawned crystal clear and fresh. And what to my wondering eyes should appear, but two big horns, a ram and an ewe wearing a radio collar which permanently defurred her neck. Totally unabashed, they enjoyed the eggs they had gracefully waltzed down the rocks to lap up. Apparently, they were familiar with humans and had no reason to fear, or at least they had not found one yet.

Their favorite delicacy was crackers—Ritz, Clubhouse, saltines. Gracefully knocking down unattended packs and choosing only the best, they searched for this staple of the backpacker. Their plundering complete, they almost flew up the steep hillside and slipped back into the cool shadows of their home.

After the big horns that morning, nothing else was looking quite so special when we entered Horsethief Meadows. These were the longest, thinnest meadows I've ever seen. They sat right in the 'v' created by two adjacent mountains. It was as if God carved a piece of the prarie and plopped it in the Rockies and said, "See what else there is to my world." A minute stream, barely a trickle, winked through the meadows, merrily, the actual creator of the thin strip of gold in the crotch of two mountains. The sunlight angled off of the air itself, a mist from a hailstorm not fifteen minutes past still lingering. In the protection offered by the aged pines, little piles of tiny white stones, hailstones, lay waiting for the sun to turn them to water. Around noon that day we walked right over a saddle into a meadow—huge, barren, rocky—and under a storm. At a fork in the trail, the group split, sending half up to make camp and the other half to tackle Santa Fe Baldy. A good portion of that monster, reaching 12,600 feet into the thin air, is bare of trees—hence, the name, "baldy." Below the timber line, which is about fifty yards from the summit, a short green plant grows, sending wiry roots deep into piano sized boulders and hanging on for dear life. It looked very much like a miniature (barely an inch high) pine tree. From my vantage point, the baldy looked conquerable. I believed that until I was half way up, too far to turn back, almost too exhausted to go on. Up, up we climbed, resting almost every five feet. The starting elevation was barely 11,500 feet. That left a climb of over 1,100 feet. With every step, my range of view broadened by miles, the sense of conquering the mountain giving me the energy to go on. I reached the line where the green became scarce, almost disappearing completely, and I was now above timberline. Lumbering onward, at long last I reached three false summits before I hit the tippy top of the mountain. The view from there was literally breathtaking. I managed a breathless whoop of triumph. I turned round and round trying to absorb everything I saw and to store it in my mind as a permanent memory. I wanted to be able to set my future grandchildren on my knee and share this with them.

Exploring the baldy, I discovered it must look like a 'C' from an airplane. The summit was not a mere point but extended for nearly a hundred yards. Below us, about 2,500 feet, Santa Fe Baldy Lake rested serenely, only a dot, yet clear enough to sparkle up at me. Snow banks lay all along that side, melting in a small incessant trickle. To the southwest, opposite the lake and snow were the Jimez Mountains, which is where my hometown nestled safely; to the north, I saw Colorado's San Antonio Mountain, the Colorado Rockies; to the south, Albuquerque, small as a quarter. Around on the southeast, Las Vegas, and even further south, Socorro. Beyond the lake, almost as high as the baldy, were the rest of the Pecos Wilderness, the burns of the past fifty years scarring the land, the alternating shades of green as pines opened to fields of aspen, and over all, the dappling of thunderhead shadows lit occasionally by a great fork of lightning. To the north, equally imposing but made to appear less so by distance, the Truchas Twin Peaks challenged a storm set in around its crown. Then my eye caught the Santa Fe Ski Basin, where raw beauty had been marred for man's pleasure. It reminded me that this throne was not a permanent one, that civilization would not seem so pretty as it did from this dizzying height, once we reached it. I turned, absorbed, remembered and felt nature until I was giddy. Then I lay down and joined the overcurious shy yellow-bellied marmits sunning on the rocks (when they weren't busy trying to sneak up on us and take a peek). Their shrill whistles kept the silence from being deafening.

Soon the air became ominously heavy, threatening rain. Getting caught in an electrical storm above timberline was not desirable at all. I slowly revolved three times making sure the picture in memory was just right, adjusting the focus before running pell mell down the sides of the mountain. "And God saw everything that He had made, and behold, it was very good." Genesis 1:31.

As we have said, the language of Arlene's second draft is obviously more vivid than was the language of the first draft. In the second draft her language does not merely tell us about an experience; it shows us the things she experienced. She effectively chooses words that express the sights she saw and her feelings upon viewing these sights. She does not—indeed, she cannot—simply describe what was there or narrate what happened. Rather, she describes what she saw there and narrates what she remembers to have happened.

Far from lessening the worth of her essay, this subjective element gives it its real value or significance. If Arlene could have simply described what was there, what would be the difference between this essay and a snapshot brought back from the trip? Would anyone wish to read her description when he could look at the picture instead?

Fortunately, we do not have to face such a question, because expressive writing is inherently subjective. When we attempt to tell what we see in a certain situation, we are attempting to express how we feel about that situation. We do so by comparing this new thing, or experience, with familiar things and experiences. This comparison involves "expressive" language that often helps us, and our readers, understand how we feel about the subject being treated.

Sometimes the comparisons in expressive language are rather obvious. For example, in one of his prose pieces E. B. White makes some straightforward comparisons in describing the school experiences of a young lad, saying the school bus "was as punctual as death."* With this comparison (*school bus* to *death*), White reveals his feelings about the school.

One way, then, to find how we feel about a thing or experience is to compare it with other things or experiences. However, our writing would be rather cumbersome if it consisted of nothing but one comparison after another. Moreover, we would not always find something with which to compare our subject. Thus, we are often called upon to be more inventive in our use of language than simple comparisons require us to be.

Straightforward comparison requires little of this inventiveness. For exam-

---

*E. B. White, "Education," *One Man's Meat* (New York: Harper and Row, 1944), p. 53.

Writing an Expressive Essay

ple, a person can tell us something of her attitude toward John by saying, "John is a lion." Such a comparison is made rather simply by equating (comparing) one word, *John*, to another word, *lion*. But more effective than this direct comparison would be an indirect comparison such as the one in the following sentence: "John growled his answer." Such an indirect comparison requires us to use language inventively, for we do not normally use the verb *growl* in reference to a human being. By putting these two words—*John* and *growl*—together, the writer is making an implicit comparison between John and a lion, or some other such beast.

Our first reaction to such inventive language is often negative. We see it as "frilly" or overly ornate and wonder why one would go the long way round to say, "John growled his answer" when he could just as easily have said, "John was gruff," or "John was mean." There are two very good ways to answer this objection. The first is to say that this inventive language helps a writer to "show" rather than to "tell," and thus to stay within the bounds of expressive writing. The person who says, "John was gruff" has provided little information about the specific situation in question. What did John do? Did he stare fixedly? Did he leave the room in a huff? Did he speak sharply? We do not know. The writer has not really shown us anything about John but has given us an evaluation of this situation. We do get an answer to these questions in the other sentence. At the same time, we get some insight into how the writer viewed John's actions.

A second, and more direct, answer to this objection that such language is "frilly" is simply to say that it is not. Rather, it exhibits a primary feature of all successful communication. We can never make words express exactly what we want them to, but the more we bend and shape them to our needs, the closer we can come to making our words serve our purposes.

<table>
<tr><td>EXERCISES</td><td>

1. Arlene changes the structure of her essay considerably in her second draft. Using the ordering principles of association, dissociation, and sequence, divide her second draft into its beginning, middle, and end.

2. We would label both of Arlene's drafts narratives because the overriding structure of both of them is provided by chronology. However, as we have said, the second draft is much richer in descriptive detail than is the first draft. What was the first draft about? What is the second draft about? Can you see any connection between the change in topic from the first to the second draft and the aforementioned change in descriptive detail?

3. Find at least three places in the second draft in which Arlene uses language effectively to express the beauty of these mountains. Does she use direct or indirect comparisons in these places? What is she comparing to what? Are there places in which Arlene's attempts to use inventive language fail for you? If so, can you account in any way for this failure?

4. After she analyzed the second draft, Arlene wrote the following introduction, designed to replace the first six paragraphs of the second draft.

</td></tr>
</table>

I awoke slowly, letting the filtered light in the little two-man tent send its subtle signals into my brain. At first I could not remember where I was or what I was doing in a sleeping bag on top of a stick the size of the leg bone of a Christmas turkey. Pictures flashed through my mind. I saw the fourteen of us, eleven high school aged young people and the two other chaperones, and myself, hoisting thirty to forty pound backpacks onto strong shoulders. Two big horn sheep, a ram and ewe, who had gracefully leaped down the steep embankment bordering our first night's camp waltzed through my mind. I shuddered at the thought of the "saddle," a ridge joining two mountain peaks, we had to cross, the memory of yesterday's saddle fresh in my mind. That saddle had been nearly a vertical rise out of the slight depression we had been in, and the "switch-backs," the winds in the trail, had been so small, numerous, and tight that the trail resembled a zipper sewn askance on the hillside. I remembered . . . . My stomach rumbled, reminding me that I would need a hearty breakfast if I were to make any progress that day. The cool, fresh Rocky Mountain air exhilerated me and by the time the camp was down and everyone else was ready, I had long been ready. We set off on the third day of our four day backpack trip in the Pecos Wilderness.

Was this a wise revision? What effect will it have on the next draft of Arlene's essay?

Step 6: Write a second draft of your essay. Pay particular attention to finding exact, vivid language that will help you express your feelings about your topic.

WRITE A FINAL DRAFT

Once Arlene had written her second draft, producing the final draft was a rather simple task: She had only to refine and correct the second draft. Here, then, is the finished product of Arlene's writing process.

Purple Mountains' Majesty

I awoke slowly, letting the subdued light in the little two-man tent filter through my eyelids and slowly activate my consciousness. I could not remember where I was or what I was doing in a sleeping bag lying uncomfortably on top of a stick the size of the leg bone of the Christmas turkey. Then snapshots of the last two days sequenced through my mind. I saw the fourteen of us, eleven high school-aged people, the two other chaperones and me, most of us from the church I worked for, hoisting thirty to forty pound packs onto our backs. I saw the two bighorn sheep, a ram and ewe, gracefully leaping down the steep embankment bordering our first night's camp. I visualized the saddle we had to cross that day, and I breathed a sigh of relief at the picture of yesterday's saddle. It had risen nearly vertically from the slight depression we were in, and the switchbacks in the trail were so small, numerous, and tight that the trail resembled a zipper sewn askance on the hillside. I remembered. . . . My stomach rumbled, demanding a hearty breakfast to take me through the day. As I emerged from the tent, the cool, fresh Rocky Mountain air whetted not only my appetite for food but also my appetite for whatever adventure lay on today's trail. With all of the gear packed, we finally set off on the third day of our four-day backpacking trip.

Around noon we walked down a saddle into a huge, barren, rocky meadow, right into a storm. At a fork in the trail, the group split, with half going on to make camp, the rest waiting until the rain had moved on and then tackling Santa Fe Baldy. A good portion of the upper half of the mountain, which rises to 12,600 feet, is bare of trees, hence the name "Baldy." Up to fifty yards short of the summit, Baldy is green. The ground is covered with miniature (one inch worth of miniature) pine trees which send wiry roots deep into the hard rock and hang on for dear life. From my vantage point, the mountain looked conquerable.

I believed that until I was halfway up, too far to turn back, almost too exhausted to go on. Go on we did, though. Up and up we climbed, resting almost every twenty feet. The meadow we started from had an elevation of 11,500 feet, and Baldy rose seemingly straight out of it, making the climb extremely strenuous. But with every step, my range of vision expanded by tens of miles. And with this new vision came a sense of conquering the beast. I found the strength to go on. Upon reaching the uneven line where the little pine trees disappeared and only tiny, fragrant flowers struggled to survive, I realized that I was now above timberline. Lumbering onward, I finally reached the crown of the mountain. I let out a triumphant but breathless whoop.

The view from that elevation was breathtaking, literally. I slowly pivoted, turning round and round trying to absorb all that I saw, smelled, and felt. I wanted to store it all in my memory permanently. I wanted to be able to share this scene with my future grandchildren. To fulfill this dream, I decided to explore this baldy and all that I saw.

The baldy itself did not come to a pointed peak; rather the summit formed a large letter 'C' of rocks. The top provided an excellent viewing platform. Twenty-five hundred feet below, Santa Fe Baldy Lake perched on the east side, a small blue-gray dot of water sparkling up at me. All along the steep east side of the baldy, huge snowbanks melted slowly. With my back to the lake, I faced west to the Jimez Mountains rising from a great flat expanse. In the bosom of the Jimez, my hometown nestled comfortably. To the north, the New Mexico Rockies faded into the Colorado Rockies. To the south, lay Albuquerque, small as a quarter, then Socorro, and off to the left, Las Vegas. All over the east and northeast, the rest of the untamed Pecos Wilderness rose defiantly to the crisp, clear blue sky. On the mottled shades of green that all the mountains and hills blended into were the scars of fires, fields of aspen, and spring-green meadows. Over this vast expanse of wilderness, the sun shone through and around clouds, creating a dappled effect. To the north, jutting above their surroundings, were the baldy's twin equals, Truchas Peaks, lightning forking from the storms surrounding their crowns.

Then my eye caught the Santa Fe Ski Basin. There was raw beauty marred for man's pleasure. The basin reminded me that this throne on the top of Santa Fe Baldy was only temporary. When we joined it again, civilization would not seem as tantalizing as it did from such dizzying heights. I could even see, I fancied, the road that would lead us down from the high country and eventually home. Shaking the unwanted thought free, I again whirled round, viewing my kingdom. Then I lay down and joined the overly curious, yet shy, yellow-bellied marmots sunning on the rocks. Their shrill whistles penetrated the keen silence and kept it from overwhelming. I dozed.

Jerking awake, I noticed that the air had become ominously heavy, threatening rain. Getting caught in an electrical storm above timberline was not what any of us wanted. Before running pell-mell down the steep side of the mountain, I slowly revolved three times being sure my memory had the fine tune in focus. With a heavy sigh, I turned to leave. Glancing back I thought, "And God saw everything that He had made, and behold, it was very good" (Genesis 1:31).

As Arlene's essay illustrates, the seven-step model we have presented in this chapter is recursive and based on revision; it loops backward while moving forward. The significance of Arlene's essay is buried within its discovery draft, but it took Arlene two more drafts before she found and said fully what she had to say. Thus, Arlene moved backward while moving forward; she read back over the first draft to produce the second, and she read back over the second draft to produce the final. Arlene discovered the significance of this trip only as she revised—first expanding her prewriting into the first draft, then expanding parts of her first draft into the second draft, then sharpening the focus by collapsing the first six paragraphs of the second draft into a single introductory paragraph and, thus, selecting only the trip to Santa Fe Baldy as the focal point for the final draft.

Earlier we said that the move from the second to the final draft was a rather simple task. In a sense this is true, because most of the material of the final paper is present in the second draft. However, there is a sense in which some of the most important revising in the whole process occurs between the second and final drafts. The second draft is so long as to be completely unmanageable. At this stage Arlene has not made the commitment to deal with the climb to the Pecos Baldy; she is still attempting to tell about the whole backpacking trip. At the final draft stage Arlene recognizes the fact that one essay cannot do everything. She chooses, then, to tell of one of her experiences on this trip. We think she has done this one thing well.

WRITING ASSIGNMENT

Step 7: Write the final draft of your essay. In this draft you should pay particular attention to editing skills. Be sure that all words are spelled correctly and that there are no grammatical errors. While you are editing, be open to any other revisions that will improve the overall essay.

Writing an Expressive Essay

Shaping Meaning

The title of this section is actually something of a misnomer, in that we have already spent a good bit of time talking about shaping meaning, and you have obviously shaped meaning in every piece of writing you have done to date. What we intend the title of this section to do is to focus you on the more complex processes at work in transactional writing, the writing that gets the world's— and the writer's—work done.

In expressive writing, you write for an audience close to home, because you write primarily for yourself. When you use expressive writing for an audience beyond yourself, you write so that the reader watches the subject of the writing unfold with you. Transactional writing makes different demands on the writer than expressive writing makes. Essentially, transactional writing fulfills one of three purposes: (1) it transmits information to the reader, telling him something the writer thinks he should know; (2) it argues a point or attempts to persuade the reader of something; or (3) it reports the results of the writer's probing of a topic, with those results presented in some way that makes them of worth to a reader. Expressive writing is more writer-centered, transactional writing more reader-centered. Thus, the writer's job is not just to make sense of a particular topic for himself but to help that topic make sense for his reader as well. The writer's task becomes one of shaping meaning to create that sense for his reader.

The five chapters of Part Two are designed to help you shape that meaning. Chapter Five focuses on the structures most often employed in transactional writing, with these structures, or modes, seen as ways of ordering a topic. It is important to note that, in all probability, none of the modes we outline will be used solely to provide structure for a piece of writing. Most often, transactional writing uses a blend of several modes, although one mode will provide the overall structuring principle for a given piece of writing. Working in tandem with Chapter Five is Chapter Six in which we take you through a transactional writing assignment designed to meet the first of the purposes we outlined for transactional writing, that of giving a reader information. In fulfilling this assignment, you will write an essay with a student essay as a guide, just as you did in Chapter Four. Chapters Seven and Eight also work together, with Chapter Seven focusing on ways of structuring an argument and Chapter Eight on writing a persuasive essay. Chapter Nine focuses on research and writing, with research activities seen as offering the writer the chance to explore or probe a topic, so that the research paper is seen as the result of an active inquiry into a topic rather than simply a rehashing of other people's ideas.

No matter which transactional purpose is at work in your writing, no matter for which audience you write, you still need to discover and report significance in your topic. While it is true that transactional writing is for audiences beyond the writer, it is nonetheless imperative that the writer base his writing on what counts for him in the topic. Transactional writing requires just as much subjectivity as expressive writing—both types of writing require the writer to report his interpretation of his topic.

Chapter Five

Structuring Transactional Writing

In our last chapter we concentrated on that type of writing through which an author can "express" herself to an audience. We now turn our attention to a different type—transactional writing. We get some insight into transactional writing from its name; it helps us make "transactions." However, we can understand this type of writing more fully by comparing its focus with that of expressive writing. The writer of an expressive piece focuses on herself in order to express an experience; the writer of a transactional piece, however, focuses on the information being conveyed to the readers in order to convey that information to readers.

The specific purposes for individual examples of transactional writing can vary greatly despite their similarities in focus. The following are all examples of this type of writing: a letter to a friend giving directions to your house, a dessert recipe, a summary of the happenings in a corporate business meeting, an analysis of the steps being taken by nuclear energy producers to make their plants as safe as possible, and a paper arguing that nuclear energy either is, or is not, safe.

All of these examples would produce writing with a transactional aim. In order to produce them, the writers would employ words that help readers form concepts, ideas, and thoughts, and the final product would contain information that the speaker wished to convey to his readers. But this contrast between the writer's knowledge and the reader's lack of knowledge, which is implicit in the use of *convey*, works only so long as we are referring to a final product. After the writer has worked through the writing process, he should have information that his readers do not have, and thus we can think of the words on the page as vehicles through which he can transmit, or convey, this information to readers.

But we should not allow this message-oriented model alone to shape our view of transactional writing. Rather, we should ask ourselves just how the writer comes to know something that the readers do not know. Certainly, we cannot accept the overly simple answer that she heard or read the information. If the writer is simply delivering information that she heard, she is transcribing, not writing. If the writer is presenting information that she read somewhere else, we must wonder why she does not simply point her readers to that writing in which she found the information.

No, the writer is not merely conveying information. Transactional writing is that process by which the writer discovers and conveys these concepts, ideas, and thoughts. But how?

TRANSACTIONAL STRUCTURES

We have actually been developing an answer to this question from the beginning of our text. In Chapter Two, we illustrated the inherent connection between form and content; there we offered procedures through which a writer can find what he wants to say by examining the potential ordering principles—What goes with what? What opposes what? What follows (from) what? Then in Chapter Four we examined the specific ordering devices that help us create meaning in expressive writing. In this chapter we will examine the ordering devices that help us discover what we want to say in transactional situations.

The ordering devices that we employ in these situations are more varied than those we use in expressive writing. The primary organizing principle in transactional writing is exposition, a mode more complex than either narration or description because its explicit structure may involve all three ordering principles introduced in Chapter Two—association, dissociation, and sequence. The complexity of exposition has given rise to six different expository structures.

1. process (based on sequence)
2. analysis (based on association)
3. comparison and contrast (based on association and dissociation)
4. causal analysis (based on sequence and association)
5. classification (based on association)
6. definition (based on association)

You may use each of these structures as something of a pattern to impose on your writing topic to help you discover and create order in that topic. As such, these structures are not ends in themselves. Seldom will you write an essay that is wholly comparison/contrast, or classification, or causal analysis; instead, these structures most often work together, so that you may use several in a given essay, even though one of the structures will be the primary structuring device.

Structuring Transactional Writing

(One example we can give of this is the section in Chapter One which *defines* writing as a recursive, three-part process and then briefly *analyzes* each of the three stages.) So structures are not ends; they are means, organizational patterns you may use to order a topic.

In discussing each of these six structures, we provide writing assignments that you may wish to use not only as part of your work with this chapter but also as the basis for the essay we will have you write in Chapter Six. As you work through this chapter, consider the suggested topics carefully.

PROCESS

At the heart of the process structure is the what-follows-what? relationship. This is not to suggest that sequence is responsible for all the order in a paragraph or essay that is based on process; rather, it is to suggest that in the simplest example sequence can provide the order for a process. The following is an example of such a simple process.

> Go to the red light at the President's house and turn left onto Highway 93. Take 93 to the fork and bear right there. Continue on through town until you come to an intersection with a red light. Turn left there and you'll find McDonald's on your right.

Although there are few time connectors in this passage, it is evident that the basic relator is the what-follows-what? connector. We know that the writer means: "You go to the red light at the President's house. 'Then' you turn left. 'Next' you take Highway 93. . . ." Thus, this simple process paragraph relies on the sequence relationship for its order. But what about a more complicated process essay? The following is an excerpt from a rather complicated piece.

Learning Speech
John Holt

1   Bill Hull once said to me, "If we taught children to speak, they'd never learn." I thought at first he was joking. By now I realize that it was a very important truth. Suppose we decided that we had to "teach" children to speak. How would we go about it? First, some committee of experts would analyze speech and break it down into a number of separate "speech skills." We would probably say that, since speech is made up of sounds, a child must be taught to make all the sounds of his language before he can be taught to speak the language itself. Doubtless we would list these sounds, easiest and commonest ones first, harder and rarer ones next. Then we would begin to teach infants these sounds, working our way down the list. Perhaps, in order not to "confuse" the child—"confuse" is an evil word to many educators—we would not let the child hear much ordinary speech, but would only expose him to the sounds we were trying to teach.

2   Along with our sound list, we would have a syllable list and a word list.

When the child had learned to make all the sounds on the sound list, we would begin to teach him to combine the sounds into syllables. When he could say all the syllables on the syllable list, we would begin to teach him words on our word list. At the same time, we would teach him the rules of grammar, by means of which he could combine these newly learned words into sentences. Everything would be planned with nothing left to chance; there would be plenty of drill, review, and tests, to make sure that he had not forgotten anything.

Suppose we tried to do this; what would happen? What would happen, quite simply, is that most children, before they got very far, would become baffled, discouraged, humiliated, and fearful, and would quit trying to do what we asked them. If, outside of our classes, they lived a normal infant's life, many of them would probably ignore our "teaching" and learn to speak on their own. If not, if our control of their lives was complete (the dream of too many educators), they would take refuge in deliberate failure and silence, as so many of them do when the subject is reading.

Last summer, in a supermarket, a young mother came with her baby to the meat counter, and began to discuss with him, in the most lively and natural way, what meat they should get for supper. This piece of meat looked nice, but it was too expensive—terrible what was happening to food prices. This piece might be all right, but it would take too long to cook; they had many other errands to do and would not get home before four o'clock. These chops looked good, but they had had them just two nights ago. And so on. There was nothing forced or affected in her words or her voice; she might have been talking to someone her own age.

A year or more ago, some friends and I dropped in on some people who had a six-month-old baby. She was well-rested and happy, so they brought her in to see the visitors. We all admired her before going on with our talk. She was fascinated by this talk. As each person spoke, she would turn and look intently at him. From time to time she would busy herself with a toy in her lap; then after a few minutes she would begin watching and listening again. She seemed to be learning, not just that people talk, but that they talk to each other, and respond to each other's talk with smiles, and laughter, and more talk; in short, that talk is not just a kind of noise, but messages, communication.

Babies and young children like to hear adult conversation, and will often sit quietly for a long time, just to hear it. If we want to help little children as they learn to talk, one way to do it is by talking to them— provided we do it naturally and unaffectedly—and by letting them be around when we talk to other people.*

Obviously this essay is shaped by various connectors. However, the overall order of the first three paragraphs is provided by the what-follows-what? connector. Once the central question of how we would go about teaching children to speak is raised, chronological connections take over. Holt tells us, "First, some

---

Structuring Transactional Writing

committee of experts would. . . ." After this sentence, he elaborates, telling how this feat would be accomplished. Two sentences later, the process continues with "Then we would begin to teach infants these sounds. . . ." Thus, even though the chronological relator is not responsible for all, or even most, of the connections between the sentences in this essay, it does provide the primary structuring frame for the essay.

We should not, however, be misled into assuming that the writer of a process essay has a simple task. Like narration, process is likely to appear deceptively simple. In fact, the basic similarities between narration and process make it possible for us to learn a great deal about one from the other. The writer of a narrative is tempted to think that she has only to recount the events that compose that narrative in the precise order in which they occurred. But as we found in analyzing sample narratives, there is no way for a writer to capture all of the events that occur. And, even if she could, the result would be a host of meaningless details, not a meaningful narrative. Thus, the key to ordering a narrative is to find reasons for including certain details of the event and for excluding others.

Similarly, the writer of a process essay must carefully select the material for the essay. To reveal the complexity of process, we can examine the decisions involved in giving directions to a place. For example, what if Ron Lunsford, one of this book's authors, wished to tell a friend how to find his house? How would he begin? Depending upon the knowledge of the person for whom he is writing, he could begin with either of the following "first steps."

1. As you leave the library parking lot, turn left.
2. Head toward Seneca on Highway 123.

The first "first" step could be written for an entering freshman at Clemson University who knows very little about the Clemson area. Ron is attempting to give this person every detail he will need in the process of finding his house. Of course, the student could find Highway 123 on a map; he could also find Ron's house by following someone else to it or in any number of other ways. But Ron wishes to write directions that in and of themselves will allow this person (with his knowledge of Clemson and its surrounds) to find his house.

On the other hand, the "first" step in the second example is written for someone who knows quite a bit about the Clemson area. This person will find Highway 123 approximately two and one-half miles from the library parking lot, the place we assume to be the starting point. To a person who knows where Highway 123 and Seneca are, any directions to 123 would be unnecessary.

<table>
<tr><td>EXERCISE</td><td>Compare the directions on some household product such as dishwashing soap with the directions on some prescription medicine. For what type of person are these directions written? Is either of these insulting to your intelligence? Why, or why not? Are the instructions equally clear?</td></tr>
</table>

EXERCISE

Often the knowledge that a reader brings to the process she is being introduced to is crucial to the writer describing that process. To get some insight into how this is so, perform the following exercise.

First, in a paragraph or so, describe to someone who is familiar with table tennis the process by which one plays the game of tennis. Then describe this process to a person unfamiliar with table tennis or any other similar game.

WRITING ASSIGNMENT

Use process as the primary structure for an essay on one of the following topics. Be sure that you choose an audience who will benefit from the information you are offering. (Write a paragraph in which you explain why you selected the particular audience you are writing for.)

1. Explain how the electoral college is chosen in your state.

2. Explain how you resolve a major disagreement with a parent, a friend, or a boyfriend or girlfriend.

3. Explain how you write a research paper.

ANALYSIS

A simple analysis depends upon one connecting agent—What goes with what? The following is such a simple analysis.

> Every good teacher possesses to some degree three essential characteristics. He must, above all else, like people. He must enjoy learning, himself. And finally, he must be flexible enough to know when the best laid plans should be put aside in favor of spontaneous learning.

In this example, the first sentence introduces a "whole," and the following sentences break this whole down into parts. Thus, the relationship between each of these sentences is, What goes with what? The sentences "go together" because they are parts of one whole.

But only the most simple analysis will rely exclusively on this associative connecting agent. The following is a more complex analysis.

WRITING
SAMPLE

The Typical
Science Fiction Film
Susan Sontag

1 The typical science fiction film has a form as predictable as a Western, and is made up of elements which, to a practiced eye, are as classic as the saloon brawl, the blonde schoolteacher from the East, and the gun duel on the deserted main street.

2   One model scenario proceeds through five phases.

(1) The arrival of the thing. (Emergence of the monsters, landing of the alien spaceship, etc.) This is usually witnessed or suspected by just one person, a young scientist on a field trip. Nobody, neither his neighbors nor his colleagues, will believe him for some time. The hero is not married, but has a sympathetic though also incredulous girl friend.

(2) Confirmation of the hero's report by a host of witnesses to a great act of destruction. (If the invaders are beings from another planet, a fruitless attempt to parley with them and get them to leave peacefully.) The local police are summoned to deal with the situation and massacred.

(3) In the capital of the country, conferences between scientists and the military take place, with the hero lecturing before a chart, map, or blackboard. A national emergency is declared. Reports of further destruction. Authorities from other countries arrive in black limousines. All international tensions are suspended in view of the planetary emergency. This stage often includes a rapid montage of news broadcasts in various languages, a meeting at the UN, and more conferences between the military and the scientists. Plans are made for destroying the enemy.

(4) Further atrocities. At some point the hero's girl friend is in grave danger. Massive counter-attacks by international forces, with brilliant displays of rocketry, rays, and other advanced weapons, are all unsuccessful. Enormous military casualties, usually by incineration. Cities are destroyed and/or evacuated. There is an obligatory scene here of panicked crowds stampeding along a highway or a big bridge, being waved on by numerous policemen who, if the film is Japanese, are immaculately white-gloved, preternaturally calm, and call out in dubbed English, "Keep moving. There is no need to be alarmed."

(5) More conferences, whose motif is: "They must be vulnerable to something." Throughout the hero has been working in his lab to this end. The final strategy, upon which all hopes depend, is drawn up; the ultimate weapon—often a super-powerful, as yet untested, nuclear device—is mounted. Countdown. Final repulse of the monster or invaders. Mutual congratulations, while the hero and girl friend embrace cheek to cheek and scan the skies sturdily. "But have we seen the last of them?"*

Sontag obviously makes use of various types of connectors in this essay. However, the overriding structure of the essay is provided by association. The "whole" that forms the framework for the essay is the science fiction film. The various parts of these films "go together" to form this whole.

Our discussion of analysis should help us begin to see more clearly the inherent connection between the transactional aim and the expository mode. Analysis, an expository tool that the writer can employ in discovering information that she can then share with her readers, makes use of the basic principle that wholes are composed of parts that "go together." This principle can be used as a tool for learning in situations as different as one in which a literary critic analyzes (breaks into parts) the code of the Hemingway hero and one in which

---

*From Susan Sontag, "The Imagination of Disaster," *Against Interpretation* (New York: Farrar, Straus & Giroux, Inc.). Copyright © 1965, 1966 by Susan Sontag. Reprinted with permission.

a gourmet cook analyzes (breaks into parts) a sauce made by another cook. In both cases the analyzer confronts a "whole" that she does not fully understand but may well come to understand by examining its parts, some of which may be familiar.

EXERCISE

We said earlier that the overriding purpose in analysis is to understand more about a whole as a result of an analysis of its parts. In a paragraph or two, analyze the following ordinary things and events. Then write a paragraph in which you discuss what you learned in doing so.

1. A typical day for you

2. The procedure by which you go about getting something that you want badly from your parents, or your husband or wife

3. An argument with your girlfriend or boyfriend

4. The grading policies of your favorite (least favorite) teacher

5. A typical first date

WRITING ASSIGNMENT

Use analysis as the primary structure of an essay in response to one of the following topics. (Write a paragraph in which you identify your audience and explain why you chose this particular audience for this essay.)

1. Analyze your writing process.

2. Analyze the plot of your favorite kind of movie, music, or reading matter (for example, novels, romances, comics, sports magazines).

3. Analyze a physical action (for example, throwing a particular pitch in baseball, moving into a dorm room, meeting a new roommate).

4. Analyze some aspect of your education (for example, a successful or unsuccessful class, the curriculum for your major, an experience unrelated to school).

COMPARISON AND CONTRAST

Another basic principle by which we form concepts and ideas is comparison. (We will use *comparison* in the broad sense in which it can refer to likenesses and differences.) In order to see how basic comparison is to the learning process, you need only observe a young child as he attempts to make sense of the world. He sees a small fur-covered animal that has two eyes, a nose, a mouth, four legs, and a tail—among many other characteristics that escape the child's notice.

His parents inform him that this strange-looking creature is a "doggie." A few minutes later, the child sees another small animal and exclaims "doggie." His parents will be pleased, but they may not fully realize just what a feat this child has accomplished. The child recognizes this second dog even though he has never seen it before and even though it is not just like anything he has ever seen before. This dog's hair color is not just like that of the first dog, its weight is not the same, its nose is not the same length, and so forth. But the child has learned something by means of comparison. Of course, the child may also "recognize" several cats as dogs for a time, but as his ability to make comparisons sharpens, he will reach a point at which he "knows" what a dog is. He could never do so without mastering the comparative mode of thinking.

As its name indicates, this structure is organized by the what-goes-with-what? relationship. Of course, because comparison includes both likenesses and differences, the other side of the associative coin—the what-opposes-what? relationship—is also at work in structuring comparisons. A simple comparison such as the following can be structured entirely by either of these relationships.

> I found that my new school had a system of dealing with students which was almost opposite to that of the old school. For example, in Baskinville we were placed in classes by a thoughtful procedure that put gifted people into demanding sections and people needing more help into sections where they got more help. In Smithfield, we were placed by a "thoughtful" procedure that determined where our names came in the alphabet.

The first sentence of this passage contains the contrast that is the connecting device for the second and third sentences of the paragraph.

Of course, more complex connections will be found in longer pieces that are structured by comparison. The following essays, one written by an undergraduate and the other by a graduate student, illustrate these connections.

The Town Made of Copper
Karen Pinckley

Things were different fifty years ago. Morenci's economy was warm and comfortable, although clad nakedly in a false security blanket spun from copper. Miners cruised in shiny Chevys and two-stepped with their darlin's to country-western twang every Friday night at the Wagon Wheel Bar. Copper was worth big bucks then, and the Morenci pit was surrounded by rich stocks. Crews and equipment cranked day and night like windmills in a hurricane to extract the valuable metal from the ground while the price was still high. An iron pumping station, located in the bottom of the mine, roared ceaselessly, keeping the mine dry and collecting the solvated copper leached to the bottom of the pit. Swivelling crane-
1 like shovels called draglines chomped up tons of blasted ore and dropped it into ore cars. A single bite piled a car to capacity. Sharply cut benches stain-stepped the slopes in forty foot intervals and supported a switch-back rail network for hauling the ore from the upper level benches down to be processed. The towering smelter, an immortal creature, puffed

imperishably around the clock, swallowing loaded ore cars through its metal mouth and spitting them out the other side empty. Heavy anode plates composed of copper and traces of gold and cadmium traveled out of the smelter on conveyors and were slam-stacked into railroad cars for transport. To the miners the anode plates were shiny Chevys and pitchers of beer.

2. The price of copper dropped suddenly. Morenci was left as vacant as the abandoned shell of a crab. A couple of wrecked Chevys rust in the alley behind the Wagon Wheel Bar, whose entrance is still marked by a weathered splintered wagon wheel clinging to the falling door supports. In the spring, the old shack hosts a howling wind dance for the night creatures, rodents and spiders. The eight-by-three-mile pit lies agape like a huge ugly mouth, exposing its soft rotting teeth and green infected gums. The abandoned pumping station drowns helplessly and silently in the green lake of copper of the bottom of the pit. Slumping and caving, the deformed benches relinquish their glory to the forces of gravity and erosion. Greenish channels, carved by the acidic copper sulphide water, streak and gulley the benches. Rusty remnants of rail and broken ore cars litter the slopes. The smelter monster lies defeated and vandalized, its smokestack clear, its furnace cold. No more anode plates, no more shiny Chevys. No more Friday night dances.

Friends

Elizabeth Ann Sandry

1. I have this wonderfully interesting friend. We grew up together in the same tiny town in Northeastern New Mexico. We attended the same elementary school and the same Sunday school. We worked for the same badges in Girl Scouts, ditched the same classes in junior high and sighed over the same boys in high school.

2. Then we graduated the same year in the early 1960's and went off to college and the sameness ended. She went on in her education to attain three degrees at colleges and universities in Minnesota, Colorado and Washington. I earned both my B.A. and M.A. degrees at the University of New Mexico. The year I began teaching in Tacoma, Washington, she was in Viet Nam. While she was cleaning wounds and changing bandages on soldiers, I was washing obscenities off desks and changing idealistic attitudes about teaching. She can tell stories like the one about the taxi cab wreck in Paris, France, and I can tell about experiencing vapor lock in Polvadera, New Mexico.

3. While she is the self-directed type who gets up and jogs at six in the morning, I can endure physical strain only if I see fifteen others suffering in the same exercise class. Last summer she climbed Mt. Rainier; I painted the kitchen. While she has changed careers and decorated new homes, I have changed schools and designed new curriculum. She collects signatures to save the nation's wildernesses; I collect paperback books to save the department budget. Over Easter weekend this year she did some late winter snow camping. I graded thirty-two research papers.

4. Last weekend I looked around her garage. A sleek, new kayak hangs from the ceiling and the walls are lined with backpacking, hiking and camping equipment. In my garage an ancient three-speed bicycle leans against the freezer and the walls are lined with garden tools and, this

4 summer, stacks of grammar books to be perused for the state textbook
evaluation committee.

In my heart of hearts I know that I would never trade my collection of
classical music for hers of country and western nor my set of the complete
5 works of Shakespeare for her "Gray's Anatomy" nor my life for hers. But
at times like this, when required to "tell something about yourself," she
sounds so much more interesting.

Both of the preceding essays are organized by comparison, but they illustrate
two different comparison structures. In "The Town Made of Copper," Karen
Pinckley uses what is commonly called the "divided" method of comparison.
The two things being compared—the town as it was during the life of the copper
mine and the town as it is after the copper mine was abandoned—are presented
separately. Karen first gives the readers a description of the town as it was, then
paints the picture of the town as it is now.

The second essay, "Friends," makes use of a second method, commonly
called the "alternating" pattern. Ann introduces each of the two subjects being
compared—Ann and her friend—and then alternates between telling something about herself and something about her friend.

Why did these two writers choose these patterns? Another way of asking
this question would be to ask what would be the effect were the two writers to
switch patterns. We think neither essay would be as effective as it now is. Karen
wants to give her readers a feeling for what has happened to this town. Her
powerful description does so in a fashion that a point-by-point contrast would
not. The alternating method of comparison would not have given a clear vision
of just how the town was and is, because the readers would have been too busy
working through these individual comparisons to see the whole that Karen wants
to paint for them.

On the other hand, Ann wants to give her readers some insight into just
how different, and yet similar, she and her friend are. The alternating method
is suited to her essay because there are so many comparisons that lead to contrasts. That is, both she and her friend went to school, both have careers, both
have hobbies, both support the causes they believe in. But they went to different
schools, began different types of careers, and so forth. The cumulative effect of
these comparisons would certainly be lost if Ann had used the divided method
of structuring her comparison.

EXERCISE

These two essays illustrate the fact that modes are not mutually exclusive.
Obviously, Karen's essay employs the descriptive as well as the comparative
ordering device, and Ann's essay employs both narration and comparison.

Though both of these essays are rather personal and tend to express certain
feelings of the authors, one of the writers could be said to have a transactional
aim. Which one? (Hint: You may begin your analysis by examining the conclusions of the two essays. Does either writer feel that she has discovered information that she wishes to share with her readers?)

Use comparison and contrast as the primary structure of an essay in response to one of the following topics. (Write a paragraph in which you identify your audience and explain why you chose this particular audience for this essay.)

1. If you have traveled very much in the United States, you are aware of certain differences in climate and culture. Write an essay in which you envision a move to another part of the country. How would life be different in this new home?

2. If you have traveled abroad, you have no doubt compared other countries to your own. Is there another country in which you would rather live? If so, write an essay in which you explain your preference.

3. If you are now living away from home, you have probably noticed some changes in your home or hometown since you left. Write an essay in which you explain some of these changes.

4. Before you enrolled in your present college or university, you probably visualized what life in this school would be like. Have your views changed? Write an essay in which you explain the similarities and/or differences between what you imagined your school life would be and what it is really like.

CAUSAL ANALYSIS

Causal analysis is the name we give to another process by which we learn. We have learned something about a thing or event if we can determine what thing(s) caused it or what thing(s) it causes.

As its name implies, causal analysis involves two separate relationships— What follows from what? and What goes with what? In attempting to prove that *A* caused *B*, we are required to analyze the whole of the situation in which *A* and *B* are found. That is, we must break it into its component parts and help our readers see that *A*—not *X*, *Y*, or *Z*—caused *B*, or that *A*, *X*, and *Y*—but not *Z*—caused *B*.

Perhaps we can illustrate the complexity of causal analysis by offering a sample essay for discussion. The following is Ralph Harper's "The Appeal of the Thriller."

<table>
<tr><td></td><td>The Appeal of the Thriller
Ralph Harper</td></tr>
</table>

What do readers wish for? There is no single and simple answer. Not even the usual one—escape. For while it may be true enough of "escape literature" that the reader wants to escape "real life," this is probably just as proper a motive for reading any kind of fiction and drama. For some people the everyday world is boring; for others, who also read

1 thrillers, the everyday world is far from boring, and they do not wish to leave it for that reason. Sometimes very busy, responsible people leading lives of high tension admit that they read thrillers to relax rather than escape. But how can one relax if he has only exchanged one kind of tension for another? Many do, and we must look first at the shape of the fictional tension in order to understand this.

2 Admittedly, life is boring and fatiguing to a great many people, and not all of them get any satisfaction or excitement out of thrillers. Edmund Wilson is not the only person who is bored by all thrillers. Too many people who cannot write well think they have found in the thriller an easy way to make money. All they have found is a way to add to readers' exasperations. The thriller writer does not really lead a privileged life, no matter what the lending libraries say. A bad thriller is worse than other bad writing, shoddier, and if we read the first page of a great number of thrillers it is because we hope to find in them certain satisfactions that we do not find in our everyday world.

3 Vicarious experience may not be as good as real experience. But it is a lot safer and cheaper. Compare the cost of a Caribbean vacation with the price of an Ian Fleming paperback. It is different in other ways too. Morality aside, and Dr. No and Honeychile Rider, few of us would choose a life of tension so explosive. Why then do so many choose the same tension vicariously?

4 One answer comes to mind immediately. A world of vicarious experience does offer the satisfaction of having a beginning and an end. So much of life is not satisfying, even when not boring, only because it is always unfinished. Except in some deliberately open-ended works of the imagination, most fiction and drama represent experience as unified, in time and in fulfillment of intention. If life seems boring, part of the reason is that it also seems unending. Even when life is unbearably tense, from pain or responsibility, part of the reason is that one cannot let go. When we read thrillers we do let go, not only of the tensions that strap us, but of the finale as well. One way or another there is a resolution, either a final episode to the course of events, one that sums up the whole course, or a discovery of the meaning of the events. In a real world, where there is all too often neither meaning nor finality to look forward to, even vicarious experience is a welcome change.*

The overall structure of this essay can best be described as cause and effect. The author begins with a given effect, the appeal that thrillers seem to have, and analyzes the whole of the context in which this appeal is set. He begins by dismissing what he sees as a false cause, the boring and fatiguing nature of life and consequent desire for escape. After dismissing this false cause, he offers what he sees as two real causes of this effect: the fact that vicarious experience is safer and cheaper than real experience and the fact that vicarious experience can provide a sense of structure—beginning, middle, and end—that life seldom provides.

---

*From Ralph Harper's *The World of the Thriller.* Copyright 1969 by Case Western Reserve University Press. Used with permission.

When a writer is involved in sorting out false causes or effects from the real causes or effects, as is the case in Harper's essay, she is dealing in "multiple causation." This is the approach to causality that we take when we expect some disagreements concerning causes or effects. However, it is not the only approach to causality. There are times when it is more important that our readers see a chain of causes and effects than that they see the entire context into which any one statement regarding a cause or effect is set; in such situations we may feel that most of the causes and effects will be rather obvious to our readers once we present them. Thus, we may choose a "serial" approach to cause, an approach that provides an overview of the causal situation rather than a carefully reasoned explanation of causes and effects. For an example of "serial causation," see Elisabeth Kübler-Ross's "The Fear of Death" later in this chapter. (For more information on causal reasoning, see pp. 185–192.)

WRITING ASSIGNMENT

Use causal analysis as the primary structure of an essay on one of the following topics. (Write a paragraph in which you state whether you will choose a "serial" or "multiple" causal structure and explain how your choice of audience influenced this decision.)

1. Examine the causes of a fear that you have.

2. Examine the causes for your decision to major in your chosen field of study.

3. Discuss the effects, as you now see them, of your decision to get a college education.

4. Discuss the effects of the worst experience you have ever had.

CLASSIFICATION

We have actually already referred to a situation that illustrates how our minds employ classification to explain things. The hypothetical language learner referred to earlier in this chapter uses associations and oppositions to differentiate between the various animals he comes into contact with. In doing so, he ultimately begins to form a classification system; that is, he uses his comparisons to form the parts of a whole, the animal life in this neighborhood.

Classification, then, is a basic tool by which we learn about the world in which we live. We often resort to classification unconsciously to name and, thus to a degree, to control, our world. Such a seemingly insignificant question as What type of person is he? reflects our basic need to analyze people in our world and place them into categories that we develop.

The following essay by John Holt makes use of classification. Study the essay and then respond to the questions that follow it.

Kinds of Discipline
John Holt

1   A child, in growing up, may meet and learn from three different kinds of disciplines. The first and most important is what we might call the Discipline of Nature or of Reality. When he is trying to do something real, if he does the wrong thing or doesn't do the right one, he doesn't get the result he wants. If he doesn't pile one block right on top of another, or tries to build on a slanting surface, his tower falls down. If he hits the wrong key, he hears the wrong note. If he doesn't hit the nail squarely on the head, it bends, and he has to pull it out and start with another. If he doesn't measure properly what he is trying to build, it won't open, close, fit, stand up, fly, float, whistle, or do whatever he wants it to do. If he closes his eyes when he swings, he doesn't hit the ball. A child meets this kind of discipline every time he tries to *do* something, which is why it is so important in school to give children more chances to do things, instead of just reading or listening to someone talk (or pretending to). This discipline is a great teacher. The learner never has to wait long for his answer; it usually comes quickly, often instantly. Also it is clear, and very often points toward the needed correction; from what happened he can not only see that what he did was wrong, but also why, and what he needs to do instead. Finally, and most important, the giver of the answer, call it Nature, is impersonal, impartial, and indifferent. She does not give opinions, or make judgments; she cannot be wheedled, bullied, or fooled; she does not get angry or disappointed; she does not praise or blame; she does not remember past failures or hold grudges; with her one always gets a fresh start, this time is the one that counts.

2   The next discipline we might call the Discipline of Culture, of Society, of What People Really Do. Man is a social, a cultural animal. Children sense around them this culture, this network of agreements, customs, habits, and rules binding the adults together. They want to understand it and be a part of it. They watch very carefully what people around them are doing and want to do the same. They want to do right, unless they become convinced they can't do right. Thus children rarely misbehave seriously in church, but sit as quietly as they can. The example of all those grownups is contagious. Some mysterious ritual is going on, and children, who like rituals, want to be part of it. In the same way, the little children that I see at concerts, or operas, though they may fidget a little, or perhaps take a nap now and then, rarely make any disturbance. With all those grownups sitting there, neither moving nor talking, it is the most natural thing in the world to imitate them. Children who live among adults who are habitually courteous to each other, and to them, will soon learn to be courteous. Children who live surrounded by people who speak a certain way will speak that way, however much we may try to tell them that speaking that way is bad or wrong.

The third discipline is the one most people mean when they speak of discipline—the Discipline of Superior Force, of sergeant to private, of "you do what I tell you or I'll make you wish you had." There is bound to be some of this in a child's life. Living as we do surrounded by things that can hurt children, or that children can hurt, we cannot avoid it. We can't afford to let a small child find out from experience the danger of playing in a busy street, or of fooling with the pots on the top of a stove, or of eating up the pills in the medicine cabinet. So, along with other precautions, we say to him, "Don't play in the street, or touch things on the stove, or go into the medicine cabinet, or I'll punish you." Between him and the danger too great for him to imagine we put a lesser danger, but one he can imagine and maybe therefore wants to avoid. He can have no idea of what it would be like to be hit by a car, but he can imagine being shouted at, or spanked, or sent to his room. He avoids these substitutes for the greater danger until he can understand it and avoid it for its own sake. But we ought to use this discipline only when it is necessary to protect the life, health, safety, or well-being of people or other living creatures, or to prevent destruction of things that people care about. We ought not to assume too long, as we usually do, that a child cannot understand the real nature of the danger from which we want to protect him. The sooner he avoids the danger, not to escape our punishment, but as a matter of good sense, the better. He can learn that faster than we think. In Mexico, for example, where people drive their cars with a good deal of spirit, I saw many children no older than five or four walking unattended on the streets. They understood about cars; they knew what to do. A child whose life is full of the threat and fear of punishment is locked into babyhood. There is no way for him to grow up, to learn to take responsibility for his life and acts. Most important of all, we should not assume that having to yield to the threat of our superior force is good for the child's character. It is never good for *anyone's* character. To bow to superior force makes us feel impotent and cowardly for not having had the strength or courage to resist. Worse, it makes us resentful and vengeful. We can hardly wait to make someone pay for our humiliation, yield to us as we were once made to yield. No, if we cannot always avoid using the Discipline of Superior Force, we should at least use it as seldom as we can.

There are places where all three disciplines overlap. Any very demanding human activity combines in it the disciplines of Superior Force, of Culture, and of Nature. The novice will be told, "Do it this way, never mind asking why, just do it that way, that is the way we always do it." But it probably *is* just the way they always do it, and usually for the very good reason that it is a way that has been found to work. Think, for example, of ballet training. The student in a class is told to do this exercise, or that; to stand so; to do this or that with his head, arms, shoulders, abdomen, hips, legs, feet. He is constantly corrected. There is no argument. But behind these seemingly autocratic demands by the teacher lie many decades of custom and tradition, and behind that, the necessities of dancing itself. You cannot make the moves of classical ballet unless over many years you have acquired, and renewed every day, the needed strength and suppleness in scores of muscles and joints. Nor can you do the difficult motions, making them look easy, unless you have learned hundreds of easier ones first. Dance teachers may not always agree on all the details

4. of teaching these strengths and skills. But no novice could learn them all by himself. You could not go for a night or two to watch the ballet and then, without any other knowledge at all, teach yourself how to do it. In the same way, you would be unlikely to learn any complicated and difficult human activity without drawing heavily on the experience of those who know it better. But the point is that the authority of these experts or teachers stems from, grows out of their greater competence and experience, the fact that what they do *works,* not the fact that they happen to be the teacher and as such have the power to kick a student out of the class. And the further point is that children are always and everywhere attracted to that competence, and ready and eager to submit themselves to a discipline that grows out of it. We hear constantly that children will never do anything unless compelled to by bribes or threats. But in their private lives, or in extracurricular activities in school, in sports, music, drama, art, running a newspaper, and so on, they often submit themselves willingly and wholeheartedly to very intense disciplines, simply because they want to learn to do a given thing well. Our Little-Napoleon football coaches, of whom we have too many and hear far too much, blind us to the fact that millions of children work hard every year getting better at sports and games without coaches barking and yelling at them.*

1. What connecting agent accounts for the overall structure of this essay? (Hint: The transition words Holt uses should help you answer this question.)

2. List all the ways in which the Discipline of Culture and the Discipline of Nature are alike; list all the ways in which they differ. Is Holt's explanation of these two classes sufficient for you to find an example of each not mentioned in Holt's essay? If so, list an example of each.

3. Holt entitles his article "Kinds of Discipline," and there is a sense in which we could say that the essay supports the following assertion: There are three kinds of discipline that humans come under the influence of. However, that assertion would not be a satisfactory thesis statement for the essay; it does not give us any real insight into why Holt wrote the essay. Certainly, he had a reason for wanting his readers to know what the kinds of discipline are. Write a thesis that captures this reason.

Banal Classifications

The last entry in the preceding exercise points to one major problem students often encounter when attempting to use the classification process. Even though classification is a natural part of our thought processes that we use unconsciously every day of our lives, academic exercises in classification may produce rather banal writing. This is because it is easy to fall into the trap of treating a clas-

---

*From John Holt's *Freedom and Beyond.* Copyright © 1972 by John Holt. Reprinted with permission of E. P. Dutton, Inc.

sification as an end in itself, rather than as a means to an end. Just as analysis helps us to sort out a whole into parts that are more meaningful to us than the whole, the analyzing and comparing that we do in classifying should be a means by which we come to know more about a whole and its parts than we did before performing the classification. No matter how neatly structured, a classification that is nothing more than a neat system is useless. For example, Holt wishes to do more than provide three categories into which we can lump all of the instances of discipline in our world. He uses this classification system to express his opinions that the most effective type of discipline is that which comes to us quite naturally—the Discipline of Nature—and that authority figures often manufacture unnatural discipline when it would be much better to rely on the Discipline of Nature. Thus, Holt is using classification to evaluate and interpret the discipline in our society.

Stereotypical Classifications

Classification is, as we have said, one of the basic tools by which we think. However, we must be extremely careful to guard against stereotypes in using the classificatory process. In Chapters Seven and Eight, we will have more to say about this problem, but for now we can make a few general statements about the difference between classifying and stereotyping by referring to an example of classifying that we mentioned earlier. Are we indeed "classifying" when we ask the question: What type of person is he? What kind of answer to this question would be a legitimate classification, and what kind would be a stereotype? As we will see in Chapter Eight, there is no simple way to make this distinction. But there is quite a difference between these two responses:

> Response 1: He is a hard-working farm boy who enjoys solitary activities such as hunting and fishing and who is not very comfortable in large crowds.

> Response 2: He is a redneck.

In the first response the individual is placed into a class—farm boys—and some of his characteristics are given: He likes solitary sports and is uncomfortable in crowds. The writer may assume that these characteristics are typical of "farm boys," but she does not assume that "all" farm boys have exactly the same set of characteristics, because she does take the time to list some of the characteristics of this individual. In the second response, however, no real attention is given to the individual. Rather the writer assumes that the term *redneck* will somehow tell all that is necessary to tell about this person.

Illogical Classification

The last classification problem we will examine occurs when writers do not give sufficient attention to the mechanics of classifying. A successful classification system must be exclusive and complete. A system that classifies students at a major university as full-time students, part-time students, and students taking night classes does not contain exclusive categories. There are surely full-time students who also take classes at night. Thus, one particular student may belong in two different classes.

Anytime a writer allows categories to overlap in this fashion, the overall effectiveness of the system will be threatened. To avoid this error, the classifier must be sure that the criterion he is using to form one class is used in forming all classes. In our example, one criterion—number of hours taken—was used to establish the first two classes, but in establishing the third class, the writer used another criterion—time of day when classes are taken.

A second aspect of this problem occurs when a classification system will not accommodate all the parts of the whole being analyzed. As an example, consider a classification system for schools of higher learning that contains the following classes: highbrow private institutions with stringent academic requirements for admission, private institutions with stringent monetary requirements for admission, and public schools with moderate academic and monetary requirements. How would such a system accommodate such a public institution as the University of California at Berkeley, which sets very high academic requirements? Obviously, the criteria by which these classes have been formed require a much more extensive list of classes if all the various colleges are to be properly placed. However, the writer's purpose may not be best served by completing this list of classes. She could be attempting to devise a classification system when she really needs to employ comparison; for example, the concepts may be more adequately treated in a comparison of two or three different private schools.

<table>
<tr><td>EXERCISE</td><td>

Developing a piece of writing by means of classification requires you to sort the various elements of your subject into appropriate bins, and then to distinguish the features of each of those bins from each other by listing the characteristics of each that set it apart from the others. As for structure, a paragraph of classification usually has a topic sentence that contains the subject (the whole to be analyzed) and the parts of that whole. Wayne Booth, in the following sentence, illustrates this pattern.

> As I try to sort out the various possible cures for those batches of boredom . . . I find them falling into three groups: efforts to give the students a sharper sense of writing to an audience, efforts to give them some substance to express, and efforts to improve their habits of observation and of approach to their task—what might be called improving their mental personalities.*

Write a paragraph in which you develop a topic by classifying. Be sure that your paragraph contains a Topic Sentence of the type just illustrated. For a subject, reflect upon your personal experience. What types of people live in your dorm or in your neighborhood? What types of teachers have you had? What types of informal educational experiences have you had?

</td></tr>
</table>

---

*Wayne C. Booth, "The Rhetorical Stance," *College Composition and Communication*, 14 (1963).

1. Survey the weekly television guide (either *TV Guide* or a guide from your local newspaper), and classify a week's worth of prime-time viewing. (Prime time is usually defined as the three-hour period from 8 P.M. to 11 P.M. in the eastern time zone and from 7 P.M. to 10 P.M. in the rest of the country.) Sort the programs by type. Which type is most prevalent? What is your interpretation of this classification? What do the types of programs offered say about viewer tastes and/or concerns?

2. Survey the Top-20 tunes of your favorite kind of music—rock, country and western, and so on. Take a representative line from each (either the title or a single line that captures each song's theme); then classify the lines. What kind of song is most prevalent? What is your interpretation of this classification? What do the types of songs say about listener tastes and/or concerns?

WRITING ASSIGNMENTS

1. Develop either of the preceding two exercises (the ones based on TV and music) into an essay. Consider expanding it by surveying television programming or Top-20 tunes from ten or twenty years ago. How do the results compare and/or contrast? What conclusions do you draw from your surveys?

2. Conduct a poll of at least fifteen people on an issue requiring more than a yes or no answer to your question(s). (For example, ask, "What do you like or dislike about this university?" instead of "Do you like this place?") Classify the responses you receive. What is your interpretation of these responses? What recommendations could you make based on this limited survey?

DEFINITION

Our final structure, definition, is the most complex of the processes we will examine in this chapter. As is no doubt obvious, there are many different ways of defining, but we will limit our discussion to three types of definition: analytical, associative, and stipulative.

Analytical Defining

By far the most frequently used method of defining, analytical definition makes use of those same analytical processes that classification employs. It is the natural process that we engage in when we attempt to give someone a precise statement of what a particular thing or concept is. For example, how would we define a term such as *socialism*? The following are all analytical definitions.

Socialism is a form of government in which the state owns all industry and provides all services for the people.

Socialism is a means of structuring society based on the concept that all people should have equal access to the goods produced by the society.

Socialism is an economic philosophy emphasizing the need to curb the greed which individual citizens are capable of exhibiting.

Although these definitions differ in content, they are structured similarly. In each, the term to be defined, the subject of the sentence, is followed by *is*, the present tense of the verb *be*. This verb is then followed by a noun that precedes some type of modifying phrase or clause.

These similarities in structure indicate that all three definitions are based on the same process. In each sentence the term to be defined (the subject of the sentence) is placed into a class. In the first example, *socialism* is a "form of government"; in the second, *socialism* is a "means of structuring society"; in the third, *socialism* is an "economic philosophy." The modifying phrases that follow then serve to differentiate socialism from the other members of the given class. In the first example another form of government is capitalism, a system in which the individuals own most of the industry and the government is not responsible for providing all services for the people.

As we have said, analytical defining is a natural process that we often employ unconsciously. Though an analytical definition can be as short as the three one-sentence examples just presented, there are also times when an analytical definition process provides the overriding structure for an entire piece, as is the case in the following essay.

Read the following essay and answer the questions after it.

Instinct
Paul H. Landis

1   For the daily routine of living and meeting the need for food and shelter, nature has provided animal life with built-in patterns known as instincts.

2   All birds of a given species build a similar nest. The orioles swing their cradle from the weeping-willow branch. Robins plaster their sturdy nest bowl in the shaded crotch of a maple, elm or oak tree.

3   Migratory birds have a built-in sense of direction which guides them to their destination on their annual migrations of thousands of miles from north to south in response to climatic changes. The geese form their V in the sky and start south in fall, led by the call of the lead gander. They do not argue about the reasonableness of it, or debate whether to set their compass to right or left. Day and night they fly on, through bright moonlight or stormy sky, reaching their destination close to schedule. It is traditional that the swallows of Capistrano, California, will arrive on March 19. They vary little from schedule year after year as they return to build their nests in the old Spanish mission.

4   On the West Coast the salmon return after four years at sea to the stream where they were hatched. There they lay their eggs and die, completing nature's life cycle for them.

Nature provides some insects with the built-in equipment for a very complicated social life. Instinct accounts for the complex community organization of bees and the complicated homes and habits of ants. Among such social insects one sees cooperation, specialization of work, and even division of labor. These patterns work perfectly, or nearly so, yet they are not learned.

Instinct is never learned by an animal. It is by definition a behavior pattern provided by nature, which functions when environmental forces are brought to bear on the creature.*

1. Identify the sentence holding the analytical definition of "instinct," and divide the definition into its various parts: term defined, class, and modifying phrases. How clearly stated is this definition?

2. Landis withholds the analytical definition completely until the essay's last sentence. How effective is this placement of the definition? How does Landis guide you into the essay while withholding the definition until the end? How effectively does he do so?

3. Landis develops the definition by giving examples of birds, fish, and insects whose lives are characterized by instinct. How many examples does he give? Why do you think Landis chose the examples he did? How effective are these examples in helping you understand what Landis means by "instinct"?

Associative Defining

Analytical defining is the process that we naturally employ when we attempt to explain to ourselves and to others, just what a word means. Associative defining, on the other hand, is the process by which we learn what words mean, as the following passage from S. I. Hayakawa's *Language in Thought and Action* reveals.

We learn the meanings of practically all our words (which are, it will be remembered, merely complicated noises), not from dictionaries, not from definitions, but from hearing these noises as they accompany actual situations in life and then learning to associate certain noises with certain situations. Even as dogs learn to recognize "words," as for example by hearing "biscuit" at the same time as an actual biscuit is held before their noses, so do we all learn to interpret language by being aware of the happenings that accompany the noises people make at us—by being aware, in short, of contexts.

The definitions given by little children in school show clearly how they associate words with situations; they almost always define in terms of physical and social contexts: "Punishment is when you have been bad and they put you in a closet and don't let you have any supper." "Newspapers are what the paper boy brings and you wrap up the garbage with it." These are

---

*From Paul H. Landis's *Social Living*, 3rd ed., © copyright 1958, by Ginn and Company. (Xerox Corporation. Used with permission.)

good definitions. They cannot be used in dictionaries mainly because they are too specific; it would be impossible to list the myriads of situations in which every word has been used. For this reason, dictionaries give definitions on a high level of abstraction, that is, with particular references left out for the sake of conciseness. This is another reason why it is a great mistake to regard a dictionary definition as telling us all about a word.*

At the center of defining by association, then, is the simple what-goes-with-what? connector. A word's meaning is tied directly to those things or situations with which we associate that word. As in Hayakawa's example of the dogs and their biscuits, the sound represented by the letters *b-i-s-c-u-i-t* means everything involved in what the dogs perceive as a "biscuit situation." That is, that sound "means" the physical object itself, the setting in which the object is found, even the feeling in dogs' stomachs before and after the object has been eaten. The same is true to a greater degree in Hayakawa's example of the term *punishment*. To these children, *punishment* is not a "means of controlling behavior which makes use of negative rewards." They would probably not know the meaning of many of the crucial words in this definition. To them *punishment* is the lost supper and the dark closet they associate it with. They will approach the more abstract definition of the term only after they have associated scores of other individual situations with the sound and have reached a point at which they want to abstract in order to determine what all of these individual punishments have in common. At that point, they will be ready to attempt an analytical definition of the type we have just examined.

They will not, however, lose their initial associations in the process. Two individuals will never attach exactly the same "meaning" to a sound. The emotional impact of *punishment* cannot be as great for the person who first associated a decrease in his weekly allowance with the word as is the impact for a person who first associated a darkened closet and no supper with the term. Their subsequent experiences may lead them both to a common analytical definition of the term, but they will always have different associations, or connotations, for the word.

As we will see in Chapter Eight, these connotations that arise from the things, or situations, that "go with" a word, are as much a part of that word's meaning as the information in the analytical, or denotative, definition.

The analytical definition is the most precise way of attempting to communicate with people who have not made the associations we have made. It is not, however, the only way. We often attempt a shortcut involving synonyms, or words that capture some of the meaning we associate with a term. For example, we might define *punishment* as "penalty." The obvious advantage to this type of defining is its simplicity. Compared with "a means of controlling behavior which makes use of negative rewards," this one-word definition seems very economical.

There are, however, some important disadvantages to defining by synonym. We can point to the first by examining the audience for whom we would define the word *punishment*. A moment's reflection should help us see that only a

---

*Hayakawa, 1978.

linguistically unsophisticated audience such as one composed of very young people or an audience composed of people who do not speak English natively would benefit from having this word defined for them. But there is the very real danger that these audiences will not know what the word *penalty* means.

Even if the readers do know the meaning of the synonym, this type of defining has its limitations. Just as no two readers will make exactly the same associations for a particular word, no individual will have exactly the same associations for two different words. Although many associations will be the same, there will always be some slight differences. Though *penalty* may be seen as a synonym for *punishment*, it falls short of capturing all the meaning of this second word, even for the person offering the definition.

<table>
<tr><td>EXERCISE</td><td>Listed here are several pairs of words that are quite similar in their meanings. However, our associations for the words are not exactly the same. For each pair, write a phrase or sentence that captures any differences you feel. Then check an authoritative dictionary to see whether it corroborates your analysis.</td></tr>
</table>

Example	mad	person with violent tendencies
	insane	person mentally deranged, but without violent tendencies
Dictionary Corroboration	mad	temporarily or apparently deranged by violent sensations, emotions, or ideas
	insane	exhibiting a persistent mental disorder

1. delight   joy
2. skid   slide
3. vertical   upright
4. series   sequence
5. normal   regular

Stipulative Defining

The last of our three types of defining is the easiest to explain. The writer of a stipulative definition does not attempt to give the reader any insight into how the term in question came to have the meaning that it now has. Rather, she simply states, or "stipulates," this meaning as a given.

Many areas in our lives call for stipulative defining. In any scientific study it is crucial that definitions be clear and unquestionable. The only way definitions can meet these requirements is to be given and accepted as stipulated definitions. For example, a geometry student may have a personal definition for "right angle," but he must accept his geometry text's definition if his learning is not to be hindered by differences in definitions.

To explore this concept further, we offer an analogy between learning and playing games. There is a sense in which all learning is like that learning we do

   Structuring Transactional Writing

when we encounter a new game. Stipulative definitions are the very essence of games; without them we would never learn the rules of a game. In baseball, for example, an *inning* is stipulated to consist of three *outs*. In such a stipulative situation the person being initiated to the game does not pause to discuss the logic by which it was decided that three, rather than two or four, outs make an inning. The definitions exist only as facilitators to allow the game to be played, and the initiate simply accepts these definitions.

The same is true in our example involving the geometry student. He is engaging in the "game" of learning as much as he can about the subject area. In order to play the game, he must accept certain definitions without question. At some point, however, he may want to change his role from participant in the learning game to shaper of the game. At that time, he will begin to question all definitions, and if the questions he asks cause other scientists to change definitions that have been stipulated in the past, the one-time student will be seen as a genius in the field.

Keep in mind what we have said about stipulative defining as you consider the following situations.

Situation A

We will define *strike* as a pitched ball that crosses a diamond-shaped piece of rubber and is in the vertical plane bounded by the shoulders and the knees of a batter standing beside the piece of rubber.

A ball is thrown and the catcher receives it, shouting, "Strike." The batter immediately retorts that the ball was too low. Two observers see this scene: One agrees with the catcher, but the other agrees with the batter. Will either of these observers ever be able to prove to the other absolutely that she is wrong? Will either of the observers ever be able to convince the other to change her mind?

Situation B

We will define a *strike* as a pitched ball that an umpire judges to have met the qualifications outlined in Situation A.

Assume the same situation as described in Situation A, the only difference being the different definition of *strike*. In this situation will it be possible for either observer to prove to the other that she is wrong? Will it be possible for one observer to cause the other to change her mind?

WRITING ASSIGNMENT

Use definition as the primary structure of an essay on one of the following terms: *democracy, education, politics, feminist, male chauvinist pig, moral majority, pornography.* (If you wish, pick a term that does not appear in this list but is similar to these terms.) You may use either the analytical or associative process of defining, or you may combine the two.

We will conclude this chapter with a brief analysis of a very effective transactional essay, "The Fear of Death," by Elisabeth Kübler-Ross. Read it and answer the questions that follow it.

The Fear of Death
Elisabeth Kübler-Ross

1 The ancient Hebrews regarded the body of a dead person as something unclean and not to be touched. The early American Indians talked about the evil spirits and shot arrows in the air to drive the spirits away. Many other cultures have rituals to take care of the "bad" dead person, and they all originate in this feeling of anger which still exists in all of us, though we dislike admitting it. The tradition of the tombstone may originate in this wish to keep the bad spirits deep down in the ground, and the pebbles that many mourners put on the grave are left-over symbols of the same wish. Though we call the firing of guns at military funerals a last salute, it is the same symbolic ritual as the Indian used when he shot his spears and arrows into the skies.

2 I give these examples to emphasize that man has not basically changed. Death is still a fearful, frightening happening, and the fear of death is a universal fear even if we think we have mastered it on many levels.

3 What has changed is our way of coping and dealing with death and dying and our dying patients.

4 Having been raised in a country in Europe where science is not so advanced, where modern techniques have just started to find their way into medicine, and where people still live as they did in this country half a century ago, I may have had an opportunity to study a part of the evolution of mankind in a shorter period.

5 I remember as a child the death of a farmer. He fell from a tree and was not expected to live. He asked simply to die at home, a wish that was granted without questioning. He called his daughters into the bedroom and spoke with each one of them alone for a few minutes. He arranged his affairs quietly, though he was in great pain, and distributed his belongings and his land, none of which was to be split until his wife should follow him in death. He also asked each of his children to share in the work, duties, and tasks that he had carried on until the time of the accident. He asked his friends to visit him once more, to bid good-bye to them. Although I was a small child at the time, he did not exclude me or my siblings. We were allowed to share in the preparations of the family just as we were permitted to grieve with them until he died. When he did die, he was left at home, in his own beloved home which he had built, and among his friends and neighbors who went to take a last look at him where he lay in the midst of flowers in the place he had lived in and loved so much. In that country today there is still no make-believe slumber room, no embalming, no false makeup to pretend sleep. Only the signs of very disfiguring illnesses are covered up with bandages and only infectious cases are removed from the home prior to the burial.

Why do I describe such "old-fashioned" customs? I think they are an indication of our acceptance of a fatal outcome, and they help the dying patient as well as his family to accept the loss of a loved one. If a patient is allowed to terminate his life in the familiar and beloved environment, it requires less adjustment for him. His own family knows him well enough to replace a sedative with a glass of his favorite wine; or the smell of a home-cooked soup may give him the appetite to sip a few spoons of fluid which, I think, is still more enjoyable than an infusion. I will not minimize the need for sedatives and infusions and realize full well from my own experience as a country doctor that they are sometimes life-saving and often unavoidable. But I also know that patience and familiar people and foods could replace many a bottle of intravenous fluids given for the simple reason that it fulfills the physiological need without involving too many people and/or individual nursing care.

The fact that children are allowed to stay at home where a fatality has stricken and are included in the talk, discussions, and fears gives them the feeling that they are not alone in the grief and gives them the comfort of shared responsibility and shared mourning. It prepares them gradually and helps them view death as part of life, an experience which may help them grow and mature.

This is in great contrast to a society in which death is viewed as taboo, discussion of it is regarded as morbid, and children are excluded with the presumption and pretext that it would be "too much" for them. They are then sent off to relatives, often accompanied with some unconvincing lies of "Mother has gone on a long trip" or other unbelievable stories. The child senses that something is wrong, and his distrust in adults will only multiply if other relatives add new variations of the story, avoid his questions or suspicions, shower him with gifts as a meager substitute for a loss he is not permitted to deal with. Sooner or later the child will become aware of the changed family situation and, depending on the age and personality of the child, will have an unresolved grief and regard this incident as a frightening, mysterious, in any case very traumatic experience with untrustworthy grownups, which he has no way to cope with.

We would think that our great emancipation, our knowledge of science and of man, has given us better ways and means to prepare ourselves and our families for this inevitable happening. Instead the days are gone when a man was allowed to die in peace and dignity in his own home.

The more we are making advancements in science, the more we seem to fear and deny the reality of death. How is this possible?

We use euphemisms, we make the dead look as if they were asleep, we ship the children off to protect them from the anxiety and turmoil around the house if the patient is fortunate enough to die at home, we don't allow children to visit their dying parents in the hospitals, we have long and controversial discussions about whether patients should be told the truth—a question that rarely arises when the dying person is tended by the family physician who has known him from delivery to death and who knows the weaknesses and strengths of each member of the family.

I think there are many reasons for this flight away from facing death calmly. One of the most important facts is that dying nowadays is more gruesome in many ways, namely, more lonely, mechanical, and dehumanized; at times it is even difficult to determine technically when the time of death has occurred.

Dying becomes lonely and impersonal because the patient is often taken out of his familiar environment and rushed to an emergency room. Whoever has been very sick and has required rest and comfort especially may recall his experience of being put on a stretcher and enduring the noise of the ambulance siren and hectic rush until the hospital gates open. Only those who have lived through this may appreciate the discomfort and cold necessity of such transportation which is only the beginning of a long ordeal—hard to endure when you are well, difficult to express in 13 words when noise, light, bumps, and voices are all too much to put up with. It may well be that we might consider more the patient under the sheets and blankets and perhaps stop our well-meant efficiency and rush in order to hold the patient's hand, to smile, or to listen to a question. I include the trip to the hospital as the first episode in dying, as it is for many. I am putting it exaggeratedly in contrast to the sick man who is left at home—not to say that lives should not be saved if they can be saved by a hospitalization but to keep the focus on the patient's experience, his needs and his reactions.

When a patient is severely ill, he is often treated like a person with no right to an opinion. It is often someone else who makes the decision if 14 and when and where a patient should be hospitalized. It would take so little to remember that the sick person too has feelings, has wishes and opinions, and has—most important of all—the right to be heard.

Well, our presumed patient has now reached the emergency room. He will be surrounded by busy nurses, orderlies, interns, residents, a lab technician perhaps who will take some blood, an electrocardiogram technician who takes the cardiogram. He may be moved to X-ray and he will overhear opinions of his condition and discussions and questions to 15 members of the family. He slowly but surely is beginning to be treated like a thing. He is no longer a person. Decisions are made often without his opinion. If he tries to rebel he will be sedated and after hours of waiting and wondering whether he has the strength, he will be wheeled into the operating room or intensive treatment unit and become an object of great concern and great financial investment.

He may cry for rest, peace, and dignity, but he will get infusions, transfusions, a heart machine, or tracheotomy if necessary. He may want one single person to stop for one single minute so that he can ask one single question—but he will get a dozen people around the clock, all busily preoccupied with his heart rate, pulse, electrocardiogram or pulmonary functions, his secretions or excretions but not with him as a human being. He may wish to fight it all but it is going to be a useless fight since all this is done in the fight for his life, and if they can save his life they can consider the person afterwards. Those who consider the person first may lose precious time to save his life! At least this seems to 16 be the rationale or justification behind all this—or is it? Is the reason for this increasingly mechanical, depersonalized approach our own defensiveness? Is this approach our own way to cope with and repress the anxieties that a terminally or critically ill patient evokes in us? Is our concentration on equipment, on blood pressure our desperate attempt to deny the impending death which is so frightening and discomforting to us that we displace all our knowledge onto machines, since they are less close to us than the suffering face of another human being which would remind us once more of our lack of omnipotence, our own limits and failures, and last but not least perhaps our own mortality?*

<table>
<tr><td>EXERCISES</td><td>

1. Divide "The Fear of Death" into its three main parts—beginning, middle, and end. Then explain how you decided upon these divisions. Did the author's use of causal analysis and comparison and contrast structures help you make these decisions?

2. With the exception of the last two sentences, all of paragraph 5 is narrative. Explain how this narrative's function is different from the function of a narrative in an expressive essay.

3. Examine Kübler-Ross's use of comparison. Is this essay structured by the divided pattern, the alternating pattern, or some other pattern?

4. There is a sense in which paragraph 3 provides the basic structure for this essay. However, no sentence in paragraph 3 would serve as the thesis, because none reveals the basic assertion that the writer wishes to make. Construct a thesis that would do so. (Remember that the author is using comparison, causal analysis, and description to write an essay that is basically argumentative.)

</td></tr>
</table>

Our analysis of "The Fear of Death" is not intended to do more than to show that various modes can be at work in the same paragraph, indeed, in the same sentence. The last paragraph of the essay illustrates this principle quite effectively. In the first sentence of that paragraph, Kübler-Ross *describes* the kind of treatment a patient may want and *compares* this treatment with a description of the kind of treatment he often gets. Later in this paragraph, she posits the cause of this kind of treatment—the inability of people in our society to accept their own mortality.

We offer Kübler-Ross's essay as an antidote for the necessarily oversimplified approach to transactional structures we presented in this chapter. In order to introduce these processes, we have isolated the various structures as if an essay should be structured entirely by any of them. In reality, an essay of any length will employ more than one of these structures. Our analysis shows that Kübler-Ross uses description, causal analysis, and comparison to write an essay with a transactional aim. We label hers a transactional essay, even though it makes extensive use of description, because her focus is on the information she elicits by comparing the two approaches to death she is describing and by analyzing the causes and effects of each of these approaches.

---

*From *On Death and Dying* by Elisabeth Kübler-Ross. Copyright © 1969 by the author. Published with permission of Macmillan Publishing Co., Inc.

Though we have labeled this a transactional essay, we have not called it a descriptive, causal analysis, or comparison essay. Our purpose here is to show that it would be impossible to do so. The discussion of modes in this chapter should not lead us to believe that a "causal analysis essay" exists anywhere other than in a composition textbook. Outside of this limited context, causal analysis is a process by which we shape our thoughts, as are all of the other structures treated in this chapter.

WRITING ASSIGNMENT

Write an essay in response to one of the following assignments. (Write a paragraph in which you tell what audience you would choose for this essay and why the information in the essay would be important to this audience.)

1. Discuss a fear that you now have or that you have had at some time in your life. What caused this fear? What has the fear caused in your life? How is it different now from the way it was at an earlier period? How do you think it may change in the future? How is it like other fears that you or other people have? How do you suppose that analyzing and naming this fear will affect it?

2. Compare some custom or tradition of your family with a custom or tradition of other people you know. (The other people may be of a different race, religion, section of the country, social class or country.) How did these customs or traditions come to be? What are their effects on your lives? How have they changed over time? How may they change in the future?

Chapter Six

Writing a Transactional Essay

We continue our discussion of transactional writing in this chapter with an extended writing assignment similar to the one offered in Chapter Four. Although most of the decisions concerning the writing process will be left to you, we will stipulate that the aim of this essay be transactional.

The shift from expressive writing to transactional writing is at times not an easy one. Whereas expressive writing tends to employ the narrative and descriptive modes, which are organized by rather simple processes, transactional writing usually employs more complicated expository devices. These organizational problems, however, must take a backseat to the task of finding something to say in a transactional writing situation. Most of us have a story that we can narrate and know of a person or place that we can describe; but when we come to the transactional aim, we often have difficulty settling on a suitable subject.

In expressive writing we "express" ourselves to our audience. As we have said, there are few potential audiences that would be unsuitable for an expressive essay; all that is required of them is an inherent interest in other human beings. Things are a bit different in the transactional writing situation. Here we are to inform or persuade our readers; thus, we must have something to say that has inherent worth for the intended audience.

This is not, however, the herculean task that we often try to make it, for each of us has specific experiences that can give rise to thoughts that will be of interest to our readers. Our task, then, in a transactional writing situation is to connect the specifics of our experience with the abstractions we formulate in shaping, or giving order to, these specifics. In other words, we are asked to think. In a sense, this is not much to ask, because thinking is as natural to humans as is eating or sleeping. But in another sense, there is no way to ask anything more difficult. For it is to require something that only humans can do—to make meaningful that which possesses no meaning in itself.

In order to think, we must begin with specifics that our minds can form and shape in the process of thinking. We cannot think about a subject such as "farm life" in the abstract. If we are to offer our thoughts on this subject, we must generate memories of specific events and characters that are a part of "farm life." As we reflect upon these, we may decide that "farm life" is "hard," "good," "different today from what it was in years past," or whatever. But the process must begin with these specifics.

Our discussion in the previous paragraph draws attention to a basic similarity between transactional writing and expressive writing that is often overlooked. Even though the writer of a transactional piece must move toward generalizations through the process of abstracting, she must begin with specific experiences. These experiences are often provided by narrative and descriptive processes. When a writer offers a generalization such as "Living on a farm was good for me," he must help readers see why he thinks so. In this chapter we will offer a writing assignment that will allow you to form generalizations from your experience. In doing so, you will be able to help your readers understand your thoughts.

COMPOSING A TRANSACTIONAL ESSAY

In Chapter Four, we led you through a series of steps that produced an expressive essay. In this chapter we will produce a transactional essay, using that same series of steps.

WRITING ASSIGNMENT

Write a transactional essay in which you explore your thoughts and ideas on a subject that interests you. Your task is to present information that will benefit the audience it is intended for.

FREEWRITE

The essay that will serve as a model for this chapter is entitled "High" and was written by Amy Smith, a student at New Mexico State University. The following is Amy's freewriting.

WRITING
SAMPLE

transactional writing; sounds like making a contract or something. Something serious. I don't think I'll do that. social, moral, academic issues. problems

                                                          Writing a Transactional Essay

How about Mr. Cooper's scholarship? American. I know someone who is German. Because her fathers great-grandfather came over from Germany. presents. from NUSU reminds me of journalism ethics. compare with both sides, presentor as advertiser and critic as indifferent reporter. Planned parenthood. Journalism paper. I remember going to interview director as student reporter. Got quite a bit of information, but interviewed another with contradictory reports. After researching problem I wrote my paper and the teacher submitted it to Sun News. Yet because the woman didn't know the paper would be turned into one paper instead of another (our college paper) she threw a fit afraid it would cause or instigate a scandal. Because of journalistic "ethics" we dropped the copy. Yet everything in the paper was true. Jane asking for more time. Too much work in Italian class. Funny, graduate level Italian, and we rarely even spoke it in class. She's honors-student, terribly intelligent, even won a trip to Italy after she graduated from High School . . . but talk about cheating!
I remember twice. Once in the fourth grade once in the seventh. Silly. Issues. Then there is the water-suit and the woman who ran over the kid, ran off and was sentenced to go to college by the judge. Funny. In Rome they finally made it illegal to be a lawyer. Beginning to be more concerned with the rights of the rapists, killers, and thieves than their victims.
Dr. Smith and Zen. Another had relatively the same idea—econ. CLEP 99.9 percent across the board, but my brother still dropped out of college three times before finally graduating. Changing grades and Kline's method of failing the entire class then giving the top half As and the bottom half Bs. No one could complain as they had really failed the class anyway. The man who said Gabriel had visited him and his dog Queenie. Somehow I just don't believe him.
I don't know where some people get these ideas. Look at John. Imagine thinking one should smoke pot because it's a gift from God. With that excuse we might as well go smoke hemlock or chew on some arsenic!

The freewriting you will do in preparation for a transactional essay will be like that you do for an expressive essay. As we saw in Chapter Four, expressive writing is the foundation for both expressive and transactional essays. For example, consider a specific piece of freewriting in which the writer talks about her favorite sport, running. This freewriting could give rise to a piece of expressive writing in which the writer would recount her thoughts while running a 10 km. road race so that the reader would experience the race with the writer. But she could also base a transactional essay on this freewriting, using it as the springboard into essays about equipment (for example, types of running shoes), training techniques, race strategy, or why more people should become runners. In such transactional essays, the writer would focus not on giving the readers insight into her but on giving them information about the topic or on persuading them about an aspect of the topic.

<table>
<tr><td>EXERCISE</td><td>Look again at your answers to the Interest Inventory that you wrote at the beginning of the semester for a possible topic for a transactional essay. Choose two different topic areas to examine with the Questions for Analysis. For exam-</td></tr>
</table>

ple, you might single out item 1, the community you live in. Rather than answering the Questions for Analysis mechanically, simply keep them in the back of your mind as you freewrite about your community. Start by describing aspects of your community or by narrating things that have happened in your community. But be sensitive to the potential for transactional focuses about specific things or experiences. In talking about your community, you may find that you have said that there is little for teenagers to do. From this statement could come a transactional essay carrying your analysis of the effect on both the teenagers and the community of a lack of things to do or an essay arguing for the establishment of more recreational facilities and programs in the community.

As the preceding exercise implies, one way of generating information for a transactional essay is simply to use something like the Interest Inventory to help you generate specific details of your experience that you can then think about. There is probably no better way to discover what thoughts interest you. But there are other ways. Another method is to examine the thoughts of other people in light of the experiences you have had. Thus, a frequently used tool of writing teachers is the provocative essay. In order to generate information for an essay, the student has only to read the article and respond to the thoughts expressed in it. Whatever method you choose, a successful transactional essay is based upon your experience just as is a successful expressive essay.

WRITING ASSIGNMENT

Step 1: Freewrite for fifteen minutes on a subject that you wish to explore. You may choose to react to a provocative essay supplied by your teacher, or to some other article that interests you. Or you may go back to your Interest Inventory and freewrite concerning concepts it raises for you. As always in freewriting, do not be concerned with grammatical or mechanical matters.

SELECT AND EXAMINE YOUR TOPIC

As she examined her freewriting, Amy found herself drawn to the comment about marijuana made at the very end. Thus she asked the Questions for Analysis of this topic. The following is Amy's Questions for Analysis.

AMY'S QUESTIONS FOR ANALYSIS

What goes with marijuana?
  What is marijuana
    a hallucinatory drug
  What do you associate with marijuana?
    Kirk's time in the business, Kevin's loss in The Pizza Connection, John and
    his "gift from God," and paraphernalia stores.

In what context is marijuana set?

> Most of the pressure was in high school, I rarely am exposed to it anymore.

In what class do you place marijuana?

> dangerous drugs

What physical entities go with marijuana?

> One usually has a pusher, a transaction, a place to get together with other smokers (that is, pot party), and finally a high.

How is marijuana like other things?

> It's a lot like alcohol—in its effects, reasons to use it, and moral stipulations surrounding it.

What opposes marijuana?

> What theoretical or philosophical opposition is there to marijuana?

> > Many people feel that it is harmful to one's health; many people oppose it morally because it blocks inhibitions.

> How is marijuana unlike other similar things?

> > Unlike cigarettes or alcohol, marijuana is illegal regardless of age.

What follows (from) marijuana?

> What are the causes of marijuana use?

> > peer pressure and unhappiness

> What does smoking marijuana cause?

> > serious health problems

Note that Amy has taken quite a bit of liberty with the Questions for Analysis, asking and answering only those questions that seem pertinent to her topic. The questions are intended as prompts to help generate material, not as hoops the writer must jump through.

Step 2: Select a topic for your essay and answer the Questions for Analysis for that topic.

DEVISE A PLANNING PAGE

In Chapter Four we said that planning the order of the discovery draft of an expressive essay is relatively easy because of the role the narrative and descriptive modes play in expressive writing. Order in transactional writing is more complicated, as we saw in Chapter Five. After we have generated thoughts by responding to the Questions for Analysis, how do we turn them into a first draft? No organizational process such as the what follows what? of narration or the what goes with what? of description takes over. Surely we cannot simply go back to the Questions for Analysis and devote a paragraph in our essay to the answers in each section. So what do we do?

The answer to this question is implicit in our discussion of exposition in the previous chapter. There we saw that each of the expository structures involves one or more of our basic connecting principles. Once we decide that one of the structures is helping us think about our discovery draft, we know something about the structure of that draft.

As we have said, no one structure will account for all of the order in an essay. However, at this stage in the writing process, it can be helpful to decide which mode seems to be predominant. We can make this decision by asking ourselves some basic questions about our purposes in this essay. With the exception of process essays, all transactional essays will do one or more of the following things.

1. Tell what the topic is   *Definition*

2. Discuss the causes of and/or the results of the topic   *Cause*

3. Make a value judgment regarding the topic   *Value*

It is relatively easy to see a connection between these overriding purposes and the categories in the Questions for Analysis. Answers to the what-goes-with-what? and what-opposes-what? questions will produce information as to what the topic is. As we saw in our discussion of definition in Chapter Five, we tell ourselves what something is by finding out what we associate with that thing and how it compares and contrasts with other things. Thus if we find ourselves drawn to the information in one or both of these sections of the Questions for Analysis, it is likely that our essay is going to tell us what our topic is.

If we find ourselves drawn to the answers to the what-follows-from-what? questions, it is likely that we will write an essay in which we explain what caused our topic and/or what the effects of our topic will be.

The final category is a bit more complex than either of the first two. Value judgments would seem to be tied to the what-follows-what? questions because one of these is the question: Is the topic good, bad, and so on? One way we have of placing a value on something is to examine its causes and its effects. If something causes cancer, we know automatically that it is bad. Or if someone's wealth is caused by his work as a hired assassin, we know that his wealth is bad. But not all of our value judgments are based on causal reasoning. We often arrive at a value judgment by associations. For example, lying is bad because it is a form of (that is, is associated with) deception. Ultimately, we may have to resort to a causal statement to show that deception is bad, but we have used association in the process of evaluating. Thus, we may find value judgments in the information generated by asking the what-goes-with-what? and what-opposes-what? questions.

At the planning stage, one of these three overriding purposes can provide the writer with a focus for her discovery draft. That focus will be represented by the Lead Sentence on your Planning Page. Once the writer has chosen a Lead Sentence, she can then develop several other topic sentences from it that will

                                          Writing a Transactional Essay

suggest ordering possibilities for the essay. For example, as we will see later, Amy's Lead Sentence is "Attitudes in our society tend to cause tolerance of marijuana among those who are neutral or opposed to it." Amy develops her topic sentences by analyzing these attitudes that cause tolerance. When the Lead Sentence is causal, as is Amy's, the topic sentences will simply identify the various causes and/or effects. When the Lead Sentence is a definition, the writer's topic sentences will serve to develop the various parts of that definition. To construct the topic sentences for a Lead Sentence expressing a value judgment, the writer must determine whether his judgment is based on association, causality, or a combination of the two. When he has done so, he can construct these sentences as if the Lead Sentence were definitional or causal.

Though our explanation may make this step sound rather complicated, it is really rather simple, as Amy's Planning Page illustrates.

AMY'S PLANNING PAGE

Lead sentence

Attitudes in our society tend to cause tolerance of marijuana among those who would otherwise oppose it.

Topic sentences

Many people openly use marijuana and assume everyone approves.

School officials seem to feel its use is inevitable.

The government's laxity in dealing with drug offenders seems to say: "it's illegal, but go ahead."

Many people from various walks of life are now dealing drugs.

Many people assume that marijuana is not harmful to one's health.

EXERCISE

Examine Amy's answers to the Questions for Analysis in light of her Planning Page. Which materials generated by these questions do you think will appear in her first draft and which will not? Then compare your response with her actual draft on pp. 153–156.

EXERCISE

Following are two additional Planning Pages. Russ Peterson's plan for his essay on the 1981 baseball players' strike makes use of a value Lead Sentence. Sondra Smith's Planning Page, for her essay, "Honesty," is based on a definition Lead Sentence. After examining these Planning Pages, answer the questions that follow them.

RUSS'S PLANNING PAGE

Lead sentence

The 1981 Baseball Players' Strike was bad.

Topic sentences

Both the causes and the effects of the baseball strike make the baseball strike bad.

The strike is caused by the players' greed.

The strike causes many innocent people such as workers in ball parks to suffer.

In the long run, the strike will cause the players themselves to suffer, because it will cause less interest in the sport.

SONDRA'S PLANNING PAGE

<table>
<tr><td>Lead
sentence</td><td>Honesty is being yourself in all situations.</td></tr>
<tr><td>Topic
sentences</td><td>One normally associates such Honest Abe and George Washington things as returning books and not telling lies with honesty.</td></tr>
<tr><td></td><td>But, true honesty is characterized by openness in all situations and to every person, including oneself.</td></tr>
<tr><td></td><td>Many people are like my friends Janie and Dorothy, who are basically dishonest with themselves.</td></tr>
</table>

1. Russ's Planning Page makes it obvious that he intends to support his value judgment by means of causal analysis. He could, however, offer support by defining important terms for his readers. What are some of the important terms that Russ might define? How might he define them in light of the position he is taking?

2. In her Planning Page, Sondra is shaping an associative definition. In light of what we have said in Chapter Five about associative defining, it is obvious that different people would make different associations with her term. Write other topic sentences for this essay that reflect some of your associations with the term.

3. At some point Sondra could find it helpful to define her term analytically. Write a Planning Page for an analytical definition of *honesty*. Then write a paragraph in which you discuss the difference between the essay that this Planning Page could lead to and one that might derive from Sondra's plan.

As we said in Chapter Four, there is a temptation to see the Planning Page as nothing more than a sentence outline. But we must resist this temptation. It is a device that will lead us into a first draft, but it should not be seen as a strait jacket that completely binds us to certain materials. At the Planning Page stage we want to provide, not a formula for organizing the paper, but a procedure for getting something on paper, which can then be shaped and formed into a final draft. Our procedure is artificial; we know this at the outset. There is little likelihood that any essay is going to deal with definition to the total exclusion of causality or vice versa. It is equally unlikely that an essay will support a value judgment by causal reasoning alone or by definition alone. As an essay develops, all of these reasoning processes will help shape it.

Writing a Transactional Essay

Thus, at the Planning Page stage any essay could be organized from the perspective of any one of the three Lead Sentences we have offered. Furthermore, an essay that was initially organized by a definition Lead Sentence may have shifted to a causal pattern by the time it reaches its final draft form. The function of the Planning Page, then, is only to provide a means of getting to a first draft.

Step 3: Construct a Planning Page for your essay.

WRITE A DISCOVERY DRAFT

The following is Amy's discovery draft. Note that at this point Amy has not titled her draft yet. That title came with the second draft, when Amy had found her essay's significance.

After our usual and slightly questioning "Hi?" and Kirk's sardonic "I wish. . ." he invited Deanne and me over to Gordon's for "some sort of party." We didn't go over immediately, however, so later, after Deanne and I had cruised the strip a couple of rounds, we decided to check it out.

The party provide to be private, and only Deanna, Kirk, Gordon, and I showed up. When we'd first gotten there, I thought we'd gone to the wrong house; it was too quiet, and I knew Gordon's taste for wild parties. But when Gordon answered the door and I saw Kirk behind him on the couch, I realized that not only was it the right house, but that there was a special reason for the quiet.

"Wanna beer?" Gordon asked. I said I wasn't thirsy, but Deanna said she'd go ahead and hav e one. Instructed to make ourselves comfortable while he got it, Deanna sprawled across the floor as I sank into a rather dirty king-sized beanbag. Kirk, sitting across from me and adjacent to Deanna, was fussing over some sort of rubber tubing and lighter.

"Just a minute, Kirk," Gordon called, "I've got some good stuff straight Brazilian. Beats your homegrown anyday."

"Drag?" Kirk asked me after his preparations were finally complete.

This is a situation which, unfortunatly, I found myself all too often in. I seems odd to me that, while the use of marijuana is still illegal in the US, one would invite another to join him if he wasn't sure that the other would even consider it. Yet, through what little experience I've gained in high school and now in college, I've learned that excessive caution is rarely the case. While studying with a friend at his dorm one vening, for example, and meeting a amazing number of people during that short time who were "just passing through," he commented on how funny it was how many friends he seemed to have as soon as it was discovered he had some pot.

So, in spite of the fact that marijuana use is still illegal, and that one could be expelled from school or university just for possession, its use is nevertheless considered inevitable, if not actually acceptable. This can be seen in the fact that an introduciton to the drug world i s often given to children by the schools themselves, often even before an upperclass user or pusher can recommend it. In the seventh grade, for instance, my classmates and I underwent a six-month study of drugs. We learned not only the psychological, emotional and physical effects of amphetamines, barbituates, marijuana, cocaine, and even heroin, but also how to identify quality and use them.

Government also, through its laws concerning these drugs combined with its laxity concerning "headships or paraphenalia stores, seem to say "It's illegal, but go ahead."

An even more imporant factor than this is the widespread familiarity with drug abuse. The person who used to be considered an evil, greedy, and downright demonic "Pusher" by many is now your friendly neighborhood "Contact" who'll supply whatever whenever. And no longer are they found solely within a certain class, but distributed throughout the social strata. What was once a big thing, reverently and carefully passed from selective pushers to reliable customers, is now passed form stranger to stranger. Once while I was walking with a friend of mine, two girls approached

and asked where they could get a couople lids. Then they and my
friend proceeded to carry on business. Ironically, we were
standing directly in fromt of our high shbool central office.

One knows that the realm of pusheres had indeed spread when he
learns that members of his own group are "in the business." "Why?"
one such friend answered me, "I made a couple hundred &ast month,
six the month before, and hey, it's good business,--on the side
money." (Turns out he quit when his parents found out and flushed
away one hundred sixty dollars worth.)

Acceptance and familiarity have reached an all time high when
another friend, Kevin, could lose ten dollars' worth in a pizza
place, go back and ask for it, and get it back. Yet, even through
this, some still refurse to take part. I overheard a boy telling
some girls, after she refused a toke, that he "never drank booze
because it ruined your brain cells, and cigarettes give you cancer.
That's why," he said,"""pot is good for you!. Hmmm. And one can
really see how attitudes have changed through this one: "Imagine,
you're standing there on judgement day, God is pointing his finger
at you and asking 'Why didn't you smloke my marijuana? It was a
gift from me to you."

It's hard to have a really anti-marijuana, anti=drug outlook,
or be truly straight. Once when asked how I felt about a friends
toking-up, I finally had to admit that even though I couldn't condone
it, I couldn't condemn him either. Even when one may not approve,
through familiarity and common acceptance it's hard to be adamane about
it.

In the face of this abundance, its practically impossible to
be shocked or offended. The question is, how far will our resignation
go? It may be hard to stand back and accept something one objects
to, but it is even harder to turn in or betray one's friends.

"I said, do you want a drag?" Kirk asked again.

Declining, I said Deanna and I needed to leave anyway. As we
walked out he door, Kirk laughed and said good-naturedly, with only

the slightest hint of warning, "Keep you nose clean."

    "I've got a hadkerchief in my back pocket," I answered.

add: effect of drugs (mind, body)
studies of marijuana } *research*
potential damage

Step 4: Using your Planning Page as a guide, compose a discovery draft of your essay.

SELECT AND ANALYZE YOUR AUDIENCE

As we said earlier, the writer of a transactional essay must have a clear concept of his audience; he must be aware of what they already know about the topic and consider what they need or would like to know about it.

Thus, the writer must choose his audience with care. Far too often writers get into trouble in the composing process because they never select a real audience to write for. Rather than choosing an audience such as "the members of the Parent-Teacher Association at Ravenel Elementary School," they choose an audience such as "people between the ages of seventeen and twenty-two who like rock music but who do not smoke pot." Where will the writer find such a group of people—where do they hold their meetings? And if the writer could find these people, would they not differ in ways that might jeopardize his chances of speaking to them on his chosen topic? The members of this audience may differ in such important matters as the social class they belong to, the region of the country they live in, the political party they belong to, and so forth. If the writer could find two people who meet the narrowly defined criteria, they could still be so different as to make it almost impossible to speak to both of them in the same fashion about a given topic.

The objection, of course, to choosing a real audience is that we cannot be sure about their beliefs. We will have more to say about this matter in Chapter Eight, where we talk about the audience for a persuasive essay, but for now we can say that although these limitations exist, they are a part of the real writing situations we must deal with. We can never be sure that all of our generalizations about a specific audience will be correct; in fact, if our audience is large, we can be sure that there will be exceptions to any generalizations we make.

Despite these limitations, if the writer chooses a group of people that he could actually address, he automatically knows certain things about this group by virtue of the fact that they meet together for certain purposes. The more specific the requirements for belonging to this group, the more the author knows about the audience to whom he is writing. For example, an author who chooses to write for "the members of my English Composition class at Clemson University" knows a great deal about his audience. He can assume that a large percentage of the members are between the ages of seventeen and nineteen, that a large percentage of them are Southerners, that few of them are from very wealthy homes and likewise few of them are from extremely poor families, that most have parents who value education and are willing to support their children in their educations, and so forth.

Because any of the more than 2000 members of the freshman class could be in the writer's audience, there are surely many differences among these individuals. If the writer wishes to remove some of these, he can choose a more specific group, say the Clemson Chapter of Youth for Christ, or the Young Democrats on campus, or the student staff of Harcomb Dining Hall. Although Clemson's students differ considerably in their religious beliefs, the members of the Clemson chapter of Youth for Christ will be in agreement concerning their basic religious beliefs. Although most of Clemson's freshmen come from rather con servative political backgrounds, the members of the Young Democrats can be counted on to be more liberal than the average Clemson student. A good many of Clemson's students depend upon their parents for tuition, but the members of the Harcomb Dining Hall staff are working to earn money to put themselves through school.

As you select an audience for your essay, you must choose people who have some interest in and need for the information in that essay. No matter how good your writing, as judged by other criteria, if it contains no "news" for the intended audience, it is not good writing. You will be more likely to produce writing that is worthwhile to the intended audience if you select a group that you could actually address and that you can analyze thoroughly. Many such groups meet regularly on your campus. Also there are many suitable groups within your home community. As we have said, the PTA is such an organization. A more specific group would be the faculty of a school or the faculty within a certain discipline in an entire school system. The County School Board would be an appropriate audience for certain topics. Other potential audiences are civic clubs such as the Lions club, political action groups, or groups composed of civic-minded citizens (the Red Cross, for example). As you can see, your ability to find a proper audience for your essay is limited only by your ingenuity.

Once you have decided upon an audience for your essay, a modified form of the Questions for Analysis may prove useful in analyzing that audience.

What does my audience associate with my topic?

What does my audience not associate with my topic?

What should cause my audience to want or need the information I am going to give them in talking about my topic?

What should possession of this information cause in their lives?

As you can see, we are simply asking the what-goes-with-what?, what-opposes-what?, and what-follows-from-what? questions. In asking what her audience associates with her topic and what they do not associate with that topic, the writer is attempting to determine just what in her essay will be "news" to this particular audience. Of course, there is a sense in which the second question—What does my audience not associate with my topic—is open to almost any answer. The purpose of the question is to focus attention on those things that the writer associates with her topic but which the readers do not associate with the topic. This is the material that will be information to the audience. If the audience analysis indicates that the essay will contain no information for this audience, the writer must find another audience for the essay.

The first of the what-follows-what? questions is designed to generate some common ground between writer and readers. What does the writer know about the audience that will help her introduce this topic to them? For example, if she is to talk to college students about the problems with the Social Security system, she must keep in mind that they cannot imagine a time when they will draw Social Security. Thus, she must choose another common ground as the foundation from which to talk. Perhaps, she will talk about the fact that their parents, whom they care about, will soon be eligible to draw Social Security payments and point to the effects that the current problems in Social Security could have on their parents. Or, she could discuss the higher Social Security payments that young people are going to have to make because of the problems in the Social Security system. Answers to these questions should provide some means of drawing this particular audience into this topic, which is an important task because most readers decide whether they will continue reading an essay by the time they have finished the introduction.

The last question, of course, addresses the ultimate effect the essay should have on the audience. Just what will this information do for them? Will it help them make money, be better parents, be more happy, or what?

The following is Amy's analysis of her audience.

AMY'S AUDIENCE ANALYSIS

Audience   Students at New Mexico State University (first, the members of her composition class and, then, the entire student body, should her essay be selected for publication in an anthology of student writing sponsored by NMSU's English department).

    What does my audience associate with marijuana?
        alcohol, parties, things that help a person relax, loosen up and take life less seriously—respectable young people having a good time

    What does my audience not associate with marijuana?
        "pushers," hard drugs, damage to health

    What should cause my audience to want or need the information I am going to give them about marijuana?

Writing a Transactional Essay

They will be interested in the topic because they use the drug or are confronted by people who do use it. The opening should catch their attention because they will have encountered similar situations.

What should possession of this information cause in their lives?
They need the information because it will help them to recognize the pressure which is being exerted upon them, even though it is subtle. The information may help them to understand why they react as they sometimes do in the marijuana using situations.

Step 5: Choose an audience for your essay and analyze that audience using the guide presented on pp. 157–158.

WRITE A SECOND DRAFT

As we enter the second draft stage of our essay, we need to reflect upon the step that separates the first and second drafts. The difference between these two drafts points to the dual purpose of transactional writing: It entails both discovery *and* communication. In the discovery draft the writer's emphasis is on discovering what he thinks about the topic. The emphasis in the second draft is on finding information in that discovery draft that will be relevant to a given audience and on communicating that information to this audience.

Reflecting upon her first draft, Amy finds that although she has done a good job of enunciating some of her thoughts on marijuana, she needs to do quite a bit of work to clarify those thoughts and to shape them so that they will be of interest to a specific audience. Her purpose in the discovery draft was simply to explore the context in which marijuana is used. At the second draft stage she has decided to write for students at New Mexico State University. Thus, she must do more than show them the situations in which marijuana is used; many of them experience these situations themselves. She must shape her material so as to give them some insights into the pressure that pervasive marijuana use places on nonusers.

Here we will present Amy's second draft. However, we do not mean to suggest that she went from her discovery draft to her second without a planning stage. As it happens, she did not submit another Planning Page, but no doubt she did some planning, if only by scribbling in the margins of her first draft. Note that in those scribblings (p. 156), Amy says that she needs to research her topic. Although she obviously is familiar with the topic, Amy recognizes the need to go to sources beyond her immediate experience for support. Often, this is the case in transactional writing. At this stage you may find it helpful to go back to your original Planning Page and rewrite some of the sentences to reflect changes in the paper that you see evolving. You should also consider whether you need to research your topic.

"Hi!?" Deanna called out from her new spicy red Mustang. Kirk, catching the question implicit in her greeting called back "I wish. . ." before telling us about the party at Gordon's.

Deanna had been to Gordon's a couple of times before, so when the light turned green we spun off, leaving Kirk and his old '67 chevy eating dust. We didn't go over immediately however, but later after Deanna and I had cruised the strip a couple of rounds, decided to check it out.

The party proved to be private, and only Deanna, Kirk, Gordon and I were there. When we'd first gotten there, I thought we'd gone to the wrong house. It was too quiet, and I knew Gordon's taste for wild parties. But when Gordon answered the door and I saw Kirk behind him on the couch, I realized that no only was it the right house, but that there was a special reason for the quiet.

"Wanna beer?" Gordon asked. I said I wasn't thirty, but Deanna said she'd go ahead and have one. Instructed to make ourselves comfortable while he got it, Deanna sprawled across the floor as I sank into a rather dirty king-sized beanbag. Kirk, sitting across from me and adjacent to Deanna, was fussing over some sort of rubber tubing and a lighter.

"Just a minute, Kirk," Gordon called, "I've got some good stuff. Straight Brazilian. Beats your homegrown anyday."

"Drag?" Kirk asked after his preparations were complete.

This was a situation, unfortunately, I found myself all too often in during my high school years. Although peer pressure was never like its commonly illustrated on tv where some ugly black-jacketed thug is ready to force either the point of his knife or the drugs he's selling on you, it was there nevertheless.

Instead, in the form of a cute date or a little out- of-the-ordinary fun at a party, it was much harder to recognize as such, much less resist.

The fact is,though, marijuana was and still is illegal. It's
illegal not only to smoke or eat, but illegal to even have one's possession as well. By definition, marijuana (also known as hemp, grass,
tea, or pot) is a drug from the plant "cannabis sativa" which when
dried leaves and flowers are burnt will yeild up a narcotic. The
effect of the narcotic may last anywhere from one to five hours depending on the manner in which it was taken, the dosage, and the
physical and emotional state of its user at the time.[1] (note)

Until only recently, marijuana has been considered essentially
a "safe" drug. In Asia Minor and the Orient, for example, it has
been held social acceptible to use it for some centuries now. Even
in the United States where marijuana is illegal, its popular disap-
probation is due to its connection with the contemporary drug scene
rather than its medical repurcussions. As a result, marijuana is commonly"mixed up with the whole drug subculture, which is permeated with
criminality and psychological illness,"[2] rather than judged of itself. (note)

This is slowly changing. Those who used to feel marijuana, hard
drugs, pimps, crim and hard time all go hand in hand are becoming
fewer are fewer. Marijuana is dropped from the list again and agin.
To most students today, marijuana just isn't that big a thing. So, in
spite of the fact that marijuana use is still illegal and that one
could be expelled from school or university just for possession, its
use is nevertheless considered inevitable, if not actual accetable.

The man who used to be considered an evil, greedy and downright
demonic "pusher" by many is now your friendly neighborhood "contact"
who'll supply whatever whenever. No longer is he found solely within

a certain class, but distributed throughout the social strata. What
was once a big thing, reverently and carefully passed from selective
pushers to reliable customers, is now passed from stranger to stranger. Once while I was walking with a friend of mine, two girls ap-

proached and asked where they could get a couple of lids. Then they and

my friend proceeded to carry on their business. Ironically, we were

standing directly in front of our high school central office.

It is difficult to maintain the picture of the black leering

ogre type pusher when one's friends have become "contacts," even less

when one finds they are educated and far from needy. "Why?" one such

friend answered me, "I made a couple hundred last month six the month

before, and hey, it's good on the side money." (Turns out he quite when

his parents found out and flushed away one hundred sixty dollars'

worth.)

Acceptance of and familiarity with marijuana have reached an all time high. Another friend, Kev in went with Deanne and me to The Pizza Connection, one

of the best pizza places around. Two pizzas later, we left, and Kevin

remembered that he'd left his satchel of pot underneath his chair,

went back and got it, while one of the waiters kid him about it.

It seems odd that, while the use of marijuana is still a

punishable crime in the United States, people should be so open about

using it or even inviting others to use it with them. I overheard

a boy telling some girl, after she had apparently refused a toke,

that he "never drank booze because it ruined your brain cells, and

never smoked because it gives you cancer. That's why," he said,

"pot is good.for you." Hmmmm. But I didn't fully realize how attitudes have

changed until I heard this line: "Imagine, you're standing there on judgement

day, God is pointing His finger at you and asking 'Why didn't you

smoke my marijuana? It was a gift from me to you!"

Why the change? Marijuana obviously is more known, more common.
One cannot neglect it.
With freinds involved, it comes home. But even more than this,

it is now an open subject between friends and in school classroms,

often to be laughed at and joked about.

An introduction to the drug world is commonly given to children
through drug ed. programs
by the schools themselves, often before an upperclass user or pusher

can even recommend them. Although this ~~is~~ outwardly a deserving ~~idea~~ [idea has merit,]

it ~~must~~ [has to] be handled carefully. In the seventh grade, for instance, ~~my~~ [language]

classmates and I underwent a six-month study of drugs. We learned not

only the psychological, emotional and physical effects of amphetamines,

barbituates [r], marijuana, cocaine, ,adn even heroin, but also how to

identify the quality of the drugs and how to administer them. A num-

ber of the kids, whether seriously or not desn't make too much differ-

ence, then told of their personal experiences with pot and so on.

Treatment of drugs as a joke in the schools is a s serious [a]

hypocajcy [r] as what the government is involved in now. ~~Although using~~ [Despite the illegality]

~~marijuana and heroine are illegal,~~ [of m. and other such drugs,] the paraphenalia or "head" shops

continue ~~their~~ business ~~is~~ [of] selling one all the supplies ~~he would~~ [necessary]

~~need~~ to use ~~such drugs~~ [them]. The combined "don't-worry-its-not-real"

attitude of some schools and the laxity of the government ~~in both~~ [both in permitting the]

selling of paraphenalia and [in] the punishing of those actually charged

and convicted of drug commerce, all seem to be saying, "It's illegal,

but go ahead."

It's hard to have a really anti-marijuana, anti-drug outlook

with these ideas so prevalent. Once when asked how I felt about a

friend toking-up, I finally had to admit that even though I couldn't

condone his actions, I no longer could condemn him either. Even

when ~~one~~ [you] may not approve, through familiarity and common acceptance,

it's hard to be adamant about it.

It's hard to be adamant, that is, until ~~one~~ [you] looks past most of

the popular myths about uses and abuses of marijuana. ~~One~~ [you] must look

first at the actual and most recent studies on marijuana, and then

look for ~~themselves~~ [yourself] at the changes in friends who use it heavily.

One of the most popular myths about marijuana is that it is

safer than ~~cigarettes and~~ alcohol,. ~~One of~~ [Probably] the most common excuses

I hear for for smoking pot is "If you can drink your booze, why can't

I soke my pot? It's safer anyway." ~~Yet~~ According to Dr. Nicholas

[I've often wondered if this was really the case.]

Pace, cofounder and past president of New York City's Affiliate of
the National Council on Alcoholism, alcohol is made up of only one
chemical and ~~it~~ is water soluble, ~~Thus, if~~ so that one oz. of alcohol, is metabolized and
completely excreted from the body within 24 hrs. Marijuana, on the
other hand, is an extremely complex drug made up of some 421 known
chemicals, 61 of which are known cannabinoids, and 4 of which are
also considered "psychoactive" or "mind-altering."[3] (note)

~~With this in mind,~~ It is not ~~entirely~~ then surprising that "clinical
observation indicates that people might drink for years before serious
brain damage occurs. But . . . you have to use marijuana for only a
relatively short time in moderation to heavy use before evidence of
brain damage begins to develop."[4] (note)

The chairman of the department of neurology and psychiatry at
Tulane Medical School, Dr. Robert Heath, found this to be true in his
studies with Rhesis monkeys. Certain portions of the Rhesis monkey
brain are extraordinarily similar to that of humans. By exposing the
monkeys to proportional levels of pot (about ¼ the average human joint
at 3% THC [rather than the regular 6% THC,*)] then taking cross sections of
the limbic area (that area which controls sex drives, appetite, and
emotions) Heath found the brain cells structually abnormal with extraneous materials and gaps in the synaptic clefts between neurons.[5] (note)

~~What this then means to the marijuana smoker~~
What this means ~~then~~ is that "chronic or extensive use of marijuana may cause brain damage and/or sterility."[6] (note) Not only has Heath
found this to be true, but it is backed up as well by the International Symposluim on Marijuana held in Reims, France, the National
Institute on Druge Abuse, and the New York University Medical School
to name only a few.[7]

Marijuana's impairmant of the brain and its harm to the reproductive systems pose a great physical kthreat to the user, but[9] (note)
marijuana has psychological threats as well. Dr. Harold Voth, of

Minniger Foundations School of Psychiatry and chief of staff at the

Topeka VA Med Center, found"diminished willpower, concentration,

attention span, ability to deal with abstract or complex problems,

increased confusion in thinking, impared judgement and hostility

towards authority," to be general attitudes and syymptoms ~~among~~ *in* his

studies.

It is man's mind, personality and spirit that makes him what he

is. That marijuana dulls these same attributions ~~of man~~, making him

little more than a dazed charicature of man, ~~reveals~~ *speaks for* itself.

To take these studies at face value without application to

those around one leaves them more studies. ~~Yet~~ *But*, applied, they come

to life. xxx In the face of ~~the~~ *widespread* acceptance and familiearity with

marijuana, it is practically impossible to be shocked or offended.

The question is, how far will our resignation go? ~~Yet with the~~ It

may be hard to stand back and accept something one objects to, but

it is even harder to turn in or betray one's friends. Yet, the

evidence demands a verdict.

"I said, do you want a drag?" Kirk asked again.

Declining, I said Deanna and I needed to leave anyway. As we

walked out the door, Kirk laughed and said good-naturedly, with only

the slightest hint of warning, "Keep your nose clean."

"I've got a handkerchief in my back pocket," I answered/

<table>
<tr><td>EXERCISE</td><td>

In Chapter Five, we emphasized the fact that no one expository structure will account for all of the order in an expository essay. That is, a single essay will often make use of, say, comparison, analysis, classification, and so on. However, these comments should not obscure the fact that good writers often use these expository structures as the framework for an entire essay. The fact that comparison provides the order for the essay "Learned Words and Popular Words" (mentioned in Chapter Three, p. 81) is made clear by the following sentence, which is found in the introduction to that essay: "Such words are called 'learned,' and the distinction between them and 'popular' words is of great importance to a right understanding of linguistic process."

To this point we have been reluctant to use the term "Thesis Sentence," preferring to introduce our own term, "Lead Sentence." Our reluctance should

</td></tr>
</table>

not be taken as an assumption that good writers do not use something like the traditional Thesis Sentence. As we saw when examining the structure of essays in Chapter Three, good writers always give their readers insight into the form and content of their essays, often doing so in one compact statement, which we may refer to as a Thesis Sentence.

This exercise and the one that follows should help you see the connection between Thesis Sentences and the overall structure of essays. After examining Amy's second draft, construct a Thesis Sentence that will give readers insight into the form and content of her essay.

1. As we have said several times before, every successful essay must have a beginning, a middle, and an end. What paragraph or paragraphs constitute the introduction of Amy's essay? The conclusion?

2. Examine the organization of the paragraphs within the body of Amy's essay. Does each paragraph help her develop and support her thesis idea? Note any paragraph that does not and decide whether the thesis idea should be expanded to include the material in that paragraph or whether the paragraph should be deleted.

3. Do any of Amy's paragraphs lack unity or coherence? Explain any problems you see.

4. In this second draft, Amy has incorporated information she found in researching her topic. How effectively has she used that information? How well does it support her position?

WRITING ASSIGNMENT

Step 6: Compose the second draft of your essay. Pay particular attention to the overall shape of your essay.

WRITE A FINAL DRAFT

The following is the final product of Amy's writing process.

High

"Hi?" Deanna called out from her spicy red Mustang. Kirk, catching the question implicit in her greeting, called back "I wish . . ." before telling us about the party at Gordon's.

Deanna knew where Gordon's place was, so when the light turned green we spun off, leaving Kirk and his old '67 Chevy eating dust. We didn't go over immediately, however; we made a couple trips around the strip before deciding to check out the party at Gordon's.

The party proved to be private; when we first got there, I thought we'd gone to the wrong house. It was too quiet, and I knew Gordon's taste for wild parties. But when Gordon answered the door and I saw Kirk behind him on the couch, I realized that there was a special reason for the quiet.

"Wanna beer?" Gordon asked. I said I wasn't thirsty, but Deanna said she'd go ahead and have one. After being instructed to make ourselves comfortable, Deanna sprawled across the floor and I sank into a rather dirty king-sized beanbag. Kirk, sitting across from me and adjacent to Deanna, was fussing over some sort of rubber tubing and a lighter.

"Just a minute, Kirk," Gordon called. "I've got some good stuff. Straight Brazilian. Beats your homegrown anyday."

"Drag?" Kirk asked after his preparations were complete.

This was a situation I found myself in all too often during my high school years. Although peer pressure was never like it is commonly illustrated on television where some ugly black-jacketed thug is ready to force the drugs he is selling at the point of a knife, it was there nevertheless. In the form of a cute date or a little out-of-the-ordinary fun at a party, the pressure was much harder to recognize, and still harder to resist.

This pressure is a part of a society which considers marijuana a "safe" drug. Few teens associate marijuana with hard drugs, pimps, and crime. Rather, it is part of normal, everyday life. The man who used to be considered an evil, greedy and downright demonic "pusher" is now your friendly neighborhood "contact" who will supply whatever, whenever. No longer is he found exclusively in the low class. Once while I was walking with a friend, two girls approached and asked where they could get a couple of lids. Then they and my friend proceeded to carry on their business. Ironically, we were standing directly in front of our high school central office.

It is difficult to maintain the picture of the leering ogre-type pusher when one's friends have become "contacts." One such friend confided that he had made "a couple hundred last month, six the month before." Asked about the morality of the practice, he responded " . . . hey, it's good on-the-side money."

Acceptance and familiarity with marijuana have reached an all time high. Another friend, Kevin, went with Deanna and me to The Pizza Connection, one of the best pizza places around. Two pizzas later, we left and Kevin realized that he had left his satchel of pot underneath his chair, went back and got it, and was kidded about it by one of the waiters. I overheard another user telling some girl, after she had apparently refused to toke, that he never drank booze because "it ruins your brain cells," and never smoked cigarettes because "they give you cancer." He went on to tell her that he smoked pot because "it is good for you."

These experiences helped make me aware of the fact that most teens accept marijuana as a fact of life, but I was not aware of the importance some people placed on marijuana use until a friend asked me to imagine myself "standing there on judgment day with God pointing His finger at you and asking 'Why didn't you smoke my marijuana? It was a gift from me to you.'"

How has marijuana come to have such an important place in the lives of high school students? One factor in its acceptance may be our schools, themselves. An introduction to the drug world is commonly given to children in the schools' drug education programs. In the seventh grade, for instance, my classmates and I underwent a six-month study of drugs. We learned not only the psychological, emotional and physical effects of various drugs, but also how to identify the quality of the drugs and to administer them. A number of the kids, whether seriously or not doesn't make much difference, then told of their personal experiences and how they compared with what we were learning.

With the proliferation of drug use and the pressure exerted by peer groups, it's hard to take an anti-drug position. Hard, that is, until you look past the popular myths about uses and abuses of marijuana.

One of the most popular myths about marijuana is that it is safer than alcohol. According to Dr. Nicholas Pace, cofounder and past president of New York City's Affiliate of the National Council on Alcoholism, marijuana is considerably more dangerous than alcohol. While alcohol is made up of only one chemical, which is water soluble so that one ounce of alcohol is metabolized and completely excreted from the body within twenty-four hours, marijuana is an extremely complex drug made up of some four hundred twenty-one known chemicals, sixty-one of which are known cannabinoids, and four of which are also considered "psycho-active" and "mind-altering."[1] In "Alert I: Brain and Sex Damage," Peggy Mann cites several noted medical authorities who report that relatively moderate use of marijuana can lead to the death of brain cells and to damage to the reproductive system.[2]

Marijuana's threat is psychological as well as physical. Dr. Harold Voth, of Menninger Foundations School of Psychiatry and chief of staff at the Topeka V.A. Medical Center, found "diminished willpower, concentration, attention span, ability to deal with abstract or complex problems, increased confusion in thinking, impaired judgment and hostility towards authority," to be effects of marijuana use.[3]

Such studies as these are merely words on paper until we apply them to the situations, and people, we encounter daily. Then, they come to life. In light of the widespread acceptance of marijuana, it is practically impossible to be shocked or offended by marijuana. But what is this acceptance leading to? Did those who are now harming themselves physically and mentally begin by finding it impossible to object to something that "all" of their friends were into? At what point does a person have to be willing to speak up for what she knows to be right? Can she be silent and safe?

"I said, do you want a drag?"

Declining, I said Deanna and I needed to leave anyway. As we walked out the door, Kirk laughed and said good-naturedly, with only the slightest hint of warning,

"Keep your nose clean."

"I've got a handkerchief in my back pocket," I answered.

Notes

[1] Peggy Mann, "Marijuana: the Myth of Harmlessness goes up in Smoke," *Saturday Evening Post* 252 (1980), p. 41.

[2] Peggy Mann, "Alert I: Brain and Sex Damage," *Reader's Digest* 115 (1979), p. 141.

[3] Peggy Mann, "Marijuana Alert III: the Devastation of Personality," *Reader's Digest* 119 (1981), p. 83.

Rather than discussing Amy's final draft, we offer the following exercises that should help you analyze it for yourself.

EXERCISES

1. Find at least three sentence structures that are changed from Amy's second draft to her final draft. Are these sentences better? Why or why not?

2. As she moved from her second draft to her final draft, Amy deleted some paragraphs, telescoped others—that is, she shortened two or three paragraphs into one—and simply restructured others, adding, deleting, and rearranging materials. Find at least three of these changes from the second to the third draft. How effective are these changes?

3. At the end of Amy's second draft, we asked you to divide that essay into its beginning, middle, and end. Do the same for this draft and compare the shape of these two drafts.

4. Amy's second draft is considerably longer than her final draft. Does she omit any material in the last draft that she should have kept? If so, what should she have kept? Why?

5. Reread Amy's audience analysis on pp. 158–159. Does the final draft of Amy's essay do what she intended to do for her audience? Can you detect any changes in her purpose as she moved from the second to the final draft?

WRITING ASSIGNMENT

Step 7: Write the final draft of your essay. After writing this draft pay particular attention to editing skills. Be sure that all words are spelled correctly and that there are no grammatical errors. At the same time that you are editing, be open to any other revisions that will improve the overall essay.

Write a Final Draft

Chapter Seven

Shaping an Argument

In this chapter we want to raise and, in part, answer a question that is fundamental to human nature: Why do humans argue? We can begin to develop our
answer to this question by examining the word *argue*. This word, along with
its variant, *argument*, can be used in such seemingly different contexts as the
following.

The man and woman argued heatedly before she shot him.

The boys played together well during the morning, but by afternoon they
had begun to argue.

The basic argument was whether children were necessarily better adjusted
in homes in which the mother kept house full-time than in homes in
which the mother had an outside job.

His argument was that coffee in excess is as unhealthy as cigarette
smoking.

As these examples reveal, *argue* can mean a variety of different things. However,
there is an underlying similarity in all four uses cited: In each case, the word
refers to differences—disagreements—between humans in their interpretations
of the world around them. In the first sentence this difference is taken to its
extreme form. In each successive example the difference between the individuals

is lessened to the point that there is no apparent disagreement in the last sentence—only one person speaking on a given topic. However, even in this situation, there is the implication that some disagreement is possible. Someone might reject the assertion; thus the speaker must offer some support for it.

Someone will probably disagree, because humans are basically argumentative. As we saw in Chapters Two and Three, we are predisposed by our language to perceive the world in different ways. Because no two individuals use language in identical ways, it follows that no two people perceive the world in identical ways. These perceptual differences give rise to our arguments.

In order to translate the abstract discussion in the preceding paragraph to everyday arguments, consider the "argument" between a parent and a teenage son as to whether the son should have the car for a date on Saturday evening. On the surface it would seem that such a disagreement is rather far removed from such esoteric matters as how one perceives the world. The teen wants the car, and the parent does not think he should have it. However, if we role-play such an argument, we will soon find differences in the way the two parties are using language. For example, the young man may begin by arguing that he is a good driver and, thus, should be trusted with the car. His father may disagree, saying that no one who has less than three months' experience as a driver can be considered a "good" driver—in which case we have isolated a problem in definition underlying their disagreement. However, the father may agree that his son is a good driver but still feel that he should not take the car. The son's next tactic may be to say that he has not had the car very much during the past month. But the father may respond, "Very much, indeed, I would say five times is very much." Again, we have found a potential problem in definition. On the other hand, the father may agree with the son on this point. Pressed for his reasons, the father may tell the son that he needs the car on Saturday evening more than the son does. In that case, the young man must either give in to his father's argument or begin to show that he disagrees with his father's definition of *need*.

Of course, we are not suggesting that all disagreements between humans arise from problems in definition. A husband and wife may argue about who should wash the dishes tonight because they disagree as to who washed them last night, one of them having forgotten. But there are important differences between such a disagreement as this, which involves a lapse in memory, and the disagreement a husband and wife could have as to whether such household chores as washing the dishes should be shared equally. The disagreement about who should do the dishes does not lend itself to absolute resolution in the way that the disagreement about who washed them last evening does. One of them actually did the dishes yesterday, and if that person, say, the wife, works hard enough, she will find a way to prove the point. But there is no way she can be sure of convincing her husband that he *should* share the housework. Her task will be to cause him to "see things her way," and she will do so by causing him to use language in the way she uses language. In her argument she may find herself discussing some of the following terms: *husband, wife, breadwinner, man's work, woman's work, household chores.*

Describe the most recent argument you were involved in. What was it about? With whom did you argue? What was the basis or cause of the disagreement? To what extent was definition of terms a problem? What was the outcome of the argument? If the conflict was resolved, how did the resolution take place?

Which of the following assertions lend themselves to the kind of absolute proof that the husband–wife argument about who did the dishes last evening does? Which would involve an attempt to cause another person to use language in the way the arguer is using it? What words would be central to these latter arguments?

1. Stealing is illegal.

2. Stealing is abnormal behavior.

3. Stealing is immoral.

4. Sometimes, stealing is justifiable.

5. Water boils at 212° F.

6. Water is essential for life.

7. Water is the most important ingredient in beer.

8. Water tastes good.

In the preceding exercise we are attempting to make a distinction between "pseudo" and "real" arguments. By "real" arguments, we mean those differences that arise from different ways of perceiving the world. This distinction leads us naturally to some discussion of the connection between writer and reader. If an argument is to be successful, certain relationships must exist between the two.

The writer of an argument always has designs on her readers; that is, there is at least one area of disagreement between the two and the writer would like the reader to come to see things her way in this area. This basic disagreement causes tension between the two, but this tension is lessened by some very important agreements. If the writer and reader do not share certain fundamental agreements, the writer cannot hope to persuade the reader to accept her point of view. These agreements are often as basic as the assumptions that kindness and humanity are good and unkindness and inhumanity are bad, or, to take the process one step further back, the assumption that humans should strive to be good and avoid being evil. Obviously, these agreements are very basic and probably not the kinds of things a writer would spend any time in trying to convince most audiences. But they are fundamental to many of the arguments humans spend their time debating. In fact, it is hard to imagine that people would expend much energy on matters that do not at some point touch upon what is good and noble as opposed to what is bad and reprehensible.

Shaping an Argument

Deduction

The process by which we connect an argumentative thesis, or generalization, to the underlying assertions upon which it is based is called *deduction*. A *Deductive Chain*, sometimes called a syllogism, is a set of three assertions connected in such a fashion that the third assertion, the conclusion, can be deduced (understood to be true) from the first two. It often happens in deduction that one of the first two assertions is a fundamental agreement between writer and reader, whereas the second is the point of disagreement that occasions the argumentative essay. Such is the case in the following Deductive Chain.

Rising unemployment is a bad thing.

Unemployment rises in Republican administrations.

A bad thing happens in Republican administrations.

If we can cause our readers to agree with these first two assertions, we can be sure they will agree with the conclusion. Not many readers will have difficulty agreeing with the first assertion, but we will have to give these readers good reasons for accepting the second assertion. But how will we do so?

Induction

Presented with such an assertion as "Unemployment rises in Republican administrations," we have two avenues of potential support. For one, we can construct another deductive chain with this general statement as the conclusion and spend our time helping our readers accept one or both of the assertions in this new chain. For another, we can abandon the deductive process and try to "prove" our assertion by *induction*—that is, by examining the particular aspects of a situation and inferring a conclusion from them. As we examine these two approaches in connection with the conclusion stated earlier, we should gain insight into the essential difference between induction and deduction. The following is a Deductive Chain.

Republican administrations always enact policies that protect the wealthy from inflation.

Policies that protect the wealthy from inflation cause unemployment to rise.

Unemployment rises in Republican administrations.

The following is an Inductive Chain.

Unemployment rose in the Hoover administration.

Unemployment rose in the Ford administration.

Unemployment rose in the Reagan administration.

Unemployment rises in Republican administrations.

As this example illustrates, rather than working from general assertions to a specific conclusion, which follows from them, induction moves from specific assertions to a more general conclusion. Thus, the conclusion is not contained in the supporting assertion. To illustrate this point more clearly, we offer another pair of Deductive and Inductive Chains.

All cats have tails.   *Deductive Chain*

X is a cat.

X has a tail.

Cat X has a tail.   *Inductive Chain*

Cat Y has a tail.

Cat Z has a tail.

All cats have tails.

In the Deductive Chain the specific assertion—X has a tail—is contained in the general assertions that precede it. We can illustrate this point by drawing a circle (Figure 7.1). Let us say that the circle represents the quality of "having tails." The first assertion—all cats have tails—has the effect of placing all cats in this circle (Figure 7.2). Now let us say that we come to X not knowing whether it has a tail or not, indeed, not knowing what it is. Then the assertions—X is a cat and all cats have tails—place X in this circle: "having tails." Thus, the conclusion—X has a tail—gives us no new information. It merely makes explicit what we already knew implicitly from the first two assertions.

The situation is quite different in an Inductive Chain. If we again think of the condition, "having tails," as being represented by a circle, the three assertions—cat X has a tail, cat Y has a tail, and cat Z has a tail—place only those three individual cats within the circle, as Figure 7.3 illustrates.

To get to the general statement—all cats have tails—we must move from the circle (representing the condition of having tails) and the individual cats that fall within the circle to a generalization about cats. This generalization—

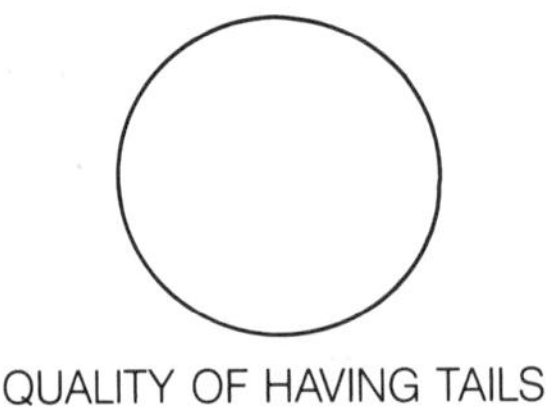

Figure 7.1

Shaping an Argument

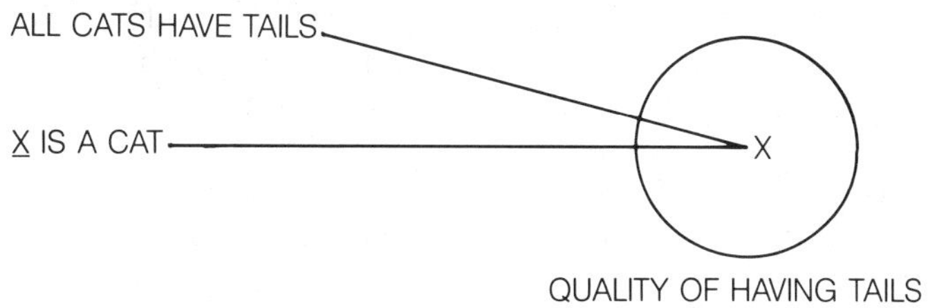

Figure 7.2

all cats have tails—is new information that is not contained in any of the supporting assertions. Thus, in framing our generalization, we must move into the realm of the unprovable.

This last statement should not lead us to dismiss all generalizations as "mere conjecture" or to think all generalizations of equal worth. To label them as "mere conjecture" is to fail to recognize them as the basis for our thinking process. As we saw in Chapters Five and Six, every new thought that we have is the result of going beyond the specific experiences of our lives to explain those experiences to ourselves and to others. These explanations are always in the form of generalizations. When an unfortunate experience with a football player causes us to explain to ourselves that one should not attempt to get a date with a football player's girlfriend, we are going beyond the realm of what is provable in any deductive process. But, we may well feel that it is important to do so.

To assign equal worth to all generalizations—to assume one thought is as good as another—is to deny the validity of our thinking. Is our earlier generalization—all cats have tails—no better than another generalization—for example, all cats are black? Our experience with cats makes us know immediately that it is not. But suppose for a moment that we have never seen a cat and are presented with these two generalizations—all cats have tails, all cats are black. We would then have to judge these generalizations on the basis of the leap the writer is asking us to make from specific instances to these generalizations, not

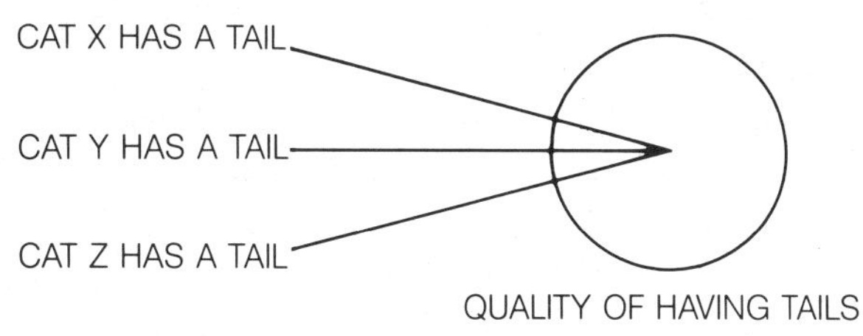

Figure 7.3

on the basis of our knowledge of cats. If the framer of the first generalization has seen three cats—*X*, *Y*, and *Z*—all of which have tails and makes this generalization, he is using a valid reasoning process. If the framer of the second generalization has seen two cats, *A* and *B*, which are black, and a third, *C*, which is white, we know she is not reasoning properly. The generalization does not follow from the evidence. But what if this person has seen three cats—*A*, *B*, and *D*—all of which are black? Forgetting what we know about cats, we must say at this point that the two generalizations are of equal value. However, what if the framer of our first generalization goes on to examine a thousand cats and finds that all of them have tails? His generalization will then be much better than the second one. The second will be as good as the first only after the investigator has examined a thousand cats and found them all black. Of course, our knowledge of cats suggests that this latter person will find a contradiction to her generalization long before she examines the thousandth cat.

The preceding example is purposefully simple to help us make our point. We will find more complex generalizations in most argumentative situations. For example, we are not likely to accept or reject immediately the generalization that unemployment rises in Republican administrations. Thus, we must determine its validity by examining the specifics upon which it is based. The individual who cites ten different Republican administrations that have experienced a rise in unemployment has framed a better generalization than the person who cites only one Republican administration.

SUPPORTING INDUCTIVE ARGUMENTS

How may we convince readers to accept our arguments? Perhaps we should ask this question in another form: Given that we believe in a certain generalization, how may we convince our readers to believe in that generalization?

Even though we are talking in this chapter about argumentation, which is often associated with facts, figures, and calculations of various sorts, our choice of the word *believe* in the preceding sentence is appropriate. When humans argue, they are attempting to persuade other humans to adopt certain beliefs; they are not developing proofs that will force others to see "the truth."

Our tendency to equate argumentation with scientific proof may well result from our failure to understand just how deductive and inductive arguments are connected with each other. A deductive argument is no stronger than the inductive argument(s) upon which it rests.

The assumption that inductive arguments always support deductive arguments follows from our earlier statement that no new information is contained in a deductive argument. If a writer supports a conclusion—for example, unemployment rises in Republican administrations—with assertions—for example, Republicans always enact policies that protect the wealthy; policies that protect the wealthy cause unemployment to rise—one of two results can be expected. Either his reader already agrees with the supporting premises and has, thus, already accepted, implicitly, the conclusion; or she will not automatically accept the supporting premises. In the latter case, the framer of the argument must offer some support for one or both of these premises. If he is to convince his readers of something they were not already convinced of, he must offer an inductive argument at some point. Otherwise, there was no real disagreement to begin with.

Framing Inductive Arguments

Given an understanding of the connection between deduction and induction, we can rephrase the question posed at the beginning of this section in yet another way. Rather than asking how we can cause readers to accept our arguments, we can ask, How may we frame our inductive arguments so that readers will make the leap from the specifics we offer to the generality we propose to induce from them?

We may begin to develop an answer to this question by examining the basic principles at work in the inductive process. These are the very same principles by which we learn any new thing about ourselves or the world we live in. We do not learn by simply looking at the world around us and "taking it all in." Our experiences are filtered by the language we use to tell ourselves what experiences mean. This is not to suggest, however, that identical language results in identical meanings. Even though speakers of a common language use very many of the same terms as filters for their experiences, they do not use these common terms in identical ways. S. I. Hayakawa makes this point in an essay that we have referred to in Chapter Five. The following is the ninth paragraph of his essay entitled "Contexts."

> We learn the meanings of practically all our words (which are, it will be remembered, merely complicated noises), not from dictionaries, not from definitions, but from hearing these noises with certain situations. Even as dogs learn to recognize "words," as for example by hearing "biscuit" at the same time as an actual biscuit is held before their noses, so do we all learn to interpret language by being aware of the happenings that accompany the noises people make at us—by being aware, in short, of contexts.*

In order to be considered speakers of a common language, individuals must use a large number of common words to refer to the various phenomena in their worlds. However, because their definitions of these words come from the contexts in which they have encountered them and because no two of these contexts have been identical, it follows that no two people define any one word exactly alike. Of course, in many cases the contexts, and subsequent definitions, are so similar as to make it appear that individuals have identical definitions for common words. If this were not the case, communication as we know it would not be possible.

On other occasions, however, individuals use the same term when in fact their perceptions of the thing or situation it refers to differ markedly; these are

---

*From S. I. Hayakawa's *Language in Thought and Action,* Fourth Edition.

argumentative situations. In many cases the common language being used by these individuals hides the differences in their underlying perceptions. But when they get beyond this apparent agreement, these individuals often find profound differences.

As an example, consider the argument that centers on the word *abortion*. In this case, two people could appear to share a definition of this word: "Induced termination of pregnancy before the fetus is capable of survival as an individual." Nevertheless, their perceptions of the situations referred to by this word may differ greatly. One may have shaped his meaning of the term, in part, in an abortion clinic where many teens aborted children they had never intended to have and were unwilling to take responsibility for. The other may have formed her definition, in part, in a medical practice that treats women who are fearful that the children they are carrying will be born with deformities.

As we examine the language these two associate with the term *abortion*, we find that the dictionary definition they share hides completely different perceptions of *abortion*. One of these two would elaborate on this dictionary definition as follows.

Abortion is killing unborn babies.

The other would completely reject this definition and offer in its place:

Abortion is a means of preventing birth defects.

Thus, the two are in obvious disagreement. How, then, will one of them go about convincing the other to accept her viewpoint? She will do so by examining the associations and implications of the words that cluster around the term *abortion*. In doing so, she should be able to arrive at a *key term* that represents the way she perceives the situation. The person in favor of abortion will discover that she sees the abortion situation as a *protection* for pregnant women and for unborn children. She must be aware that someone opposed to her viewpoint will see the situation through another filter, or key term, the *killing* of unborn babies. Her task is to do all within her power to show her reader just how it is possible to see abortion as *protection*.

She may accomplish this task by availing herself of several different avenues of persuasion. For example, she may relate examples. If she has known of a person who has refused, or been refused, an abortion and who has subsequently given birth to a deformed child, she may recount the details of this example, emphasizing the pain and suffering involved. She may also avail herself of facts and figures, such as the number of individuals who die each year in illegal abortion attempts where abortions are not permitted. She may cite statistics regarding the number of deformed children born in places where abortions are not available. Or, she may offer causal arguments in favor of her viewpoint. That is, she may detail the various reasons that one may have for wanting an abortion and discuss the effects on people's lives when unwanted or deformed children are born into the world. Or, the writer may offer opinion statements in favor of her point of view. Of course, it is her opinion that abortion is not killing. In support of this opinion, she will show what words she associates with killing and explain why abortion does not "go with" these words. She may also elect to bolster this opinion statement with the opinions of persons whose education and/or position make them authorities on the subject. She may seek statements by physicians as to just how *life* should be defined; she may cite the opinions of religious leaders who do not see abortion as killing or as immoral.

As we have said before, this argument will not back the readers into a logical corner where they must relinquish their opinions on the subject or be seen as simpletons. That was not the aim of the writer in the first place. Rather, she hoped to help these readers see her perception of the topic. All these argumentative tools—examples, facts, figures, causal statements, and opinion statements—were designed to allow this to happen. If they have done so, the argument is successful, whether or not the effect is to change the reader's mind.

EXERCISE

We have just offered five tools of argumentation: examples, facts, figures, causal statements, and opinion statements. We have also implied that these tools may be used on either side of an argument. Write a paragraph explaining how each of these could be used to frame an argument in opposition to abortion.

Using Argumentative Processes

We must note here that the five elements of the abortion argument are not the only tools available to the writer and that the writer is not obligated to use all these tools in a given piece of writing. Different topics, different arguments call for different tools. As Joseph Wood Krutch's "Lightning Water" illustrates, the writer need use only those tools that will develop her argument.

WRITING
SAMPLE

Lightning Water

Joseph Wood Krutch

1 Flash floods, those wildly beautiful desert hallmarks, serve as a healthy reminder that nature on the rampage can quickly reduce to utter helplessness the careless individual or the person who naively assumes that the whole of the natural world has been "conquered." Strangers to the desert cannot believe that a sandy gully, which looks like a good place to camp, may become, without warning, a raging flood—a wall of water several feet high plunging forward with enormous speed and force.

2 Reclamation engineers, operating under a variety of names, are making a concerted effort to tame or conquer these floods—along with everything else that is free and natural. Their rationale often alludes to the fact that people have sometimes been drowned in them; but people have been killed rather more often in highway accidents, and no one talks about the necessity of eliminating automobiles. Perhaps the real reason for the often intemperate enthusiasm of the reclaimers is that the projects they dream up will provide them with jobs.

Like the road builders, the reclaimers are inclined to see needs where no one else can, and their consequent boondoggling threatens to destroy a large portion of the remaining natural environment. When every stream has been dammed and all the countryside has become a mere network of roads, their triumph will be complete—America the Beautiful will have become America the Conquered.

If we would only begin to question our naive faith that the road and dam builders "must know best because they are experts"; if, instead, we would only realize that the first concern of all of them is their vested interest in their own jobs, rather than in the public good, then their pointless vandalism of our countryside might be stopped. But this realization is likely to be too late in coming.

It doesn't rain often in the desert and the total annual rainfall is small. But when it does rain, the water often comes down in torrent proportions. This is one reason why the flash flood is primarily a desert phenomenon. Death Valley in California furnishes an extreme example. It is the driest spot in the United States. Average rainfall is about 1.5 inches and more than a year has been known to pass without a measurable trace. Yet in July, 1950, a cloudburst (a convenient but not very meaningful term) produced a flood which cut a six-foot-deep gully across the main road and rolled along boulders five feet in diameter. In Arizona more than five inches of rain has fallen in a twenty-four-hour period; as much as eleven inches in the course of one storm. These are exceptional figures, but very heavy downpours within a short time are usual.

The other principal reason why the flash flood is almost exclusively a feature of the desert is that nearly all the water that falls in a torrential rain runs off. Vegetation ground cover is sparse or nonexistent. The surface of the ground is often baked to an almost bricklike consistency. Very little water is absorbed. Most of it runs off into the dry riverbeds cut by previous floods. These gullies are among the most characteristic features of arid lands and are called by a variety of names—dry wash or draw in Arizona, arroyo in California, wadi in the Near East. Some of the floodwaters that periodically rage through an arroyo sink into its usually sandy or rocky bottom. A few feet below the surface, the soil may be damp while that of the surrounding desert floor is completely dry. The difference in moisture creates a special environment for plant life. Near the borders of the dry wash there may be cottonwoods that cannot survive the desert and a special species of palo verde trees, which needs just a bit more water than the easily distinguishable species that grows in more arid situations.

Another geomorphic feature created by the flash floods is the alluvial fan—characteristic of desert regions bordered by mountains. These are delta-shaped accumulations of sand and rock, deposited at the point where mountain ravines open onto the desert floor. Torrents arising from storms in the mountains plunge down these ravines, finally dumping their debris when their speed is reduced by emergence onto the flatness of the desert. Especially striking specimens can be seen in Death Valley. They look rather more like glaciers than like the flood deltas of moister regions, and they are among the most graceful of land forms.

Most paved roads in the desert are crossed at frequent intervals by dips that conduct the water across the roadbeds. These dips, too, may be dangerous in flood season. Neither the pedestrian nor the motorist can quite believe the force of the water that occasionally rushes through these dry beds. But the presence of automobile-sized boulders in the arroyos attests to the carrying force of the water which increases enormously with an increase in speed.

It is said that the carrying power of a stream varies as the sixth power of its velocity. But whether or not this figure is entirely accurate, all the lay traveler needs to remember is that an increased speed of flow increases manyfold the stream's power to sweep heavy objects along with it. He must not assume that because the flood doesn't look much swifter than it did when he crossed it safely a short time before, it is probably still safe. If he makes that assumption, he may be in for trouble. Flash floods are dangerous only if you don't take the trouble to know what they are and why they exist. But to some of us it seems that it would be better to teach people how to travel or live in the few remaining natural areas than to destroy their unique characteristics.

The ultimate endeavor of the reclaimers is to homogenize the American earth, which today presents an infinite variety. The more it is crossed by freeways and the more its streams and lakes are regularized by engineers, the more every part of it will look like every other part. It will no longer be worth taking the journeys from one region to another that the superhighways are supposed to make so easy and so quick.

The Southwest without the flash floods would be no longer recognizable, no longer unique, no longer beautiful in its own way. We have begun to hear some talk about preserving a few wild rivers, and the flash flood is the wildest of all wild rivers. On the other hand, the reclaimers seem determined to tame everything capable of inspiring awe and to put everywhere in its place the tame, the uniform, and the convenient. They are making this a far less interesting world.*

Though he does not state a thesis explicitly, the first two paragraphs make it clear that Krutch is opposed to what he sees as an attempt to prevent all flash floods in the desert. Krutch uses several different argumentative tools in the attempt to cause his readers to perceive this situation as he does.

The *key term* for Krutch's view of this situation is *conquer*. He sees the work of reclamation engineers as an attempt to conquer nature, and he supports his viewpoint with examples, facts, causal statements, and opinions. In paragraph 2 he recognizes a fact that his opponents will use to argue their case and offers a fact of his own to counter their argument. They will argue that these floods must be controlled because people lose their lives in them. Krutch points out the fact that more people lose their lives in automobile accidents than in flash floods but that no one suggests that we should do away with highways. In this same paragraph he offers his opinion as to the "real" motive of these reclamation engineers. They say they want to prevent deaths, but Krutch believes they really want to protect their jobs. He offers no support for this opinion, apparently assuming that his audience—the readers of *Natural History*—will accept the opinion at face value.

---

*Joseph Wood Krutch, "Lightning Water," *Natural History*, Vol. 77, No. 7. Copyright The American Museum of Natural History, 1968. Used with permission.

He continues this line of argument in paragraphs 3 and 4. In paragraph 3, he compares these engineers to highway engineers whom he accuses of destroying the natural beauty of our country. In paragraph 4, he once again offers the opinion that these engineers are self-serving; "the first concern of all of them is their vested interest in their own jobs."

In paragraph 5, Krutch begins another line of argument. He is aware that his opponents could respond to his first argument by asserting that we have to sacrifice a certain number of deaths on our highways because of the importance of these highways to our way of life. In this section of the essay, Krutch wishes to make his readers aware how important our deserts are. He does so not by explaining but by showing the process by which this beauty is created. In paragraph 5, he describes Death Valley; in paragraph 7, he describes the beauty of an alluvial fan.

In paragraphs 8 and 9, Krutch returns to the potential dangers of these flash floods. He recognizes this danger but in paragraph 9, he offers his opinion that "Flash floods are dangerous only if you don't take the trouble to know what they are and why they exist." This opinion is in part supported by the descriptions and examples in paragraphs 5 through 7. In paragraph 9 Krutch offers another opinion, which is in effect the thesis of his essay: "But to some of us it seems that it would be better to teach people how to travel or live in the few remaining natural areas than to destroy their unique characteristics."

He closes in paragraphs 10 and 11 by stating his opinion that the effect of these reclamation engineers will be to "regularize" our country. In his conclusion he implies his opinion that in losing this variety we will have lost as much or more than we would lose if we lost highways. Without them we would have no way to travel from one part of the country to another. Without this variety, we would have no reason to do so.

<table>
<tr><td>EXERCISE</td><td>As we have said, Krutch's key term for his argument is conquer. An opponent could choose as a key term control and argue that we must control these events in nature. Write a paragraph in which you plan the types of supports that one could use in developing this counterargument.</td></tr>
</table>

<table>
<tr><td>EXERCISE</td><td>Krutch says in his ninth paragraph that "Flash floods are dangerous only if you don't take the trouble to know what they are and why they exist." Throughout his essay he characterizes victims of flash floods as careless people who cannot be protected from themselves, much less from acts of nature. He begins this characterization in paragraph 1 with the word careless. Find other words in the essay that cluster with this word to form Krutch's description of these people. What is Krutch's attitude toward them? Does that attitude add to, or hinder, the overall effect of the essay?</td></tr>
</table>

Shaping an Argument

Of the argumentative tools outlined earlier, we need not discuss facts and figures at any greater length, except to say that the writer's job in using them is to interpret their meaning for the reader. Both opinion statements and causal statements, however, require more attention, and to them we need to add another tool of argument: the analogy.

Opinion Statements

We found several opinion statements in the preceding essay. At first, you may think that an argumentative essay should contain one opinion statement and a host of fact and example statements supporting that opinion. But that just is not the way we argue, or think, for that matter. We do not link all opinion statements directly to the facts or examples that support them. If we did, our minds would be much less complex than they are. For example, we could support the assertion that Alfred would be a good candidate for school president by such fact statements as the following: Alfred made an "A" in his history class, Alfred made a "B" in chemistry, or Alfred works three hours a night in the library. But rather than offering such specifics in support of the assertion that Alfred should be elected class president, we would be more likely to offer another opinion statement: Alfred is a disciplined person. If we feel it is necessary, we can then offer specifics in support of the second opinion. But we need this second opinion to help our readers see the relevance of these facts to the matter at hand. They may not know exactly what Alfred's making an "A" has to do with his candidacy for school president, but they will probably be able to see why we offer the opinion that he is a disciplined person as support for the opinion that he would make a good president.

Of course, this is the very process we talked about earlier when we said that at least one of the supporting premises for a conclusion would be an arguable assertion. At some point every arguable thesis will depend upon an opinion statement for support. If the argument is to be successful, the writer must find some way to make his supporting opinion statement more acceptable to his readers than the thesis it supports.

What factors will make one opinion statement more acceptable than another? Before we answer this question, we should distinguish between three different types of opinion statements, as represented by the following three specific opinion statements.

1. Murder is bad.

2. Milk tastes good.

3. Alfred would be a good candidate for school president.

Sentence 1 is the type of opinion statement that needs no support. It is fortunate that it does not, because anyone who would not automatically accept this opinion might very well reject the assertions we would use in support of it. Like sentence 1, sentence 2 presents an opinion that is difficult to support. Even though many people like milk, that fact is support only for the assertion that they think milk tastes good. How would one offer any real support for the assertion that milk actually does taste good? This is literally a matter of personal taste and a type of opinion that you will do well to avoid in your arguments.

The third sentence is an example of the type of opinion we concern ourselves with in constructing argument essays. It is not a truism accepted by everyone, and it is a statement that lends itself to support. If we think Alfred would make a good president, we can use any or all of those methods of support outlined earlier: examples, facts, figures, causal statements, and opinion statements.

Once we determine that an opinion statement belongs in this third category, we judge it on the principles that we introduced in talking about the inductive process. We will want to know how careful the writer has been in examining specifics that underlie the induction and in relating them to the opinion. We will have more to say about this matter later in the chapter when we talk about potential problems in arguments.

Analogies

The analogy is a form of support that does not fit very neatly within the system of argumentative tools we have outlined. Perhaps it comes closest to being an extended example. However we classify it, the analogy is an important argumentative tool. If we can convince our readers that a certain thing or situation is like another thing or situation, we can make them feel about the first thing as they feel about the second. For example, if we can convince our readers that the current laws against marijuana are like the laws against alcohol during Prohibition, we can predict that many readers will think these marijuana laws ought to be changed.

There is an inherent strength and weakness in every analogy. An analogy allows a writer to tap feelings, responses, and opinions that he knows his reader already possesses; but no one can prove to the reader that she should accept the comparisons that are the basis of the analogy. No matter how similar the two things being compared, if the reader finds a dissimilarity that is integral to the argument from her perspective, she will reject the analogy. For example, a writer could argue that boxing should not be considered a brutal sport by comparing it to football, which is fast becoming our national sport. He could refer to the number of injuries in both sports and insist that if these injuries are acceptable in one sport, they are acceptable in the other. He might also list the various types of protections such as pads, helmets, headgear, gloves, and padded rings in the sports. However, an unsympathetic reader could cite a crucial difference between the two: The ultimate goal in football is to score points *by crossing a goal line*; the goal in boxing is to score points *by doing damage to an opponent's body*. Thus, for this reader, the analogy will not work.

Because an analogy is a comparison of two separate things, there will always be differences between the two. When you make an analogy, it is crucial, however, that those differences do not draw attention to themselves at the very point of your argument. In our example, the writer's thesis concerns "brutality." The difference in the way in which points are scored in boxing and football draws attention to this very issue; thus, the analogy is not likely to work for most readers.

Shaping an Argument

We have already seen an analogy that avoids this problem rather well. In "Lightning Water" Krutch compares reclamation engineers to highway engineers. He assumes that his audience will react negatively to highway engineers. Reclamation engineers are like them in that they destroy the natural environment because of their own vested interest. Many other points of similarity may occur to the readers. Both types of engineers work for the government and are given seemingly unlimited budgets for their projects. As government employees, both seem very remote from the concerns of the average person. Both are trained in engineering massive changes in the landscape. Both introduce great amounts of concrete and other man-made materials into what was a natural setting.

There does not seem to be a difference between these two types of engineers that would interfere with Krutch's argument. In terms of the destruction they occasion and the relative importance of their work, they seem very much alike. Thus, this comparison helps Krutch develop his perception of the work being done to prevent floods in the desert.

<table>
<tr><td>EXERCISE</td><td>Create at least one analogy that would help you support one side of each of the following arguments. Then choose the analogy you consider most workable and write a paragraph in which you use it to support your point of view in the argument. Then choose an analogy that looks less promising and write a paragraph in which you discuss possible problems with that analogy.</td></tr>
</table>

1. Busing students for racial integration.

2. Scheduling television programs in accordance with the wishes of the Moral Majority.

3. Informing parents of underage children who secure birth control devices.

Causal Statements

As we said earlier, one way of helping readers perceive things as we do is to support our viewpoint with causal statements. But once we have made a causal statement, how can we help readers to believe in the causal relations it expresses? In order to examine this question, we return to an assertion—for example, unemployment rises in Republican administrations. Even though the word *cause* does not appear in this statement, the writer is obviously implying that Republican administrations cause unemployment to rise. She is arguing that Republicans should not be supported, and her key term might be something like *ineffectiveness in economical matters*. This term is then supported by the causal statement.

How will this writer persuade her readers to share her belief that Republican policies cause unemployment? How does one ever persuade someone to "believe in" a causal relation? An answer to this last question is hinted at in the way the writer frames her generalization. We noted earlier that she does not feel it necessary to assert that the Republican policies cause the unemployment. She merely offers the statement that this phenomenon happens in Republican administrations. If she can make her readers believe this statement, she will make them believe that the policies of Republicans cause this unemployment.

Just why is this the case? Why will readers tend to see this what-follows-what (chronological) connection as a what-follows-from-what (causal) connection? They will do so because the causal connection provides a means of ordering their lives and because the chronological connection is the closest thing to a causal connection in their lives. We may get some insight into just how this is so by examining the following causal statements.

1. Frank's dismissal caused Bill to resign.

2. The rise in temperature caused the ice to melt.

3. The removal of the base domino caused the stack of dominoes to fall.

4. His refusal to accept her role as a working person caused their divorce.

5. The opening of the new market caused the old market to go out of business.

6. Policies that protect the wealthy from inflation cause unemployment to rise.

There are two types of statements here.

Those acceptable at face value:	Statements 2, 3
Those needing support:	Statements 1, 4, 5, and 6

We are hardly tempted to question the causal assertions in the first category, but most of us would require quite a bit of support for the assertions in the second category. Why do we automatically accept statements 2 and 3? Both of these concern the physical laws of the universe as we know them; these are matters that we all just naturally know about and accept. Rises in temperature cause certain changes in ice. Bodies, such as dominoes, just do not remain suspended in air without support. But why do we accept them? How do we know that a rise in temperature actually *causes* ice to melt? You may be tempted to offer as an answer that because ice melts at a temperature above 32°F, any rise above 32°F will result in the melting of ice. But how do we know that this rise in temperature causes ice to melt? How would we go about proving this assertion?

This last question leads us back to a distinction made earlier in this chapter: Some arguments lend themselves to resolution by discussing the meaning(s) of words, whereas other arguments are resolved by referring to nonverbal phenomena. We would "prove" that ice melts at a temperature above 32°F, not by discussing the issue—that is, defining the words *ice*, *melt*, and so forth—but by raising the temperature around ice above 32°F over and over and over to determine whether the solid becomes a liquid at that temperature every time. Will such experiments "prove" that a rise in temperature causes ice to melt?

The answer to this question will depend, of course, on what we mean by this word *prove*. Actually, such statements as "ice melts at a temperature above 32°F" are the very principles upon which our scientific proofs are based; but they, themselves, cannot be proved in the same deductive manner as the con-

Shaping an Argument

clusions we use them to prove can be. For example, we might construct the following deductive chain, using the premise "Ice melts at a temperature above 32°F."

Ice melts at a temperature above 32°F.

This substance is ice.

This substance will melt at a temperature above 32°F.

By means of a Deductive Chain, we have "proved" that this substance will melt at a temperature above 32°F. But what kind of Deductive Chain could we frame in support of our initial premise? You might be tempted to scoff at this whole line of questioning, asserting that such a basic "fact" needs no proof. But, for just a moment, assume that someone you know is not convinced of this assertion. How will you prove it to this person? You will not prove it by deduction.

Because it is so hard to prove such seemingly obvious causal relations, it is no wonder that less obvious causal relations are difficult to prove. Despite their difficulty, these less obvious relations lend themselves to the same principle of proof we rely upon in dealing with the obvious causal relations: the shift from what-follows-what? to what-follows-from-what? relations. We convince doubters that a rise in temperature causes ice to melt by repeating the chronological connection over and over again; that is, we raise the temperature and observe that *after* doing so, the ice melts. Finally, the doubter is convinced that there is more than a chronological connection here—that the rise in temperature not only preceded but caused the ice to melt.

Matters are not so simple in a situation such as the one referred to in the following sentence: Frank's dismissal caused Bill to resign. We cannot dismiss Frank over and over to see whether Bill resigns every time. However, we can examine the situation thoroughly to see if there are any other factors that could have caused Bill's resignation. Were any other variables changed? Did Bill receive a cut in salary? Did any other working condition change? Also we might examine Bill's relation with Frank. Were they friends? Did Bill think Frank was a valuable employee? Did Frank make it easier for Bill to perform his job? Did Bill threaten to resign if Frank were fired? If after examining all of these factors, we find no other change in the working situation that might have caused Bill to resign, and if we find reason to believe that Bill thought Frank had been treated unfairly or that Bill thought his work would be more difficult as a consequence of Frank's dismissal, we may come to see this chronological relationship—that is, the fact that Frank was fired just before Bill resigned—as a causal relationship. We may believe, and hope to convince our readers to believe, that Frank's dismissal caused Bill to resign.

WRITING ASSIGNMENT

Write an essay in which you examine the causes of a major event in your life. Following are some examples.

1. Why did you choose to attend your present college instead of any others you considered? As you consider your choice, ask yourself whether the real rea-

sons for your choice were the same as the ones you gave your parents. Your friends. Yourself. Assuming that you will continue your education at this college, will your reasons for staying here be the same ones you chose the school for?

2. Why did you decide to major in the field you are in? What factors influenced you more? Job satisfaction, job security, money, parental pressure, friends, other?

3. Have you experienced a major problem in your life? What was the problem? In what situation did it arise? What were its causes? What was the outcome?

4. Have you undergone a major change in your thinking about something important in your life? What is that change? What factors were most important in bringing about the change? What will be the effects of the change?

An effective persuasion essay makes use of many different argumentative tools in supporting its author's viewpoint. However, often one of these tools will predominate. In the following essay, Gore Vidal relies heavily upon causal supports for his thesis.

Drugs

Gore Vidal

    It is possible to stop most drug addiction in the United States within a very short time. Simply make all drugs available and sell them at cost. Label each drug with a precise description of what effect—good and

1 bad—the drug will have on the taker. This will require heroic honesty. Don't say that marijuana is addictive or dangerous when it is neither, as millions of people know—unlike "speed," which kills most unpleasantly, or heroin, which is addictive and difficult to kick.

    For the record, I have tried—once—almost every drug and like none,

2 disproving the popular Fu Manchu theory that a single whiff of opium will enslave the mind. Nevertheless many drugs are bad for certain people to take and they should be told why in a sensible way.

    Along with exhortation and warning, it might be good for our citizens to recall (or learn for the first time) that the United States was the creation

3 of men who believed that each man has the right to do what he wants with his own life as long as he does not interfere with his neighbor's pursuit of happiness (that his neighbor's idea of happiness is persecuting others does confuse matters a bit).

    This is a startling notion to the current generation of Americans. They reflect a system of public education which has made the Bill of Rights,

4 literally, unacceptable to a majority of high school graduates (see the annual Purdue reports) who now form the "silent majority"—a phrase which that underestimated wit Richard Nixon took from Homer who used it to describe the dead.

    Now one can hear the warning rumble begin: if everyone is allowed to take drugs everyone will and the GNP will decrease, the Commies will

5 stop us from making everyone free, and we shall end up a race of Zombies, passively murmuring "groovie" to one another. Alarming thought. Yet it seems most unlikely that any reasonably sane person will become a drug addict if he knows in advance what addiction is going to be like.

6 Is everyone reasonably sane? No. Some people will always become drug addicts just as some people will always become alcoholics, and it is just too bad. Every man, however, has the power (and should have the legal right) to kill himself if he chooses. But since most men don't, they won't be mainliners either. Nevertheless, forbidding people things they like or think they might enjoy only makes them want those things all the more. This psychological insight is, for some mysterious reason, perennially denied our governors.

7 It is a lucky thing for the American moralist that our country has always existed in a kind of time-vacuum: we have no public memory of anything that happened before last Tuesday. No one in Washington today recalls what happened during the years alcohol was forbidden to the people by a Congress that thought it had a divine mission to stamp out Demon Rum—launching, in the process, the greatest crime wave in the country's history, causing thousands of deaths from bad alcohol, and creating a general (and persisting) contempt among the citizenry for the laws of the United States.

8 The same thing is happening today. But the government has learned nothing from past attempts at prohibition, not to mention repression.

9 Last year when the supply of Mexican marijuana was slightly curtailed by the Feds, the pushers got the kids hooked on heroin and deaths increased dramatically, particularly in New York. Whose fault? Evil men like the Mafiosi? Permissive Dr. Spock? Wild-eyed Dr. Leary? No.

10 The government of the United States was responsible for those deaths. The bureaucratic machine has a vested interest in playing cops and robbers. Both the Bureau of Narcotics and the Mafia want strong laws against the sale and use of drugs because if drugs are sold at cost there would be no money in it for anyone.

11 If there was no money in it for the Mafia, there would be no playground pushers, and addicts would not commit crimes to pay for the next fix. Finally, if there was no money in it, the Bureau of Narcotics would wither away, something they are not about to do without a struggle.

12 Will anything sensible be done? Of course not. The American people are as devoted to the idea of sin and its punishment as they are to making money—and fighting drugs is nearly as big a business as pushing them. Since the combination of sin and money is irresistible (particularly to the professional politician), the situation will only grow worse.*

Vidal argues that laws regarding drugs should be abolished. He bases his argument on a series of causal chains, which shows what removing the laws would cause and what the laws as they now exist are causing.

---

*From *Homage to Daniel Shays: Collected Essays 1952–1972* by Gore Vidal. Reprinted with permission of Random House, Inc.

Vidal's solution to the drug problem, and his thesis for the essay, can be found in the essay's second sentence: "Simply make drugs available and sell them at cost." Vidal begins his support of this proposal in the second paragraph, which offers an answer to a potential counterargument, also based on causal reasoning. Many would argue that these drugs are capable of enslaving people and that the laws against them protect people from experimenting with drugs and becoming hopelessly addicted. Vidal offers a personal example in response to this argument: "I have tried—once—almost every drug and like none, disproving the popular Fu Manchu theory that a single whiff of opium will enslave the mind."

In paragraph 5, Vidal introduces a line of reasoning that he continues through paragraph 10. Once again he refutes a counterargument based on causal reasoning. Some will say that we need drug laws to prevent our society from becoming a race of "Zombies." Vidal argues that this will not happen and offers his opinion that "forbidding people things they like . . . only makes them want those things all the more." As support for this latter opinion statement, he offers the example of what happened when alcohol was prohibited in the United States. He develops this example further by showing the various effects that Prohibition had in the United States and comparing those effects to the effects of present drug laws.

In paragraph 11, Vidal introduces another supporting premise. Drugs should be legalized to take away the profits of organized crime and, thus, cause it to stop trafficking in drugs. Vidal apparently believes his readers will accept this causal generalization at face value, for he offers no support for it. His final argument is also introduced in this paragraph: When we made drugs illegal, we made the Bureau of Narcotics necessary. If drugs were legalized, we would need no such agency.

EXERCISE

In the preceding we have presented Vidal's argument and explained the structure of support in that argument. However, we have said little about the argument's effectiveness. Consider Vidal's argument and then answer the following questions.

1. How convinced are you that drugs will not enslave people if they experiment with them? How would you evaluate the support that Vidal offers for this assertion? (After you have answered this question for yourself, look ahead in this chapter to the section entitled "Weak Arguments," pp. 199–208. What error(s) could an opponent accuse Vidal of making in regard to this premise?)

2. In paragraphs 5 through 10, Vidal argues that removing drug laws will not result in wholesale addiction to drugs, and he supports this assertion by comparing the drug laws to the laws that once prohibited alcoholic consumption. How do you react to this analogy? Write a brief answer to Vidal's analogy from the standpoint of someone who believes drug laws are necessary.

As practice in arguing from cause, write one or both of the following papers.

1. Write an essay in which you take the opposing side of Vidal's argument. Base your essay on causal reasoning.

2. Write an essay in which you refute Vidal's argument in a parody—that is, an essay that satirizes Vidal's method of arguing. The following essay by Sydney J. Harris should serve as a model for that parody.

Fantastic Piece of Logic
Sydney J. Harris

One of the most fantastic pieces of logic I've ever seen in print is the rationale of capital punishment recently offered by Dr. George Crane, the only syndicated columnist who signs himself, "Ph.D., M.D."

He writes: "Clergymen should stress the fact that without capital punishment, there would be no Christianity at all. If Jesus had not been sentenced to death on the cross, how could there be any Catholic or Protestant churches today? So Christianity owes its very existence to capital punishment."

With the use of this tremendous reasoning device, what cannot be justified in history? For instance, without the madness and despotism of King George I, there would have been no American Revolution and no United States of America.

Many of the King's advisers and members of Parliament were in favor of giving the colonies more freedom and self-government and lifting the harsh taxes that had been imposed on them.

But George I, who eventually went mad, bitterly resisted such advice, and clamped down on the colonists. So we should be grateful to insanity and despotism for resulting in the U.S.A. Ergo, insanity and despotism are good things, just as capital punishment is.

Let's keep in mind, too, that the Inquisition in Spain was a marvelous thing—because it inaugurated the resistance to Roman Catholicism all over Europe, culminating in the Protestant Reformation. So without the Inquisition, there might have been no Protestant Church, which owes its very existence to religious repression.

Ergo, once more, Inquisitions are good, just as capital punishment is right, because they result in the creation of a new, reformed church. Praise be to all Inquisitors everywhere.

There is no limit to what the imaginative historian can do with this device, henceforth to be known as "Crane's Equation." Since most good things have arisen from the bad conditions that caused them, we should therefore support all bad things on the basis that they will stimulate truth, reason, justice, freedom, and reform.

Slavery is excellent, because it precipitated the Civil War, and thus took the blacks out of bondage. Obviously, without slavery there could have been no Emancipation. Infectious and contagious diseases are marvelous things, too, since without them we never would have developed our anti-toxins.

A man needs both a Ph.D. and an M.D. to figure these matters out. I am eternally indebted to Dr. Crane for a whole new slant on history.*

ORGANIZING PERSUASIVE ESSAYS

The same principles we discussed in regard to the order of expressive and non-argumentative transactional writing apply to the order of argumentative essays. Like these types of writing, arguments must have a beginning, a middle, and an end. However, there are some additional concerns that come into play in argumentative writing. In addition to stating a thesis, the introduction of an argument will often introduce a problem that occasions the essay. The body of the essay will do more than support the thesis: It will offer *refutation* to the counterthesis. Finally, the conclusion often goes beyond the summary or statement of implications found in nonargumentative writing to what is known as a *call for action*. The writer wants not only to convince his readers of his argument, but also to motivate them to take some specific action; this action is made clear in the conclusion.

In order to illustrate organization in arguments, we will reexamine the structure of the argumentative essays we have discussed in this chapter. First we look at the overall structure of "Lightning Water."

Introduction	Paragraphs 1 and 2
Body	Paragraphs 3 through 9
Conclusion	Paragraphs 10 and 11

In the introduction to this essay Krutch gives the readers a clear understanding of what the issue of the essay is to be and of the side he will take. He does not state a thesis at this point, but the last two sentences of the second paragraph make it clear that he and the reclamation engineers are adversaries. Krutch begins to make his case against their work in paragraphs 3 and 4, comparing them to road builders who are willing to destroy the environment for their own gain.

To this point, the structure of this essay looks very much like that of a nonargumentative transactional essay. However, the writer of an argument is responsible to do more than show readers why she has arrived at the generalization in the thesis; she must refute the arguments of her opponents.

Krutch begins his refutation in paragraph 5. These reclamation engineers would argue that saving the desert is not as necessary as building roads and that Krutch's analogy, offered in paragraph 2, fails for this reason. In paragraphs 5, 6, and 7, Krutch relates the process by which the various parts of a desert are formed and describes the beauty that results. Krutch would maintain that this beauty is well worth what it would take to preserve it.

---

*Reprinted by permission of Sydney J. Harris and Field Newspaper Syndicate.

In paragraphs 8 and 9, Krutch offers a refutation to another argument. He mentions the fact that some would argue that these dams must be built to save lives, but he offers his opinion that carelessness, rather than the floods themselves, is responsible for deaths in desert floods.

Krutch concludes his essay in paragraphs 10 and 11, where he examines the ultimate effects of these dams. If these dams are continued, "The Southwest would be no longer recognizable, no longer unique, no longer beautiful in its own way."

EXERCISE   We have said that all of the modes can be used in an argumentative essay. How many different modes can you find operating in this essay? Is there any connection between the modes and the various divisions of the essay? (Hint: Does there seem to be a change in mode at paragraph 5?)

Our second argument for analysis was Gore Vidal's "Drugs." Although the overall structure of that essay is similar to the structure of "Lightning Water," there is a sense in which its structure is quite different internally. The similarities in overall structure are apparent in the following representation of this essay's structure:

Introduction	Paragraph 1
Body	Paragraphs 2 through 11
Conclusion	Paragraph 12

Within this pattern, however, Vidal adopts a much more conversational structure than does Krutch. Rather than presenting his case and then dealing with objections, Vidal offers his thesis and then counters the objections to that thesis, much in the fashion of a speaker interacting with an audience.

After introducing the thesis in the second sentence of the first paragraph, Vidal immediately raises and answers an objection in paragraph 2. He does not believe that drugs enslave everyone who experiments with them.

Paragraphs 3 and 4 illustrate the freedom that an experienced writer will often allow himself in structuring his essay. The opinions in this paragraph describe the problem that forms the context for Vidal's argument. A more formal structure would place them immediately after paragraph 1 and allow the three paragraphs to form the introduction. However, Vidal apparently wishes to emphasize the conversational nature of his argument; thus, he introduces this background material in paragraphs 3 and 4 almost as an afterthought.

In paragraphs 5 through 10, Vidal raises and answers a second objection to his thesis—that Americans could turn to drugs in great numbers if his plan were adopted. Finally, having countered these two primary objections, Vidal offers a scantily developed argument in paragraph 11. There he asserts that the overall effect of drug laws is to make money for the Mafia and to keep the Federal Bureau of Narcotics in business.

Vidal's conclusion is an ironic illustration of the call for action. Vidal knows that one of the purposes of an argument's conclusion is to show readers exactly what they should do and to encourage them to take action. However, he simply states his opinion that no action will be taken in regard to this matter. If Vidal has been serious in writing the essay, as he no doubt has been, this conclusion cannot be straightforward. That is, by taking this negative approach, Vidal hopes to arouse his audience even more than a call to action would have.

EXERCISE

A major support in Vidal's argument is his analogy between present drug laws and the laws against alcohol during Prohibition. We foreshadowed this analogy in our discussion of analogies, where we said that if a writer could convince an audience that our present drug laws are like the laws of Prohibition, she could tap into their negative feelings about Prohibition. But an opponent to Vidal's argument will not necessarily accept the analogy. Write a paragraph in which you refute Vidal's analogy. You will need to find important differences between our present drug laws and the Prohibition laws, or between alcohol and those drugs that Vidal is talking about.

EXERCISE

The following is another persuasive essay for your consideration. Read it and then answer the questions that follow it.

How to Mark a Book

Mortimer J. Adler

1 You know you have to read "between the lines" to get the most out of anything. I want to persuade you to do something equally important in the course of your reading. I want to persuade you to "write between the lines." Unless you do, you are not likely to do the most efficient kind of reading.

2 I contend, quite bluntly, that marking up a book is not an act of mutilation but of love.

3 You shouldn't mark up a book which isn't yours. Librarians (or your friends) who lend you books expect you to keep them clean, and you should. If you decide that I am right about the usefulness of marking books, you will have to buy them. Most of the world's great books are available today, in reprint editions, at less than a dollar.

4 There are two ways in which one can own a book. The first is the property right you establish by paying for it, just as you pay for clothes and furniture. But this act of purchase is only the prelude to possession. Full ownership comes only when you have made it a part of yourself, and the best way to make yourself a part of it is by writing in it. An illustration may make the point clear. You buy a beefsteak and transfer it from the butcher's icebox to your own. But you do not own the beefsteak in the most important sense until you consume it and get it into your bloodstream. I am arguing that books, too, must be absorbed in your bloodstream to do you any good.

5 Confusion about what it means to own a book leads people to a false reverence for paper, binding, and type—a respect for the physical thing—the craft of the printer rather than the genius of the author. They forget that it is possible for a man to acquire the idea, to possess the beauty, which a great book contains, without staking his claim by pasting his

Shaping an Argument

bookplate inside the cover. Having a fine library doesn't prove that its owner has a mind enriched by books; it proves nothing more than that he, his father, or his wife, was rich enough to buy them.

6 There are three kinds of book owners. The first has all the standard sets and best-sellers—unread, untouched. (This deluded individual owns woodpulp and ink, not books.) The second has a great many books—a few of them read through, most of them dipped into, but all of them as clean and shiny as the day they were bought. (This person would probably like to make books his own, but is restrained by a false respect for their physical appearance.) The third has a few books or many—every one of them dogeared and dilapidated, shaken and loosened by continual use, marked and scribbled in from front to back. (This man owns books.)

7 Is it false respect, you may ask, to preserve intact and unblemished a beautifully printed book, an elegantly bound edition? Of course not. I'd no more scribble all over a first edition of *Paradise Lost* than I'd give my baby a set of crayons and an original Rembrandt! I wouldn't mark up a painting or a statue. Its soul, so to speak, is inseparable from its body. And the beauty of a rare edition or of a richly manufactured volume is like that of a painting or a statue.

8 But the soul of a book *can* be separated from its body. A book is more like the score of a piece of music than it is like a painting. No great musician confuses a symphony with the printed sheets of music. Arturo Toscanini reveres Brahms, but Toscanini's score of the C-minor Symphony is so thoroughly marked up that no one but the maestro himself can read it. The reason why a great conductor makes notations on his musical scores—marks them up again and again each time he returns to study them—is the reason why you should mark your books. If your respect for magnificent binding or typography gets in the way, buy yourself a cheap edition and pay your respects to the author.

9 Why is marking up a book indispensable to reading? First, it keeps you awake. (And I don't mean merely conscious; I mean wide awake.) In the second place, reading, if it is active, is thinking, and thinking tends to express itself in words, spoken or written. The marked book is usually the thought-through book. Finally, writing helps you remember the thoughts you had, or the thoughts the author expressed. Let me develop these three points.

10 If reading is to accomplish anything more than passing time, it must be active. You can't let your eyes glide across the lines of a book and come up with an understanding of what you have read. Now an ordinary piece of light fiction, like say, *Gone with the Wind*, doesn't require the most active kind of reading. The books you read for pleasure can be read in a state of relaxation, and nothing is lost. But a great book, rich in ideas and beauty, a book that raises and tries to answer great fundamental questions, demands the most active reading of which you are capable. You don't absorb the ideas of John Dewey[1] the way you absorb the crooning of Mr. Vallee.[2] You have to reach for them. That you cannot do while you're asleep.

[1]John Dewey was a modern educational philosopher whose influence on learning was profound.

[2]Rudy Vallee was a singer, popular in the 1920s.

If, when you've finished reading a book, the pages are filled with your notes, you know that you read actively. The most famous *active* reader of great books I know is President Hutchins, of the University of Chicago. He also has the hardest schedule of business activities of any man I know. He invariably reads with a pencil, and sometimes, when he picks up a book and pencil in the evening he finds himself, instead of making intelligent notes, drawing what he calls "caviar factories" on the margins. When that happens, he puts the book down. He knows he's too tired to read, and he's just wasting time.

But, you may ask, why is writing necessary? Well, the physical act of writing, with your own hand, brings words and sentences more sharply before your mind and preserves them better in your memory. To set down your reaction to important words and sentences you have read, and the questions they have raised in your mind, is to preserve those reactions and sharpen those questions.

Even if you wrote on a scratch pad, and threw the paper away when you had finished writing, your grasp of the book would be surer. But you don't have to throw the paper away. The margins (top and bottom, as well as side), the end-papers, the very space between the lines, are all available. They aren't sacred. And, best of all, your marks and notes become an integral part of the book and stay there forever. You can pick up the book the following week or year, and there are all your points of agreement, disagreement, doubt, and inquiry. It's like resuming an interrupted conversation with the advantage of being able to pick up where you left off.

And that is exactly what reading a book should be: a conversation between you and the author. Presumably he knows more about the subject than you do; naturally, you'll have the proper humility as you approach him. But don't let anybody tell you that a reader is supposed to be solely on the receiving end. Understanding is a two-way operation; learning doesn't consist in being an empty receptacle. The learner has to question himself and question the teacher. He even has to argue with the teacher, once he understands what the teacher is saying. And marking a book is literally an expression of your differences, or agreements of opinion, with the author.

There are all kinds of devices for marking a book intelligently and fruitfully. Here's the way I do it:

1. *Underlining:* of major points, of important or forceful statements.

2. *Vertical lines at the margin:* to emphasize a statement already underlined.

3. *Star, asterisk, or other doo-dad at the margin:* to be used sparingly, to emphasize the ten or twenty most important statements in the book. (You may want to fold the bottom corner of each page on which you use such marks. It won't hurt the sturdy paper on which most modern books are printed, and you will be able to take the book off the shelf at any time and, by opening it at the folded-corner page, refresh your recollection of the book.)

4. *Numbers in the margin:* to indicate the sequence of points the author makes in developing a single argument.

5. *Numbers of other pages in the margin:* to indicate where else in the book the author made points relevant to the point marked; to tie up the

20 ideas in a book, which, though they may be separated by many pages, belong together.

21   6. *Circling of key words or phrases.*

   7. *Writing in the margin, or at the top or bottom of the page, for the sake of:* recording questions (and perhaps answers) which a passage

22 raised in your mind; reducing a complicated discussion to a simple statement; recording the sequence of major points right through the books. I use the end-papers at the back of the book to make a personal index of the author's points in the order of their appearance.

   The front end-papers are, to me, the most important. Some people reserve them for a fancy bookplate. I reserve them for fancy thinking. After I have finished reading the book and making my personal index on the

23 back end-paper, I turn to the front and try to outline the book, not page by page, or point by point (I've already done that at the back), but as an integrated structure, with a basic unity and an order of parts. This outline is, to me, the measure of my understanding of the work.

   If you're a die-hard anti-book-marker, you may object that the margins, the space between the lines, and the end-papers don't give you room enough. All right. How about using a scratch pad slightly smaller than

24 the page-size of the book—so that the edges of the sheets won't protrude? Make your index, outlines, and even your notes on the pad, and then insert these sheets permanently inside the front and back covers of the book.

   Or, you may say that this business of marking books is going to slow up your reading. It probably will. That's one of the reasons for doing it. Most of us have been taken in by the notion that speed of reading is a measure of our intelligence. There is no such thing as the right speed for intelligent reading. Some things should be read quickly and effortlessly, and some should be read slowly and even laboriously. The sign of intelli-

25 gence in reading is the ability to read different things differently according to their worth. In the case of good books, the point is not to see how many of them you can get through, but rather how many can get through you—how many you can make your own. A few friends are better than a thousand acquaintances. If this be your aim, as it should be, you will not be impatient if it takes more time and effort to read a great book than it does a newspaper.

   You may have one final objection to marking books. You can't lend them to your friends because nobody else can read them without being

26 distracted by your notes. Furthermore, you won't want to lend them because a marked copy is a kind of intellectual diary, and lending it is almost like giving your mind away.

   If your friend wishes to read your *Plutarch's Lives, Shakespeare,* or

27 *The Federalist Papers,* tell him gently but firmly to buy a copy. You will lend him your car or your coat—but your books are as much a part of you as your head or your heart.*

---

*From Mortimer J. Adler, "How to Mark a Book," *Saturday Review of Literature,* July 6, 1940. Copyright © 1940; copyright © 1967 by Mortimer J. Adler. Reprinted with permission.

We can find a key term for Adler's essay in paragraph 2. He wants us to perceive marking a book as *an act of love* as opposed to *an act of mutilation*. The following questions have to do with the way in which Adler supports this viewpoint.

1. Find at least two places where Adler supports his viewpoint with analogies. What things does Adler compare marking a book to? Do the comparisons seem appropriate? How might a person who disagrees with Adler question these comparisons?

2. Find at least one place where Adler supports his argument by means of an example. Is the example effective? If so, why? If not, why not?

3. In paragraph 6, Adler supports his argument with an opinion statement— the first sentence of the paragraph. Does Adler offer sufficient support for this opinion? Can you think of any "book owners" who do not seem to fit into one of the categories posited here? Explain how this opinion statement and the classification system it occasions support Adler's argument.

4. Paragraph 9 begins as if it is to present a causal statement in support of the argument. However, it presents instead several opinion statements. What are these statements? Are they supported at all? If so, how? If not, are they acceptable without support?

Questions of Structure

1. Divide the essay into beginning, middle, and end. Then answer the following questions.

   a. Is there a sentence that states Adler's thesis? If so, what is it? If not, how would you state his thesis?

   b. Does Adler include discussion of a problem in the introduction? If so, what is the problem? If not, why not?

   c. Does Adler offer any refutation to the argument those not in agreement with his thesis might make? If so, explain where these refutations occur and what arguments they answer.

   d. Is there a call to action in the conclusion? If so, what does Adler ask his readers to do? If not, why not?

2. Adler uses nearly all of the expository processes in shaping this essay. Which process organizes each of the following paragraphs: 4, 6, and 9?

3. Even though there are many different processes at work within this essay, one of these serves as an organizing device for the entire essay. Which is it? Point to as many places as you can where this process shapes the essay.

Questions of Style

1. We have often been told to avoid trite or clichéd phrases. Yet Adler begins his essay with such a phrase: "You know you have to *read between the lines*

Shaping an Argument

to get the most out of anything." Explain why this cliché is effective in this context, whereas it would be ineffective in many other contexts.

2. In paragraph 4, Adler says that buying a book is "the prelude to possession" of that book and that one does not own a beefsteak until he "consume[s] it." The two words *prelude* and *consume* are rather formal, but they are appropriate for the contexts in which they are found in a way that such synonyms as *first step* and *eat* would not be. Explain why.

3. In paragraph 5, Adler makes the following statement: "Having a fine library doesn't prove that its owner has a mind enriched by books; it proves nothing more than that he, his father, or wife, was rich enough to buy them." What would be lost in this sentence if *rich* were replaced by *wealthy*? Find at least two other places where Adler repeats a word in the same sentence but with a variation in its meaning or in the structure in which it functions. Explain why the repetitions are effective.

WEAK ARGUMENTS

We have spent quite a bit of time in making the point that there is no way to structure an irrefutable argument. However, there are certain types of arguments that are much easier to refute than others. In the following pages we will discuss factors that make arguments ineffective.

There are many ways to weaken an argument, and there is no one correct classification system for problematic arguments, though many different ones have been offered. You are probably aware of various lists of *fallacies*, or false methods of reasoning. We will use some of the terms found in these lists, but we will frame them in a classification system based upon our discussion of potential supports for arguments given earlier in this chapter. The classes within our system are mutually exclusive only so long as one views them from the perspective we offer. As we shall see at the end of this section, if that perspective shifts, the categories within the system begin to blend. Nevertheless, we feel the system will help give you some insight into problems people often have when structuring arguments.

We have offered the following methods of support for argumentative theses: facts, figures, statistics, causal statements, and opinions. Using these various supports, we have developed three different types of errors. Problems in the use of facts, figures, and statistics give rise to the first type of error; problematic causal statements constitute a second type of error; and problematic opinion statements, the third.

Fallacies of Irrelevance

Writers and speakers often go awry when using facts, figures, and statistics because they fail to make the proper connection between these supports and the thesis of their argument. Of course, facts and figures do not have to be irrelevant to be useless in arguments. If one offers something as a fact—say, that Columbus discovered America in 1942—which turns out not to be true, then the argument that this fact is being used for is doomed. We assume, however, that the arguer will begin by getting the facts straight and by being sure of figures and statistics.

Problems arise even when the arguer gets these facts correct, because he assumes a connection between them and his thesis that readers are not willing to accept. The most prevalent of these fallacies are the following: *argumentum ad hominem, stereotyping, bandwagon fallacy, argumentum ad ignorantiam,* and *hasty generalization.*

Argumentum Ad Hominem This fallacy involves name calling, arguing by attacking a person instead of issues. Anytime a speaker attacks someone rather than speaking to the issues at hand, these attacks are irrelevant. For example, a politician may argue that her opponent should not be elected because he has been divorced, but if the politician fails to show how this "fact" is related to the thesis—that one should not vote for her opponent—she is making an error of relevance and reducing her chances of convincing her audience.

This is not to suggest that facts concerning a politician are never relevant to questions of whether that politician should serve in an office. The fact that a candidate for county treasurer has been convicted of embezzlement is hardly an irrelevant one. Our point is that the shaper of an argument must be sure that the relevance of his facts to the question at hand is clear to his audience.

Stereotyping Stereotyping is the attempt to attribute certain characteristics to an individual by placing her into a certain group, often, but not always, a racial, ethnic, or religious group. Examples of stereotypical thinking include the following: Girls do well in English; boys do well in mathematics; civil servants are plodding, bureaucratic types who do not really care for people. An example of reasoning by stereotype is "I wouldn't hire him; he belongs to some strange religious group." In such a statement, the assumption is that this person's membership in the group will have some bearing on the way he performs his job. Of course, if the person offering this argument can show that the religious group in question believes that employees should undermine their capitalistic employers, she can show the relevance of this fact. Otherwise, it is irrelevant.

Bandwagon Fallacy We often see this type of problematic reasoning in advertisements: Kangaroos have outsold the competition for two consecutive years. When are you going to drive a Kangaroo? The argument offers no relevant reason for buying this type of car. It could be that many people are buying Kangaroos because they are well-built cars. However, it could also be that many people are buying Kangaroos because they have been convinced that "many people are buying Kangaroos." The advertisement asks us to do something without giving us a good reason for doing so.

Shaping an Argument

Argumentum Ad Ignorantiam Loosely translated *argument from ignorance*, this error occurs when the arguer fails to take responsibility for his assertions. Children are noted for this type of reasoning: My dad is Superman; you can't prove he isn't. Our court system has recognized the fact that a defendant's failure to prove his innocence is irrelevant to the question of whether he is in fact innocent—thus the maxim, innocent until proven guilty. When arguing, the one who asserts is responsible to support his assertions with relevant information.

Hasty Generalization This problem results when a writer connects facts, figures, and statistics to an argumentative conclusion without examining them as closely as she should. We have already discussed a hasty generalization in our introduction to inductive reasoning. There we said that the fact that cats *A*, *B*, and *D* are black does not give us the necessary support for the conclusion that all cats are black. As it turns out, the fact that we happened upon three black cats is irrelevant to the color of cats. The same would be true with such an argument as "Boxing is safer than football, because each year twice as many football players as boxers are injured." A close examination of these statistics would show that they are irrelevant to the question of safety in the two sports because of the large number of people who play football as opposed to the small number who box.

As we said earlier, if we are ever to learn anything new, we must generalize, and there is no way to be absolutely sure that we are not making a hasty generalization. However, we can improve our arguments by being careful not to leap from one or two specifics to a generalization. We do not want to judge all cats on the basis of the three we have seen. Likewise, we want to be sure of all the relevant factors that may influence the connection between our figures and statistics and the conclusions we draw from them. For example, we would not want to determine how Americans feel about contact sports by interviewing people leaving football stadiums. No matter how large our sample, we will not get relevant results because these are people who have chosen to attend a football game.

<table>
<tr><td>EXERCISE</td><td>The following is the first paragraph of "For Pollsters, 'More' Doesn't Always Mean 'Better'" by John Shelton Reed.</td></tr>
</table>

Just before the election of 1936, *The Literary Digest*, a widely read and influential magazine, announced the results of its presidential preference poll. The New Deal was going to be repudiated; FDR would be swept out of office. Alf Landon would be the next president, taking nearly 60 percent of the two-party popular vote. The announcement was made with a great deal of hoopla. The *Digest* quoted a reference to itself as an "oracle, which, since 1920, has foretold with almost uncanny accuracy the choice of the nation's voters. . . ." And, after all, hadn't they mailed out over 10 million "secret ballots" to voters all over the nation, after ransacking tax rolls, telephone directories, automobile registration and magazine subscription lists for names? And hadn't they heard from more than 20 percent of the nation's voters in return?*

Of course President Roosevelt won by a large margin. Explain in a paragraph any problems you see in the reasoning of those who conducted the poll, using the terms of the discussion we have just completed.

Causal Fallacies

Whereas the errors we talked about in the previous section arose from problematic connections between supporting statements and the conclusions based upon those statements, here we will concern ourselves with problems within the causal statements themselves. Of course one could well fail to connect an acceptable causal statement properly to the conclusion he is attempting to induce from it. But causal supports are more often a problem because the readers question the causal statements themselves.

Given the difficulty of proving that one thing causes another, it is little wonder that many arguments fail because the readers cannot accept the causal statements they are offered. When working with causality, we must be aware of the same principles of generalizing that control our other inductions, because causal statements are, in fact, inductions. If a writer says that Alfred will be a good president because he makes good grades, the writer must be aware that this generalization must have many specifics to support it. It will not stand by itself. An opponent may argue that Alfred's good grades are a sign that he will work too hard at being a good student to pay the proper attention to his role as school president. Thus, the person who proposes this causal generalization must support it with examples of individuals who have been good presidents (in the opinions of students and faculty) and who have made good grades, or by offering his opinion that the same intelligence and discipline that cause Alfred to make good grades will cause him to be a good president, or, perhaps with the opinions of authority figures. In any case, the writer cannot simply present the generalization and expect his audience to accept it at face value.

As the preceding example illustrates, we can fall prey to faulty causal reasoning by assuming a cause and effect relationship at a point where our audience is unwilling to make such an assumption. But there are two other causal errors, *oversimplification* and the *either/or dilemma*, that are more frequent culprits in causal reasoning.

Oversimplification The writer who focuses on one of a number of causes for a phenomenon as if it were *the* cause of that phenomenon is oversimplifying. A classic example of this error in reasoning occurs when a motorist blames another

---

*John Shelton Reed in *Society by Agreement: An Introduction to Sociology*, Earl R. Babbie (Belmont, Calif.: Wadsworth, 1977).

Shaping an Argument

motorist for an accident by accusing her of not signaling a stop. Certainly, the failure to signal a stop could be a contributing cause of an accident. However, could that accident have occurred if the following motorist had been traveling at a proper speed and distance from the first car, had been paying careful attention to his driving, and had been operating a car with no mechanical defects? No. The first motorist would have been able to stop even though the other motorist failed to signal a stop. The person who blames the high price of petroleum on the greed of large oil companies, or on Mideast conflicts, or on the policies of one particular administration—or on any *one* cause—is guilty of the same type of oversimplified causal reasoning.

When framing arguments, we will do well to resist the temptation to find *the* cause of any complicated event or human situation. Things are usually more complicated than that. However, we are not suggesting that we must account for all the potential causes of any one event. For example, there is a sense in which the invention of the automobile is a cause for our current oil shortage, but that cause is so far removed from the effect as to not be a valid factor. How then may we decide which causes are appropriate to an analysis? There is no easy way to answer this question, but there are three distinctions among causes that may help us make the decision concerning the relevance of causes. A cause may be seen as *necessary, sufficient,* or *contributory.*

A *necessary cause* is one that is essential to produce the effect. In the hypothetical car accident, negligence on the part of the following driver is a necessary cause for the accident. He was driving too fast, too close to the car in front, or without proper attention to the situation. Or, the following driver had failed to maintain his car properly. In a more literal sense, both cars are necessary causes for the accident. In this sense, of course, it is also necessary for the car in front to come to a stop.

As the name would imply, a *sufficient cause* is one capable of producing the effect in question. In our example, any of several errors on the part of the following driver is sufficient to have caused the accident. No matter what other factors prevailed—that is, no matter how carefully the first driver signaled her stop, or how carefully the second driver was watching the situation—if the second driver was following too close to the first car, the crash would have occurred. Thus, following too close is a sufficient cause for the accident. (Of course, there is a sense in which this speed is not sufficient without a stop on the part of the front driver. However, in this instance, we are treating the stop of the first car as a given, because at some time, a stop will always occur.)

In addition to the necessary and sufficient causes we have examined for our hypothetical accident, there may be *contributing causes*. The brakes of the following car may not have been as effective as they were when the car was new; these less-than-optimal brakes may be, then, a contributing cause to the accident. However, if they are not severely deficient, they are not a sufficient cause for the accident, because they would have stopped the car had the driver been thoroughly attentive and been driving at a safe speed and at a proper following distance.

In sum, you would be well advised not to say what *the* cause of an event or a situation is unless you can show that cause to be necessary for the effect. You must also be aware that any effect will have many more contributing causes than you can possibly treat; thus you should devote most of your energies to necessary and sufficient causes.

The Either/Or Dilemma Actually a specific type of oversimplification, the either/or dilemma occurs when a writer pretends only two causes or two effects exist when in reality there may be multiple causes or effects. An example of the either/or fallacy is the following: Either the allocation for education in our state budget must be held at its present level, or the taxpayers are going to have to pay more taxes in the future. Such an either/or statement is based on the following assumed causal relations: more money for education causes higher taxes to pay for that education budget; no more money for education requires no higher taxes. However, these are not the only possible effects of these causes. For example, taxes could be raised even if the amount of money spent on education is not increased. Other factors such as increased expenditures for welfare and unemployment compensation could cause this need for increased taxation. By the same token, an increased budget for education will not necessarily increase the overall tax burden of citizens. If the increased expenditure on education produces more people capable of assuming jobs, and thus, paying taxes, individual taxpayers may even pay lower taxes at some time in the future. Also, if the increased money spent on education ultimately causes fewer people to need welfare and/or unemployment compensation, the increase in education funds could well be balanced by less money needed for these services.

The purpose in pointing to such problems with the either/or reasoning is not to prove that such a statement as our example is patently false, because it could be that increased monies spent on education will require increases in taxation. Rather, the point is to show the oversimplification in such either/or statements. Even though they are frequently used by many politicians who are trying to simplify matters for what the politicians apparently believe to be a "simple" electorate, they are cases of fallacious reasoning. The only way that such a politician can convince a sophisticated voter to accept this assertion is to offer support for the implicit assertions in the generalization he is offering.

EXERCISE   Find and explain the errors in causal reasoning in the following statements.

Example Detroit automakers say they are building better cars and it must be, for since 1973 the number of highway deaths has decreased significantly.

Explanation This is a rather obvious case of oversimplification. Automakers may be building better cars, but many other factors may be contributing to this decrease in highway deaths. A very important factor that must be taken into account is the reduction of maximum highway speed to 55 mph. Other factors such as safe driving campaigns and reduced travel due to the increase in fuel cost may also have been causes.

     Shaping an Argument

1. The wives of successful men wear expensive clothing, so the best way for a woman to help her husband to be successful is to buy expensive clothing.*

2. Mr. Smith will surely support the E.R.A. After all, he has been active in civil rights work for twenty years.

3. Either you are for an increase in teachers' pay or you prefer your own pocketbook to the welfare of the youth of our society.

4. It was obvious from the time that Jimmy Carter became president that Russia would become more aggressive in countries like Poland. An American president just cannot afford to give any indication of weakness to Russia.

5. We should never cut taxes again. We cut them in 1981 and unemployment rose immediately.

6. You were bound to be mugged sooner or later. A person just cannot subject herself to crowds the size of those at baseball games continually without being mugged.

7. If I were you, I would take German from a native German. After all, you do want the best instruction for your money.

8. If I were you, I would take German from a nonnative speaker. After all, you do want to pass the course, don't you?

When labelling a given assertion an example of faulty reasoning, we are not implying that it is impossible to treat the topic of that assertion in a reasonable and convincing fashion. For example, there is quite a bit of difference between the basic reasoning at work in statements 1 and 2 in the preceding exercise. Whereas statement 1 is unreasonable to the point of being humorous, there is some degree of reason involved in statement 2, even though we cannot accept the assertion as it stands. If you were going to argue that Smith will back the E.R.A., how would you develop your argument? Write a paragraph in which you plan a strategy for such an argument.

Fallacies of Definition

Fallacies of definition occur when arguments are supported by opinion statements. We call them fallacies of definition because all opinion statements hinge on definitions. If a writer asserts that Joe fought with Bill, readers will probably see little point in arguing the fact. They may not believe the statement and, indeed, they may decide to investigate to see whether it is true, but they will not argue it. However, if the speaker goes on to offer the opinion that Joe is brave, readers may be inclined to disagree and to question the speaker's defi-

---

*Irving M. Copi, *Introduction to Logic* (New York: The Macmillan Company, 1953).

nition of *brave*. Opinion statements are labelled as such, then, because they have one or more such arguable terms.

To be successful, the writer of an argumentative paper must be sure that the definitions of terms in his opinion statements are clear and that he offers support for those definitions that need support. If he fails in either of these tasks, his argument will be less effective. A failure in clarity is called *equivocation*, and a failure in support is called *begging the question*.

Equivocation Equivocation is the stuff of the slick advertising slogan. As an example, consider the following slogan: "When guns are outlawed, only outlaws have guns." Here there is a shift in meaning of the word *outlaw*. In its verb form, this word means simply "to declare illegal, or against the law." However, in the noun form, it comes to mean "an habitual criminal," the kind of person who can be shot on sight in some states. Although it is true that when guns are outlawed only people who are going against a certain law will have guns, it is not true that when guns are outlawed only notorious or habitual criminals will have guns.

For another example, suppose a person offers as a supporting premise the assertion that anyone who would commit a premeditated murder is insane and then moves from this premise to the conclusion that such a person should be found "not guilty by reason of insanity." The equivocation here is on the word *insane*. In the conclusion, the word must mean "mentally deranged to the point of not knowing the difference between right or wrong and/or not being in sufficient control of oneself to keep from doing wrong things." However, if readers accept the premise, they are probably ascribing a less technical meaning to *insane*: "disturbed in thinking, not normal." They would accept the premise that a person who would kill is "disturbed," but they would not necessarily believe a person has to be "out of control" to kill.

Begging the Question Whereas the problem in equivocation is a shift in meaning of an important word, the problem in begging the question is that a conclusion is deduced from a premise that masks the same assertion made in the conclusion. Both of these assertions contain a crucial term that is never defined satisfactorily. The following is an example of begging the question: You should not major in a liberal arts field because it will do you little good. This pair of assertions is really but one assertion repeated: A liberal arts major is not *good* because it does one little *good*. Both sentences, then, assert that a liberal arts major is not good, but neither of them helps a reader to understand what the writer means by *good*.

In many cases the writer who falls into the trap of begging the question could frame a workable argument by carefully defining terms. For example, the preceding argument could have been structured as follows.

A college education should provide one with marketable skills.

A liberal arts major does not provide one with marketable skills.

One should not choose a liberal arts major in college.

Shaping an Argument

Of course, the writer has much work to do in helping readers to accept the two supporting premises, but she is no longer begging the question.

<table>
<tr><td>EXERCISE</td><td>Label the fallacies of definition in the following examples and explain which term(s) cause(s) the difficulty.</td></tr>
<tr><td>Example</td><td>That film should be given the Academy Award because it was the best picture of the year.</td></tr>
<tr><td>Explanation:</td><td>This is a simple case of begging the question. There is really only one assertion stated twice. The film is the best because it is the best. The writer offers no insight into what "best film" means, or why he considers this the best film.</td></tr>
</table>

1. We all agree that each company should be free to set its own price. Therefore, how can we deny the companies the freedom to set prices as a group?

2. I wouldn't choose only children to be camp counselors because they are not good in group situations.

3. Dad, how can you say I'm not dependable enough to have the car? Yesterday, you said you could depend on me to ask for the car every weekend.

4. I can't believe you voted for a Democrat.

5. The West wasn't won with a registered gun.

By this time it should be clear that these three types of reasoning errors remain mutually exclusive only so long as they are viewed from the perspectives we offer. By changing our perspective, we can see the same error as a definitional error, a causal error, or an error of irrelevance. To illustrate the point, consider the fourth statement in the previous exercise: I can't believe you voted for a Democrat.

Because this exercise followed our discussion of definitional errors, you probably found a definitional problem in it. To reveal the problem, you may have phrased the argument as follows: One should not vote for a Democrat—she is a Democrat—thus, you should not vote for her. Or, to make the question begging even more obvious, the argument could be phrased as follows: Democrats are bad (should not be voted for) because they are Democrats. It is obvious that there is no premise given in support of the assumption that Democrats are bad.

But if this particular example had followed our section on causal errors, you could well have discussed its problems in the terminologies we developed there. In order to do so you might have phrased the underlying assumption as follows: The fact that she is a Democrat will cause her to do a bad job in office. Of course the writer offers no support for this implicit causal assertion.

From a third perspective, this may be seen as an error of irrelevance, specifically as a stereotype. The writer is attempting to determine the worth of a certain individual by placing her into a class. No support is offered for the assumption that all Democrats are unworthy candidates. Thus, the sophisticated reader is likely to see the implied premise—the candidate is a Democrat—as irrelevant to the conclusion—you should not vote for her.

Although the three categories of problematic arguments we have devised may be helpful to you, the preceding discussion should make the point that the basic principles of logical argument are much more important than any classification system for fallacious arguments. *The* basic principle is that disagreements arise because of differences in the perceptions of those who are arguing. A corollary to this principle is that in any case where there is a real argument, the short, albeit witty, statement will not suffice. Arguments such as "When guns are outlawed only outlaws have guns" and "The West wasn't won with a registered gun" will work only for people who already share the point of view of the writer or for people who are not sophisticated enough to see the problems with these statements.

PRACTICAL APPLICATION

The following essays—"The Efficacy of Prayer" by C. S. Lewis and "Why I Am an Agnostic" by Clarence Darrow—are rather complicated pieces of argumentation. Read each, and then respond to the exercises for each.

The Efficacy of Prayer
C. S. Lewis

1. Some years ago I got up one morning intending to have my hair cut in preparation for a visit to London, and the first letter I opened made it clear I need not go to London. So I decided to put the haircut off too. But then there began the most unaccountable little nagging in my mind, almost like a voice saying, "Get it cut all the same. Go and get it cut." In the end I could stand it no longer. I went. Now my barber at that time was a fellow Christian and a man of many troubles whom my brother and I had sometimes been able to help. The moment I opened his shop door he said, "Oh, I was praying you might come today." And in fact if I had come a day or so later I should have been of no use to him.

2. It awed me; it awes me still. But of course one cannot rigorously prove a causal connection between the barber's prayers and my visit. It might be telepathy. It might be accident.

3. I have stood by the bedside of a woman whose thigh-bone was eaten through with cancer and who had thriving colonies of the disease in many other bones as well. It took three people to move her in bed. The doctors predicted a few months of life; the nurses (who often know better), a few weeks. A good man laid his hands on her and prayed. A year later the patient was walking (uphill, too, through rough woodland) and the man who took the last X-ray photos was saying, "These bones are as solid as rock. It's miraculous."

4. But once again there is no rigorous proof. Medicine, as all true doctors admit, is not an exact science. We need not invoke the supernatural to explain the falsification of its prophecies. You need not, unless you choose, believe in a causal connection between the prayers and the recovery.

The question then arises, "What sort of evidence *would* prove the efficacy of prayer?" The thing we pray for may happen, but how can you ever know it was not going to happen anyway? Even if the thing were indisputably miraculous it would not follow that the miracle had occurred because of your prayers. The answer surely is that a compulsive empirical proof such as we have in the sciences can never be attained.

Some things are proved by the unbroken uniformity of our experiences. The law of gravitation is established by the fact that, in our experience, all bodies without exception obey it. Now even if all the things that people prayed for happened, which they do not, this would not prove what Christians mean by the efficacy of prayer. For prayer is request. The essence of request, as distinct from compulsion, is that it may or may not be granted. And if an infinitely wise Being listens to the requests of finite and foolish creatures, of course He will sometimes grant and sometimes refuse them. Invariable "success" in prayer would not prove the Christian doctrine at all. It would prove something much more like magic—a power in certain human beings to control, or compel, the course of nature.

There are, no doubt, passages in the New Testament which may seem at first sight to promise an invariable granting of our prayers. But that cannot be what they really mean. For in the very heart of the story we meet a glaring instance to the contrary. In Gethsemane the holiest of all petitioners prayed three times that a certain cup might pass from Him. It did not. After that the idea that prayer is recommended to us as a sort of infallible gimmick may be dismissed.

Other things are proved not simply by experience but by those artificially contrived experiences which we call experiments. Could this be done about prayer? I will pass over the objection that no Christian could take part in such a project, because he has been forbidden it: "You must not try experiments on God, your Master." Forbidden or not, is the thing even possible?

I have seen it suggested that a team of people—the more the better— should agree to pray as hard as they knew how, over a period of six weeks, for all the patients in Hospital A and none of those in Hospital B. Then you would total up the results and see if A had more cures and fewer deaths. And I suppose you would repeat the experiment at various times and places so as to eliminate the influence of irrelevant factors.

The trouble is that I do not see how any real prayer could go on under such conditions. "Words without thoughts never to heaven go," says the King in *Hamlet*. Simply to say prayers is not to pray; otherwise a team of properly trained parrots would serve as well as men for our experiment. You cannot pray for the recovery of the sick unless the end you have in view is their recovery. But you can have no motive for desiring the recovery of all the patients in one hospital and none of those in another. You are not doing it in order that suffering should be relieved; you are doing it to find out what happens. The real purpose and the nominal purpose of your prayers are at variance. In other words, whatever your tongue and teeth and knees may do, you are not praying. The experiment demands an impossibility.

Empirical proof and disproof are, then, unobtainable. But this conclusion will seem less depressing if we remember that prayer is request and compare it with other specimens of the same thing.

We make requests of our fellow creatures as well as of God: we ask for the salt, we ask for a raise in pay, we ask a friend to feed the cat while we are on our holidays, we ask a woman to marry us. Sometimes we get what we ask for and sometimes not. But when we do, it is not nearly so easy as one might suppose to prove with scientific certainty a causal connection between the asking and the getting.

Your neighbour may be a humane person who would not have let your cat starve even if you had forgotten to make any arrangement. Your employer is never so likely to grant your request for a raise as when he is aware that you could get better money from a rival firm and is quite possibly intending to secure you by a raise in any case. As for the lady who consents to marry you—are you sure she had not decided to do so already? Your proposal, you know, might have been the result, not the cause, of her decision. A certain important conversation might never have taken place unless she had intended that it should.

Thus in some measure the same doubt that hangs about the causal efficacy of our prayers to God hangs also about our prayers to man. Whatever we get we might have been going to get anyway. But only, as I say, in some measure. Our friend, boss, and wife may tell us that they acted because we asked; and we may know them so well as to feel sure, first that they are saying what they believe to be true, and secondly that they understand their own motives well enough to be right. But notice that when this happens our assurance has not been gained by the methods of science. We do not try the control experiment of refusing the raise or breaking off the engagement and then making our request again under fresh conditions. Our assurance is quite different in kind from scientific knowledge. It is born out of our personal relation to the other parties; not from knowing things about them but from knowing *them*.

Our assurance—if we reach an assurance—that God always hears and sometimes grants our prayers, and the apparent grantings are not merely fortuitous, can only come in the same sort of way. There can be no question of tabulating successes and failures and trying to decide whether the successes are too numerous to be accounted for by chance. Those who best know a man best know whether, when he did what they asked, he did it because they asked. I think those who best know God will best know whether He sent me to the barber's shop because the barber prayed.

For up till now we have been tackling the whole question in the wrong way and on the wrong level. The very question "Does prayer work?" puts us in the wrong frame of mind from the outset. "Work": as if it were magic, or a machine—something that functions automatically. Prayer is either a sheer illusion or a personal contact between embryonic, incomplete persons (ourselves) and the utterly concrete Person. Prayer in the sense of petition, asking for things, is a small part of it; confession and penitence are its threshold, adoration its sanctuary, the presence and vision and enjoyment of God its bread and wine. In it God shows Himself to us. That He answers prayers is a corollary—not necessarily the most important one—from that revelation. What He does is learned from what He is.

Petitionary prayer is, nonetheless, both allowed and commanded to us: "Give us our daily bread." And no doubt it raises a theoretical problem. Can we believe that God ever really modified His action in response to

Shaping an Argument

the suggestions of men? For infinite wisdom does not need telling what is
best, and infinite goodness needs no urging to do it. But neither does
God need any of those things that are done by finite agents, whether living
or inanimate. He could, if He chose, repair our bodies miraculously
without food; or give us food without the aid of farmers, bakers, and
butchers; or knowledge without the aid of learned men; or convert the
heathen without missionaries. Instead, He allows soils and weather and
animals and the muscles, minds, and wills of men to co-operate in the
execution of His will. "God," said Pascal,[1] "instituted prayer in order
to lend to His creatures the dignity of causality." But not only prayer;
whenever we act at all He lends us that dignity. It is not really stranger,
nor less strange, that my prayers should affect the course of events than
that my other actions should do so. They have not advised or changed
God's mind—that is, His over-all purpose. But that purpose will be realized in different ways according to the actions, including the prayers,
of His creatures.

For He seems to do nothing of Himself which He can possibly delegate
to His creatures. He commands us to do slowly and blunderingly what
He could do perfectly in the twinkling of an eye. He allows us to neglect
what He would have us do, or to fail. Perhaps we do not fully realize
the problem, so to call it, of enabling finite free wills to co-exist with
Omnipotence. It seems to involve at every moment almost a sort of divine
abdication. We are not mere recipients or spectators. We are either
privileged to share in the game or compelled to collaborate in the work,
"to wield our little tridents." Is this amazing process simply Creation
going on before our eyes? This is how (no light matter) God makes something—indeed, makes gods—out of nothing.

So at least it seems to me. But what I have offered can be, at the very
best, only a mental model or symbol. All that we say on such subjects
must be merely analogical and parabolic. The reality is doubtless not
comprehensible by our faculties. But we can at any rate try to expel bad
analogies and bad parables. Prayer is not a machine. It is not magic. It
is not advice offered to God. Our act, when we pray, must not, any more
than all our other acts, be separated from the continuous act of God
Himself, in which alone all finite causes operate.

It would be even worse to think of those who get what they pray for as
a sort of court favorite, people who have influence with the throne. The
refused prayer of Christ in Gethsemane is answer enough to that. And
I dare not leave out the hard saying which I once heard from an experienced Christian: "I have seen many striking answers to prayer and more
than one that I thought miraculous. But they usually come at the beginning: before conversion, or soon after it. As the Christian life proceeds,
they tend to be rarer. The refusals, too, are not only more frequent; they
become more unmistakable, more emphatic."

Does God then forsake just those who serve Him best? Well, He who
served Him best of all said, near His tortured death, "Why hast thou
forsaken me?" When God becomes man, that Man, of all others, is least
comforted by God, at His greatest need. There is a mystery here which,

---

[1]Blaise Pascal was a seventeenth-century French philosopher and mathematician.

21 even if I had the power, I might not have the courage to explore. Meanwhile, little people like you and me, if our prayers are sometimes granted, beyond all hope and probability, had better not draw hasty conclusions to our own advantage. If we were stronger, we might be less tenderly treated. If we were braver, we might be sent, with far less help, to defend far more desperate posts in the great battle.*

Questions of Content

1. What is Lewis's thesis in this argument? The complexity of the essay may make it necessary for you to reread the entire essay and then frame a Thesis Statement different from any sentence in the essay. Do you find any difference between Lewis's expressed purpose in the essay and what you feel to be his real aim?

2. Lewis uses many different types of support in this essay, among them several opinion statements. Find at least two of these and determine what definitions these opinions hinge upon. What support does Lewis offer for the viewpoint reflected in these definitions?

3. Lewis also relies heavily on negative causal reasoning. That is, he asserts that it is impossible to prove causality. What supports does he offer for this assertion? What is the relation of this negative causal argument to his thesis?

4. Does Lewis offer any facts, figures, or statistics? If so, are they used effectively?

5. Assuming that you oppose Lewis's argument, can you find any places where you could question his reasoning? If so, explain the problem you see in terms of our discussion of fallacies in this chapter.

Questions of Structure

1. Divide the essay into its three parts—beginning, middle, and end.

2. What objections to his thesis does Lewis anticipate? Where do his refutations come? All at one place or throughout the essay?

3. Lewis's essay illustrates the fact that argumentation often employs many different modes. In addition to definition and causal analysis—already mentioned in the Questions of Content—Lewis shapes his essay with examples, which he uses in comparative structures. Point out several of these examples.

4. Lewis supports his argument by one central comparison, or analogy. What is the analogy? How successful is it? Could an opponent question the validity of this comparison? If so, how?

5. What modes does Lewis use in the introduction to the essay? (Remember that the introduction is not necessarily limited to the first paragraph.)

---

*From C. S. Lewis's "The Efficacy of Prayer," copyright © 1958 by The Atlantic Monthly Company. Used with permission of Curtis Brown, LTD.

Shaping an Argument

1. As we will see in Chapter Eight, tone is in part the result of a writer's attitude toward his readers and, in the case of argumentative essays, toward those who oppose his argument. How would you describe Lewis's attitude toward those who might disagree with him? Are there places where he insults these people? How is a nonbeliever likely to react to Lewis's argument? To Lewis, himself?

2. Even though his argument is very serious, Lewis shows that he does not take himself too seriously by introducing humor into the essay. Where is that humor? What effect does it have by being placed where it is? At whom, or what, is the humor directed?

<table>
<tr><td>WRITING
SAMPLE</td><td>

Why I Am an Agnostic
Clarence Darrow

1   An agnostic is a doubter. The word is generally applied to those who doubt the verity of accepted religious creeds of faiths. Everyone is an agnostic as to the beliefs or creeds they do not accept. Catholics are agnostic to the Protestant creeds, and the Protestants are agnostic to the Catholic creed. Anyone who thinks is an agnostic about something, otherwise he must believe that he is possessed of all knowledge. And the proper place for such a person is in the madhouse or the home for the feeble-minded. In a popular way, in the western world, an agnostic is one who doubts or disbelieves the main tenets of the Christian faith.

2   I would say that belief in at least three tenets is necessary to the faith of a Christian: a belief in God, a belief in immortality, and a belief in a supernatural book. Various Christian sects require much more, but it is difficult to imagine that one could be a Christian, under any intelligent meaning of the word, with less. Yet there are some people who claim to be Christians who do not accept the literal interpretation of all the Bible, and who give more credence to some portions of the book than to others.

3   I am an agnostic as to the question of God. I think that it is impossible for the human mind to believe in an object or thing unless it can form a mental picture of such object or thing. Since man ceased to worship openly an anthropomorphic God and talked vaguely and not intelligently about some force in the universe, higher than man, that is responsible for the existence of man and the universe, he cannot be said to believe in God. One cannot believe in a force excepting as a force that pervades matter and is not an individual entity. To believe in a thing, an image of the thing must be stamped on the mind. If one is asked if he believes in such an animal as a camel, there immediately arises in his mind an image of the camel. This image has come from experience or knowledge of the animal gathered in some way or other. No such image comes, or can come, with the idea of a God who is described as a force.

Man has always speculated upon the origin of the universe, including himself. I feel, with Herbert Spencer, that whether the universe had an origin—and if it had—what the origin is will never be known by man.

</td></tr>
</table>

The Christian says that the universe could not make itself; that there must have been some higher power to call it into being. Christians have been obsessed for many years by Paley's argument that if a person passing through a desert should find a watch and examine its spring, its hands, its case and its crystal, he would at once be satisfied that some intelligent being capable of design had made the watch. No doubt this is true. No civilized man would question that someone made the watch. The reason he would not doubt it is because he is familiar with watches and other appliances made by man. The savage was once unfamiliar with a watch and would have had no idea upon the subject. There are plenty of crystals and rocks of natural formation that are as intricate as a watch, but even to intelligent man they carry no implication that some intelligent power must have made them. They carry no such implication because no one has any knowledge or experience of someone having made these natural objects which everywhere abound.

To say that God made the universe gives us no explanation of the beginnings of things. If we are told that God made the universe, the question immediately arises: Who made God? Did he always exist, or was there some power back of that? Did he create matter out of nothing, or is his existence coextensive with matter? The problem is still there. What is the origin of it all? If, on the other hand, one says that the universe was not made by God, that it always existed, he has the same difficulty to confront. To say that the universe was here last year, or millions of years ago, does not explain its origin. This is still a mystery. As to the question of the origin of things, man can only wonder and doubt and guess.

As to the existence of the soul, all people may either believe or disbelieve. Everyone knows the origin of the human being. They know that it came from a single cell in the body of the mother, and that the cell was one out of ten thousand in the mother's body. Before gestation the cell must have been fertilized by a spermatozoön from the body of the father. This was one out of perhaps a billion spermatozoa that was the capacity of the father. When the cell is fertilized a chemical process begins. The cell divides and multiplies and increases into millions of cells, and finally a child is born. Cells die and are born during the life of the individual until they finally drop apart, and this is death.

If there is a soul, what is it, and where did it come from, and where does it go? Can anyone who is guided by his reason possibly imagine a soul independent of a body, or the place of its residence, or the character of it, or anything concerning it? If man is justified in any belief or disbelief on any subject, he is warranted in the disbelief in a soul. Not one scrap of evidence exists to prove any such impossible thing.

Many Christians base the belief of a soul and God upon the Bible. Strictly speaking, there is no such book. To make the Bible, sixty-six books are bound into one volume. These books are written by many people at different times, and no one knows the time or the identity of any author. Some of the books were written by several authors at various times. These books contain all sorts of contradictory concepts of life and morals and the origin of things. Between the first and the last nearly a thousand years intervened, a longer time than has passed since the discovery of America by Columbus.

When I was a boy the theologians used to assert that the proof of the divine inspiration of the Bible rested on miracles and prophecies. But a miracle means a violation of a natural law, and there can be no proof imagined that could be sufficient to show the violation of a natural law; even though proof seemed to show violation, it would only show that we were not acquainted with all natural laws. One believes in the truthfulness of a man because of his long experience with the man, and because the man has always told a consistent story. But no man has told so consistent a story as nature.

If one should say that the sun did not rise, to use the ordinary expression, on the day before, his hearer would not believe it, even though he had slept all day and knew that his informant was a man of the strictest veracity. He would not believe it because the story is inconsistent with the conduct of the sun in all the ages past.

Primitive and even civilized people have grown so accustomed to believing in miracles that they often attribute the simplest manifestations of nature to agencies of which they know nothing. They do this when the belief is utterly inconsistent with knowledge and logic. They believe in old miracles and new ones. Preachers pray for rain, knowing full well that no such prayer was ever answered. When a politician is sick, they pray for God to cure him, and the politician almost invariably dies. The modern clergyman who prays for rain and for the health of the politician is no more intelligent in this matter than the primitive man who saw a separate miracle in the rising and setting of the sun, in the birth of an individual, in the growth of a plant, in the stroke of lightning, in the flood, in every manifestation of nature and life.

As to prophecies, intelligent writers gave them up long ago. In all prophecies facts are made to suit the prophecy, or the prophecy was made after the facts, or the events have no relation to the prophecy. Weird and strange and unreasonable interpretations are used to explain simple statements, that a prophecy may be claimed.

Can any rational person believe that the Bible is anything but a human document? We now know pretty well where the various books came from, and about when they were written. We know that they were written by human beings who had no knowledge of science, little knowledge of life, and were influenced by the barbarous morality of primitive times, and were ignorant of most things that men know today. For instance, Genesis says that God made the earth, and he made the sun to light the day and the moon to light the night, and in one clause disposes of the stars by saying that "he made the stars also." This was plainly written by someone who had no conception of the stars. Man, by the aid of his telescope, has looked out into the heavens and found stars whose diameter is as great as the distance between the earth and the sun. We know that the universe is filled with stars and suns and planets and systems. Every new telescope looking further into the heavens only discovers more and more worlds and suns and systems in the endless reaches of space. The men who wrote Genesis believed, of course, that this tiny speck of mud that we call the earth was the center of the universe, the only world in space, and made for man, who was the only being worth considering. These men believed that the stars were only a little way above the earth, and were set in the

firmament for man to look at, and for nothing else. Everyone today knows
that this conception is not true.

The origin of the human race is not as blind a subject as it once was.
Let alone God creating Adam out of hand, from the dust of the earth, does
anyone believe that Eve was made from Adam's rib—that the snake
walked and spoke in the Garden of Eden—that he tempted Eve to persuade
Adam to eat an apple, and that it is on that account that the whole
human race was doomed to hell—that for four thousand years there was
no chance for any human to be saved, though none of them had anything
whatever to do with the temptation; and that finally men were saved
only through God's son dying for them, and that unless human beings
believed this silly, impossible and wicked story they were doomed to hell?
Can anyone with intelligence really believe that a child born today should
be doomed because the snake tempted Eve and Eve tempted Adam? To
believe that is not God-worship; it is devil-worship.

Can anyone call this scheme of creation and damnation moral? It
defies every principle of morality, as man conceives morality. Can anyone
believe today that the whole world was destroyed by flood, save only Noah
and his family and a male and female of each species of animal that
entered the Ark? There are almost a million species of insects alone. How
did Noah match these up and make sure of getting male and female to
reproduce life in the world after the flood had spent its force? And why
should all the lower animals have been destroyed? Were they included in
the sinning of man? This is a story which could not beguile a fairly
bright child of five years of age today.

Do intelligent people believe that the various languages spoken by man
on earth came from the confusion of tongues at the Tower of Babel,
some four thousand years ago? Human languages were dispersed all over
the face of the earth long before that time. Evidences of civilizations are
in existence now that were old long before the date that romancers fix
for the building of the Tower, and even before the date claimed for the
flood.

Do Christians believe that Joshua made the sun stand still, so that the
day could be lengthened, that a battle might be finished? What kind of
person wrote that story, and what did he know about astronomy? It
is perfectly plain that the author thought that the earth was the center of
the universe and stood still in the heavens, and that the sun either went
around it or was pulled across its path each day, and that the stopping of
the sun would lengthen the day. We know now that had the sun stopped
when Joshua commanded it, and had it stood still until now, it would not
have lengthened the day. We know that the day is determined by the
rotation of the earth upon its axis, and not by the movement of the sun.
Everyone knows that this story simply is not true, and not many even
pretend to believe the childish fable.

What of the tale of Balaam's ass speaking to him, probably in Hebrew?
Is it true, or is it a fable? Many asses have spoken, and doubtless some
in Hebrew, but they have not been that breed of asses. Is salvation to
depend on a belief in a monstrosity like this?

Above all the rest, would any human being today believe that a child
was born without a father? Yet this story was not at all unreasonable
in the ancient world; at least three or four miraculous births are recorded

in the Bible, including John the Baptist and Samson. Immaculate conceptions were common in the Roman world at the time and at the place where Christianity really had its nativity. Women were taken to the temples to be inoculated of God so that their sons might be heroes, which meant, generally, wholesale butchers. Julius Caesar was a miraculous conception—indeed, they were common all over the world. How many miraculous-birth stories is a Christian now expected to believe?

In the days of the formation of the Christian religion, disease meant the possession of human beings by devils. Christ cured a sick man by casting out the devils, who ran into the swine, and the swine ran into the sea. Is there any question but what that was simply the attitude and belief of a primitive people? Does anyone believe that sickness means the possession of the body by devils, and that the devils must be cast out of the human being that he may be cured? Does anyone believe that a dead person can come to life? The miracles recorded in the Bible are not the only instances of dead men coming to life. All over the world one finds testimony of such miracles: miracles which no person is expected to believe, unless it is his kind of a miracle. Still at Lourdes today, and all over the present world, from New York to Los Angeles and up and down the lands, people believe in miraculous occurrences, and even in the return of the dead. Superstition is everywhere prevalent in the world. It has been so from the beginning, and most likely will be so unto the end.

The reasons for agnosticism are abundant and compelling. Fantastic and foolish and impossible consequences are freely claimed for the belief in religion. All the civilization of any period is put down as a result of religion. All the cruelty and error and ignorance of the period has no relation to religion. The truth is that the origin of what we call civilization is not due to religion but to skepticism. So long as men accepted miracles without question, so long as they believed in original sin and the road to salvation, so long as they believed in a hell where man would be kept for eternity on account of Eve, there was no reason whatever for civilization: life was short, and eternity was long, and the business of life was preparation for eternity.

When every event was a miracle, when there was no order or system or law, there was no occasion for studying any subject, or being interested in anything excepting a religion which took care of the soul. As man doubted the primitive conceptions about religion, and no longer accepted the literal, miraculous teachings of ancient books, he set himself to understand nature. We no longer cure disease by casting out devils. Since that time, men have studied the human body, have built hospitals and treated illness in a scientific way. Science is responsible for the building of railroads and bridges, of steamships, of telegraph lines, of cities, towns, large buildings and small, plumbing and sanitation, of the food supply, and the countless thousands of useful things that we now deem necessary to life. Without skepticism and doubt, none of these things could have been given to the world.

The fear of God is not the beginning of wisdom. The fear of God is the death of wisdom. Skepticism and doubt lead to study and investigation, and investigation is the beginning of wisdom.

The modern world is the child of doubt and inquiry, as the ancient world was the child of fear and faith.*

Questions of Content

1. What is Darrow's thesis in this essay? Can you find any discrepancy between what Darrow says his purpose is in the first paragraph and what you feel his real aim is?

2. Like Lewis, Darrow offers many opinions in support of his argument. Find at least two of these opinions and determine what definitions they hinge upon. What support does Darrow offer for these definitions?

3. Find several causal supports in the essay. Does Darrow assume these causal statements will be self-evident, or does he offer insight into why he accepts them?

4. Does Darrow offer any facts, figures, or statistics in support of his argument? If so, are they used effectively?

5. Assuming that you oppose Darrow's argument, can you find any places where his reasoning can be questioned? If so, explain these problems in terms of our discussion of fallacies in this chapter.

Questions of Structure

1. Divide the essay into its three parts—beginning, middle, and end.

2. What objections to his thesis does Darrow anticipate? Where do his refutations come? All at one place or throughout the essay?

3. In addition to definitional and causal supports, Darrow uses a good many comparisons. Find at least three different comparisons. What is being compared to what? How does Darrow use these comparisons to support his thesis?

Questions of Tone

1. How would you describe Darrow's attitude toward those who oppose his argument? Are there places where he insults them? How is someone opposed to his argument likely to react to Darrow's argument? To Darrow himself?

2. There is at least one place where Darrow uses humor in his essay. How would you characterize this humor? We said earlier that Lewis does not take himself too seriously, in that he aims his humor, at least in part, at himself. At whom or what does Darrow aim his humor? What will be the effect of this humor on those opposed to Darrow's argument?

From Verdicts Out of Court by Arthur Weinberg and Lila Weinberg. Quadrangle Books, 1963. Used with permission of the Clarence Darrow estate.

Shaping an Argument

Respond to one or both of the following writing assignments.

1. Write an essay in which you compare Lewis's essay to Darrow's essay. When writing this comparison, you may want to consider such questions as the following.

   a. What audience was each writer addressing? Is there a difference between the apparent audience and the real audience for either of the essays? If so, how do you account for this difference?

   b. Is there a difference in the quality of the reasoning in the two essays? If so, how would you characterize this difference?

   c. Is there a discrepancy between the stated purpose and the real purpose in either of the essays? That is, both essays purport to be persuasive in aim. Are they? If not, what is the purpose of each? How well does it achieve the author's real aim?

2. Write an essay that takes the opposing view to either Lewis's or Darrow's essay.

WRITING ASSIGNMENT

Write an argument of 1000 to 1500 words on one of the following topics. When you choose an audience, select one that would be indifferent, at best, or mildly hostile, at worst, to the point you wish to argue.

1. Given the proliferation of telecommunications, why should we study writing? Or even write, for that matter? (Or, why should we not study writing?)

2. Should some sort of military or public service be mandatory for everyone, either at age eighteen or within three months of graduation from high school, whichever occurs later?

3. Should the electoral college be abolished so that the president of the United States is elected directly by popular vote?

4. Are there required courses in your major that should not be required? What requirements or options would you suggest in place of these requirements?

5. To what extent does your college meet the needs of its students? *Needs* may be defined as broadly as you think necessary, so that you can talk about academic needs, recreational needs, and so on. How does your college fall short, if it does? What remedies can you offer?

6. Are there environmental issues with which you are directly concerned? Has, for example, one of your favorite spots been threatened by pollution, encroaching civilization, bureaucrats, and so forth? If so, how should these issues be resolved?

Chapter Eight

Writing a Persuasive Essay

TYPES OF PERSUASION

In our last chapter we discussed the role of argument in human interactions. In this chapter we will apply the principles of argumentation to writing a persuasive essay. Argument is but one means of persuading. We can illustrate this point by returning to our example offered near the beginning of Chapter Seven. One means of persuading the father to part with the family car on Saturday night is to develop an argument as to why he should do so. There are other ways, however. The son could attempt to make his father feel sorry for him by allowing the father to overhear a conversation with a friend, the gist of which is that if he does not get the car on Saturday his girlfriend will not date him any longer. This would not be a good argument to offer to the father, because he would probably conclude that such a girlfriend is not worthy of his son in the first place. Presented, however, not as an argument but as a piece of (overheard) information that can have its effect on the emotions, it could work.

This example illustrates two of the three different ways of persuading that Aristotle offered in his *Rhetoric*. The first is to persuade by the force of a reasoned argument. Aristotle's name for this type of persuasion was *logos*, from which we derive the word *logical*. This, of course, is the type of argument we discussed in the previous chapter, the kind illustrated by a son's attempt to convince his father that he should have the car by defining words so that the father will come to see things his way.

As our example illustrates, reason is not the only tool we use in persuading. Aristotle's name for a second type of persuasion was *pathos*, from which we derive the word *pathetic*. Humans are not thinking machines; that is, they can be persuaded to act in certain ways by emotional appeals, even when logic would dictate that they should act in another way. Or, in other situations, they need emotional persuaders to help them to act in what they have already determined to be a logical fashion but have not been able to follow through on. An example is the antismoking commercial that offers not facts and figures on the connection between smoking and certain diseases but a scene in which a young child tells her father she loves him as he debates whether to light the cigarette in his mouth.

Aristotle called the third tool of persuasion *ethos*, from which we derive the word *ethical*. Our previous example is not suited to illustrate this type of persuasion because of the close relation between the father and child. However, in most persuasive situations, the writer uses language in such a way to show herself to be a trustworthy and ethical person. Audiences are generally willing to make compromises with such a person. But when the language of the writer shows that she is refusing to enter into the persuasive situation in good faith, that is, to respect the rights and opinions of those opposed to her point of view or to offer reasonable arguments, the critical audience is not likely to be persuaded.

Despite the divisions outlined in the previous paragraphs, we must remember that these three types of persuasion are all parts of one process. To a great extent the ethical appeal of a writer rests on the character of his logical and emotional appeal. Also, contrary to what our rather simplified definitions may imply, logic and emotion are actually inseparable. Whenever we use *argument*—in the sense of the term developed in Chapter Seven—we must use words and, thus, elicit emotional reactions from readers. It is true that certain words appeal more to our emotions (and are, thus, more connotative) than other words. For example, such words as *brat, darling, scoundrel,* and *cheapskate* appeal almost entirely to our emotions, whereas words such as *child, boy, girl,* and *mailman* are primarily denotative. However, even such words as these in the latter list can become highly connotative, and thus emotionally charged, in certain situations. For example, when a slave-owner referred to a forty-year-old man as a *boy,* that name was charged with the feelings of that slave-owner toward the black man. As we will see in Sydney Harris's "A Guide to Dirty Words," the same would be true in a situation in which a twenty-five-year-old male executive referred to his forty-five-year-old secretary as his *girl*. Try as we might, we will always find it impossible to keep our emotions from surfacing in the language that we choose to describe a situation. As these emotions surface, our readers will be affected by the connotations in our language.

     Find an advertisement that attempts to convince you by the logic of its argument, a second advertisement that uses an emotional appeal, and a third based on the ethical appeal of the person used in the advertisement or of the company itself. After you have analyzed these advertisements, answer the following questions.

1. What kinds of emotional appeal or ethical appeal could the writers of the "logical" advertisement have used? Why do you suppose they chose a logical appeal instead?

2. What emotion, or emotions, does the second advertisement appeal to? Would it be possible to use a logical appeal in place of this emotional appeal?

3. What logical or emotional appeals could the writers of the third advertisement have used? Why do you suppose they elected to depend primarily upon ethical appeal?

EXERCISE

Read the following essay, Sydney Harris's "A Guide to Dirty Words," and answer the questions that follow it.

A Guide to Dirty Words
Sydney J. Harris

My column a few weeks ago, about derogatory words that at first designated both sexes and then were applied only to women, brought in the mail a copy of a recent booklet, "An Intelligent Woman's Guide to Dirty Words."

The "dirty words," of course, are not necessarily obscene in the ordinary sense. They are dirty to women in the sense that they derogate and depreciate her gender, her role, her function, and her status.

Listed as Volume One of "The Feminist English Dictionary," this bristling little booklet demonstrates how over the centuries our language has been manipulated to depict woman as "whore," "body," "animal," and other epithets and stereotypes that reinforce both conscious and unconscious male chauvinism.

"Girl" can be a "dirty word" in some contexts—such as one executive to another, "Have your girl phone me when you're ready for lunch" when the "girl" is 45 years old, has worked there longer, and puts in a more conscientious day for the company than the executive does. (No one would say of an adult male secretary, "Have your boy call me . . . ")

Our language, devised and structured by men, since women were not permitted to have an education until a century or so ago, contains relatively few deprecatory words for men, but hundreds for women.

There are few, or no, male equivalents for such terms as "bag," "bat," "witch," "chippy," "cow," "dog," "floozy," "hussy," "mol," "quail," "slut," "pig," "tart," "tramp," "trollop," "chick," "dish," "doll," "fluff," "hag," "hoyden," "wench," "crone," "filly," "hen," "ball-and-chain," "battle-ax," "harpy," "old maid," "shrew," and countless others unfit for listing in a family newspaper.

Language, we must remember, is not merely a medium of communication, the way a telephone line or a cable is a medium. Actually, the medium of language colors the message in a profound way we may be unconscious of. What we call the "real world" is built up on the language habits of the society we belong to.

Writing a Persuasive Essay

When Tom Sawyer's aunt remarked of the ship explosion, "Thank God, nobody was hurt—only two niggers killed," this otherwise kindly woman was being satirized by Mark Twain for failing to see that her language equated blacks with "nobody," and unconsciously reinforced her view of the world. The scores of epithets men use about women do precisely the same—which is why Confucius advised that any real reform of society must begin with the correct use of words.*

1. In his third paragraph Harris says that men have used language to stereotype women. As we said in Chapter Seven, stereotyping is a means of placing value judgments on all the individuals within a certain group. What value judgments are implied by *bag, cow, mol, slut, filly,* and *hen*? (Another way of asking this question would be, What do you associate with each of these terms, and what is the effect of attributing those associations to the human beings referred to by these terms?)

2. Harris quotes Confucius as saying that "any real reform of society must begin with the correct use of words." Obviously, Harris is talking specifically about negative value judgments that come about as the result of stereotyping. Can you think of situations in which actions or events have been made to seem better than they really are by our failure to use language correctly?

3. In his title Harris plays with the rather juvenile connotations of the term *dirty.* Later in the article he says that some of the words that he is about to deal with are dirty even though they are not necessarily obscene. What do you think Harris means by *dirty*? What, according to him, would be an obscene word? Are you able to think of a word (not mentioned by Harris) that he would consider dirty? ·

As Harris's article demonstrates, and as we have said throughout this text, our language does much more than transmit messages. It conveys our attitudes and viewpoints. The writer who begins an argument against abortion by calling it "legalized murder" reveals an attitude that makes it impossible for her to truly communicate with a person in favor of abortion. A person who has been called a murderer or told that she is in favor of murder will not continue to listen. By the same token there is little impetus for the writer to put herself in the place of the reader and understand what it would take to convince him to view abortion differently—the writer is convinced that the reader is unreasonable.

This last statement brings up important considerations for the shaper of any argument: The writer must ask to what audience she is directing the argument and how she wishes to interact with that audience. The failure to recognize the importance of these considerations often causes the writer to employ language not suited to her persuasive purpose. She does so because of misconcep-

---

*Reprinted by permission of Sydney J. Harris and Field Newspaper Syndicate.

tions concerning the persuasive process, misconceptions that may arise from the popular argumentation she is exposed to. For example, she may read an article in a local newspaper, perhaps an open letter to the boxing commission, in which a writer asks the members of the commission just how long they intend to continue supporting "legalized murder." Or, she may see one presidential candidate in a debate with another candidate refer to that person's economic policies as "Voodoo Economics." Because she respects these individuals, she may come to think that such tactics are effective persuasive tools. Though these tactics can be effective, they must be used only when the writer has no hope of convincing her opponent and is, thus, attempting to convince a neutral third party by attacking her opponent. The person supposedly writing to the boxing commission is in truth attempting to convince the paper's readers who have very little personal involvement with the argument, and these readers may be moved toward the writer's position by this emotionally charged language. The same is true in the hypothetical presidential debate. The person arguing against another presidential candidate has very little hope of convincing the other candidate to reconsider his point of view and call off the race. However, the emotionally charged language could help win over noncommitted voters and is not likely to cost the speaker anything as far as the other candidate is concerned—unless, of course, there comes a time when he would like to be considered as a vice-presidential candidate on the ticket with that other candidate.

These are the types of persuasive situations that receive the most publicity and, thus, the ones we recall when writing a persuasive piece. However, they make up only a small percentage of the persuasive situations we face in our everyday lives. Far more typical is our example of a son or daughter attempting to persuade a parent to grant car privileges for a weekend. In such a situation this kind of emotionally charged language can backfire. How many parents will be able to hold onto their objectivity after being told that their *primitive* views of child rearing are astonishing? Not many. Most teenagers who really want the car for an important Saturday date and who think they have a chance of getting it know enough about persuasion to avoid such language. Nevertheless, you may have rendered your writing ineffective by using such strong language when you have written persuasion papers for college courses or letters to the editor of the college paper.

Why did you make such errors? Probably you transferred what you know about "real" persuasive situations to these "academic" situations. You can remedy these problems quite simply by asking one question: Do I hope to convince the person or persons to whom this argument is addressed? If you do, you are going to have to take some risks in the persuasive process.

In order to explain just what we mean by this last statement, we need to refer to statements made in Chapters Two and Seven. You will remember that in Chapter Two we made the point, by means of the optical illusions, that the same experience or phenomenon can look different from different perspectives. In Chapter Seven, we discovered that at the heart of all true arguments is some basic difference in the way individuals are using language to interpret their worlds. If we hope to change the viewpoint of a reader, we must come to

Writing a Persuasive Essay

understand the essential difference between the way she is using language and the way we are using language. We must place ourselves in her position so thoroughly as to be able to state her point of view in language she can accept. For example, if we are against abortion and our reader is for it, we must avoid saying that an advocate of abortion wants to "kill innocent unborns." A proponent of abortion is bound to reject such a judgment on our part as ludicrous. Rather, we would have to say that she is for some method of preventing the suffering and pain that often follow when seriously deformed children are born into the world or when children are born to parents who do not want them or who do not have the ability to care for them. We may think that her language is hiding some important facets of abortion from her and we may set ourselves the task of revealing just how this is so, but if we are to do so, we must begin by demonstrating an understanding of her point of view through the language we use in describing that viewpoint.

As we said earlier, there are some risks involved in this process. When we attempt to understand the language of those opposed to our argument, we may well find that our language has hidden certain things from us and that we must rethink our position, or aspects of that position, from the standpoint of the new insights we have gained in the process of understanding the language used by our opponents.

<table>
<tr><td>EXERCISE</td><td>A network newscaster conducted an interview with a high-ranking government official. The official was under fire for spending money to remodel his offices and for renting a limousine and engaging the services of a chauffeur at a time when the services provided to citizens by his agency were being reduced because of budget cuts. In response to the second charge, the official said that he put in fifteen-hour days, from 7 A.M. to 10 P.M., as it was and that the car and driver were necessary to allow him to conduct the business he had to conduct in the various parts of the city. The implication was that if he had to wait on taxis or use public transit systems, his long day would become longer. Consider the following questions regarding this exchange.</td></tr>
</table>

1. The newscaster, in the role of adversary, chose to refer to the automobile and its operator as a *limousine* and a *chauffeur*. The official chose to call them a *car* and a *driver*. What is the emotional impact of each word? Were they proper choices for each of the speakers? If so, why?

2. Can you say that one of these persons chose language that more correctly represented the phenomena being discussed? Would you call the tactics of either person deceitful?

3. If each speaker examined with an open mind the language of the other speaker, what new insights might each get? What subsequent changes in point of view and/or actions could conceivably result?

In Chapter Seven, we suggested several argumentative topics; in all likelihood, you have already written one or more papers with a persuasive aim. In doing so, you may well have employed some of the prewriting practices we have demonstrated in our earlier chapters. At this point, however, we would like to introduce another writing assignment in the form of the assignments offered in those previous chapters.

WRITING ASSIGNMENT

Write a persuasive essay about a topic that you know a good deal about and/or would like to learn about by researching it. Your task in this essay will be to shape an essay that will be persuasive to an audience composed of people who disagree with you on this topic.

The sample paper in this chapter was written by Ron Lunsford, one of the authors of this text. We hope to make several important points in offering this sample essay. The first, and perhaps most important, is that writing is a process. No one sits down and composes a finished draft from thin air. Another point we wish to make is that even though people are supposedly "rational" animals, none of us, not even writers of chapters on argumentation, forms his or her opinions in a cold, calculating, "Mr. Spock" fashion. We do not carefully weigh the evidence and plug it into our "computer" brain and produce an objective, reasonable opinion. Rather, we form an opinion subjectively and then cast about for evidence to support that opinion. Our purpose in this chapter will not be to attempt to change this process—it is too much a part of human nature—but to help you develop your abilities to find support for your opinions and your critical skills so that you will know when you cannot find the proper support and, thus, when it is necessary to modify or give up a point of view.

One final purpose in presenting one of our own papers is to illustrate once again the process that we have outlined in this text. Ron wrote this paper after that process was fully developed and had been used by many students in the classes of both authors; he came to the paper intending to follow the process faithfully. But, as will be evident, he had to modify the procedure slightly to allow his own writing process to take over. At one point he added a step to the process, because he was not ready to move on to the next prescribed step.

Before we enter the first step, we will outline the entire process once again.

Step 1: Freewrite
Step 2: Select and Examine Your Topic
Step 3: Devise a Planning Page
Step 4: Write a Discovery Draft
Step 5: Select and Analyze Your Audience
Step 6: Write a Second Draft
Step 7: Write a Final Draft

Freewrite

As before, the first step in a persuasive essay is to freewrite. The following is Ron's freewriting.

> I am interested in the criminal system of our country. It seems to me that something has to be done, if we are to survive as a country. I certainly don't know what the answers to our problems are, things certainly get complicated in a hurry when you get into them, but I wonder if something couldn't be done to deal with some of these problems. One thing I am concerned about is our practice of putting offenders in jail who have not harmed anyone. Why not work out some system whereby they can pay back the debts they owe society rather than incurring another debt by going to prison and, of course, coming under the influence of hardened criminals. I am also concerned about the short prison sentences people are serving for heinous crimes. Of course one alternative to this is to reinstate capital punishment, but I'm not sure I would be for that. I'm not sure it is right to take an eye for an eye. The alternative to capital punishment is longer sentences, but they would certainly cost the taxpayers much money. I also think we must do something about the insanity plea. In my opinion, anyone who takes another person's life intentionally is insane; however, that does not mean that the person is not guilty of the crime, or that he should not pay society the debt owed. It's, of course, sad that some people may have to spend the rest of their lives, or a large part of them, in prison for acts that they committed while not in full possession of their faculties. However, the difficulty of proving just who is in possession of his faculties—at the time of trial and at the time of possible release—make this the lesser of two evils. There is a sense in which the attempt to incorporate an insanity plea into our system is a failure to recognize our limitations as human beings. We just do not have the wisdom to mete out the proper decisions.

Ron's freewriting may not be typical of what most people will produce. Although Ron did not intend to do so, he developed a focus around the problems with criminal justice quite quickly. His first thoughts concerned problems in this system, and he found himself devoting all of his allotted time to this topic. Ron's freewriting may also be different in that it seems quite ordered, almost like an outline. This was not the result of his intention, but rather of quite a bit of thinking about the matters in the days and weeks preceding this freewriting. He was now taking the time to put down these thoughts.

You should not be concerned if your freewriting is much less organized than this example. After all, the freewriting stage is designed to allow you to explore ideas to see what topics you are interested in. However, if you have been giving a good bit of thought to a controversial matter, your freewriting may take on quite a bit of order as did Ron's.

Another thing you will notice about Ron's freewriting is its abstract, discursive nature. He is not talking about the man down the street who has been in and out of jail five times in the last ten years, or about his Uncle Bill who was mugged on the streets of a large city. Rather, he is dealing with abstractions such as the insanity plea and the prison sentences handed down by our courts. This kind of discursive writing is the result of many specific examples that he has been aware of within the last few years. His freewriting, and certainly his final paper, could have been enriched by narratives of such specifics. As it turns out, he became lost in these abstract thoughts and never got around to the specifics. If you find yourself struggling for something to write about in the freewriting stage, you should try to make abstract argument topics more personal. If you are interested in gun control, but do not know exactly why or what to say about the subject, rely on your experiences. How many people do you know who own guns? What do they use or intend to use the guns for? How safe do they seem to be with these guns? If personal experiences are not forthcoming, think about your reading. What newspaper stories do you remember that are relevant to this issue? Have you read relevant editorials? In short, allow your mind the freedom to retrieve the pieces of information you have stored on this subject.

WRITING ASSIGNMENT

Step 1   For the next fifteen minutes write about any controversial subjects you have been concerned with recently. Recount any personal experiences or write about any readings relevant to these subjects. Do not be concerned with grammatical or mechanical matters.

Select and Examine Your Topic

The following are Ron's answers to the Questions for Analysis of his topic.

QUESTIONS
FOR
ANALYSIS

Topic

Short prison sentences given to violent criminals

What goes with short sentences?

What physical entities go with short sentences?

Rather plush prisons with TV's, exercise rooms, tennis and basketball courts, swimming pools, etc.

Overcrowded prisons

What do you associate with short sentences?

An increase in serious crimes.

An increasingly hazardous environment for those law abiding citizens subjected to these people.

In what context are short sentences set?

A society obsessed with the rights of its citizens

A society greatly affected by Behavioral psychology

A selfish society of people unwilling to take unpopular causes until some member of their own family is a victim.

                                              Writing a Persuasive Essay

What opposes short sentences?

    What theoretical or philosophical opposition is there to *X*?

        Those who believe that longer prison sentences would deter this type of crime.

        Those who fear what these people will do to society as soon as they are released.

    How do short sentences stand out against their context?

        The suffering of the affected families as compared to the punishment meted out to these felons

        Stands out against a society supposedly concerned with human rights of the individual

        Stands out against a free society which places great stress on freedom of movement and freedom from duress for its citizens

        Stands out against a society which values life

    How are short sentences unlike other similar things?

        Unlike the prison systems in other countries

        Unlike the rather harsh punishments meted out at times for lesser offenses

What follows or follows from short sentences?

    What follows short sentences chronologically?

        More convicted criminals free in our society

        More recidivism

    How did short sentences come to be?

        More and more emphasis has been placed on rehabilitation

        The change has come gradually so that the public has been lulled into accepting this phenomenon

    What are the causes of short sentences?

        Overcrowded prisons

        Behavioristic philosophy

        Rehabilitative theory in penology

    What sort of problem do short sentences pose?

        Eventually could lead to vigilante attitude among citizens

        Endangers our society of laws

    What are its solutions?

        Longer sentences with less opportunity for early parole

        More emphasis on prisoners earning their own way

When selecting a topic, you should remember two things: (1) the actual way in which you phrase the topic is important, but (2) the selection of topic at this stage is not the final word. As you will see, Ron found it necessary to narrow his topic quite a bit before he plugged it into the Questions for Analysis. At first he planned to talk about sentences given to serious offenders. However, as he began to ask the questions, he found it more helpful to treat his topic as the "short prison sentences being given to violent criminals." Thus, when he asked what these short sentences caused, he could examine implications that he would not have been able to see had the topic been in its original form. Actually what he was doing at this stage—in choosing "short prison sentences" rather than "prison sentences"—was committing himself to a point of view regarding this controversial topic; that is, he was implying that these sentences are too short. He knew he could have to change, or at least modify, his point of view, but he felt it would be difficult to continue analyzing this argumentative topic without placing the analysis within the framework of his viewpoint.

But, as we said earlier, Ron realized that this statement of topic was not the final word. At one point later in the process, Ron considered completely changing his topic to "the parole system in the U.S." As it turns out, he did not do so, but if he had, the work at this stage would not have been useless if it helped him find exactly what he did want to talk about.

Ron's answers to the Questions for Analysis provide us with an opportunity to examine the thinking of a "logical" person. Note that he associated "an increase in serious crimes" with these shorter prison terms. Note also that he accuses our society of being "selfish" and "unwilling to take unpopular causes." These are but two examples of unsupported generalizations he makes here. If such statements were to appear in an essay with no proof, as they do here, we would see them as examples of faulty reasoning. However, they are perfectly acceptable here, because Ron's purpose is not to convince an audience but rather to find exactly what he thinks about this topic. Later he will have to examine each of these beliefs to see whether he can find any support for them and, as he continues in the process, many of these assertions will have to be modified or given up completely.

Step 2   Select a topic and answer as many of the Questions for Analysis as are relevant to that topic.

Devise a Planning Page

As we have seen in the previous examples of the writing process in Chapters Four and Six, the Planning Page is designed to provide some order for the first draft of an essay. As was the case in Chapter Six, the Planning Page makes use of a Lead Sentence, which gives the writer some insight into the overall structure of the upcoming draft. But, whereas the nonargumentative transactional essay lends itself to three types of Lead Sentences—definitional, causal, and evaluative—arguments lend themselves to only two: definitional and causal. The reason for this limitation should be fairly obvious from our discussion in Chapter Seven of the roles of definition and causal analysis in the support of arguments.

This is not to suggest that the writer will structure an argument entirely on causal or definitional arguments, but rather that as he enters the argument, one of these methods of argumentation will seem to be predominant. The writer can make the decision as to which is central by referring to his Questions for Analysis. If he is attracted to the materials generated by the association and opposition questions, it may well be that he is leaning toward a definitional argument. If, on the other hand, he is drawn to information generated by the what-follows-what? question, he may be leaning toward a causal argument.

As we have said, the writer's purpose at this stage is not to commit to either method exclusively—many arguments will contain both processes—but simply to get some insight into how he may structure a first draft. As will be obvious in Ron's process, the writer may well change his Lead Sentence from the first to the second or third draft.

Once the writer has decided upon a Lead Sentence, he can then compose Topic Sentences by studying the information in his answers to the Questions for Analysis. The following is Ron's Planning Page.

PLANNING PAGE

Lead sentence	Behaviorism and a rehabilitative philosophy of penology cause short prison sentences which in turn cause many bad things in our society.
Topic sentences	Behaviorism has caused short prison sentences.
	The rehabilitative philosophy of penology has caused short prison sentences.
	Short prison sentences cause great increase in crime.
	Increase in crime causes law abiding citizens to develop a vigilante mentality.

This Planning Page prepares Ron to write an argument paper structured by serial causation; that is, he will attempt to show what factors in our society cause these short prison terms and what the chain of effects of these sentences has been. As we will see, Ron will abandon this structure after the first draft, but it does provide him with a starting place.

Step 3   After you have answered the Questions for Analysis and studied your responses, write a Planning Page for the first draft.

Write a Discovery Draft

With this Planning Page as a guide, Ron wrote the following draft.

WRITING SAMPLE	Persuasion
First draft	~~We have heard a good deal about our system of justice in~~

                    been the subject of
Our judicial system has ~~come in for~~ a good bit of discussion recently.

              the
~~To~~ Judging from ~~this~~ comments of ~~the man on~~ people ranging from "the

man on the street" to the jurors themselves, the judicial system has

been weighed in the balances and found wanting. The outrage that the

public seems ~~x~~to feel over the "not guilty by reason of insanity"

verdict rended by ~~the~~ John Hi*n*ckl*e*y, Jr(?)'s jury may well lead to re-

form of the insanity ~~laws~~ plea. P~~h~~erhaps, we *do* need to ~~xxxxxx~~ ~~look at~~ *rethink*

this complicated issue, *b*~~B~~ut in ~~charging~~ *attacking* this issue so vociferously,

we may well be straining at the pr*o*verbial nat and swallowing a camel.

~~That possibility was reared by~~ A comment by on e of the Hickley

jurors--in justifying the jury's *verdict* ~~action--should have received more~~ seems to have been lost in
the uproar created by those
~~thoughtful attention that~~   calling for reform of this insanity plea.

That juror's ~~comment~~ observation that Hickley may well spend more

time in actual confinement as a result of this insanity plea than he

would had he been convicted of the charges of ________________ ~~should~~

is worthy of more attention than we ~~x~~ given it. It is true. Had

Hi*n*ckl*e*y been ~~x~~convicted, he would have received a sentence of

___________ , with a possibility of being paroled in _______________ .

The bottom line is that he very well cou*j*ld have been back on the

streets in __________ years, and he certainly would have been, in

__________ years. Certainly, we have a right to be upset if we think

the ~~plea~~ insanity plea is ~~causing~~ ~~alloing~~ providing a few accused

murdersrs with a looph*ole*~~illw~~ which they can use to avoid conviction.

We should, however, be much more concerned over the fact that, given

the prison terms for attempted murder and murder, ~~and~~ *the* accused murder-

er has a rather difficult decision to make as to whether he/~~she~~

should avail hims*/*elf of this insanity plea.

Just how have these "wrist slapping" sentences evolved in our

judicial system? There are, no doubt, many factors involved, but in

this brief essay I should like to focus our attention on three of

them. The first, and perhaps most important, is the influence Behav-

iorism has had on 20th century America. ~~With~~ the work of~~xk~~B.F. Skin-

ner (b. 19   ) and his followers has changed the way we feel about

Writing a Persuasive Essay

"responsibility." Of course, Skinner was not the first scientist/

philosopher to b concerned with the causes of behavoir and the con-

sequent responsibility of the individual for his/her bbehavior. Sig-

mund Frued is famous for this ftheories concerning these matters. But

it was Skinner ~~who captured the~~ whose work ~~directly and~~

~~indirectly~~ has, directly and indirectly, shaped our views concerning be-

havior. Skinner has theorized, and to his satisfaction proved, that

an organism--any org. including "human organisms--can be made to do   *where does this quote end?*

virtually anything by the proper stimuli. The is behavioristic phil-

osophy has ~~triggered the work~~ caused us to be as concerned ~~if not~~

~~more con~~ with the causes of a murderer's actions as we are with ~~its~~ *their*

effects. When we investigate the horrible childhoods ~~and~~ of ~~this~~ *these*

felons and reflect that "but for the grace of God," it is little

wonder that we can be moved to lighten ~~our sentences~~ their sentences.
                 but related,
        A second, cause for these sentences is the rehabilitative phil-

osophy which has come to prevail in penology. Experts in the field

no longer see prison as chiefly designed to punish the perpetrators
                                    from
of crimes or to protect citizens fox these offenders;xbxxkx fax rather

prisons exist primarily to take pxx unfortunate individuals who, be-

cause of some negative factors in their lives, have been driven to a

life of crime and to transform them into upstanding citizens. It

stands to reason that if that is the purpose of prisonx (and if one

believes the task possible), it is as likely, if not more likely, to

be accomplish in five or ten years than in twenty to twenty five years.

Thus those who believe in this rehabilitive philsophy support these
                                  u
mild sentences which are plaging our society.

        A final cause fot these sentences is selfishness on the part of

uninvolved citizens. Many citizens do not agree with the philoso-

phies underlying our treatment of these felons, but in this "enlight-

ened"age it is not very popular, espectally among educated people, to

be for "repressive" treatment of prisoners. Thus, rather than to make waves for themserves, many citizens float along with the tide,

until some tragedy strikes close to home. Then, in many cases the

facade is dropped and the affected citizen cries for a more just sys-

tem--but to late for the loved.one who has been injured or killed.

These, then, are the causes for the sentencing practices of our

courts. With the exception of the last, reltively minor cause, they

are not terriblay controversial. That is, even those people who

are in faovr of these sentences would, for the most part, agree with

that behavioristic rehab. philsophies are

greatly responsiblef for the changes that have occurred in sen-

tanceing practices. However, they

conveniently ignore what this lenient atmosphere is causing in our

society.

The primary effect of these shortened sentences is an increase

in the number of innocent victims in our xsociety.

Since our courst have abandoned capital punishment

and have shortened the actual time in prison for many violent crimes,

every year sees an increase in serious crimes And

this increase cannot be explained away with population growth, because

the percentage of serious crimes committed per citizen is constantly

riseng. Certainly these shortened senteneces can-

not be seen as the sole cause of the problem, but a brief examination

of the rates of recidivism nationwide would support a claim that it is

a major factor. (Find support for these assertions)

If our society is going to survive as we know it, something has to

be done about this problem. Our larger cities are already greatly

threatened by the reactions of normal "law abiding" citizens. In many

cases, citizens are forming neighborhood watch groups (with the approval

of local police departments) the purpose of which is to patrol the

streets and to prevent violent crimes. These groups are not far removed

from the vigilante groups of the old west, and they are anathama to the

Writing a Persuasive Essay

American system. As the citizenry begins to arm and train itself, we head toward a society where "might makes right," a society of guns and gurella warfare rhathter than a society of laws and legal redress. As citizens watch the courts swing wide the prison gates, releasing convicted criminals to make walking the streets a harrowing experience, they feel it necessary to protect themselves. This means that they must take upon themselves decisions that officers of the court have been duly sworn to take. A proprietor of a liquor sx store or other small shop is more than liely better armed than the poiicumuax policeman walking or driving the beat. When a suspicious person enters his shop, this proprietor a will, often, not wait for this person to "get the drop" on him and take his money and, perhaps, his life. Raﬔer, he ioi will draw his weapon and order the person out of his store. In some cases a robbery aad (and imurderø) is prevented in others an innocent citizen is (athe "suspécious x character") is unnecessarily harrassed, and in other, more drastic cases, a shopewner is killed by a skilled robbbr or an innocent, but br frieghtened

xhopkeepex

citizen is injured or killed by an untrained and frightened shopkeeper.

Of course, it could be argued that the unfortunate events described in the preceding paragraph are not directly attributable to the lower sentences handed out by our courts. While the causal connected is difficult to prove absolutely, ikxisx there is strong evidence that it exists. Thexfaetxisx that more and more convicted *It is a fact* *persons* *of violent crimes* murderers are being released into our society. A second fact is that more and more of these murderers are committing additional murders. And finally, it is a fact that thecitizenry is armed as never before (find proof of this). The connection between the numbers of potentially kxiøgex dangerous (to themselves and others) armed citizens and the numbers of relaøased felons is not hard to make.

It is ironic that what has begun as *a* movement in keeping with the country's founding philosophy of freedom the respect for the worth and inalienable rights of the individual has degenerated into a snare which has the effect of taking away freedom and the rights of individual citizens. Those people who have pushed for reform in sentencing of convicted felons have pushed for reform in sentencing of convicted felons have often done so for the best of reasons. They have been concerned with the inherent worth of of individuals, those inds. convicted of the serious crime of murder. However, in guarding the "rights" of these people, they have overlooked the rights of other citizens: the right to run a shop without living in constant fear that a released felon will robe and (possibly) kill you, the right to take the subway home without fear of being molested and ossibly killed, the right to walk your dog without constantly looking over your shouldered to make certain you are not being stalked, and, finally, the right to enjoy a night's rest in your home without worrying that a *burglar* will intrude upon the sanctity of that home and possible injury you and/or your loved ones. These rights are sacred; they take precedence over the rights of any convicted felon.

But if we are convinced that something should be done about these sentances, what can we do about them? The immediate objection is likely to be that prisons are dangerously overcrow*d*ed now and that a change in sentencing policies would be the last straw which would push the entire prison system under. Th*is* is certainly a serious problem, one that should bthoroughly investigated before any actions are taken. The taxpayers are already suffering a great burde*n* for the present penal system. The average cost of keeping a prison *person in* for a year *is* __________ If we tack on extra years at ~~souh~~ *such* a cost *per* prisoner, we could soon ba*n*krupt

our system. But aren't there other solutions? Why does it cost us
so much per year to keep a prisoner incarcerated? Has it always cost
us this much? What changes could we make in the phil. of penology
that would lower this cost? These are questions that we should ask
ØØXSRïŒRS and find answers for, for XØØSØRS our society cannot toler-
ate any longer the cnntinual relase of convicted felons into its midst.

As we have already said, the purpose of the first draft is to find out what
the writer thinks. Ron is thinking on paper. Note the first paragraph in which
he leaves blanks at crucial places concerning sentences for convicted felons. He
does not know exactly what these are, but he thinks they are too short. Of
course, research into the matter could completely change the complexion of his
essay, but at this point he is just getting his ideas on paper.

The essay is filled with unsupported assertions. He says that behavioristic
philosophy has caused us to be as concerned with the causes of a criminal's
actions as with the consequences, that experts in the field no longer see prison
as chiefly designed to punish criminals, that many citizens do not agree with
the philosophy underlying our treatment of these felons, and so forth—all with
no support. What makes him think that behavioristic philosophy has caused
these effects, or that experts no longer see prison as punishment? He gives no
insight into how he formed these opinions.

The key to Ron's failure to support these assertions and to the subsequent
major changes that he makes in the next draft of his paper is in paragraph 5 of
this first draft. There he says that much of what he has said is not that controversial. Thus, he has not found it necessary to offer any real support for his
assertions. But the question one must ask is why has he spent so much time in
dealing with noncontroversial (from his point of view) assertions?

Ron will confront this question in the next stage in which he chooses and
analyzes an audience for his essay.

Step 4　Using your Planning Page as a guide, compose a discovery draft of your
essay.

Select and Analyze Your Audience

In a broad sense you already know what your aim will be in this writing assignment: to persuade an audience to accept your point of view in regard to a
controversial subject. Ron also knew what his aim would be from the beginning
of his writing process. But he was not sure of his audience. At first he thought
he would write an editorial for a local newspaper, but upon reflection he decided
that writing to the readers of that paper would be too easy a task. He estimated

that 70 to 80 percent of those readers would agree with him. That fact would not make his essay useless to them; it could offer them corroboration of their opinion and a chance to see how someone else would support the assertion. However, such an audience did not present much of a challenge.

Ron was searching for an audience that would be sufficiently different from him in its initial response to this topic to cause him to rethink completely, and perhaps modify, his position. He chose as his audience the liberal arts faculty members of the college in which he teaches. They provided him a suitable audience for several reasons. In his opinion liberal arts faculty tend to be liberal, particularly in regard to social issues; thus they are likely to approach the essay with some skepticism. However, he did not feel that their initial negative predisposition was so ingrained as to be unchangeable, as might be the case with certain audiences such as authorities on penology or individuals related to people serving time in prisons. Another advantage to choosing this audience is that Ron can speak to them as a peer. Even though they may have some definite opinions on the subject, most will not have done any real research on the topic; thus, the small amount of reading that he does in the course of writing the paper will make him as well informed as, if not better informed than, most of these people.

Having decided on his audience, Ron can return to his original intention of writing the essay as an editorial for the local newspaper. But now he will envision as his audience a small percentage of the actual readers, those who would disagree with his thesis (most of whom will be associated with the university).

At this point Ron is ready to analyze his audience, but from a different perspective than we outlined in Chapters Four and Six. Rather than just briefly identifying his audience, Ron puts himself into the place of his audience and answers the Questions for Analysis for them. The purpose of doing so is to gain as full an understanding of their point of view as possible so that he can offer them valid reasons for changing that point of view. However, in order to make this gain, he must be willing to so identify with their point of view as to make changes in his own point of view should he find it necessary to do so.

The following are Ron's answers to the Questions for Analysis for his audience.

<table>
<tr><td>AUDIENCE'S QUESTIONS FOR ANALYSIS</td><td>

According to my audience

What goes with short prison sentences?

  What are short prison sentences?

    A means of making adjustments in sentences, taking individual into consideration, a refusal to reduce justice to a formula

  What physical entities go with short prison sentences?

    Overcrowded prisons

  What do they associate with short prison sentences?

    Humane treatment of people

  In what context are short prison sentences set?

    A society that places great emphasis on the worth of the individual

</td></tr>
</table>

   Writing a Persuasive Essay

Fair, impartial parole officers

Strict rules regarding parole and probation

What opposes short prison sentences?

What theoretical or philosophical opposition is there to short prison sentences?

That philosophy which holds that the end (a safer society) justifies the means (neglecting the basic right of people to be treated as individuals)

What follows or follows from short prison sentences?

What are the causes of short prison sentences?

The desire to treat people as individuals

What sort of problems do short prison sentences pose?

The difficulty of dealing with humans as humans, not as machines

What is the implication of short prison sentences?

We will extend our belief in the worth of the individual as far as possible in this society.

Are short prison sentences good, bad, etc.?

They are good, but sometimes have bad effects.

The key to making this a useful stage in the writing of the persuasion paper is the writer's ability to choose language that allows her to see things as her audience sees them. For example, Ron says that members of his audience associate these shorter sentences with "a means of making adjustments in sentences, taking the individual into consideration." These are probably words that many members of the audience themselves could accept in describing their point of view. Ron could have said that for the audience these sentences were a means of washing their hands of guilt and allowing the rest of society to suffer the consequences. But what purpose would such language serve? It would certainly not help him shape an argument more acceptable to his audience, because it would not help him see things as his audience sees them. None of those individuals who disagree with the author would accept these words as a proper description of their point of view.

<table>
<tr><td>EXERCISE</td><td>Refer to our discussion of denotation and connotation in Chapter Ten. These concepts will help us in discussing the language used in argumentation. For example, in Ron's argument, short sentences could be referred to as "wrist-slapping sentences" by one opposed to them and as "enlightened sentences" by one who favors them. However, both these latter phrases are highly connotative (and, thus, emotionally charged) and less denotative than the original phrase, "short sentences." Examine your argument topic and find actions or situations that lend themselves to emotionally charged terms. In each one, what term would you tend to use? What term would one taking the other side of the argument tend to use? Can you find a more neutral (more denotative) word or phrase that both you and your readers can accept for each action or situation?</td></tr>
</table>

At this point perhaps we should pause and say a word about the apparent stereotyping we are doing in answering the Questions for Analysis for the members of our audience. Certainly the answers we have given cannot be the answers that every member of the audience would give for himself. We know this is true because Ron is himself a member of a liberal arts faculty, and his answers are quite different from those given in the analysis for the audience. But even though he knows that not every member of the audience fits the description he has outlined, he believes that many of them do. That is all he means to imply by offering such a description. But why is this not the same kind of stereotyping we have warned against in the previous chapter?

Although the difference between a stereotype and a generalization is not always easy to enunciate, we can say in principle that a generalization is an attempt to increase information by the inductive process, whereas a stereotype is an attempt to make value judgments. The difference between the two usually becomes clear as we see the writer's purpose for a categorization. For example, we would feel differently about the two following types of categorization. In the first, imagine that an educator argues that we should allow more boys than girls to be placed in advanced mathematics classes in high school because boys make better scores in mathematics than do girls. We would say that this is an erroneous type of reasoning, a case of basing policy decisions on a stereotype. In a second instance, imagine that a school administrator predicts that more boys than girls will sign up for the advanced class in mathematics, because boys usually like mathematics better than girls. Both of these examples involve generalizing, but the first is a case of unfair, illogical improper reasoning whereas the second is not. Why?

In the first case we are using an inductive leap to form a value judgment. It is obvious that to be good at mathematics is better than not to be good. But what may not be obvious is the way that the first statement implies that boys are inherently better in mathematics than are girls. Nevertheless, that assumption is present in the statement. Even worse, in this situation the stereotype is being used as a basis for decisions that will affect individuals negatively in the stereotyped group.

In the second instance, no value judgment is being made. The information contained in the generalization is not being used as a basis for deciding how to treat the members of either group; rather, the framer of this generalization is merely trying to use past experience to help make a prediction about the relative composition of classes. This is the same type of reasoning used by pollsters when they say that even though the Republican is ahead in the early vote counting, she may yet lose because the votes from the poorer precincts, which are usually heavily Democratic, have not been tabulated.

The previous analysis should make it clear that Ron is generalizing rather than stereotyping. He is attempting to describe the members of his audience rather than to evaluate them, and his purpose in doing so is to understand better how to present his argument to them; he does not plan to prove anything by means of these generalizations.

Step 5   Choose an audience and aim for your essay. Then analyze that audience by answering the Questions for Analysis for them. Be sure the language you attribute to them would be acceptable to them.

Write a Second Draft

At this stage Ron was to write the next draft of his essay. However, although he felt he had quite a few things to say on the topic, he was not ready to go to the next draft. Before doing so, he wrote a brief outline.

GENERAL OUTLINE

Tentative thesis

We should take some discretion away from judges and parole boards and enforce longer sentences for those who have committed violent crimes against our society.

Supports

Allowing felons back on the streets too soon causes more people to be hurt than would be the case if they were kept longer.

There is no proof that criminals have more difficulty readjusting to society after a long imprisonment than after a short one.

There is evidence that many of those who have been released have committed other crimes.

Parole boards are not possessed of the wisdom necessary to decide which criminals would be helped by early parole.

Refutation

We can combat the problem of expense in prison and consequent overcrowding by rethinking our attitudes on prisoners paying their own way.

Before writing this outline, Ron had felt his topic wavering somewhat, so he began this prewriting exercise by asking himself exactly what it was that he wished to argue for and against. Once he had decided this issue, he had a tentative thesis for the essay. He chose to frame the thesis without the constraints of the Lead Sentence because he felt his paper would surely contain both causal and definitional supports. However, as he developed his supporting sentences, he found that he was still shaping his argument by causal reasoning.

As we will see in Ron's second draft, this outline helps Ron to structure his essay, though it does not dictate the ultimate structure of the essay. When writing that draft, Ron finds that the causal arguments lead naturally to a definitional argument that is just as important as, if not more important than, the causal argument.

Note that two people reviewed this draft—Ron himself and an outside reader—as indicated by the different handwritten corrections and questions. The following is the second draft of Ron's essay.

Our judicial system has been the subject of a good bit of discussion in the weeks immediately following the trial of would-be presidential assassin, John Hinkly, Jr. Judinging from the comments pf people ranging from "the man on the street" to the jurors themselves, something must be done about the insanity plea whichx allowed Hinckley to be found "not guilty by reason of insanity." Perhaps we do need to rethink this complicated issue, but in attacking this verdict so vociferously, we may well be straining at the proverbial gnat and swallowing a camel. A comment by one of Hinckley's juror's--in justifying the jury's verdict—seems to have been lost in the uproar created by those calling for reform of this insanity plea. That juror's observation that Hinckley may well spend more time in actual confinement as a result of this "not guilty" verdict than he would had he been found guilty is worthy of more attention than we have givenx it--it is true. Certainly, we have a right to be upset if the insanity plea is providing a few accused murderers a loophole by which they can avoid a conviction. We should, however, be much more concerned over the fact that had Hinckley been convicted, he could have reenteredxour society in only three to xfour years. (Source)

Just how is this so? There are not xdoubt many factors involved, but the chief culprit is the system of parole which has developed in this country within the last one-hundred years (Source). In developing this system, penologists have been greatly influenced by x their beliefs that the purpose of prisons is to rehabilitate prisoners and that after a rather xshort period of time, the prisoner xxxxx reaches a point at which further incarceration will xhave a negative effect on him. In speaking to this matter, David Dressler, an authority on penology, asks the following question: "Is it not to our interest to see to it that those released come under supervision for some time, as they reaccustom themselves to life outside?" (Sonce: Practice and theory of Probation and Parole, p. 260). Assuming that his readers will accept this premise, Dressler continues his argument:

> We must assume, as we do with probationers, that a great
> many prisoners are susceptible to change. Assuming (for the
> sake of discussion) that the institution does something to
> help bring this about, there comes a time when an inmate has
> profited as much as he ever will from incareceration. At
> that psychological moment, if we can capture it, we should
> parolex him. To retain him further would be to countervail
> both the community's and the individual's welfare. (p. 160)

Dressler's argument should perhaps have some bearing on our treatment of people whose crimes were not directed against other individuals. However, we must reject this reasoning when it comes to situations in which a crime has been directed against an individual. If, indeed, there does come "a time when an inmate has xprofited as max much as he never will from incareration," who among us is so sagacious as to be able to discern just when this moment occurs? How do we know that this moment is more likely to occur within the first ten years of imprisonment than within the second ten years? We do not.

There are some things, however, that we can, and do, know. We know that the rate of recidivism for individuals having served time in federal prison isx high. One study conducted several years ago found that 24 of those released eventually returned to prison. (The Effects of Prison... p. 25)

We also know that a person still behind prison bars cannot commit a crime against the society outside those bars. Of course, there is room to argue, as many will, that this recidivism is so high because of the poor job of rehabilitation being done in prisons and/or because we are keeping individuals in prison too long. But before we accept the suggestions of these prison reformers, we should address a seme fundamental questions about penology.

That question has already been alluded to above: What is the purpose of a prison sentence? Should it *be to punish, rehabilitate* ~~rehabilitate, punish,~~ or

simply incarcerate the individual. Of course, this matter is not so

simple as the question might imply. It is to be hi hoped that all

three elements will be at work at times. But if we had to choose

one among these as _the_ purpose of imprisonment, which would it be?

In order to answer this questions, let us briefly examine each pro-

posed purpsose.

xIs prison, first and foremost, a punishment inflicted upon an

offender against society? To a degree, all of us feel the need to

punish and to be punished for wrongs. When we watch the bad guy

"get his" on a TV program we experience a Catharsis which is not less

real kan than the cartharsis felt by parents of a slain child when the

killer is apprehended and placed behind bars. b But is this Carthar-

sis the reason for the prison dsentence? Even these parents of the

slain child would probably say there is a reason for imprisoning this

killer which is more important than their Cartharsis. They would no

doubt feel it "more" necessary to imprison this person to prevent him

or her dexm from taking the life of another couple's child. Another

way of putting this would be to say that they wuld feel it necessary

to imprison this person even if they received no Chartharsis from

the imprisonment. And they would probably reject as uncivilized an

act which would provide catharsis foxxmr for them but no protection

for society--such as chopping off the offending hand.

If punishment is not _the_ reaons for imprisonemen, then perhaps

rehabilitation isx. The rehabilitation philosophy certainly has

carried the day among penologists in the last ten b twenty myears.

And it is an attractive philosophy. Since many penoi penologists and,

for that matter, many citizens, accept the basic tnets of behaviorism,

it is only logical that they should not want prison to be a punishment

for something that the prisoner could notkhelp and that they should

Writing a Persuasive Essay

think the prison expdrience has served its function when the stimuli
which caused the prisoner's behavior have been removed.

The problem with this approach to penology is that human behavior
is just too complicated for humans to understand. We can all agree
that the child reared by drunken parents has pooer prospects than the
one reared by upstanding, loving parents. But we have yet to find
all the factors involved in situations where the child from a "bad"
home becomes president and the child from a "good" home attempts
to assassinate the president. Likewise, we are unable to determine
exactly what factors make for rehabilitation in prisons. Surely, the
prisoner subjected to inhuman treatment would seem more likely to
have difficulty adjusting to reentering society than the person who
has been treated weel, and in fact given educational opportunities in
prison. But many of these people now in prison were treated well
and given educational opportunities outside the prison. There is no
wasy to say whether these individuals will awail themselves of these
opportunities in prison.

Because of our imperfect understanding of the various factors
involved in human behavior, I am forced to accept the third purpose
for prison. For convicted felons who have proved themselves dangerous to socity, prison is, first and foremost, a place of incarcera-
ation designed to keep them away from other citizens. If some rehabilitation can be accomplished in the process and if some carhharsis
is also provided, that is all the better. But these are secondary
matters.

The belief that we can perform this rehabilitation has allowed
for the short sentences which threaten our society. In a typical
state, Pennsylvania, one can commit the most heinous crime, murder,
and be eligible for parle in four years (<u>Prescriptions for Justice</u>

).This is the kind of sentence the Hinckley juror was referring

        to. If we understood the human psyche enough to cure a murderer (and

        to recongnize when the cure had been effected)within four years, it

        might be considered reasonable to parole a murderer in that lenght

        of time. Until we do, however, such a sentence threatens every mem-

        ber of our society.

There are a couple of points we should make about this draft before moving on to the final draft of the essay. The first has to do with the relation between this second draft and the one that preceded it. A comparison of the two will reveal that this second essay is a revision in the literal sense of the word. That is, it is a re*seeing* of the entire essay, not just an attempt to "clean up" the first version. Before we look at some specific revisions, we need to say something about the role of research in the persuasive process. Many times argumentative essays are written with no research. However, unless the writer is already an expert on a subject, he is unlikely to possess the information necessary to support a position or to understand the position of those who oppose him. Research, both that involving materials in the library and that involving sources such as students and faculty on campus and/or members of the surrounding community, will help writers remedy this situation. Thus, even though the chief aim in this writing assignment is to persuade, the writing process is, nevertheless, a learning process. No one completes an argument in good faith without learning something.

As we said earlier, the writer of an argumentative essay can use the first draft stage to find what she thinks about the topic at hand. The following questions are designed to help you examine this first draft stage.

1. Examine Ron's first draft to discover places where he needs to do research to support the opinions he brings to this draft. Obvious places will be those where he has left blanks. However, you should be able to find others. Suggest some possible sources of information for the matters that need to be researched.

2. Find two or three places in the first draft of your essay that will lend themselves to research. List possible sources for the information you need.

3. When comparing Ron's first and second drafts, can you find any places (not mentioned in the text) where he seems to have changed or modified his point of view as a result of his research? In each case, does the change seem to be a result of information he has discovered through his research or of more logical reasoning?

Now let us return to the specific comparisons between the two drafts. The quality of the revision in the second draft may not be apparent in the first paragraph, which reads very much like the first paragraph in the first draft. But there are significant changes even in this paragraph. Rather than ending with the rather caustic observation that convicted criminals have a hard decision to make as to whether they should plead insanity, an observation that would imply that all of those who plead insanity are trying to beat the system, Ron simply asserts that Hinckley could have received less time in actual confinement had he been found guilty and concludes with what he sees as a shocking statistic—the fact that a person convicted of attempted murder could reenter our society in three to four years.

The extensive nature of the revision in the second draft begins to be apparent in the second paragraph of the respective essays. In the first essay Ron had begun with a rather emotional adjective for these short sentences—*wrist-slapping*—and followed that with a paragraph dedicated to the sins of behaviorism. Then followed a paragraph dedicated to the wrongheadedness of the rehabilitative philosophy of penology. Ron's analysis of his audience convinced him that he should take a different approach in the second draft. He begins in the second paragraph of the revised draft to talk about the problems inherent in the parole system. But in this paragraph he does not repeat the logical error made in the first paper, the *argumentum ad ignorantiam* (asserting without proving). Rather he turns the tables on rehabilitative penologists by having one of them make assertions that are difficult to prove. He has Dressler say, "there comes a time when an inmate has profited as much as he ever will from incarceration." Because Dressler offers no support for this assertion and does not assert that it is possible to know when this "psychological moment" arrives, Ron can build his argument by showing the problems in Dressler's argument.

After using Dressler's statements as a springboard into his argument, Ron finds it necessary to move into a definition of *prison*. He shows the problems involved in seeing prison as a place of punishment, but his argument that it should not be seen as a place for rehabilitation falters because of fallacious reasoning. His argument is that the complexity of human nature makes it impossible to know just how to go about rehabilitating a prisoner. But his supporting examples constitute a *hasty generalization*. Does the fact that one child in a hundred or two hundred overcomes a difficult childhood to forge a successful life prove that bad environments do not usually produce troubled adults? Does the fact that some people with an education go to prison prove that educating prisoners will not rehabilitate many of them? How many of these prisoners actually did have a good education? Ron offers no support in regard to this crucial matter. Clearly, he must rework this entire section if he is to keep it in the final draft of the essay.

Step 6   Compose a second draft of your essay. You will probably find it necessary to do some research between the first and second drafts.

The following is Ron's final draft of his essay.

No More Short Sentences for Violent Criminals

Our judicial system has been the subject of a good bit of discussion in the weeks immediately following the trial of would-be presidential assassin, John Hinckley, Jr. Judging from the comments of people ranging from the "man on the street" to the jurors themselves, the public thinks something must be done about the insanity plea. Perhaps we do need to rethink this complex issue. But in attacking this verdict so vociferously, we may well be straining at the proverbial gnat and swallowing a camel. A comment by one of Hinckley's jurors—in justifying the jury's verdict— seems to have been lost in the uproar created by those calling for reform of this insanity plea. That juror's observation that Hinckley may well spend more time in actual confinement as a result of this "not guilty" verdict than he would have had he been found guilty is worthy of more attention than we have given it. It is true. Certainly, we have a right to be upset if the insanity plea is providing a few accused murderers a loophole by which they can avoid a conviction. We should, however, be much more concerned over the fact that had Hinckley been convicted, he could have reentered our society in three to four years.[1]

Just how is this so? There are no doubt many factors involved, but the chief culprit is the system whereby a judge renders an indefinite sentence and a parole board determines exactly how much time a convicted felon spends in prison. In developing this system, penologists have been greatly influenced by their belief that the purpose of the penal system is to rehabilitate prisoners and that after a rather short period of time, the prisoner often reaches a point at which further incarceration will have a negative effect on him and at which he will be ready to be released into society under the supervision of a parole officer. According to David Dressler, an authority on penology:

> We must assume, as we do with probationers, that a great many prisoners are susceptible to change. Assuming (for the sake of discussion) that the institution does something to help bring this about, there comes a time when an inmate has profited as much as he ever will from incarceration. At that psychological moment, if we can capture it, we should parole him. To retain him further would be to countervail both the community's and the individual's welfare.[2]

People who have committed nonviolent crimes should reenter our society as soon as possible. However, we must rethink our treatment of those who have committed violent crimes which were directed against individuals. If, indeed, there does come "a time when an inmate has profited as much as he ever will from incarceration," who among us is so sagacious as to be able to discern just when this moment occurs? How do we know that this moment is more likely to occur within the first ten years of imprisonment than within the second ten years? We do not.

There are some things, however, that we do know. We know that the rate of recidivism for individuals having served time in federal prisons is high. One study conducted several years ago found that 24% of those released from federal prisons eventually returned to prison.[3] While there is little data breaking down recidivism according to the seriousness of crimes committed, it is reasonable to assume that in some prisons where violent criminals have been placed, the rate is even higher. One inmate's analysis of the situation in his prison offers some support for this assumption:

> In January of this year, in the prison where I served thirteen years of a life sentence, 20 per cent of the inmates had done a single previous jolt in that or another penitentiary, 16 per cent were three-time losers and 37 per cent had four or more prison commitments on their records. Only 27 percent of the inmate body were first-timers, and of this group 6 percent were twenty-one years of age or under and therefore hadn't yet had a fair chance to demonstrate their capacity for long-haul jousting with the law.[4]

Of course, there is room to argue, as many will, that recidivism is so high because of the poor job of rehabilitation being done in prisons and/or because we are keeping individuals in prison too long. But before we accept the suggestions of these prison reformers, we should address a fundamental question about penology.

That basic question has already been alluded to above: What is the purpose of a prison sentence? Should it punish, rehabilitate, or simply incarcerate the individual? Of course, this matter is not so simple as the question might imply. It is to be hoped that all three elements will be at work at times. But, if we had to choose one among these as *the* purpose of imprisonment, which would it be? In order to answer this question, let us briefly examine each proposed purpose.

Is prison, first and foremost, a punishment inflicted upon an offender against society? To a degree, all of us feel the need to punish, and to be punished for, wrongs. When we watch the bad guy "get his" on a TV program we experience and enjoy a catharsis which is imitative of the "real" catharsis which the parents of a slain child experience when the killer of that child is apprehended and placed behind bars. But is this catharsis the reason for the prison sentence? The parents of the slain child would probably feel that the "real" reason for imprisoning this killer is to prevent him from taking the life of another couple's child. They would feel it necessary to imprison this person even if they received no cathartic effect from the act, and they would probably reject, as uncivilized, an act which would provide catharsis for them but no protection for society— such as chopping off the offending hand. If these reactions are typical, then the American public does not see punishment as *the* reason for imprisonment.

If not for punishment, then perhaps prison is for rehabilitation. The rehabilitative philosophy certainly has carried the day among penologists in the last ten to twenty years. And it is an attractive philosophy. Since many penologists and, for that matter, many citizens, accept the basic tenets of Behaviorism, it is only logical that they should not want prison to be a punishment for something the offender was not totally responsible for and that they should think the prison experience has served its function when the stimuli which caused the prisoner's behavior have been removed.

The problem with this approach to penology is that human behavior is too complicated to allow it to work. Parole boards just do not possess the Solomon-like wisdom it would take to know when an individual has "learned his lesson" in prison. Those states which have adopted the rehabilitative philosophy and have thus left the actual sentences of prisoners in the hands of parole boards—by means of the indefinite sentence— have had the highest rates of recidivism. In two such states, California and New York, recidivism for an entire year was 44% in each state.[5] The rate of recidivism for youthful offenders has also been particularly high, in part because so many of these youths have been given indefinite sentences and released on parole after serving very short sentences. In one year, our federal reformatories had a recidivism rate of 58%.[6]

The purpose of citing the preceding figures is not to suggest that we should develop a "lock 'em up and throw away the key" philosophy toward all offenders. It is, rather, to suggest that our sentencing practices in regard to individuals who have committed violent crimes against other members of our society should be changed. We must give them longer sentences.

This suggestion is based on a concern for human life. According to a noted penologist, Daniel Glaser, one way to protect human life is to keep these offenders in prison longer. He makes this point in talking about the effects our sentences for murderers have had on their rate of recidivism. In his words:

> Today most murderers are given long prison terms, usually designated life, although most are eligible for parole in fifteen to twenty-five years. The parole violation rate for murderers is the lowest of any offense, and less than 1 percent of those released repeat this crime. (Age at release is doubtless a factor in this.)[7]

Glaser's last statement, though in parenthesis, is a significant one. It shows that he still believes in a hypothesis he stated in an earlier work: "The older a man is when released from prison, the less likely he is to return to crime."[8] It may seem harsh, but we should age these violent offenders more than three or four years before turning them back onto the streets. After all, in many cases such as Hinckley's the difference between the act of a person who serves three years of an eight to ten year sentence for attempted murder and that of a person who serves fifteen years of a life sentence for murder is marksmanship. But if a person is capable of a violent act which could have resulted in death, we must guard ourselves against this person as carefully as we guard ourselves against the person whose attempt was successful.

We should indeed make a distinction between those offenses directed against individuals and those which are not. That person who has not shown himself to be a danger to society should be given every opportunity to right himself before being sent to prison. In some states, many such offenders are given suspended sentences and ordered to make monetary restitution for the goods they have stolen and/or destroyed. More and more states should look into this option.

Such probationary sentences will be a start toward relieving our overcrowded prisons. They will not remedy the situation, however. Only a completely different attitude toward prisoners and the prison system will provide a solution. We must be willing to build as many prisons as necessary to accommodate those who are a danger to our society and to adopt an attitude toward the prison system which will allow us to find ways to make prisoners self-supporting. This will be no easy task, but it is one that will be worth the effort it will require.

The belief that we can truly rehabilitate violent criminals has resulted in these short sentences. If we understood the human psyche enough to cure a potential murderer (and to recognize that cure) within three to four years, the kind of sentence that the Hinckley juror was referring to might be considered a reasonable one. Until we do, such sentences threaten every member in our society.

Notes

[1]Jack M. Dress, *Prescription for Justice* (Cambridge: Ballinger Publishing Company, 1980), pp. 265, 273.

[2]David Dressler, *Practice and Theory of Probation and Parole* (New York: Columbia University Press, 1951), p. 60.

[3]Daniel Glaser, *The Effectiveness of a Prison and Parole System* (New York: The Bobbs-Merrill Company, Inc., 1964), p. 25.

[4]Hal Hollister, "I Say Prisons Are a Failure," *The Saturday Evening Post*, 234, No. 34, August 26, 1961, 13.

[5]Glaser, p. 25.

[6]Glaser, p. 26.

[7]Daniel Glaser, *Adult Crime and Social Policy* (Englewood Cliffs, New Jersey: Prentice-Hall, Inc., 1972), p. 35.

[8]Glaser, *The Effectiveness of a Prison and Parole System*, p. 36.

<table>
<tr><td>EXERCISE</td><td>Rather than commenting on the final draft, we offer this exercise as a tool by which you can examine this last draft for yourself.</td></tr>
</table>

1. Introducing quotes is often a tricky business. Compare how Ron introduced the Dressler quote in the final draft with the way he introduced it in the second draft. Why is the final version better?

2. For the most part, Ron does not make major changes in the final draft. But he continues to work with sentences to get them to say exactly what he means. Note the difference between the following sentence in the second draft and the way it is realized in the final draft: "When we watch the bad guy 'get his' on a TV program, we experience a catharsis which is no less real than the catharsis felt by parents of a slain child when the killer is apprehended and placed behind bars." What is the effect of this change in wording? Find at least two other such changes from the second to the final draft. How do they differ? What is the effect of the change?

3. One significant change that Ron makes in the final draft is in the way he defines the term *prison*. In the second draft, he explicitly states that prisons are for the purpose of incarceration. In the final draft the paragraph in which he makes this statement is dropped. What effect does this change have on the last draft? Is it clear in the last draft that Ron sees prisons as places for "incarceration"? If so, how is this definition made clear? What does Ron put in the place of the paragraph in which he makes the definition clear? Is this new paragraph a significant addition to the essay? If so, how?

4. As the handwritten material on the second draft shows, Ron asked another reader to comment on that draft. This reader's comments are printed. What kind of advice did this reader offer? To what extent did Ron follow it? What effect did that reader have on the final draft?

Tone

Ron's final draft provides us a springboard into a discussion of a concept that has been an overriding concern throughout this chapter, though we have talked about it only indirectly to this point. Though we all know what the word *tone* means when parents tell a child not to "use that tone" with them, we may be a bit unsure what the term means in literary contexts. However, reconsideration of this chapter may help us to understand the term better and thereby to write more effective persuasive essays.

Before applying the term to persuasive situations, we should consider its meaning in contexts with which we are familiar. When a parent tells a child not to use a certain tone, the child may assume the objection is to the sounds he has made, that perhaps he was talking in a harsh "tone" of voice. But in reality the parent is objecting to an attitude that those particular sounds represent. The parent feels that the child should remember who is the child and who is the parent and show a certain amount of respect for those roles, even in the midst of an argument. Thus, many parents will reject the harsh or loud sounds because they associate them with a lack of respect for these roles.

Of course, if sounds were the only way in which tones could be transmitted, we would not be talking about tone in a writing text. But that is not the case. One can reveal her attitude toward another person by means of the words she uses. We could not hear Darrow's tone of voice when he said, "Many asses have spoken, and doubtless some in Hebrew, but they have not been that breed of asses," but we did recognize a certain attitude toward those being called "asses."

Is tone, then, the writer's attitude toward the reader? In great part, it is, but matters are not quite that simple. In order to explore fully the concept of tone, we need to examine two other factors: the writer's attitude toward his subject, and his attitude toward his opponents, if his subject is argumentative.

A writer's attitude toward a subject can vary greatly in nonargumentative transactional situations. However, we can get some insight into the various attitudes writers bring to these situations by using a continuum with two poles—

Writing a Persuasive Essay

serious and nonserious. An expository piece by a nuclear scientist having to do with the dangers of nuclear energy is likely to be near the serious pole. On the other hand, an article by Erma Bombeck in which she talks about her problems with salespersons in department stores is likely to be near the other pole on the continuum. Most examples of nonargumentative transactional writing will be somewhere between these two extremes, and we will do well to begin our investigation of tone by locating the writer's attitude on this continuum.

This continuum is not very helpful in evaluating the tone of persuasive writing because a serious attitude toward the subject is a given in the persuasive situation. Of course, the framers of argumentative essays do sometimes say things they do not mean, as when Jonathan Swift proposes that the Irish sell their children as food for the English. We say that such an essay has an *ironic tone*, because the writer attempts to cause us to act or react in one way by pretending to want us to act or react in an opposite way. Swift wants his readers to rise up in revolt and protect Irish children, but he pretends to want them to kill Irish children. Nevertheless, Swift's essay is extremely serious in tone.

The various tones in persuasive writing are more likely the result of the writer's relationship with her audience than of her relationship with her subject. We can investigate the tone of a persuasive essay by determining the author's attitude toward those people who are opposed to her argument and her attitude toward her readers. Of course, there is only one group to consider when the author is addressing those opposed to her argument.

When choosing a less hostile or neutral audience, writers sometimes dismiss those who are diametrically opposed to their argument (remember our example of the political debate earlier in this chapter). In doing so, they often produce essays with harsh or satirical tones. When a writer shows little regard for those who take an opposing viewpoint and shows how ludicrous the viewpoint is—often by making the viewpoint and/or its proponents the butt of humor—we label his tone *satirical*. We saw an example of such an essay in Chapter Seven. Though in "Fantastic Piece of Logic," Sydney Harris argues against Dr. Crane's position on capital punishment, his essay is not designed to convince Crane, or for that matter, anyone who has espoused the type of argument Crane offers. From the beginning of his essay where he refers to Crane as "the only syndicated columnist who signs himself, 'Ph.D.,' 'M.D.,' " Harris displays a lack of respect for Crane.

If Harris's essay is not written for Dr. Crane or those who espouse his point of view, who then is it written for? Harris would probably see his audience as those who are truly neutral in regard to the argument. What is his tone toward his audience? He attempts to show respect for them by asking them tacitly to join him in satirizing Crane. That is, they are too smart to accept the type of reasoning that Crane offers. Of course, Harris never says so, but the humor he directs at Crane implies this.

We saw a similar tone in another essay offered in the previous chapter. In "Why I Am an Agnostic," Darrow argues against Christians rather than to them. Darrow knows that no one who believes in God will be convinced by his arguments; rather than trying to convince these people, he belittles their beliefs, thus adopting a superior tone toward them. But what will the effect of such a tone be on those who are neutral in regard to this issue, if indeed, they are the intended audience? We would guess that Darrow's tone would hinder his chances of convincing these people. It would seem to jeopardize his ethical appeal with such readers; they are not likely to be convinced by someone who resorts to such slanted terms and who thus shows himself unwilling to be fair and open-minded. Thus, as we suggested in one of our questions in the exercise following Darrow's essay, there is a sense in which his essay is not really persuasive. He is somewhat like a preacher addressing the already-converted.

We close our discussion of the tone in Darrow's essay by examining two of the words Darrow uses in paragraph 13 of that essay. In one sentence Darrow says that those who wrote the Bible were influenced by "barbarous morality" and that they lived in "primitive times." Obviously, Darrow is not attempting to use language that those opposing his argument could accept. The associations that most people bring to these words are extremely negative. For example, we make the following sets of associations.

barbarous	*primitive*
savage	unskilled
hostile	naked, unclothed
uneducated	incapable of communicating
uncivilized	uneducated
unkempt	uncivilized
smelly	

By describing people whom Christians have great respect for with these words, Darrow shows his lack of concern for the feelings of these believers.

<table>
<tr><td>EXERCISE</td><td>We said earlier that in many persuasive situations you may need to address your argument toward those who disagree with you and, thus, to attempt to see things from their point of view. Thus, we have suggested that you write your essay to those opposing your point of view and that your attitude (tone) toward them be one of respect. Examine the two drafts you have written to this point to see if you can find any places where you have made a change that improves the tone of the first draft in the second draft. Then examine the second draft to see if you can find any words that need to be replaced. What associations are your readers likely to bring to these problematic words?</td></tr>
</table>

WRITING ASSIGNMENT

Step 7   Compose the final draft of your essay, paying particular attention to achieving an appropriate tone for your persuasive purpose.

Writing a Persuasive Essay

Chapter Nine

Researching and Writing

We imagine that you have written at least one research paper in the past. What was it like? How would you characterize any research papers you have done? At times, student research papers seem to amount to little more than a collection of facts and quotes, strung together in some semblance of order but not really making any particular point. Such papers have no definite shape; they have no discernible beginning, middle, and end. They have been written for no particular purpose or audience, so they lack direction. This is not always the case. Certainly, there are times when a research paper carries a ring of authenticity, a ring created by the writer's interest in the topic, by that writer's having found significance in the topic.

Ideally, research writing will involve in-depth inquiry into a subject of the writer's choosing. It should be a springboard to discovery as the researcher attempts to find new information to help him settle his own mind about a topic and/or to help him support or modify a tentative position on the topic. In *Searching Writing*, Ken Macrorie comments on discovery in the research process.

> Look at a two-year-old grabbing books off a shelf, seeing how they open, ripping pages, finding out how they taste. Not much different from a kitten first time out of his box. Apparently, we're all born curious. Inside or outside school, research should be like that, but usually it isn't.*

---

*Ken Macrorie, *Searching Writing* (Rochelle Park, N.J.: Hayden Book Company, 1980), p. 54.

Implicit in Macrorie's comment is that most assigned research is artificial. But it need not be.

At least part of the problem students have with research writing stems from a misconception of what a research paper should be and what it means to research. Research writing should begin as a question the writer has about a particular topic, so that the writer's initial job is to probe the topic in search of an answer. Once she has found an answer, or at least a tentative stance on the topic, she may structure her research writing to fulfill any of three transactional purposes: (1) to report the results of a probe or exploration of the topic, (2) to present information and an interpretation of it, and (3) to argue a point. A research paper written to fulfill one of these three purposes will not be merely a rehashing of other writers' ideas, which is what many students see the research paper to be. Beginning an assigned research project, many students groan as they envision themselves seated in a library till late at night, slaving away at huge piles of books, picking a pithy quotation from one source, taking a telling statistic from another. But research should not entail this kind of drudgery. Although it is true that research requires you to use sources beyond yourself, a research paper should be authentic; it should carry your personal stamp as it reports your inquiry into your subject. In short, your research paper should begin in curiosity and convey the excitement you feel in making discoveries.

At the same time there are particular conventions you must follow. You must avoid plagiarism while using someone else's thoughts. You must also report the results of your inquiry in such a way that other researchers can use your findings, if they so desire. The purpose of this chapter is to help you achieve what we see as a necessary balance between content and convention in research writing, so that you may probe a topic with curiosity and then report your findings in a more or less standard format.

TOPICS

Sometimes you will have free choice of topics for your research. Your task becomes, then, one of finding the right topic, one you want to spend a good bit of time with. But how to find this topic?

What are your interests? That is the most logical starting point. When you begin a research assignment, you may know, or at least have some idea of, a topic. If you are blank, however, look through your Interest Inventory (see pp. 19–20) to see if any topic appeals to you immediately. Your inventory should tell you that you are an expert on any number of subjects. It should also tell you that you feel strongly about a number of issues. From such topics as these— ones in which you have expertise, ones about which you feel strongly—can come research papers fulfilling any of the three purposes of research writing we outlined earlier in this chapter.

Here is an example. One of the authors, Bill Bridges, recently published an essay on publishing student writing. The topic was one in which Bill was greatly interested because of his belief that publishing student writing is an excellent means of motivating students to write, and write well. From this topic could have come an essay presenting information (how to publish student writing), reporting a probe (results of formal and/or informal surveys and results of interviews with teachers who publish or do not publish student writing), or arguing a point (that publishing student writing is important). Bill's essay is something of all three, though it is primarily persuasive, a justification of the importance of publishing projects and a call for teachers to publish student writing. But although the essay is persuasive, it also conveys information, listing thirteen ways teachers can publish student writing. It also involves research.

When preparing the article, Bill drew on the work of James Britton and Donald Graves in outlining the benefits of having students write as much as possible, on the work of Rebekah Caplan, Rhoda Maxwell, Stephen Judy, and Linda Chittenden in showing ways of publishing student writing, and on his own observations of how publishing projects motivate students to write. He was knowledgeable about the topic, having published his students' writing on several occasions, but Bill thought it necessary to use outside sources for additional ideas and for support for his own ideas. In the end, Bill's essay was the final stage in a research project that began with his interest in publishing student writing.

Although you will at times be free to choose any subject you wish, at other times you will not. Either your instructor will ask you to find a subject in a specific context (for example, the American colonial period) or will limit you to an even narrower subject (for example, George Washington's battle strategies in several important battles during the American Revolution). In such instances, your job is to make the subject your own—that is, to find a topic of significance in it so that the paper you write carries your ideas about or assessment of the topic.

One of the best ways to begin searching for a topic is to freewrite, so that you uncover what you do and do not know. You probably will know or will learn a good deal about such subjects as the colonial period or Washington's battle plans, primarily because such subjects will be assigned in the context of a course, in this case, a class in early American history. If you are not assigned a subject specifically but may choose your own, then we suspect you will pick one you are familiar with or one you want to know more about. Whichever the case, begin by freewriting. Ask such questions as What interests me about this topic? and What do I know about this topic? Then work toward answering them as you freewrite.

<table>
<tr><td></td><td>

1. Pick one of the following subjects and freewrite on it for fifteen minutes, asking questions you think to be appropriate. Then read back over your freewriting and look for a focal point, something that might serve as the basis of a research project. If you find such a point, why do you think it might work into a research paper?

nuclear energy

alternatives to nuclear energy

good (bad) study habits

</td></tr>
</table>

history of a favorite sport or hobby

buying something (for example, the best camera or microcomputer)

benefits of some kind of exercise (for example, running, swimming, biking)

job opportunities for college students

a social issue (for example, drunk driving)

an environmental issue

a campus issue

the draft

alternatives to the draft

2. Later in this chapter, you will be assigned to write a research paper. Begin thinking now about potential topics, if you may select your own, or ask your instructor for suggested or assigned topics. Pick one, and freewrite on it for fifteen minutes, asking appropriate questions. Then read back over your freewriting, and look for a focal point, something that might serve as the basis of a research project. If you do not find one, freewrite for another fifteen minutes; then look again. If you do find such a point, why do you think it might work into a research paper?

Searching a Topic

We assume at this point that you have found at least a tentative topic, one you are curious enough about to spend some time probing or exploring. How do you search the topic? How do you find, record, and make sense of information about the topic?

Sources of Information Once you have found a tentative topic, your next step is to survey sources to see what information is available. Depending on your topic, you may rely wholly on your library to support your research; then again, you may find it necessary or desirable to do some kind of field search. No matter where you find sources of information, your job is not merely to string together facts and quotes; your job is to make some meaning of the information you survey so that you report what you find of significance or importance in your topic. In this light you should see sources of information as springboards to discovery. With what do you agree or disagree in those sources? At what points are the thoughts of others consistent or inconsistent with your experience? What do you find of consequence in the information? Is there some action you think should be taken, or was some action taken that should not have been? Answering such questions as these as you explore sources can help you to focus your thinking. What you find in researching a topic you should use first to help you settle your mind about the topic, to find a position on the topic, and then to support your position.

Reading Sources One of the more difficult tasks students face in conducting research is learning how to make the best use of the printed information—for example, books, articles, and news items—they find. To discover what you think to be important in a printed source, you can do the following before you read, while you read, and after you have read. We do not intend this list to be exhaustive; instead, we intend it to serve as a model of the kinds of things you can do so that you may devise your own as necessary.

1. Preview a book by scanning the title, subtitle, table of contents, foreword, introduction, and conclusion. What was the author's purpose in writing the book? How pertinent is that purpose to your topic? Similarly, preview an essay or news item, using the title, introduction, conclusion, headings, and any graphics (for example, tables, charts, or pictures).

2. Use the index of a book to locate particular information about your topic.

3. Use the bibliography of a book or article to locate additional sources relevant to your topic.

4. As you read, note those parts of what you are reading with which you agree or disagree. After you have finished reading, return to those parts you noted and comment about your agreement or disagreement.

5. After reading, outline the main points of what you have read. Which of these are most important? Why? Which are consistent or inconsistent with your experience? How?

6. Before you read, ask several questions you think should be answered by what you will read. After you have read, answer your questions, based on your reading.

7. After reading, frame several questions you would ask the author, were you to meet him. Or frame several questions you would ask any of the key figures in your reading, were you to meet them.

Taking Notes As you work with your sources, you will need to find some way to use the information you gather. One convenient way is the traditional note card system. As you take notes, use 3 × 5 note cards, recording one bit of information (for example, a summary of a certain passage or a direct quote) per card. Listing one bit per card makes it easy for you to use information later as you shuffle notes and move various citations around to find the most effective way to use them.

Note card formats vary, but each card should carry at least this information: (1) the last name of the person you are citing (for example, author or interviewee) or some other identification of the source (for example, key word of the title); (2) the source's call number, if it has one; (3) the note itself; and (4) the page number you took the note from, if the source is printed. Figure 9.1 is a sample note card carrying a direct quote and brief introduction to it.

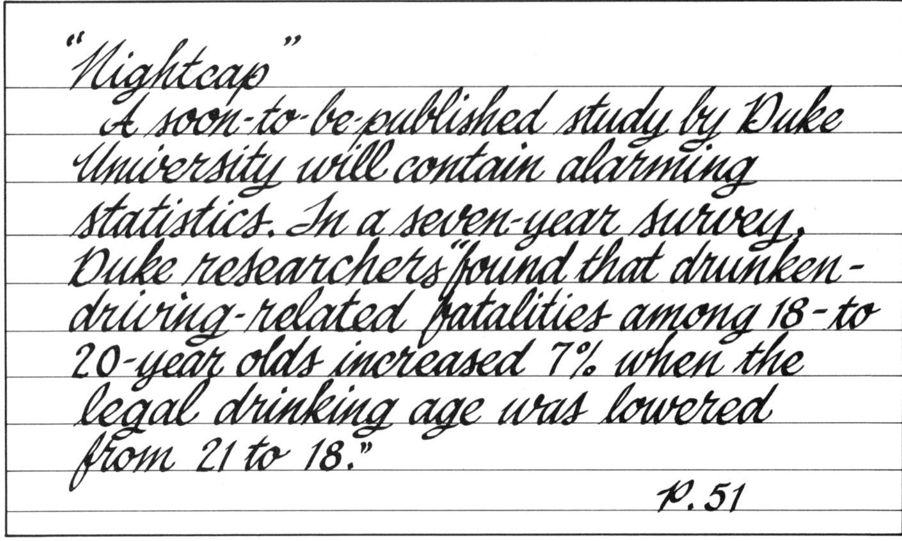

Figure 9.1

This passage is from an unsigned or anonymous article, "Nightcap: Raising the Drinking Age," which appeared in the January 3, 1983, issue of *Time*. Because the author was not identified, we identified the passage using a key term from the article's title.

Summarizing and Paraphrasing At times, a source will not contain specific facts, statistics, or language that you will want to quote directly, or it will be too long for you to quote directly. Still it may contain ideas you wish to use. If this is the case, you will need to summarize those ideas, putting in your own words what you interpret as the passage's main point or points. To write a summary, first read the entire passage you wish to summarize. Then identify the key terms and ideas of the passage, jotting them down in your own words. Next, using your jottings as a guide, write the summary. Finally, check your summary for accuracy by rereading both the passage and your summary of it.

Compare this short passage by Otto Friedrich with the summary that follows it.

In medicine, the computer, which started by keeping records and sending bills, now suggests diagnoses. CADUCEUS knows some 4,000 symptoms of more than 500 diseases; MYCIN specializes in infectious diseases; PUFF measures lung functions. All can be plugged into a master network called SUMEX-AIM, with headquarters at Stanford in the West and Rutgers in the East. This may sound like another step toward the disappearance of the friendly neighborhood G.P., but while it is possible that a family doctor

Researching and Writing

would recognize 4,000 symptoms, CADUCEUS is more likely to see patterns in what patients report and can then suggest a diagnosis. The process may sound dehumanized, but in one hospital where the computer specializes in peptic ulcers, a survey of patients showed that they found the machine "more friendly, polite, relaxing, and comprehensible" than the average physician.*

The following is one possible summary of this passage.

Computers are applied widely in medicine to enhance a doctor's diagnosis of a patient's symptoms. And while computers do not yet replace doctors, in at least one hospital, patients seemed to prefer the "bedside manner" of a computer able to deal with peptic ulcers to that of a typical physician.

If this summary were to be used in a research paper, it would need documentation; that is, it would need to be identified in some way, most commonly by footnote or end note. The information it carries would be borrowed from Friedrich; therefore, it would not be original material and would need documenting. (For details on documentation, see pp. 268–273.)

A summary carries your subjective decision about the importance of a passage's ideas and is generally less than half the length of the original. Note that the preceding summary focused in general on the computer's role in making diagnoses and in particular on the amusing idea that a computer may be more personable than a human. Another summary could be written focusing on the network of computer assistance available to doctors. The content of any summary you write will be determined by your interpretation of the passage's significant or key points.

Akin to the summary is the paraphrase, but whereas the summary requires you to capture a passage's main ideas in abbreviated form, the paraphrase requires you to rewrite the passage in other words. A paraphrase is a complete rendition of the original passage and generally approaches the original's length. Paraphrasing can be helpful when you wish to include a passage but find the original language to be inconsistent with your purpose. If, for example, you wish to use a passage from a scientific paper that your readers would have trouble understanding, you should paraphrase that passage, "translating" it for your audience. The following is a paraphrase of Friedrich's paragraph on computers and medicine.

In medicine, computers no longer do only routine bookkeeping and billing. Instead, several new computers work at diagnosing illnesses. CADUCEUS is like a G.P., able to recognize 4,000 symptoms of over 500 diseases; MYCIN deals with infectious diseases, PUFF with lung functions. All may become part of a national network called SUMEX-AIM, headquartered at Stanford and Rutgers. These computers will not replace a doctor, but machines like CADUCEUS see patterns quickly in patients' complaints and then diagnose accordingly. Patient response to these computers seems positive; in at least one hospital, patients preferred one computer's "bedside manner" to that of a typical doctor.

---

*Otto Friedrich, "The Computer Moves In," *Time*, January 3, 1983, pp. 14–24.

In this paraphrase there are 101 words, only a slight reduction of the original 139. It recounts faithfully the information carried in the original. Just as with the summary of this passage, the paraphrase would need documenting; its information would be borrowed from Friedrich.

EXERCISE   Write a summary and then a paraphrase of this passage by William Pfaff.

> There is no longer agreement among Western governments about what the Soviet danger is. To some in the Reagan Administration, there appears to be an active threat of attack. They, accordingly, want unqualified American military superiority and stepped-up economic warfare against the U.S.S.R. They take with utter seriousness the traditional Soviet ideological insistence that our two systems are permanently irreconcilable—that we coexist merely because history has conceded the Western democracies a temporary stay of execution. In Europe, however, the position of these Americans is highly controversial. It is accepted by only a narrow segment of opinion, and is not the view of West European foreign offices or governments.*

Reliability of Sources Not all sources of information are equally reliable, and part of your job as a researcher is to determine just how reliable your sources are. The more reliable the source, the more weight the information you take from it will carry. But how do you determine such reliability? To evaluate a book, essay, or news item, determine the author's standing in his field. What are his credentials as an authority on this topic? Then you should determine how well researched the writing is. From the bibliography, footnotes, or sources quoted, decide how complete the author's treatment of the topic seems to be. Is the book published by a national or a university publishing house? Both national and university presses generally require their publications to be well researched and well written, so that books from such houses are usually thought of as constituting reliable sources. Where does the essay or news item appear— in a national, regional, state, or local publication? We do not mean to imply that national sources are necessarily better than local sources. A statewide publication such as *Texas Monthly* (a well-written magazine concerning issues and topics in Texas) may well be a more reliable source of information on a particular topic than a nationally circulated gossip tabloid. Whatever the level of publication, your job is to determine the quality of the writer's treatment of the subject. The better that quality, the more reliable the source is likely to be.

If the source is a person you will interview or correspond with, what is the person's status as an authority on your topic? Does she, for example, have national standing; is she a nationally known figure? What is her background or education in the field? If your topic is more local than national in scope (for example, if your topic involves a community issue such as whether a new indoor swimming pool should be built at city expense), what standing does your source have with

---

*William Pfaff, "Reflections: The Waiting Nations," *The New Yorker*, January 3, 1983, pp. 57–65.

    Researching and Writing

respect to your topic? What qualifies her as an expert or authority? Is she sponsor of a local swim team? Is she your city's mayor or a city council member? The more expertise such sources have, the more reliable they may be.

Library Search Obviously, a library, whether your school's or a nearby public library, is a logical place to start. From past experience you probably are familiar with some of the services and research opportunities a library offers. The following are typical.

1. Card catalog: a listing of the library's holdings, usually alphabetized by author's last name, by book title, and by subject matter.

2. Periodicals: current newspapers and popular, scientific, and professional journals to which the library subscribes. Most libraries will have a reference section to house periodicals.

3. Interlibrary loan: a system enabling a library to borrow books and periodicals it does not have from other libraries. If you cannot find a source you need, look into the feasibility of using the interlibrary loan.

4. Micromaterials: collections of various materials (for example, *The New York Times*) on microfilm or microfiche. Most libraries have microreaders available for patrons' use.

5. Government documents: collections of studies commissioned by agencies of the U.S. government. Some libraries around the nation are designated document repositories and make these documents available to the public.

6. Various guides to periodicals and reference works: indices or bibliographies or summaries of various reference works. The most widely used of these guides is the *Readers' Guide to Periodical Literature*, which lists articles in magazines and journals arranged alphabetically by subject matter and by author's last name.

Another valuable source of information is the reference librarian, whose job it is to help people find what they are having trouble finding. If you have a particular problem in locating information or the sources you need, ask the reference librarian for help.

EXERCISE

Using the topic you wrote about in an exercise earlier in this chapter (pp. 257–258), or using the tentative topic you have chosen for your research paper, locate in your library the following sources relating to your topic, listing the title, author, and call number for each.

1. two books

2. two essays in popular journals (for example, *Time, Newsweek, Better Homes and Gardens, Popular Mechanics, National Geographic*), if applicable

3. two essays in scholarly or professional journals, if applicable

4. two items from a newspaper, including one from *The New York Times*

How reliable is each potential source? On what do you base your decision?

Field Search Oftentimes, students overlook the value and appropriateness of using sources beyond those they find in a library. Field sources can be especially important on current community or campus issues, even on topics of national scope. If you have such a topic, you should not limit yourself to searching only a library for information. Similarly, if one of your professors is a noted authority on your topic, you should arrange to interview him, even though his writings may be available in your library.

Survey your campus or local community to locate potential sources. Begin with a local telephone book to find, for example, businesses or chapters of local and national civic organizations and special interest groups (for example, environmental protection groups) that may be able to provide information about your topic. Many groups can furnish trade publications, pamphlets, brochures, and newsletters relevant to your search. To discover who is most concerned with your topic, read local and campus newspapers. Many individuals will be willing to talk with you about their points of view. Whereas using printed materials from groups is a relatively easy task, preparing to talk with someone is more difficult.

Interviewing An interview is a face-to-face meeting in which some topic is discussed. It may vary in formality. The discussion may be limited only to questions submitted by the interviewer prior to the interview, or it may be unlimited, with the interview becoming informal talk between two people interested in the same subject. Whatever the circumstances may be, there are some general guidelines you may follow in preparing for and then conducting an interview.

1. Call the person you want to interview as far in advance as possible to set up the interview. Identify yourself and your purpose clearly so that the interviewee will have some time to think about the general subject of the interview.

2. Prepare questions ahead of time to help you think your way through the interview. Decide what information you would like to receive and frame questions to elicit it. Although you may use only some of these questions in the actual interview, preparing them will help you focus the interview.

3. Ask pertinent, relevant questions; stick to the subject. Include questions designed to establish the interviewee's credentials—for example, who she is and how she came to be an expert on your subject.

4. Ask open-ended questions, those designed to elicit the interviewee's ideas and whatever facts she may know that you need. Ask for definition of terms

or for clarification of points that are not clear to you. Open-ended questions let the interviewee talk at length about the subject and should elicit the information you seek.

5. In devising and asking questions, remember that more than likely you are not an investigative reporter out to champion a cause or to expose criminal activity. Questions should ask for information; they should not be of the do-you-still-beat-your-wife type.

6. Take notes or use a tape recorder, but do not record secretly. Get the interviewee's permission to record ahead of time. If the interviewee is nervous, just talk with her and jot notes immediately after the interview. (When exploring a potential topic for a master's thesis on folklore, one of the authors found that many of the older people he contacted were especially nervous about being interviewed and recorded, and he had to stop recording on several occasions and simply rely on his memory to provide notes once the interview was over.)

7. At appropriate intervals and again at the end, summarize the interview. Tell the interviewee what you have understood her to have said so that she can clarify her position if need be.

8. As a courtesy, provide the interviewee with a transcript of the interview and a copy of your paper—before the paper is due—so that she can see how you plan to use the interview. At this time the interviewee can check facts and quotations for accuracy, which can strengthen your paper.

Questionnaires Sometimes your topic will call for a survey of a sizable group of people, so that interviewing would be inappropriate. To reach this group, you may want to devise a questionnaire, a set of questions with spaces set aside for the recipient to respond. We see questionnaires often in our society. For example, political pollsters make great use of them to ascertain voter attitudes and then to predict a candidate's chances of winning. Advertising executives use them to ascertain consumer preferences before marketing a product.

Questionnaires survey primarily for two kinds of response.

1. factual information—for example, frequency of product or facility use, kind of products or services used

2. opinion—for example, statements of agreement or disagreement with particular people (perhaps politicians or celebrities), respondents' perspectives on particular issues, short statements about topics of particular interest or concern.

The following is an example of a questionnaire that could be part of a research project on how well a school library functions. Questions 1–3 ask for factual information, whereas 4–8 seek opinion.

In responding to the following questions, circle or mark the most appropriate response.

1. How often do you use the library?

    daily   seldom

      1   2   3   4   5   6

2. What time of day do you most often use the library?

    morning   afternoon   evening

3. For what purposes do you most often use the library? (Circle all that apply.)

    reading   studying   typing   researching   other _______

4. How helpful are the following library personnel?

	very helpful not helpful	
reference librarians	1 2 3 4 5 6	no opinion
reading room librarians	1 2 3 4 5 6	no opinion
circulation librarians	1 2 3 4 5 6	no opinion
interlibrary loan staff	1 2 3 4 5 6	no opinion

5. To what extent are you able to find the resources you need in the library?

    always   seldom

      1   2   3   4   5   6

6. How adequate are the library hours for your needs?

    adequate   inadequate   undecided

7. Should the library change its hours of operation? _______Yes _______No
If *yes*, should the library *increase* or *decrease* its hours? _______

8. What are the library's two primary strengths? Weaknesses?

In addition to posing topical questions to a respondent, pollsters may seek demographic information as well in the attempt to identify particular characteristics of the group being surveyed. In a political race, pollsters might ask the respondent to identify such things as age, sex, race, income level, education level, religious preference, status as home-owner or renter, marital status, and political affiliation. For our hypothetical library survey, appropriate demographic information would include the respondent's age, class (for example, freshman), and major. Such information allows pollsters to describe a "typical" respondent so as to see trends or patterns in the responses and thereby enhance their analysis of the information. A researcher might find, for example, that 85 percent of the freshmen and 80 percent of the sophomores surveyed feel the library to be something of a maze in which they have trouble finding what they need, but only 5 percent of the graduate students surveyed feel this to be the case. Our researcher could conclude from such responses that a comprehensive library orientation program is needed to help undergraduates learn how to use the library.

Observation The last form of field search we will discuss is firsthand observation. If your topic is of some kind of physical nature (for example, an environmental issue, campus parking facilities, campus bike traffic), one of the best ways of searching is to watch or to see what you can see. If possible, observe the scene of your topic several times at different times of the day. Take notes; jot down your impressions of what you see; describe what you see; try to discern patterns in what you see.

<table>
<tr><td>EXERCISE</td><td>

1. Find a topic of current interest in your local or campus community. What is at issue? Identify the thoughts of people on both sides. What is the position of each person? Find at least two published sources (for example, newspaper items) for each side, and summarize each. Identify at least one person for each side and prepare a list of questions you would ask in an interview. If possible, interview each, and summarize the results of your interviews. How reliable do you think the sources you have uncovered are? Why?

2. Identify a current issue about which you are concerned. Devise a questionnaire of at least five questions to ascertain opinions of others on this issue. Administer the questionnaire to at least twenty people, drawing on as broad a range of respondents as possible. Summarize and analyze the results. How did your questions help to shape the results?

3. In a newsmagazine such as *Newsweek*, *Time*, and *U.S. News and World Reports*, find an interview of a national business, political, or religious leader. Summarize the interview's content and its key points. How would you characterize the questions asked? The answers? Are there any questions you would have asked that were not asked? If so, what are they? Why would you ask them?

4. Interview one of your classmates. Prepare a list of questions, asking things you would like to know about that person. After the interview, write a brief character sketch or biography of that person and have him check your writing for accuracy.

5. Spend an hour at a busy spot on campus. Describe the scene before you. Who is there? For what purpose? Are there any dominant patterns that emerge, things that are striking about what you see? If so, identify them. What makes them dominant or striking? What conclusions do you draw from your observations?

</td></tr>
</table>

Incorporating Material from Sources

To use your sources as effectively as possible, you need to be sure that each piece of information you use is clearly set in a context. Your reader needs to see just how you are using that information—for example, how particular information supports your ideas or how your interpretation of information fits with other material in your paper. You can help the reader see how things fit by introducing passages smoothly.

Unintroduced passages seldom seem anything but abrupt; often they intrude on the reader, interrupting the paper's flow. You can introduce a passage in a number of ways, as these hypothetical examples illustrate.

1. Preview the passage by identifying its main idea.

    A. B. Smith does not agree with the current criticism of President Gumbody's economic policies and vehemently attacks critics, saying, "Senator Jones can criticize our policies all he wishes—where are his alternatives? It's time for him to put up or shut up!"

2. Give the author's name.

    Of this perspective, A. B. Smith states, "Now is not the time for divisiveness but for unity."

    A. B. Smith comments on this criticism: "Let those who criticize our policies submit workable alternatives. So far, no one has, though we've continually challenged our detractors to do so."

    A. B. Smith says that "to date, no suitable alternatives have been submitted."

3. Make the passage an integral part of your own ideas.

    Despite intense criticism, President Gumbody's supporters remain loyal because "the opposition has offered no workable alternative."

Documenting Information

Documentation, an essential part of any research project, involves both honesty and courtesy. You will use sources other than yourself in preparing a research paper, and you should credit those outside sources for the information you borrowed. Documentation, from start to finish, does at least these things.

1. Gives credit where it is due (a courtesy to the author you borrow from)

2. Provides readers with points for departure, should they wish to use your research and your sources as the beginnings of their own work (a second courtesy)

3. Takes away any problem of plagiarism—that is, of your using someone else's words or thoughts without giving credit (a matter of honesty)

Documentation begins with an initial or working bibliography and ends with your use of notes and formal bibliography in the paper's final draft.

Initial Bibliography An initial bibliography is a list of potential sources, which you may keep on 3 × 5 note cards, one source to a card, as a matter of convenience. A bibliographical note card should carry such information as the author's name (last name first, to make alphabetizing the final bibliography easy), the source's title, publication data, library call number (if applicable), and a very brief summary of the work's contents. A typical bibliography card would look like Figure 9.2.

Figure 9.2 / Bibliographical Note Card

Because the type of source being used will vary, the bibliography entry format will vary accordingly. Listed here are typical formats for frequently used sources.

Essays

1. In a magazine

Mann, Charles. "The Volcano That's Changing the World." *Science Digest*, May 1983, pp. 76–83, 106–107.

2. In a professional journal

Lamb, Richard F. "The Extent and Form of Exurban Sprawl." *Growth and Change: A Journal of Public, Urban, and Regional Policy*, 14, No. 5 (1983), 40–47.

3. In a newspaper

Smith, Hedrick. "Resignations 'not helping' Reagan." *Las Cruces Sun-News*, 13 Jan. 1983, Sec. A, p. 2, cols. 2–5.

4. In a collection of essays

Larson, Richard L. "Discovery Through Questioning: A Plan for Teaching Rhetorical Invention." *College English* (Nov. 1968). In *Contemporary Rhetoric: A Conceptual Background with Readings*. Ed. W. Ross Winterowd. New York: Harcourt Brace Jovanovich, Inc., 1975, pp. 144–154.

5. An edition or collection of essays

Smith, Henry Nash, ed. *Mark Twain: A Collection of Critical Essays.* Englewood Cliffs, N. J.: Prentice-Hall, Inc., 1963.

Books

1. By one author

Manners, David X. *Complete Book of Home Workshops.* New York: Harper and Row, 1975.

2. By two or three authors

Young, Richard E., Alton L. Becker, and Kenneth L. Pike. *Rhetoric: Discovery and Change.* New York: Harcourt, Brace, and World, Inc., 1970.

3. By more than three authors

Britton, James et al., *The Development of Writing Abilities (11–18).* London: MacMillan Education Ltd., 1975.

4. A reference work (for example, an encyclopedia)

"Sparrow Hawk." *Encyclopedia Americana.* 1972 ed.

Other

1. A personal interview

Lunsford, Ronald F. Personal interview. 12 January 1983.

You probably will not use every source you survey initially, and your initial bibliography makes it convenient for you to retrieve more useful sources later. Just as you may not use all your initial sources, you may augment your bibliography as you find pertinent or appropriate sources later in your project.

Final Bibliography The final bibliography, which you submit as part of the final paper, may be either a list of only the works you cite in your paper itself or a list of all the works you survey in preparing your paper. If the latter, you may divide the bibliography into sections headed (1) "Works Cited" or "Primary Sources" and (2) "Other Works Surveyed" or "Secondary Sources." In any case, alphabetize each section of your bibliography by author's last name, and use the same entry format as that of your initial bibliography, whether that format is the one we suggested, a different one preferred by your instructor, or one established by a style manual in your field. (For more information about style manuals, see p. 273.)

Notes Textual notation formats vary as widely as bibliographical formats, ranging from page references inserted in an essay's text to footnotes placed at the bottom of each page.

In-text References Generally, in-text references are becoming increasingly popular as they provide a quick and easy form of notation. Here are four types of in-text notations.

1. In *Language*, Leonard Bloomfield advocates a commonsensical or utilitarian approach to questions of grammar, stating, "Grammatical doctrine should be accepted only where it passes a test of usefulness, and even then it should be re-shaped to suit the actual needs" (p. 506). (Here the source is identified in the sentence by title and author, and the page from which the quote was taken appears in parentheses at the end of the passage.)

2. In *Language* appears the idea that "grammatical doctrine should be accepted only where it passes a test of usefulness, and even then it should be re-shaped to suit the actual needs" (2:506). (Here the first number in parentheses refers to a numbered entry, in this case the second, in the bibliography; the second number is the page on which the quoted material originally appeared.)

3. In *Language*, we find the idea that "grammatical doctrine should be accepted only where it passes a test of usefulness, and even then it should be re-shaped to suit the actual needs" (Bloomfield, p. 506). (Here the source is identified in the sentence, and the author and page reference are listed in parentheses following the passage.)

4. Bloomfield states that "grammatical doctrine should be accepted only where it passes a test of usefulness, and even then it should be re-shaped to suit the actual needs" (1933, p. 506). (Here the publication date refers the reader to the work published by Bloomfield in 1933. If you need to use works published by an author in the same year, then identify the works with this notation: 1933a, 1933b. The *a* would refer to the first entry by the author published in 1933, the *b* to the second entry.)

In-text references are easier for the writer to use than footnotes because she does not have to gauge how much space to leave at the bottom of the page for footnotes. However, in-text references do not provide as much immediate information as footnotes do. Whether you use in-text references or footnotes will be determined by the assignment you are fulfilling.

Footnotes These are complete references placed either at the bottom of the page on which the referenced materials appear or on a separate note page at the end of the paper. If you place footnotes at the bottom of the page, gauge the space you will need using the following guidelines.

1. Double-space after the last written line on the page. (Draw a 2- to 3-inch line on this line from the left margin to separate the text from the notes.)

2. Single-space within footnotes; double-space between footnotes. Generally, you should allow two lines per footnote for simple references (for example, a book by one author, a magazine or journal article).

3. Be sure the last footnote on a given page does not intrude into the bottom margin. (Your instructor or a particular style manual will outline margin requirements for you.)

If you use a note page, place it between the paper's conclusion and bibliography. The format for note page entries and footnotes is the same. Earlier, we presented bibliography formats for the more commonly used sources. The following are sample formats for those same sources entered as footnotes. Compare each note entry with its bibliographical counterpart. What differences do you notice?

Essays

1. In a magazine

[1]Charles Mann, "The Volcano That's Changing the World," *Science Digest*, May 1983, pp. 76–83, 106–107.

2. In a professional journal

[2]Richard F. Lamb, "The Extent and Form of Exurban Sprawl," *Growth and Change: A Journal of Public, Urban, and Regional Policy*, 14, No. 5 (1983), 40–47.

3. In a newspaper

[3]Hedrick Smith, "Resignations 'not helping' Reagan." *Las Cruces Sun-News*, 13 Jan. 1983, Sec. A, p. 2, cols. 2–5.

4. In a collection of essays

[4]Richard L. Larson, "Discovery Through Questioning: A Plan for Teaching Rhetorical Invention." *College English* (Nov. 1968), in *Contemporary Rhetoric: A Conceptual Background with Readings*, ed. W. Ross Winterowd. (New York: Harcourt Brace Jovanovich, Inc., 1975), pp. 144–154.

5. An edition or collection of essays

[5]Henry Nash Smith, ed., *Mark Twain: A Collection of Critical Essays* (Englewood Cliffs, N. J.: Prentice-Hall, Inc., 1963), p. 5.

Books

1. By one author

[1]David X. Manners, *Complete Book of Home Workshops* (New York: Harper and Row, Inc., 1975), p. 73.

2. By two or three authors

[2]Richard E. Young, Alton L. Becker, and Kenneth L. Pike, *Rhetoric: Discovery and Change* (Harcourt, Brace, and World, Inc., 1970), p. 14.

3. By more than three authors

[3]James Britton, et al., *The Development of Writing Abilities (11–18)* (London: MacMillan Education Ltd., 1975), p. 87.

4. A reference work (for example, an encyclopedia)

[4]"Sparrow Hawk," *Encyclopedia Americana*, 1972 ed.

Other

A personal interview

[1]Personal interview with Ronald F. Lunsford, 12 January 1983.

Style Manuals The preceding bibliography and note formats are those prescribed by the Modern Language Association (MLA) in the *MLA Handbook for Writers of Research Papers, Theses, and Dissertations* (New York: Modern Language Association, 1977) and accepted as the standard format for papers in the disciplines of English and Foreign Languages. Such a handbook is called a style manual and contains requirements for such elements of research works as documentation, manuscript preparation (for example, spacing, margins, pagination, and binding), and mechanics of writing (for example, spelling and punctuation). For writing papers in a particular discipline (for example, agriculture, biology, anthropology), consult the style manual adopted by experts in the field. If you do not know which manual is recommended for your discipline, consult one of your professors for advice.

WRITING A RESEARCH PAPER

Research projects generally result in essays more formal than most transactional essays, though this need not always be the case. To indicate the range of formality in research papers, we include two papers, both by Karen Pinckley: "Lake Valley: A Treasure Chest of Fossils" and "The Senseless Seal Slaughter." As you read these essays, consider the following questions.

Questions for Discussion

1. The "Lake Valley" paper was written to meet the second purpose of research writing; that is, Karen intended that it primarily present information to her audience. The "Seals" paper, however, was written to meet the third purpose; its goal is to argue a particular point. How well does each paper fulfill its purpose? On what do you base your assessment?

2. How formal is each essay? Which is the more formal? The less formal? How appropriate is the formality of each? On what do you base your assessment?

3. The audiences for these papers vary greatly. Karen's "Lake Valley" paper was written for submission to *New Mexico Magazine*, a monthly magazine published by the state of New Mexico to spotlight people and points of interest in New Mexico. The "Seals" paper was written in the context of a composition class, and Karen selected the readers of such magazines as *Smithsonian*, *GEO*, *National Geographic*, and *National Wildlife* as her intended audience. How appropriate is each paper for its primary audience? On what do you base your assessment?

Lake Valley: A Treasure Chest of Fossils

Karen Pinckley

Southern New Mexico has not always been dry and hot. In fact, about 330 million years ago, a tropical sea as rich in life as the modern-day Bahama Banks drenched this now desert land. By her miracle of fossilization, Nature has captured the fascinating story of this warm sea and its life in layers of rock called formations. One of the best hunting grounds for those seeking keepsakes from this ancient sea is the Lake Valley formation in Southern New Mexico, a giant treasure chest heaped with fossils for the taking.

<u>New Mexico—A Tropical Sea</u>

The Lake Valley formation was born over 330 million years ago during the geologic time period known as the "Mississippian." Ancestral North America was unbelievably different from its present state. Europe and Africa were slammed in tight against its eastern coast, and a shallow sea, called an epeiric sea, glazed over most of the land.

Scientists believe the equator ran through the middle of the continent; in fact, New Mexico's northwest corner could have nearly hung on it. (A composite picture of North America as geologists believe it looked during Mississippian is shown in Figure 1.) The shallow sea which once covered our state was so loaded with shellfish and reef-building creatures that they left a "limey" debris on the seafloor; this carbonate-rich sediment formed the limestone rock of the Lake Valley formation, which is now wealthy with Mississippian fossil-life.

In its day, this epeiric sea was a flourishing tropical marine sanctuary, with Mississippian fauna so prolific they created an

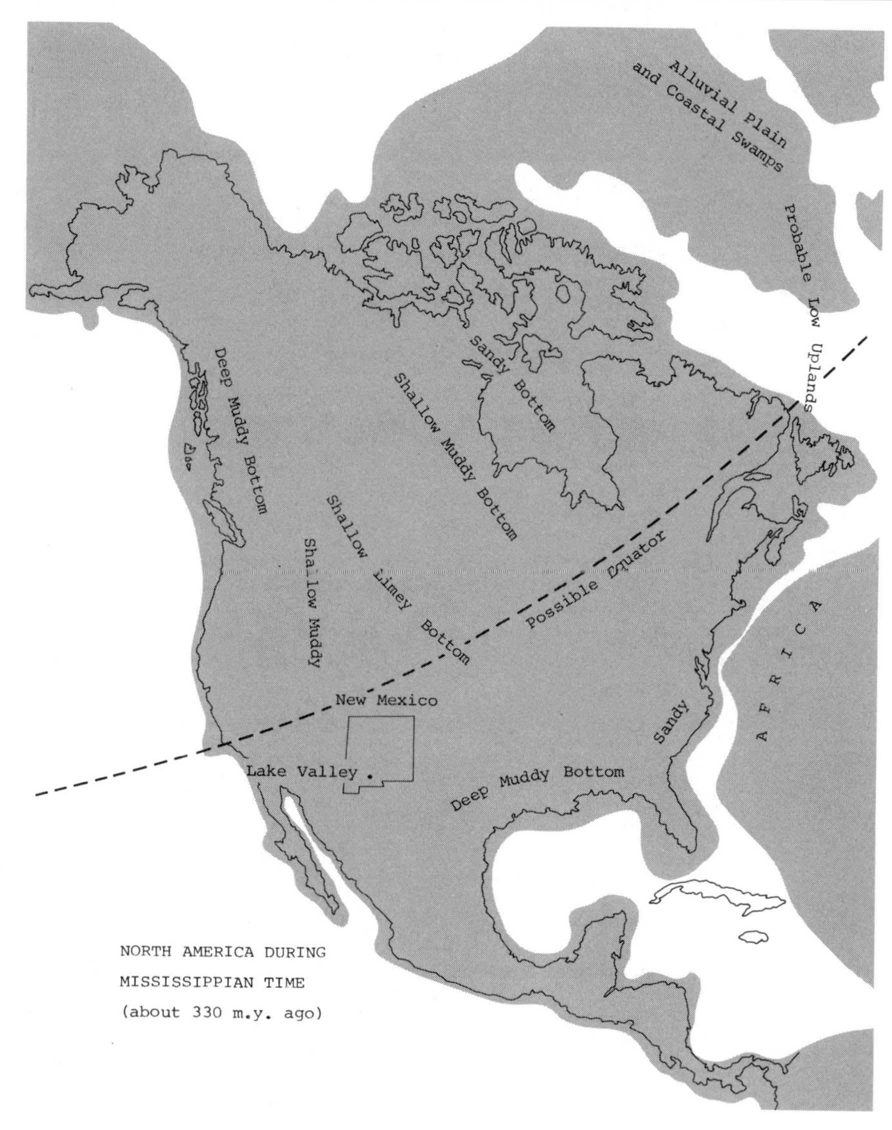

Figure 1.

Adapted from Dott and Batten, 1976, p. 279.

enchanting undersea garden. Crinoids, long-stemmed invertebrates that looked more like wildflowers, decorated the sea in "blooms" and swayed gracefully to the motion of the salty water. Shells of all shapes and sizes pebbled the garden grounds, and lacy and twiggy bryzoan, stretching up towards the warm sunshine, squeezed into the spaces between them. Horn-shaped corals and pulsating sponges, rooted firmly in the soft ocean sediments, filter-fed on the rich water. One of the most intriguing characters of this marine community was the now extinct trilobite, a strange creature that looked somewhat like a cross between a rolypoly bug and a cockroach, but was actually a crustacean. (An artist's re-creation of a Mississippian "garden" of creatures is shown in Figure 2.)

<u>From</u> <u>Life</u> <u>to</u> <u>Stone</u>

After these invertebrates died, their soft tissues decayed, putrefied, or were eaten by scavengers, so that only their hard parts, such as the shell, remained. The shell was frequently attacked by boring organisms or crushed against rocks by waves, but occasionally it was buried and sealed in the soft seafloor sediments. With time, sand, mud, and skeletal debris accumulated hundreds of feet thick over the shell, and the weight of the pile squeezed the water from the sediments and caused the temperature to increase, in effect, baking the shell and sediments into solid stone. It was by this process, called fossilization, that the Lake Valley community was captured in stone.

After Mississippian time, the epeiric sea retreated from the continent and the land dried. For the next three million years, the processes of deposition (the accumulation of new layers of sediment) and erosion (the removal of old layers of sediment) battled. Sand dunes,

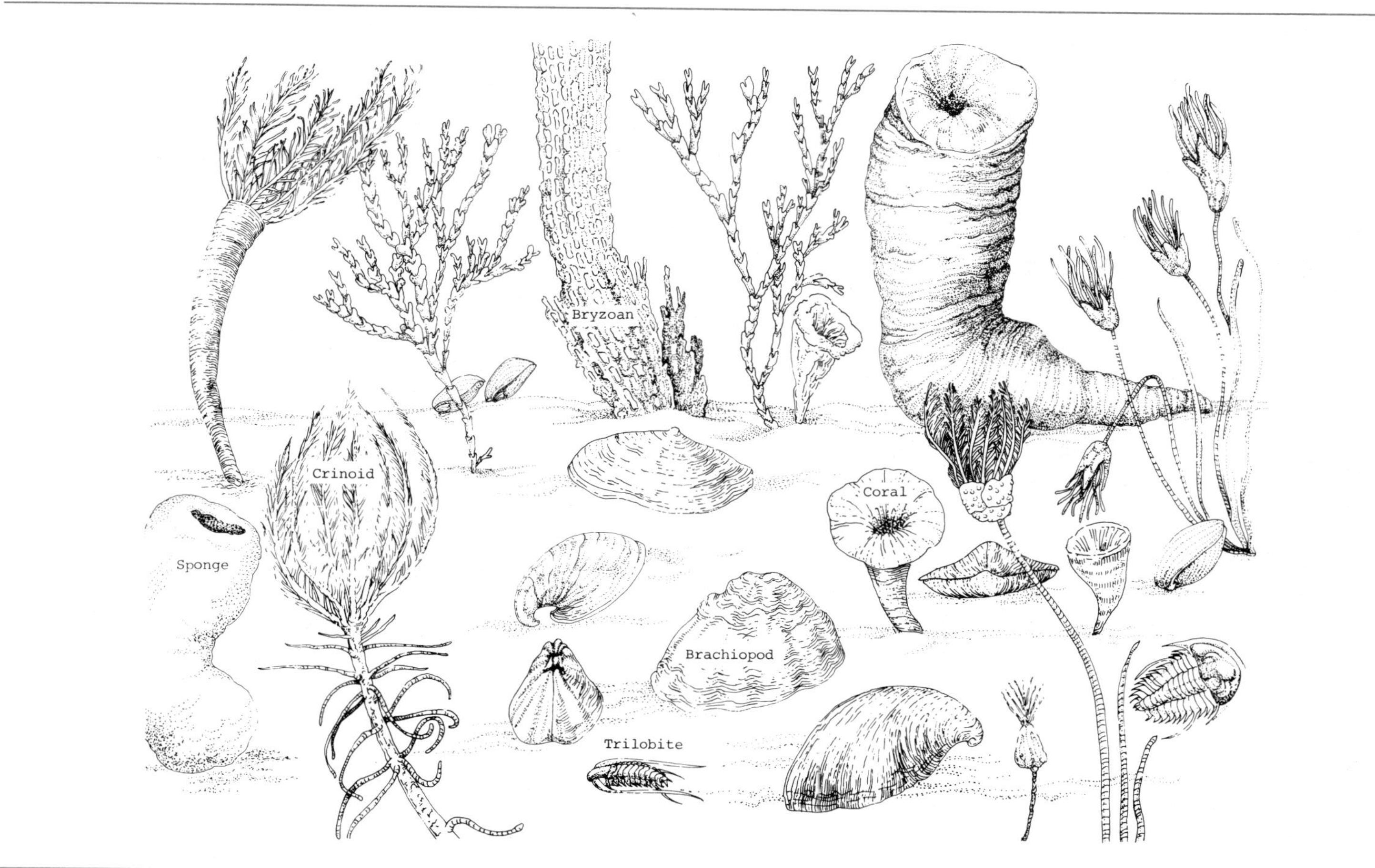

Figure 2

lava flows, ash falls, and sediment carried by water layered over the old sea floor. Sporadically, the Earth's dynamic forces attacked these new layers—wind and water stripped away sediment; heaving and faulting deformed and displaced huge sections of rock. In some areas of Southern New Mexico, the fossil-rich limestone of the Lake Valley formation ended up on top of the pile as a surface outcrop and formed tremendous fossil hunting grounds.

<u>Lake</u> <u>Valley</u>—"<u>Lousy</u>" <u>with</u> <u>Fossils</u>

Stone life is so abundant in the Lake Valley limestone that geologists say it's "lousy" with fossils. One of the "lousiest" and most accessible spots to collect Lake Valley fossils is from a weathering bluff beside New Mexico Highway 27, 13.5 miles northwest of Nutt. Directions to my favorite fossil hot-spot are given on the map below.

Location of the Lake Valley Formation Fossil-Hunting Grounds

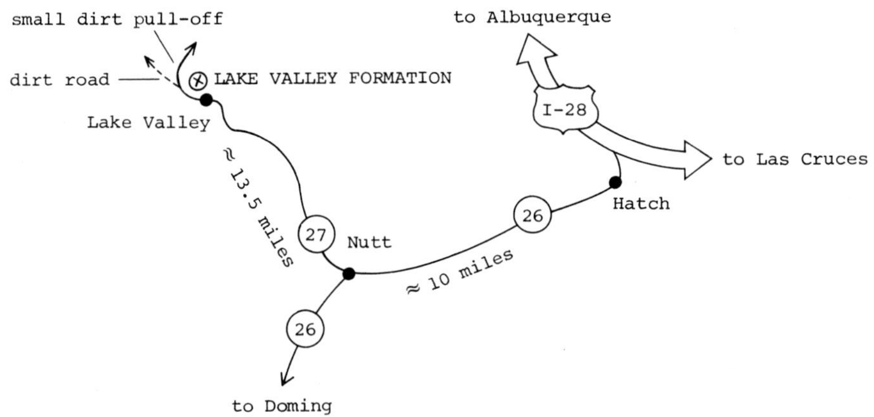

<u>Treasure-Hunting Tips</u>

On your first trip to the Lake Valley treasure chest, allow at least half a day to hunt. Finding fossil keepsakes is exciting, and you won't want to leave a stone unturned, but hiking back in the dark —through the cactus—could end your day painfully. Although the distance you'll hike is fairly short, the terrain is rugged, so wear heavy jeans and sturdy footwear. And leave your small children at home.

For the actual collecting, you won't need any special equipment. Toilet paper makes a great wrap for small, delicate specimens, and you can collect your treasures in a sturdy sack or bucket, although a daypack makes carrying them out much easier. Bring along a rock hammer if you want, but I've had better success collecting the lazy way —from small gullies or slope bases where the fossils have weathered naturally out of the rock. On my first trip to Lake Valley, I ambitiously packed out chunks of the bluff and boulders believing I could chip the tempting fossils out of them when I got home. But most cracked when I tried, so all I collected that day was a sore back.

When you find a likely place, kneel, sit, hunch over, or squat, but get close enough to the ground to inspect a small area carefully. After a few minutes of staring at the grey rock, your eyes will "fine tune" and you'll begin to spot fossils like an expert. Take the fossils you wish, but be selective—remember that whatever you collect you'll have to lug out. (See Figure 3 for an abbreviated guide to some of the fossils you're most likely to find.)

Here are just a few examples of the fossils you are most likely
to discover in the Lake Valley limestone. If you want to identify your
treasures more precisely, you'll need a book on invertebrate fossils.

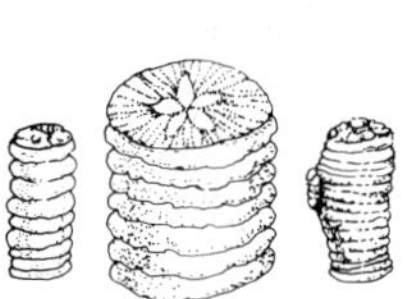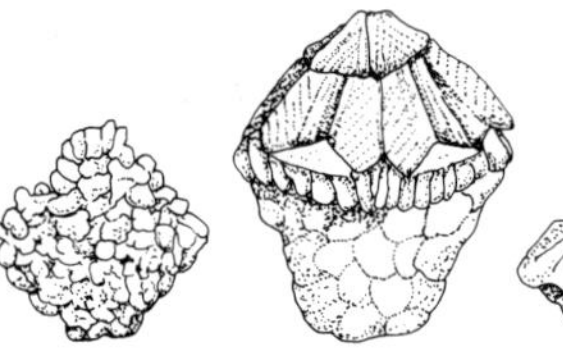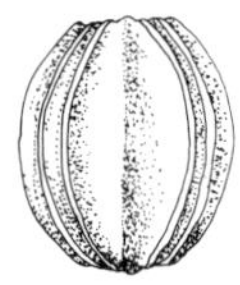

CRINOID STEMS   CRINOID TOPS   BLASTOIDS
They're everywhere!   An exciting, rare find.   The size of a pea.

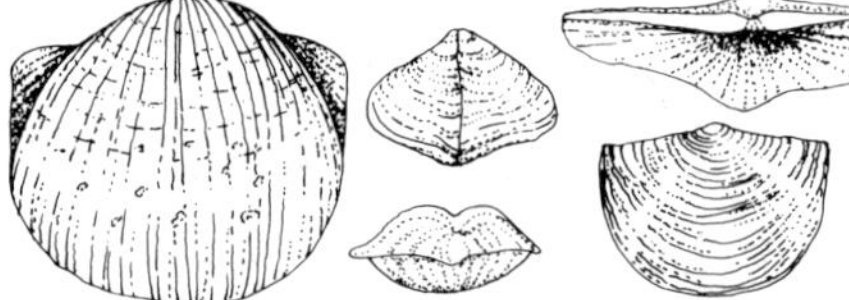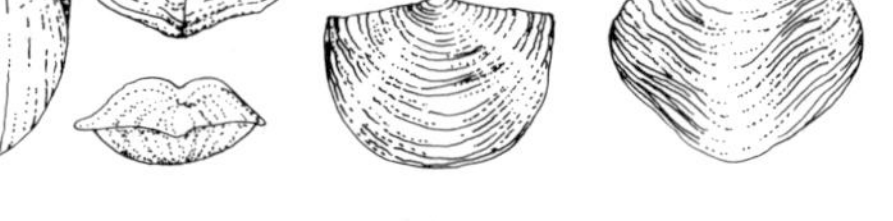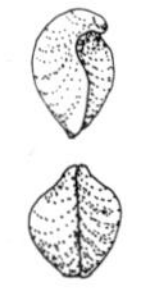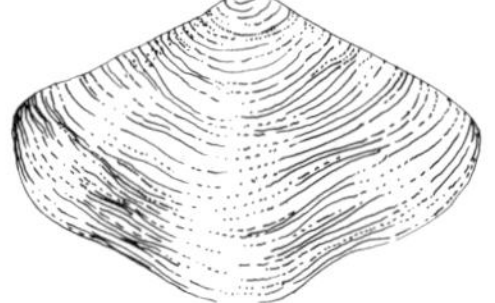

BRACHIOPODS: An endless array, in all shapes and sizes.

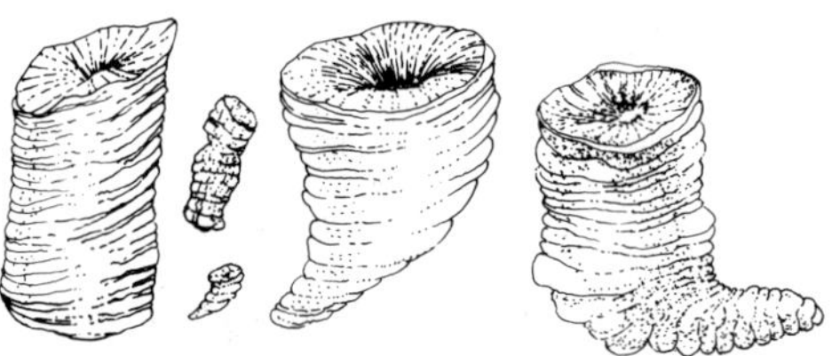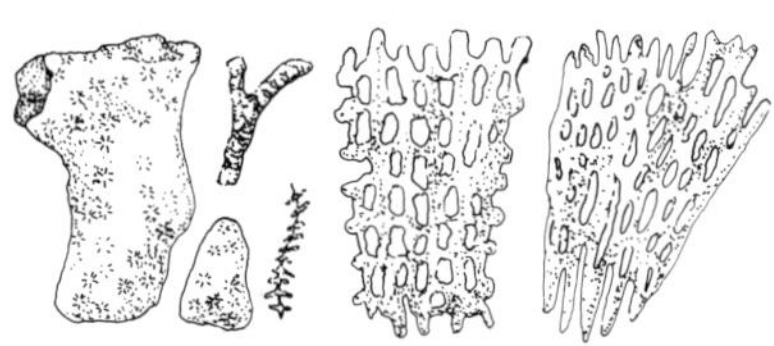

CORALS: They litter the ground!   Twiggy and lacy BRYOZOANS

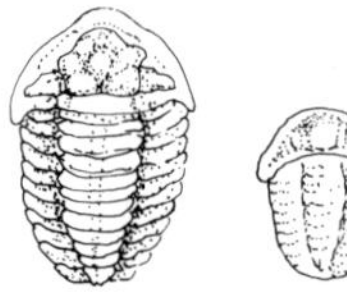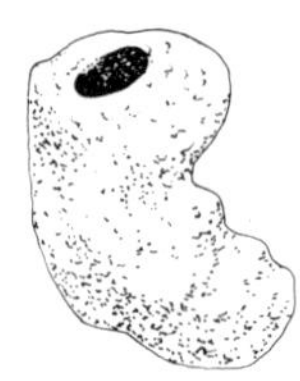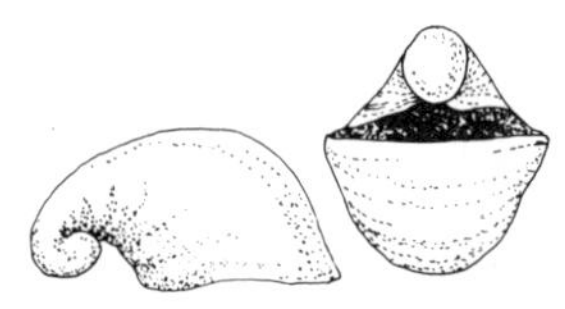

TRILOBITE: A fabulous find!   SPONGE   GASTROPODS

<u>Lake</u> <u>Valley</u> <u>Fossils</u>:   <u>Record</u> <u>of</u> <u>New</u> <u>Mexico's</u> <u>Ancient</u> <u>History</u>

Exciting events in New Mexico's history have been recorded in ballads, legends, and folk tales ever since this land was pioneered. Fierce battles between the Spaniards and Indians, adventures along the Santa Fe Trail, and wars over New Mexico's lands highlight our state's rich history. But New Mexico's ancient history, recorded in layers of stone, is just as exciting and important. The fossil life you may discover locked in the solid stone treasure chest of the Lake Valley formation is a small but vital piece of a huge geological puzzle that tells us of a tropical sea, brimming with life, that drenched this land over 330 million years ago. The Lake Valley story proves that, even from the beginning, New Mexico was The Land of Enchantment.

The Senseless Seal Slaughter

Karen Pinckley

Annually, rituals of death occur. In March, hunters slay thousands upon thousands of helpless white harp seal pups in Newfoundland; in July, hunters take adult spotted fur seals in Alaska's Pribilof Islands. Over the years, sealing has taken an enormous toll on these two species of seal. Continued sealing will eventually lead to their extinction.

Large-scale commercial exploitation of the beautiful harp and fur seal began about two centuries ago in North America. Between 1806 and 1834, Russian sealers ruthlessly massacred over 2.5 million fur seal along the rugged shores of the Pribilofs.[1] Men stalking Newfoundland's ice floes have brutally clubbed, shot and kicked to death millions of baby harp seal for their soft, white pelts over the last two hundred years.[2] Seal slaughtering is a cruel and merciless family keepsake, a bloody tradition passed from father to son. The tradition must be abolished.

In the past, no efforts were made to preserve the seal population. Before the U.S. purchased Alaska in 1867, fur sealing by the Russians was totally unregulated. Once the seals numbered in the millions, but by 1909 Russian hunters had thoughtlessly butchered the herd down to a straggling 200,000. Fortunately, an international fur treaty was

---

[1] Stephen Spotte, "Ashore with Alaska's Feisty Fur Seal," _National Wildlife_, June/July 1980, pp. 4-11.

[2] Cleveland Amory, "Let's Save the Seals," _Good Housekeeping_, March 1980, pp. 60-64.

enacted in 1911 which forbade pelagic sealing[3] and saved the herd from extinction, but it still allowed the massacre to continue.[4] No such treaty protects the harp seal pups, as Canadian officials have re-peatedly ignored pleas from conservation groups and distressed biolo-gists to regulate the harp seal hunt meaningfully. While the Alaskan fur seal slaughter is limited to 30,000 bachelor males,[5] the Canadian harp seal quota is set at a whopping 180,000 pups a year.[6]

Nearly 75% of the world's population of fur seal breed in the Pribilof Islands along the east coast of Alaska. Adult males, weighing up to 400 pounds, set up strict breeding territories along the rocky coastline during May. They aggressively guard their terri-tories and wait for the females or "cows" to reach the islands in June. Cows, normally weighing about 100 pounds, deliver one ten-pound pup in late July. Since the pups have a coarse black birth coat, they are considered worthless by hunters, who value the silvery, slick, spotted coat of the adults. Tragically, the pups are often victims of the hunt; when their mothers are slaughtered, they inevitably starve.[7]

---

[3] Pelagic sealing was a method of harvesting seal at sea which was practiced by vessels not permitted to kill seal on the Pribilofs. They harpooned and shot seal non-selectively, often killing pregnant or nursing mothers. Over one-half of their kill sank before they could retrieve it (Spotte, pp. 4-11).

[4] Spotte, pp. 4-11.

[5] Spotte, pp. 4-11.

[6] Amory, pp. 60-64.

[7] Brian Davies, _Savage Luxury_ (New York: Taplinger Publishing Co., 1970), pp. 131-133.

In March, the female harp seal gives birth to a soft white pup on the ice floes around Newfoundland. The snowy-white babies lie helplessly on the ice for their first two and a half weeks of life. Hunters take full advantage of their helpless state and club them where they lie before they reach three weeks of age, when they can fend for themselves. Harp seal parents will defend their pups to the death, if they are present when hunters attack. Of course, hunters quickly stifle the fearsome growl of the 900 pound male with a bullet. It is illegal to hunt the adults, but legal to kill them in self-defense.[8]

Fur and harp seal are slain by similar methods. The main difference between the two hunts is that adult fur seal are clubbed as they frantically bound from the rocky shores to the sea's protection, while harp seal pups are bludgeoned to death as they lie helplessly on the ice. William McCloskey vividly describes the murder and skinning procedure:

> It was done as work, impersonally. The sealer strikes the seal on the head with the steel knob of his hakapik (the other legal method is with a hardwood club). . . . The sealer is instructed to strike three times. ("Once to kill him, once for the fishery officer, and once for Greenpeace," say the sealers.) Next, he must turn the seal over and bleed it, cutting straight into the chest. A stream of blood spurts out and reddens the ice. In most cases, he straightens and pauses to sharpen his knife. He then bends

----

[8]Davies, pp. 50-52.

over and with deft slices "sculps" the sculp (pelt and fat)
from the carcass and cuts the flippers from the fat. Finally
he drags the 30-to-70-pound sculp to a central pan marked
by a red flag with the ship's name, to be picked up later in
the day as the ship breaks through the ice to the pans.[9]

Prior to 1964, hunters could legally slaughter seal in any way
that struck their fancy. The traditional Newfoundlander method was
gaffing. First, the hunter would club the seal in the head with the
flat side of a spiked board, then drive the spike into the seal's
brain. Some sealers would simply kick the baby seal in the face, roll
him over, and slice his throat. Sometimes seals were drowned by holding them under the icy polar waters in strong nets or traps. Longlining, the most gruesome killer of all, was a method by which a
cruelly sharp, baited hook was lowered into the water and swallowed
by a hungry seal. The hook sliced the seal's throat and gouged into
his belly, leaving the animal to gag and suffocate in the dark waters
as he desperately struggled to get free. Still practiced today,
shooting is generally reserved for rebellious adults who stay to defend their young; these adults the hunters claim they are forced to
kill.[10]

Legislation since 1964 allows only two murder weapons to be used:
the club and the hakapik. The club is made of hardwood and looks like
a fat baseball bat, while the hakapik is a resculptured version of the

---

[9] William B. McCloskey, Jr., "Bitter Fight Still Rages Over the Seal Killing in Canada," *Smithsonian*, Nov. 1979, pp. 54-64.

[10] Davies, pp. 14-16.

gaff, its "pik" shorter and straighter. As efficient as these weapons
are, other methods have been tested. After receiving hostile criticism concerning an especially brutal Pribilof Island hunt in 1968, the
United States Department of the Interior organized a task force to
evaluate killing methods. They ran a series of hideous tests—beating,
shooting, gassing, and shocking adult seal to death before an emotionless audience of task force observers. They concluded clubbing was
the most effective and humane method.[11] So the barbarism continues.

And for what purposes? Seals are slaughtered for their fur, to
make expensive, high-fashion coats, to line boots and mittens, and to
stuff children's toys. They are also taken for their oil and their
tough, gamy meat. But are seal fur coats worth the cost, the ruthless
destruction of a gentle and spectacularly beautiful animal? Can you
buy your child a baby seal playtoy, knowing of the brutal beating this
innocent baby has taken? Can you survive without seal oil lamps and
gamy-flavored seal meat? Can you simply watch the seals bludgeoned
into extinction? When we lose the seals—and ultimately we will if
the slaughter is not stopped—then we will lose something of ourselves:

> These animals are symbolic, and if they can't be saved,
> it probably isn't ever going to be possible to save any
> substantial population of wild creatures. The world will
> gradually fill with filth and one day, empty of all but
> man, this planet will become the loneliest place in the

---

[11]Davies, pp. 134-142.

universe. Perhaps in saving the seals, man may save himself.[12]

The bloody tradition of sealing must stop. It can be stopped only if
we join together and support organizations opposing the brutality. I
urge you to send a donation—just $10.00 will help—to The Fund for
Animals (140 W. 57 St., New York, N.Y. 10019). With your help, the
seals have a chance. Without it, they move closer and closer to
extinction.

---

[12] Davies, p. 208.

BIBLIOGRAPHY

Amory, Cleveland. "Let's Save the Seals." <u>Good</u> <u>Housekeeping</u>, March
     1980, pp. 60-64.

Davies, Brian. <u>Savage</u> <u>Luxury</u>. New York: Taplinger Publishing Co.,
     1970.

McCloskey, William B., Jr. "Bitter Fight Still Rages Over the Seal
     Killing in Canada." <u>Smithsonian</u>, Nov. 1979, pp. 54-64.

Spotte, Stephen. "Ashore with Alaska's Feisty Fur Seal." <u>National</u>
     <u>Wildlife</u>, June/July 1980, pp. 4-11.

Engage in a research project. Find a subject you are or can become curious about; explore it; then write a paper carrying your insights into that subject. Remember that a research paper will fulfill one of these three purposes: (1) report the results of your probing or exploring the topic, (2) present information and your interpretation of it to your reader, or (3) argue a point.

A research paper is a particular kind of transactional writing; thus, the process you will use in writing a research paper will be very similar to that you used in writing several papers in this course. As a reminder, here is the seven-step process we outlined earlier.

> Step 1: Freewrite
> Step 2: Select and Examine Your Topic
> Step 3: Devise a Planning Page
> Step 4: Write a Discovery Draft
> Step 5: Select and Analyze Your Audience
> Step 6: Write a Second Draft
> Step 7: Write a Final Draft

Here we will comment specifically only on steps 2 and 5 as we see them at work in a research paper.

In step 2 you may begin your initial search—reading, taking notes, forming an initial bibliography, structuring and analyzing the results of a questionnaire, interviewing, and doing whatever is appropriate for your topic. This step, then, will probably take a good bit more time in research writing than in other kinds of transactional writing.

In step 5 you should consider your discovery draft carefully in light of your intended audience and purpose. As you decide the appropriateness of your paper's purpose, its focus, and the information it presents, you may find more research to be necessary. If so, use the same procedures that you used in step 2; in essence, return to step 2 for extended searching and probing of your topic.

In this section we present a research project by Karen Pinckley that culminated in "The Senseless Seal Slaughter." To complete this assignment, Karen followed the seven-step process we suggested for transactional writing with one exception—she skipped the first step, freewriting, because she began her project with a topic in mind. Karen's involvement with environmental issues plus a particularly gory exposé of sealing on a national news broadcast led her to both a topic—sealing—and a focus—that sealing must be stopped. Her job, then, was to write a paper arguing against sealing for an appropriate audience, one that would be unaware of the specific problems Karen associated with sealing or one that would be neutral about or slightly in favor of sealing. Even though she began by knowing both topic and focus, Karen discovered much in writing her paper, learning more about seals and sealing than she knew before. What she discovered heightened her outrage at what she termed "the senseless seal slaughter."

Step 1 For the next fifteen minutes, freewrite about potential topics. If you may choose your topic but do not have one yet, look through your Interest Inventory for potential topics. If your topic is assigned by your instructor, freewrite about that topic. As you write, raise questions you would like answered, or ask questions about what in the topic interests you. Your task is to begin discovering an initial focal point that fits with one of the three purposes of research writing.

Select and Examine Your Topic

Karen's search led her to the library, where she did a good bit of reading, steered to such magazines as *Smithsonian* and *National Wildlife* by the *Readers' Guide to Periodical Literature*. She also located books by using the card catalog. Her initial note taking was messy and disorganized because she decided not to use note cards but to use notebook paper instead, often placing information from three or four sources on a single page. She also collected more than she needed. Not all the information she gathered initially appears in the final draft. During her library search, Karen wrote the following responses to the Questions for Analysis.

QUESTIONS FOR ANALYSIS

What goes with the seal hunt?

What is it?

Annual slaughter of baby harp seal and adult fur seal in the waters around Newfoundland and the Pribilof Is.

What physical entities go with the seal hunt?

The club and hakipik, blood & guts, sealing boats, hunters, ice flows along coast of Newfoundland, rocky shores of Pribilofs, Greenpeace and other conservation groups, fur coats, seal oil, seal meat, other fur items.

What do I associate with the seal hunt?

Slaughter of innocent baby seal, cruel and merciless hunters, seal conservation groups, blood, messy operation, the club & hakipik.

In what context is the seal hunt set?

Tradition—a livelihood for the sealers and a way of life. Oppositely set in a context of useless, cruel slaughter.

How is seal hunting like other things?

Like the slaying of exotic African beasts, hunted for their fur, ivory or hide rather than their meat. Like the whale hunt—severely opposed by conservation groups—yet still continues.

In what class do I place the seal hunt?

In the same class as poaching of endangered species for non-survival reasons.
What opposes the seal hunt?

What physical entities oppose the seal hunt?

The sight of a bloody, clubbed baby harp seal dead on the ice. Numbers left in the herd. Sight of hunters clubbing seal.

Theoretical or philosophical opposition to the hunt?

Many people are against cruel method used to kill seal. Conservation groups such as Greenpeace and "Save the Seal" foundation oppose the murder of the seals because they feel it's an ancient, cruel, barbaric tradition that should not be practiced and they fear extinction of the seal.

How does the seal hunt stand out against its context?

A cruel, bloody, barbaric slaughter occurring along the peaceful, serene, beautiful shores of Alaska and ice of Newfoundland.

How is the seal hunt unlike similar things?

The seal are not as close to extinction as other hunted wild animals such as the elephant or leopard.

What about the seal hunt is odd, incongruous, or unusual?

The fact that the seal hunt continues when there is so much opposition to it.
What follows from the seal hunt?

What follows the hunt chronologically?

Preparation & sale of the pelts, flippers, and meat.

How did the seal hunt come to be?

Russians began hunting the seal over 200 yrs. ago—used Aleut slaves. Those Aleuts remained on the Pribilofs and kept hunting seal—it was their livelihood.

What are the causes of the seal hunt?

The pelts bring a high price.

What results from the seal hunt?

Fur coats, mittens, seal oil, seal meat. Opposition to the hunt by conservation groups.

What sort of problems does the hunt pose?

Possible damage or extinction of herd, cruelty to animals, violent protests by Greenpeace. Loss of lives of hunters on iceflows & spotting plane.

What opportunities does the hunt offer?

Chance to make money by sale of pelts and chance to see the harp & fur seal in their natural environment.

What are the implications of the seal hunt?

A brutal, ruthless murder of a graceful, beautiful animal of the sea.

Is the hunt good, bad, etc.?

The hunt is merciless and cruel and should be stopped before permanent damage is done to herd numbers.

Step 2   Begin searching your topic, whether that search involves library or field research, or some combination of the two. Establish an initial bibliography; take notes; apply the Questions for Analysis to your topic.

Devise a Planning Page

Karen's Planning Page is primarily a checklist of points to include arranged in what she thought to be a logical order. In the margins Karen jotted particular strategies she thought might be effective in presenting her case, even though she had not selected an audience at this point. Figure 9.3 is a copy of Karen's Planning Page. Note that it does not carry a final statement of thesis—that is, her stance on the topic. Given the nature of her responses to the Questions for Analysis, however, Karen's position on the topic is clear—her paper will carry an argument against sealing.

Step 3   Using the focal point you found in step 2, however tentative that point may be, devise a Planning Page for your first draft.

Write a Discovery Draft

Karen's discovery draft is a bit incomplete and awkward in places, but it was something she could base the next two drafts on. This draft follows the Planning Page fairly well, although this draft lacks a conclusion, and the section planned about current legislation does not appear. You have already read Karen's final draft. How does it compare with this discovery draft?

WRITING
SAMPLE

First draft

The Senseless Seal Slaughter

Sealing: A Bloody Tradition

  Commercial exploitation of the beautiful harp and fur seal

began about two centuries in North America. Russian sealers ruth-

lessly massacred over 2.5 million fur seal, between 1806 and 1834,

akong the rugged shores of Alaska's Pribilof Islands (Spotte). Men

stalking the iceflows around Newfoundland have brutally clubbed,

shot, and kicked to death millions of baby harp seal for their soft,

white pelts over the last two hundred years (Amory). Seal slaughtering is a cruel and merciless family keepsake that is passed on from
father to son. The tradition must be abolished.

In the past, no efforts were made to preserve the seal population. Before the U.S. purchased Alaska in 1867, fur sealing by
the Russians was totally unregulated. Once they had numbered in
the millions, but by 1909 the Russians had thoughtlessly butchered
the herd down to a straggling 200,000. Fortunately, an international fur treaty was enacted in 1911 which forbid pelagic* sealing
and saved the herd from extinction; but it still allowed the massacre
to continue (Spotte). (bottom of page: *Pelagic sealing was a
method of harvesting seal at sea which was practiced by vessels not
permitted to kill seal on the Pribilofs. They harpooned and shot
seal non-selectively, often killing pregnant or nursing mothers.
Over one-half of their kill sank before they could retrieve it--
Spotte.) Past officials in the Canadian government have purposely
ignored please from conservation groups and distressed biologists
to regulate the harp seal hunt (Davies).

The Spotted Fur Seal

Nearly 75% of the world's population of fur seal breed in
the Pribilof Islands along the east coast of Alaska. Adult males,
weighing up to 400 pounds, set up strict breeding territories along
the rocky coastline during May. They aggressively guard their
territories and await for the females or "cows" to reach the islands
in June. Cows, normally weighing about 100 pounds, deliver one ten-
pound pup in late July. Since the pups have a coarse black birth coat,
they are considered worthless by hunters, who value the silvery, slick,
spotted coat of the adults. Tragically, the pups are often a victim
of the hunt; when their mothers are slaughtered they inevitably starve.
By the end of November, the seals abandon the Pribilof Islands for the
warmer waters along the coast of California (Davies).

<u>The White Harp Pup</u>

In March, the female harp seal gives birth to a soft white pup on the ice flows around Newfoundland. The snoey-white babies lay helplessly on the ice for their first two and a half weeks of life. Hunters take full advantage of their helpless state and club them where they lay before they reach three weeks of age, when they can fend for themselves. Harp seal parents will defend their pups to the death, if they are present when hunters attack. Of course, the hunters quickly stifly the fearsome growl of the 900 pound male with a bullet. It is illegal to hunt the adults, but legal to kill them in "self defense." The adult coat is coarse and black, which brings a lower price anyway. Immature and adult seal congregate on the ice in April to moult, then in June, head up north to the icy waters of Baffin Bay and Davis Strait, where they find peace away from the hunters for the short arctic summer (Davies).

<u>The Slaughter</u>

Fur and harp seal are slayed by similar methods. The main difference between the two hunts is the adult fur seal are clubbed as they frantically bound from the rocky shores to the sea's protection; harp seal pups are beaten to death as they lie helplessly on the ice. William McCloskey vividly describes the murder and sculpting procedure:

> It was done as work, impersonally. The sealer strikes the
> seal on the head with the steel knob of his hakapik (the
> other legal method is with a hardwood club). Biologists agree
> that it takes only moderate strength and aim over a small
> area to render the seal permanently unconscious. The sealer
> is instructed to strike three times. ("Once to kill him, once
> for the fishery officer, and once for Greenpeace," say the
> sealers.) Next, he must turn the seal over and bleed it, cut-
> ting straight into the chest. A stream of blood spurts out

and reddens the ice. In most cases, he straightens and pauses

to sharpen his knife. He then bends over and with deft slices

"sculps" the sculp (pelt and fat) from the carcass and cuts

the flippers from the fat. Finally he drags the 30-to-70-

pound sculp to a central pan marked by a red flag with the

ship's name, to be picked up later in the day as the ship

breaks through the ice to the pans. (McCloskey, 1979, p. 59)

<u>Hakapik</u> <u>and</u> <u>Club</u>: <u>Legal</u> <u>Murder</u> <u>Weapons</u>

Prior to 1964, hunters could legally slaughter seal in any

way that struck their fancy. The traditional Newfoundlander method

was gaffing. First, the hunter would club the seal in the head with

the flat side of a spiked board, then drive the spike into the seal's

brain. Some sealers would simply kick the baby seal in the face,

roll him over, and slice his throat. Sometimes seals were drowned

by holding them under the icy polar waters in strong nets or traps.

Longlining, the most gruesome killer of all, is a method by which

a cruelly sharp, baited hook is lowered into the water and swallowed

by a hungry seal. The hook slices the seal's throat and gorges into

his belly, leaving the animal to gag and suffocate in the dark waters

as he desperately struggles to get free. Shooting is generally re-

served for "rebellious" adults who stay to defend their young (the

ones the hunters claim they are "forced" to kill) (Davies). One

hunter admitted to swooping over seals congregated on an ice pack

and firing at them with a semi-automatic rifle. He complained, "I

lost 60 percent of everything I hit," in reference to the seals who

refused to die quickly (Davies).

Legislation since 1964 allows only two murder devices to

be used: the club and hakapik. The club is made of hardwood and

looks like a fat baseball bat. The hakapik is a resculptured ver-

sion of the gall, its pik shorter and straighter.

The United States Department of the Interior organized a

"task force" to evaluate killing methods after receiving hostile

criticism concerning the brutal 1978 Pribilof Islands hunt. They

ran a series of hideous tests; beating, shooting, gassing, and

shocking seal to death before an emotionless audience of task force

observers. They concluded clubbing was the most effective and

humane method. So the barbarism continues.

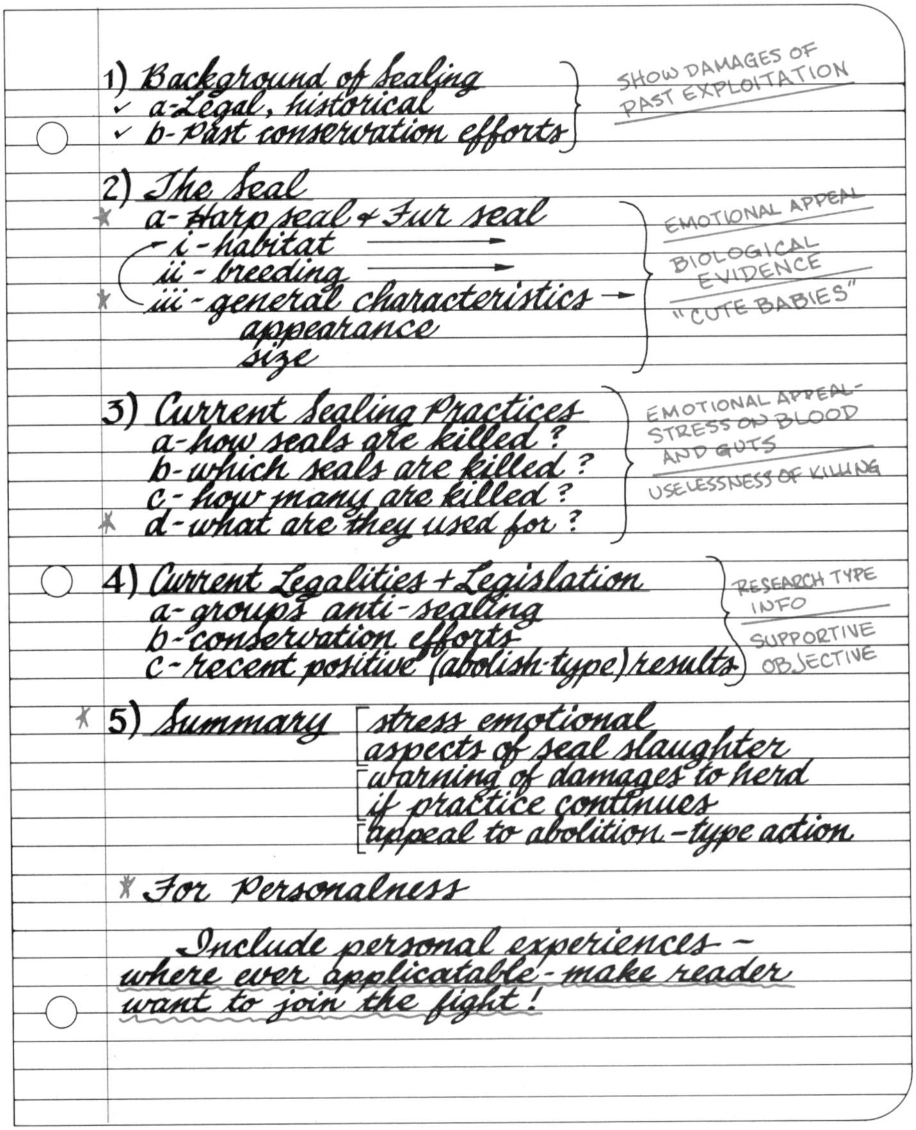

Figure 9.3

Step 4   Using your Planning Page as a guide, write the discovery draft of your research paper.

Select and Analyze Your Audience

Karen chose readers of such journals as *Smithsonian*, *GEO*, *National Geographic*, and *National Wildlife* as her audience because she thought these readers would have at least some concern for environmental issues and could be moved to take action on a particular issue, if the case for action were made strongly enough. Karen's purpose was to encourage her readers' support for organizations trying to stop sealing. To find the most effective ways of achieving that purpose, she first depicted a "typical" member of her audience, describing him as being a literate, educated, middle- to upper-middle-class person likely to act on his convictions. After she created this audience, she briefly applied the Questions for Analysis to the topic "seals and sealing," responding as she thought the members of her audience would.

QUESTIONS
FOR
ANALYSIS

According to my audience

What goes with seals and sealing?

Cute pups, kids' toys, cartoon figures, Jacques Cousteau films, playful sea clowns, circus/zoo creatures, luxurious seal fur coats

What opposes seals and sealing?

News reports in spring of harp seal harvest, unpleasant pictures, PBS programs on sealing

What follows or follows from sealing?

Various products, coats primarily, controlled harvest stressed, so sealing's regulated

Most of these points have fairly positive connotations. Although the news broadcasts are unpleasant, they last only a short while, and only the most concerned of Karen's audience is likely to act. Her analysis indicated not so much indifference on the part of the audience as a lack of awareness of sealing's brutality. So Karen decided her task was to disabuse her audience of the "cute" image they held of seals and to induce a sense of outrage at the hunts themselves. To do so, Karen decided to stress the goriness of the hunt and the helplessness of the seals. She also decided to structure a conclusion that called for some kind of action.

Step 5   Choose an audience appropriate for your purpose. (Remember the three reasons for research writing we outlined earlier: (1) to report the results of a probe into a topic, (2) to present information, and (3) to argue a point.) Describe a typical member of your audience; then apply the Questions for Analysis to your topic from your audience's perspective. Read over your first draft and decide its appropriateness for your purpose and audience. If necessary, research your topic again.

Write a Second Draft

Karen decided to keep most of her first draft; her revision of it into a second draft entailed some rewording (in the first paragraph, for example), moving information around in the paper (from the first draft's "hakapik and club" section to the second draft's "white harp pup" section), and writing a conclusion designed to move the audience to take some action. How effecive is the conclusion Karen added? If you were to write it, is there anything you would do that Karen did not? If so, what?

WRITING
SAMPLE

Second draft

```
                          The Senseless Seal Slaughter

Sealing:  A Bloody Tradition

        Large-scale commercial exploitation of the beautiful harp and

fur seal began about two centuries ago in North America.  Russian

sealers massacred over 2.5 million fur seals between 1806 and 1834

along the rugged shores of Alaska's Pribilof Islands (Spotte, 1980).

Men stalking Newfoundland's icefloes have brutally clubbed, shot and

kicked to death millions of baby harp seal for their soft, white pelts

over the last two hundred years (Amory, 1980).  Seal slaughtering is

a cruel and merciless family keepsake, a bloody tradition passed on

from father to son.  The tradition must abolished.

Our Ancestors Didn't Care

        In the past, no efforts were made to preserve the seal popu-

lation.  Before the U.S. purchased Alaska in 1867, fur sealing by the

Russians was totally unregulated.  Once they had numbered in the

millions, but by 1909 Russian hunters had thoughtlessly butchered the

herd down to a straggling 200,000.  Fortunately, an international fur
```


Researching and Writing

treaty was enacted in 1911 which forbid pelagic sealing* and saved
the herd from extinction; but it still allowed the massacre to continue (Spotte, 1980). No such treaty protects the harp seal pups, as
Canadian officials have repeatedly ignored pleas from conservation
groups and distressed biologists to regulate the harp seal hunt
meaningfully (Davies, 1970). While the Alaskan fur seal slaughter
is limited to 30,000 bachelor males (Spotte, 1980), the Canadian
harp seal quota is set at a whopping 180,000 pups (Amory, 1980).

The Spotted Fur Seal

Nearly 75% of the world's population of fur seal breed in
the Pribilof Islands along the east coast of Alaska. Adult males,
weighing up to 400 pounds, set up strict breeding territories along
the rocky coastline during May. They aggressively guard their territories and await for the females or "cows" to reach the islands
in June. Cows, normally weighing about 100 pounds, deliver one
ten-pound pup in July. Since the pups have a coarse black birth
coat, they are considered worthless by hunters, who value the silvery,
slick, spotted coat of the adults. Tragically, the pups are often
a victim of the hunt; when their mothers are slaughtered, they inevitably starve. By the end of November, the seals abandon the
Pribilof Islands for the warmer waters along the coast of California
(Davies, 1970).

The White Harp Pup

In March, the female harp seal gives birth to a soft white
pup on the icefloes around Newfoundland. The snowy-white babies lie
helplessly on the ice for their first two and a half weeks of life.
Hunters take full advantage of their helpless state and club them

----

*Pelagic sealing was a method of harvesting seal at sea which
was practiced by vessels not permitted to kill seal on the Pribilofs.
They harpooned and shot seal non-selectively, often killing pregnant
or nursing mothers. Over one-half of their kill sank before they
could retrieve it (Spotte, 1980).

where they lie before they reach three weeks of age, when they can
fend for themselves. Harp seal parents will defend their pups to
the death, if they are present when hunters attack. Of course, the
hunters quickly stifle the fearsome growl of the 900 pound male with
a bullet. It is illegal to hunt the adults, but legal to kill them
in "self-defense." The adult coat is coarse and black, which brings
a lower price anyway. Immature and adult seal congregate on the
ice in April to moult, then in June, head up north to the icy waters
of Baffin Bay and Davis Strait, where they find peace away from the
hunters for the short Arctic summer (Davies, 1970).

The Slaughter

Fur and harp seal are slain by similar methods. The main
difference between the two hunts is that adult fur seal are clubbed
as they frantically bound from the rocky shores to the sea's protection while harp seal pups are beaten to death as they lie helplessly
on the ice. William McCloskey vividly describes the murder and
sculping procedure:

> It was done as work, impersonally. The sealer strikes the
> seal on the head with the steel knob of his hakapik (the
> other legal method is with a hardwood club). The sealer
> is instructed to strike three times. ("Once to kill him,
> once for the fishery officer, and once for Greenpeace,"
> say the sealers.) Next, he must turn the seal over and
> bleed it, cutting straight into the chest. A stream of
> blood spurts out and reddens on the ice. In most cases,
> he straightens and pauses to sharpen his knife. He then
> bends over and with deft slices "sculps" the sculp (pelt
> and fat) from the carcass and cuts the flippers from the
> fat. Finally, he drags the 30-to-70-pound sculp to a
> central pan marked by a red flag with the ship's name, to
> be picked up later in the day as the ship breakes through
> the ice to the pans. (McCloskey, 1979)

Hakapik and Club: Legal Murder Weapons

Prior to 1964, hunters could legally slaughter seal in any
way that struck their fancy. The traditional Newfoundlander method
was gaffing. First, the hunter would club the seal in the head with
the flat side of a spiked board, then drive the spike into the seal's
brain. Some sealers would simply kick the baby in the face, roll him

Researching and Writing

over, and slice his throat. Sometimes seals were drowned by holding

them under the icy polar waters in strong nets or traps. Longlining,

the most gruesome killer of all, is a method by which a cruelly sharp,

baited hook is lowered into the water and swallowed by a hungry seal.

The hook slices the seal's throat and gouges into his belly, leaving

the animal to gag and suffocate in the dark waters as he desperately

struggles to get free. Shooting is generally reserved for "rebellious"

adults who stay to defend their young (the ones the hunters claim they

are forced to kill) (Davies, 1970). One hunter admitted to swooping

over seals congregated on an ice pack and firing at them with a semi-

automatic rifle. He complained, "I lost 60 percent of everything I

hit," in reference to the seals who refused to die quickly (Davies,

1970).

Legislation since 1964 allows only two murder weapons to be

used: the club and hakapik. The club is made of hardwood and looks

like a fat baseball bat, while the hakapik is a resculptured version

of the gaff, its "pik" shorter and straighter.

After receiving hostile criticism converning the brutal 1968

Pribilof Island hunt, the United States Department of the Interior

organized a task force to evaluate killing methods. They ran a series

of hideous tests--beating, shooting, gassing, and shocking seal to

death before an emotionless audience of task force observers. They

concluded clubbing was the most effective and humane method. So the

barbarism continues.

Our Empty Future Without the Seal

Are seal fur coats worth the cost, a ruthless destruction of

a gentle and spectacularly beautiful animal? Would you like to buy

your child a baby seal playtoy, knowing of the brutal beating this

innocent baby has taken? Can you survive without seal oil lamps and

gamy-flavored seal meat? Would you be willing to put forth a word or dollar to preserve a unique, gentle, beautiful creature for the

next generation to enjoy?

> These animals are symbolic, and if they can't be saved,
> it probably isn't ever going to be possible to save any
> substantial population of wild creatures. The world will
> gradually fill with filth and one day, empty of all but
> man, this planet will become the loneliest place in the
> universe. Perhaps in saving the seals, man may save
> himself. (Davies, 1970).

Step 6   Write a second draft of your paper, revising the first draft to meet the demands you expect from your audience.

Write a Final Draft

Before she wrote a final draft, Karen submitted her paper to several of her composition classmates. Their advice was as follows.

1. Write a smoother introduction. To Karen's group, the second draft's introduction was a little too abrupt and flat; they thought it opened too quickly into sealing statistics and that the sentences were too choppy.

2. Write a stronger conclusion. Karen's group found that the call to action, coming as the fourth in a series of rhetorical questions, was not strong enough. Although they liked the quote from Davies, they thought it entered too abruptly and needed a better introduction.

3. Use MLA footnote and bibliography format, because the assignment required them. (Karen knew of this requirement and had used in-text notations to help her keep citations straight; so the group's advice here served as a reminder.)

4. Drop the heading divisions in the paper. Because the paper is relatively short, the group thought the headings to be unnecessary. In longer papers with major divisions and subdivisions, such headings may be necessary to help the reader by dividing the text into more manageable "chunks." But in the seals paper, Karen's group found that the headings actually impeded the paper's flow.

5. Look again at paragraph unity. The group thought that the information at the end of the paragraphs about the breeding habits of the fur and harp seals and about the methods of killing employed was interesting information, but that it did not fit with other information in these paragraphs. So the group's advice was to drop a total of five sentences in these three paragraphs.

6. Look at spelling and mechanics. For example, one member of the group pointed out that Karen had used *icefloes* when the standard spelling is two words—*ice floes.*

7. Watch transition. Karen's group felt that the paragraph about the U.S. Interior Department's task force entered abruptly; so they recommended that Karen tie it tightly to the preceding paragraph, which talks about legal methods of taking seal.

Here, then, is Karen's final draft. After you have read it, answer the questions that follow.

The Senseless Seal Slaughter

Karen Pinckley

Annually, rituals of death occur. In March, hunters slay thousands upon thousands of helpless white harp seal pups in Newfoundland; in July, hunters take adult spotted fur seals in Alaska's Pribilof Islands. Over the years, sealing has taken an enormous toll on these two species of seal. Continued sealing will eventually lead to their extinction.

Large-scale commercial exploitation of the beautiful harp and fur seal began about two centuries ago in North America. Between 1806 and 1834, Russian sealers ruthlessly massacred over 2.5 million fur seal along the rugged shores of the Pribilofs.[1] Men stalking Newfoundland's ice floes have brutally clubbed, shot and kicked to death millions of baby harp seal for their soft, white pelts over the last two hundred years.[2] Seal slaughtering is a cruel and merciless family keepsake, a bloody tradition passed from father to son. The tradition must be abolished.

In the past, no efforts were made to preserve the seal population. Before the U.S. purchased Alaska in 1867, fur sealing by the Russians was totally unregulated. Once the seals numbered in the millions, but by 1909 Russian hunters had thoughtlessly butchered the herd down to a straggling 200,000. Fortunately, an international fur treaty was

---

[1] Stephen Spotte, "Ashore with Alaska's Feisty Fur Seal," National Wildlife, June/July 1980, pp. 4-11.

[2] Cleveland Amory, "Let's Save the Seals," Good Housekeeping, March 1980, pp. 60-64.

enacted in 1911 which forbade pelagic sealing[3] and saved the herd from extinction, but it still allowed the massacre to continue.[4] No such treaty protects the harp seal pups, as Canadian officials have repeatedly ignored pleas from conservation groups and distressed biologists to regulate the harp seal hunt meaningfully. While the Alaskan fur seal slaughter is limited to 30,000 bachelor males,[5] the Canadian harp seal quota is set at a whopping 180,000 pups a year.[6]

Nearly 75% of the world's population of fur seal breed in the Pribilof Islands along the east coast of Alaska. Adult males, weighing up to 400 pounds, set up strict breeding territories along the rocky coastline during May. They aggressively guard their territories and wait for the females or "cows" to reach the islands in June. Cows, normally weighing about 100 pounds, deliver one ten-pound pup in late July. Since the pups have a coarse black birth coat, they are considered worthless by hunters, who value the silvery, slick, spotted coat of the adults. Tragically, the pups are often victims of the hunt; when their mothers are slaughtered, they inevitably starve.[7]

---

[3] Pelagic sealing was a method of harvesting seal at sea which was practiced by vessels not permitted to kill seal on the Pribilofs. They harpooned and shot seal non-selectively, often killing pregnant or nursing mothers. Over one-half of their kill sank before they could retrieve it (Spotte, pp. 4-11).

[4] Spotte, pp. 4-11.

[5] Spotte, pp. 4-11.

[6] Amory, pp. 60-64.

[7] Brian Davies, _Savage Luxury_ (New York: Taplinger Publishing Co., 1970), pp. 131-133.

In March, the female harp seal gives birth to a soft white pup
on the ice floes around Newfoundland. The snowy-white babies lie
helplessly on the ice for their first two and a half weeks of life.
Hunters take full advantage of their helpless state and club them
where they lie before they reach three weeks of age, when they can
fend for themselves. Harp seal parents will defend their pups to
the death, if they are present when hunters attack. Of course,
hunters quickly stifle the fearsome growl of the 900 pound male with
a bullet. It is illegal to hunt the adults, but legal to kill them in
self-defense.[8]

Fur and harp seal are slain by similar methods. The main difference between the two hunts is that adult fur seal are clubbed as they
frantically bound from the rocky shores to the sea's protection, while
harp seal pups are bludgeoned to death as they lie helplessly on the
ice. William McCloskey vividly describes the murder and skinning procedure:

> It was done as work, impersonally. The sealer strikes the
> seal on the head with the steel knob of his hakapik (the
> other legal method is with a hardwood club). . . . The
> sealer is instructed to strike three times. ("Once to kill
> him, once for the fishery officer, and once for Greenpeace,"
> say the sealers.) Next, he must turn the seal over and
> bleed it, cutting straight into the chest. A stream of
> blood spurts out and reddens the ice. In most cases, he
> straightens and pauses to sharpen his knife. He then bends

---

[8] Davies, pp. 50-52.

over and with deft slices "sculps" the sculp (pelt and fat)
from the carcass and cuts the flippers from the fat. Finally
he drags the 30-to-70-pound sculp to a central pan marked
by a red flag with the ship's name, to be picked up later in
the day as the ship breaks through the ice to the pans.[9]

Prior to 1964, hunters could legally slaughter seal in any way
that struck their fancy. The traditional Newfoundlander method was
gaffing. First, the hunter would club the seal in the head with the
flat side of a spiked board, then drive the spike into the seal's
brain. Some sealers would simply kick the baby seal in the face, roll
him over, and slice his throat. Sometimes seals were drowned by holding them under the icy polar waters in strong nets or traps. Longlining, the most gruesome killer of all, was a method by which a
cruelly sharp, baited hook was lowered into the water and swallowed
by a hungry seal. The hook sliced the seal's throat and gouged into
his belly, leaving the animal to gag and suffocate in the dark waters
as he desperately struggled to get free. Still practiced today,
shooting is generally reserved for rebellious adults who stay to defend their young; these adults the hunters claim they are forced to
kill.[10]

Legislation since 1964 allows only two murder weapons to be used:
the club and the hakapik. The club is made of hardwood and looks like
a fat baseball bat, while the hakapik is a resculptured version of the

---

[9] William B. McCloskey, Jr., "Bitter Fight Still Rages Over the
Seal Killing in Canada," <u>Smithsonian</u>, Nov. 1979, pp. 54-64.

[10] Davies, pp. 14-16.

gaff, its "pik" shorter and straighter. As efficient as these weapons
are, other methods have been tested. After receiving hostile criticism concerning an especially brutal Pribilof Island hunt in 1968, the
United States Department of the Interior organized a task force to
evaluate killing methods. They ran a series of hideous tests—beating,
shooting, gassing, and shocking adult seal to death before an emotionless audience of task force observers. They concluded clubbing was
the most effective and humane method.[11] So the barbarism continues.

And for what purposes? Seals are slaughtered for their fur, to
make expensive, high-fashion coats, to line boots and mittens, and to
stuff children's toys. They are also taken for their oil and their
tough, gamy meat. But are seal fur coats worth the cost, the ruthless
destruction of a gentle and spectacularly beautiful animal? Can you
buy your child a baby seal playtoy, knowing of the brutal beating this
innocent baby has taken? Can you survive without seal oil lamps and
gamy-flavored seal meat? Can you simply watch the seals bludgeoned
into extinction? When we lose the seals—and ultimately we will if
the slaughter is not stopped—then we will lose something of ourselves:

> These animals are symbolic, and if they can't be saved,
> it probably isn't ever going to be possible to save any
> substantial population of wild creatures. The world will
> gradually fill with filth and one day, empty of all but
> man, this planet will become the loneliest place in the

---

[11]Davies, pp. 134-142.

universe. Perhaps in saving the seals, man may save himself.[12]

The bloody tradition of sealing must stop. It can be stopped only if
we join together and support organizations opposing the brutality. I
urge you to send a donation—just $10.00 will help—to The Fund for
Animals (140 W. 57 St., New York, N.Y. 10019). With your help, the
seals have a chance. Without it, they move closer and closer to
extinction.

____

[12]Davies, p. 208.

Amory, Cleveland. "Let's Save the Seals." <u>Good</u> <u>Housekeeping</u>, March
     1980, pp. 60-64.

Davies, Brian. <u>Savage</u> <u>Luxury</u>. New York: Taplinger Publishing Co.,
     1970.

McCloskey, William B., Jr. "Bitter Fight Still Rages Over the Seal
     Killing in Canada." <u>Smithsonian</u>, Nov. 1979, pp. 54-64.

Spotte, Stephen. "Ashore with Alaska's Feisty Fur Seal." <u>National</u>
     <u>Wildlife</u>, June/July 1980, pp. 4-11.

1. How much of her group's advice did Karen take? Did she improve the paper? If so, to what extent?

2. Would you rework either the introduction or the conclusion? If so, how? And why?

3. Does the final draft fulfill Karen's purpose for her chosen audience? On what do you base your assessment?

4. Footnote 3 is an example of an explanatory footnote, which has as its purpose presenting supporting information that is relevant but not essential to the paper itself. Is the information in this footnote relevant but unessential? Should Karen have incorporated this information into the paper's text? If so, where? And how?

5. What is the reason for the format of footnotes 4–6, 8, and 10–12?

6. How reliable do Karen's sources seem to be? On what do you base your assessment?

7. How well researched is Karen's paper? On what do you base your assessment?

WRITING ASSIGNMENT

Step 7   Write a final draft of your paper, revising the second draft to meet the demands of your audience and to fulfill your stated purpose.

Refining Writing: Words, Sentences, and Paragraphs

With the assistance of Margaret Marks

Much of your work with Parts Three and Four will come after you have written at least one draft of a piece of writing. Revision may involve both rewriting (that is, making substantive changes in content, wording, and structure) and editing (that is, proofreading and correcting errors in grammar and mechanics); both these aspects are important as the writer attempts to make his writing as effective as possible. Part Three concerns rewriting, Part Four, editing.

Chapters Ten, Eleven, and Twelve are about words, sentences, and paragraphs, in that order, with each chapter directing you to reconsider such aspects of your writing as word choice and sentence and paragraph structure so as to help you make your writing as effective as possible. In these three chapters we talk briefly about principles of using words, sentences, and paragraphs effectively, presenting short exercises to give you some practice at applying these various principles. But our emphasis is placed on your writing, as we always ask you to return to a piece of your writing to revise it.

Chapter Ten

Words

The language you choose to express your thoughts is an extremely important element of the writing process because only through the words you choose and the ways you arrange them can your reader understand your thoughts about the topic. Your words on a page convey more than the meanings dictionaries report; they also convey your attitudes toward your subject and toward your reader.

DENOTATION AND CONNOTATION

When we talk about the meanings of words, it is helpful to distinguish between two types of meaning: the one we find in a dictionary definition of a word—its denotation—and the type of meaning that arises from the various associations— connotation—the word evokes. All words have both denotative and connotative meanings, but not all words are alike in their connotative impact. The words we use just to name things often have little connotative meaning. For example, *tree* represents a physical thing, as do the words *flower, car, ship,* and *cow.* These words denote the things they stand for.

When a word simply "stands for" a thing, it is not necessary to involve other words (and their inherent associations) in getting to the meaning of that word. The meaning of the word is already in the thing it represents. This is not to say that such a word has no connotation. If a reader perceives meaning in a word, partly through personal associations, she is attributing connotative meaning to that term. The reader who arrives at the meaning of *flower,* for example, by associating it with the flower-giving situations she has experienced is involving connotative meaning in her total understanding of this word. To this person, *flower* means the thing it stands for, but it also "means" the pleasant feeling she gets when she hears the word. Nevertheless, words that refer to things allow readers to arrive at a denotative meaning that is usually more free of connotations than other more abstract words in our language.

Only a small percentage of our vocabulary is so largely denotative. Whenever we use words that refer to ideas and concepts, these words tend to imply, by means of their connotations, much more than they mean explicitly, or denotatively. Often such words have emotional value because of the associations a particular audience brings to them. This emotional value arises because the words we choose to represent experience often reveal our attitudes toward that experience. Suppose, for example, you are the spokesperson for a student group on your campus that is trying to change a particular academic policy. Both you and your school's president refuse to compromise on your respective positions. From your point of view, you are firm, determined, and resolute; the president, however, is obstinate, even pigheaded. From your president's perspective, you are the pigheaded one. Both of you reveal your attitudes toward each other by using these terms. The words may share similar denotations, but their connotations convey attitudes as well as exact meanings.

Why does one word carry such a different emotional impact than another word that has a denotative meaning similar to the first? Why is it good to be firm but bad to be obstinate, and even worse to be pigheaded? The key to the impact of these words is in the associations readers make with them. All of them describe a person or thing that does not give in easily. But the word *firm* is associated with other positive contexts such as those in the following sentences.

> The foundation was *firm.*
> He made a *firm* commitment to the team.
> The athlete's body was *firm* and supple.

Though the meaning of *firm* in each of these sentences differs from its meaning in the president-student disagreement, some of the positive feelings associated with each of the sample contexts seem to go with *firm* when it is used in the president-student situation. These positive associations do not, however, go with *obstinate*, as the following exercise should make clear.

1. Devise several sentences that highlight the negative associations of *obstinate*. Then replace *obstinate* with *firm* in each of these sample sentences and note the change in meaning. How much of that change is due to connotative differences between these two words?

2. Above we said that *pigheaded* contains an even more negative connotative meaning than *obstinate*. Can you account for this fact by examining the associations readers will make with the word *pigheaded*?

1. In each of the following sets of terms, which would you label as positive, which as neutral, and which as negative? On what do you base your labeling? Can all the terms in one set be applied to the same person? If so, how?

   thin, scrawny, lean, gaunt, slender, lanky, scraggy

   rash, heady, impetuous, hasty, inconsiderate

2. For each of the following words, develop a set of synonyms. Then rank your words from most positive to most negative. If you were to use each word to describe someone or something, how would your attitude towards that person or thing change as your language changed?

   lazy   small   satirical   sweet   large   motive   feisty

Which of the following statements are the most connotative and which the most denotative? What are the essential differences between those statements you see as basically denotative and those you see as highly connotative?

1. The temperature of that stream is 44° F. (7° C.).
   That stream is cold.
   That stream is icy.
   That stream is frigid.

2. War is hell.
   War is armed combat between opposing forces.
   It was war out there on the old gridiron tonight, folks.

3. The Sears Tower is a colossus among buildings.
   The Sears Tower is the world's tallest building.
   The Sears Tower is a giant.

The following sets of names are those of sports cars, football mascots, and military hardware, respectively. What do these names imply, individually and as a group? Are the names connotative? What attitudes does each term and each set of terms convey? How?

Sports Cars

Mustang	Jaguar
Spitfire	Stingray
Firebird	Triumph

Football Mascots

Tigers	Broncos
Vikings	Lions
Bengals	Colts
Bulldogs	Buccaneers
Rams	Giants
Razorbacks	Trojans
Bruins	Eagles
Raiders	

Military Hardware

Starfighter	Phantom
Flogger	Titan
Minuteman	Foxbat
Sidewinder	Strike Eagle
Superfortress	Freedom Fighter
Tomcat	Mirage

CHOOSING THE RIGHT WORD

Precise Diction

It is tempting to think of connotations as something added to the denotative meaning. In reality, the connotative element of our language is an integral part of the meaning we convey to others. To illustrate the role connotation plays in the overall impact of writing, return to Ceci Cano's "Only a Reflection," first introduced in Chapter One (pp. 24–28). Here is Ceci's first paragraph.

> Infectious sounds reached our ears as we stepped into the dim passage. My friend and I strolled towards the chattering voices and tinkling laughter coming from a larger room in which we could see small tables and chairs. As we approached the entrance, the music rose and surrounded us, deafening my ears to any other sound, and we entered a wonderland of lights, sounds, and action.

Ceci does a good job of preparing her readers for the disillusionment in her final paragraph, beginning with the choice of her first word, *infectious.* What do we associate with this word? In what contexts do we usually see it? Infectious laughter comes to mind immediately, and it seems a proper association since Ceci is describing a place of laughter and merriment. However, another association for this word that we cannot ignore is infectious disease. By the time we get to the conclusion, we find that Ceci's choice was deliberate. She feels drawn to the disco; thus the sounds are infectious in the sense that a person's laugh may be said to be infectious. However, since she also feels something foreboding and unhealthy about this disco world, the sounds are infectious in the sense that a disease is.

Like Ceci's essay, Stephanie Weikert's "Franklin Elementary School" (pp. 67–68) illustrates careful word choice, especially in the first paragraph where Stephanie expresses her negative opinion of the school. Here is this paragraph with some of the negative words underlined.

> On a chilly fall morning, Franklin Elementary School awaited the beginning of another day. Its ugly, ancient frame solemnly rose from the ground and met the morning sun. Classroom lights shone through the dirty windows and illuminated the hard ground below. The wind blew through the swings on the empty playground, making them squeak and creak like a door turning on rusty hinges. Three tall maple trees vainly attempted to hide the eyesore. A steel fence enclosed the school property, separating it from the rest of the neighborhood. Surrounding Franklin were the small, grim ghetto shanties filled with youngsters preparing for the school day.

At first it may not be obvious that such words as *hard* and *separating* are necessarily negative in connotation, although they are often found in negative contexts: for example, "the hard ground would yield no crop," "there was a wall of silence separating the child from her father." By using such strong words as *ugly* and *eyesore*, Stephanie elicits the negative contexts, ensuring that her readers will see *hard* and *separating* as negative too.

Appropriate Diction

In choosing appropriate language, a writer must be aware of the writing situation, and a major component of this is the relationship between the writer and her readers. The following passage, taken from Stephanie Weikert's "Franklin Elementary School," shows how failure to choose appropriate language can hinder the overall effect of a piece of writing:

> As I viewed these surroundings, I felt a sense of disappointment. Of the five elementary schools in Wadsworth, I had to be dumped at Franklin to work as a teacher's aide.

We underline the words *viewed* and *dumped* not because anything is inherently wrong with the words, but because they are associated with different writer-audience relationships. Words such as *viewed, surroundings,* and *disappointment* usually appear in rather formal contexts. They make Stephanie sound precise, proper, and a bit distant from her audience. If Stephanie wants to loosen up, that is, be a bit less precise and lessen the distance between herself and her audience, she could rewrite this first sentence.

> As I looked at this school and the houses around it, I frowned.

While nothing is incorrect about the words Stephanie has used, these rather formal words do not go with some of the other less formal language in the paragraph—in particular with the word *dumped*. In using *dumped*, Stephanie is greatly reducing the distance between herself and her audience. This word is found in everyday conversation between people who know each other reasonably well, but it is not often found in speeches or formal essays. Such paraphrases of *dumped* as *placed in* or *assigned to* would go better with *viewed* and *surroundings*.

We are not suggesting, though, that these more formal words are better for Stephanie's essay. The contrary is true. As we have said, the expressive essay writer creates the illusion that the reader is looking over his shoulder as she works her way through his experience. He will best create this illusion by writing his experience in the informal language he uses with close friends rather than the formal language he would use in giving a speech.

EXERCISE

Examine the following words. Then write the first sentence that comes to mind for each word. An example for the first word might be, "The jury examined the evidence."

examine	halt	notify
decapitate	rich	throw
leave	mangle	edge
gravitate		

Each of these words is related to other words (or phrases) that are either more or less formal than it is. For example, a less formal phrase for *examine* is *look at*. Find an equivalent word or phrase for the other nine words in this list. Use that word or phrase in any sentence that comes immediately to mind. For example, the sentence for *look at* could be, "The boy looked at the girl." Then switch the words between your two sentences as follows.

The jury looked at the evidence.
The boy examined the girl.

After doing this, write a sentence or two about each pair of words and state what you learned about the words in this process. Finally, compare what you discovered with the introduction and conclusion to "Learned Words and Popular Words" (p. 81 and pp. 84–85, respectively).

Figurative Language

As a writer your job is to help create images in the reader's mind so that she comes to understand your particular viewpoint on the topic. Part of creating images involves helping the reader to understand abstract concepts; to do this, you can use figurative language to make the abstract more concrete. Two of the best ways to use figurative language for this purpose are similes and metaphors, which are both based on comparisons.

Simile A simile is a figure of speech in which two things are directly compared. A famous literary simile is found in Samuel Taylor Coleridge's "The Rime of the

Ancient Mariner." Coleridge writes of a becalmed ship, saying that it is "as idle as a painted ship upon a painted ocean." Coleridge uses this simile to build an image of a ship that is not moving; he writes of an "idle" ship, one as static as a ship in a painting. In this simile, the comparison is signaled by *as*. In other similes, the comparison may be signaled by *like*, as this line from one of Robert Burns's poems illustrates: "Oh, my love is like a red, red rose that's newly sprung in June."

Metaphor A metaphor is an implied comparison in which one thing takes on the attributes of another. In the metaphor "John was a lion in battle," John assumes the ferocious and courageous attributes of a lion. In attributing these features to John, the writer builds a concrete image about how courageous John was during the fight. Because it makes an implied comparison, the metaphor is similar to the analogy (see Chapter Seven, pp. 184–185).

EXERCISE

Compose a simile and a metaphor for each of these terms.

truth	love	rewriting
freedom	justice	your writing process
hate	writing	creativity

EXERCISE

Your purpose in using figurative language is not simply to spice up your writing but to help clarify your thoughts for your reader. Look again at one expressive and one transactional essay you have written during this course. Identify the similes and metaphors you used. Why did you choose to use them? How effective were they? In rereading, did you find any other places in which figurative language would have been effective? If so, revise those passages to incorporate such language.

PROBLEMS WITH LANGUAGE

Jargon

Jargon is a word that has assumed negative connotations although in its purest sense jargon is nothing more than the specific language or terms a particular group uses. It is hard to imagine how people in business, education, or industry could communicate without using at least some jargon. Whenever two people in the same trade talk, they are likely to use jargon to communicate effectively. Two doctors could talk about coronaries, lumbar punctures, EKGs, EEGs, cat-scans, and so on, while two English teachers could talk about the objective correlative, dangling modifiers, and heuristics. When the writer uses jargon to communicate information that is more or less technical, either she should be sure her reader will understand the terms or she should define them in some way.

Jargon, however, has its darker side. It may be nothing more than gibberish, meaningless talk or writing that is characterized by pretentiousness and highly abstract diction, as the following examples illustrate.

1. The select group of local citizens, a truly representative cross-section of the community, who constituted the ad hoc Vehicular Traffic Movement Committee opted to maximize vehicular traffic flow by offering its studied opinion that all vehicular traffic moving on Main Street be directed to move in a northerly direction, while all vehicular traffic moving on Water Street be directed to move in a southerly direction.

    Translation: The Traffic Committee recommended that traffic be routed north on Main Street and south on Water Street.

2. It has been observed on several occasions by this researcher that the ingestion of bologna sandwiches, in which the bologna is green in color and has a strong, peculiar odor not unlike that of cabbage (*Brassica oleracea capitata*) left too long in an environment the temperature of which is so heated as to be incompatible with preservation of the cabbage, tends to create favorable conditions for the possibility of an intense gastronomic disturbance.

    Translation: Don't eat rotten bologna—it'll make you sick.

3. The corporation president, seeking to enhance operational efficiency and thereby to realize an optimum profit picture, selected the best, in her opinion, of the various options presented and chose to begin procedures to restructure existing physical plant and laboratory facilities instead of embarking on a new, unprecedented capital construction program, because restructuring seemed to her to be the most efficacious solution.

    Translation: To make operations more efficient and profitable, the corporation president decided to remodel existing plant facilities instead of building a new plant.

To be sure, these examples are overdrawn, but not by much. Compare these sentences, from a memorandum concerning computer use, to the examples: "A machine sensory component is an important aspect of the knowlege-based systems to be investigated. This means that the system will deal with real-time sensory information in addition to information from interaction with human users of the system and information in the system database." For a reader with little or no familiarity with computers, these sentences may well be meaningless, so that nothing is communicated.

All these samples point to the potential problem of jargon: it can confuse a reader or listener by masking the message's content; at its worst, it can hide the truth. As a writer, your job is to decide when jargon is appropriate and, if you decide to use it, whether your readers will understand the terms. If jargon—in its best sense—is not essential to your purpose, avoid using it.

The bumper sticker "The best man for the job may be a woman" points to the problem inherent in sexist language: Such language may be used to establish and maintain artificial distinctions between men and women, almost always at the expense of women. To avoid making such distinctions, you will need to decide how to handle pronouns and other language that deals with people.

Pronouns are words that take the place of or represent nouns, and they may take masculine, feminine, or neuter forms. The following list represents the pronouns we use most often.

Person	Singular	Plural
first	I	we
second	you	you
third	he, she, it	they

Of these pronouns, the third person singular causes the trouble, because this is where we make distinctions between masculine and feminine references. Until recently, the convention was to use the third person masculine form—he. But this use sometimes created problems by reinforcing stereotypes. For example, one long-standing convention was to refer to doctors, attorneys, and corporate executives as *he*, which implies that only men were capable of holding such professional positions as these. But a number of women are very competent doctors, attorneys, and corporate executives; thus, the use of the masculine pronoun in referring to such people is clearly inappropriate. More than simply being inappropriate, use of the masculine pronoun exclusively in such situations does not recognize the equality of women and therefore subtly reinforces the dominance of men in society at the expense of women.

To counteract this, you may choose other conventions in dealing with pronouns.

1. Use third person plural pronouns (*they, them, themselves*) entirely unless you are referring to some person you identify specifically. When you identify a particular person, then use third person singular masculine or feminine pronouns as appropriate.

2. Use both the masculine and feminine third person singular pronouns together: *Him* or *her, himself* or *herself, her* or *him, herself* or *himself.* You can do this when using pronouns to refer to an example rather than to someone specifically. For example, you might write, "The writer needs to make a conscious choice about what kind of pronoun reference she or he will use in her or his writing." Whichever form you choose, be consistent in using it, but do not always put the masculine pronoun before the feminine if you choose to use both.

3. Alternate the third person singular masculine and feminine pronouns as content dictates. This is the option we chose in using pronouns in this text.

As you look through this text, you will find that we use the third person singular feminine form in one passage and the third person singular masculine form in the next, whenever we refer to "the writer" or "the reader" as a typical writer or reader.

Other potential troublesome terms are those identifying a particular sex, for example, *chairman, policeman, fireman, mailman,* and *stewardess*. Chairing a committee, however, is not limited strictly to men, and women may also be police officers, fire fighters, and postal workers. Men may also be flight attendants. As a writer, you need to be conscious of such terms as these because they may signal subtle discrimination on your part, whether you intend it or not. The National Council of Teachers, in "Guidelines for Nonsexist Use of Language in NCTE Publications," provides a summary statement that addresses the importance of nonsexist language:

> Language plays a central role in socialization, for it helps teach children the roles that are expected of them. Through language, children conceptualize their ideas and feelings about themselves and their world. Thought and action are reflected in words, and words in turn condition how a person thinks and acts. Eliminating sexist language will not eliminate sexist conduct, but as the language is liberated from sexist usages and assumptions, women and men will begin to share more equal, active, caring roles.*

EXERCISE | Closely examine articles and other items in various magazines. What do you notice about the use of sexist language? Is there any? If so, in which magazines? How does such language reflect the views of the magazines? What does that language suggest about those to whom it refers?

---

*"Guidelines for Nonsexist Use of Language in NCTE Publications" (Urbana, Ill.: NCTE, 1975), p. 1.

Sentences

The sentence is one of the most important grammatical units for the writer but also one of the most difficult to define. A frequently used definition is that a sentence is a "group of words that expresses a complete thought." But this definition has its problems because a complete thought may easily be expressed in less than a sentence as well. If a friend walks into your room unexpectedly dressed in an outlandish costume, you might exclaim, "Oh, wow!" Your exclamation represents a complete thought, but there is some question as to whether it constitutes a sentence.

As this example illustrates, our difficulties in defining sentences often arise from the difference between a complete thought in conversation and a complete thought in writing. When someone greets you by saying, "What a day!" his facial expression tells you whether the day has been wonderful or depressing. But if that same person writes, "What a day!" he must go on to convey his precise meaning somehow because readers cannot see his face. Groups of words that are complete and clear in speech may not be clear at all in writing.

SENTENCE STRUCTURE

Our discussion of a sentence is to help you become aware of the constraints in a writing situation. In the following two statements and discussion, we refer to the characteristics of the sentence as the term is used in formal writing situations. A sentence contains a subject and a predicate. A group of words that does not have either a subject or a predicate is called a sentence fragment.

	subject predicate
Sentence	The <u>boy</u> <u>was</u> <u>swimming</u>.
Fragment	The boy swimming.

Here some definitions are in order to clarify what makes one group of words a sentence and another group a fragment.

Subject The subject states what the sentence is about; it identifies the focal point of the sentence. The simplest subject is a single noun. But other words in the sentence may modify, or tell us more about, that noun. The simple subject and its modifiers together are called *the complete subject.*

Example

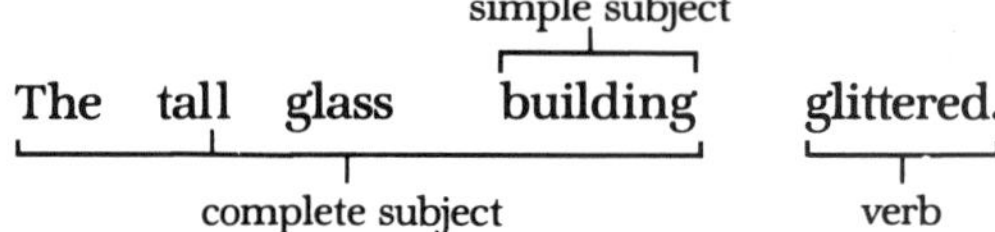

Predicate The verb of a sentence tells us something about the subject. It may tell us what the subject does, or what the subject is, or what condition the subject is in. The main verb of a sentence is often known as the *simple predicate.* Other words in the sentence that modify the verb along with the verb itself are called the *complete predicate.*

Example

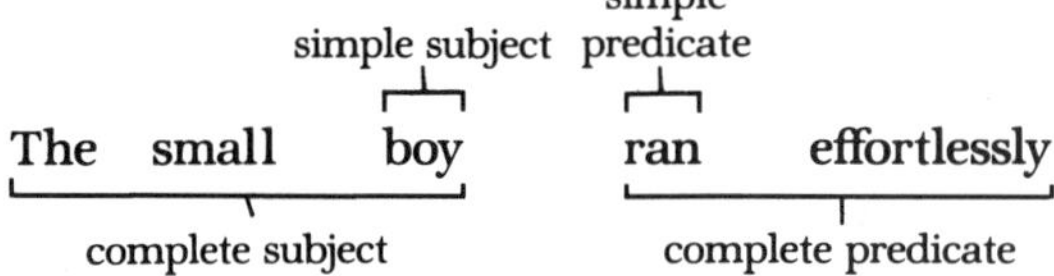

Complements Some sentences are complete with only a simple subject and verb: "John sang." Other sentences require more. The phrase "The boy threw" needs something more to make sense: "The boy threw the ball." We call the words necessary to complete the meaning *complements.* Here are the most common kinds of complements.

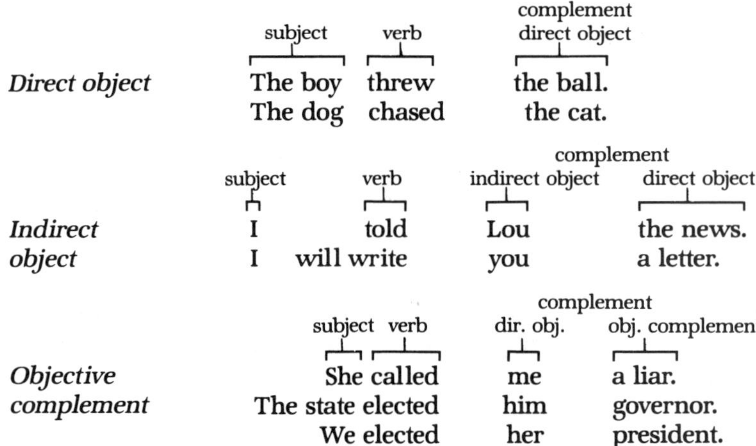

	subject	verb	complement predicate noun
Predicate *noun*	She	is	a chemist.
	My father	is	a teacher.

	subject	verb	complement predicate adjective
Predicate *adjective*	I	am	hungry.
	She	seemed	happy.

The basic sentence components are, then, a subject, a verb, and, in some cases, a complement or complements. Other words or groups of words in the basic sentence pattern serve as modifiers of the subject, the verb, or the complement.

<hr>

EXERCISE

Identify the subject, verb, and any complements in each of the following sentences. (Be specific as to what type of complement it is.)

1. The three convicts were astonished to find that all of their efforts had gotten them no farther than halfway under the prison exercise area.

2. The threatened little man slowly raised his eyebrows and shrugged his shoulders.

3. Quiet was the little mouse and watchful was the sinister cat.

4. The sergeant gave the private a look designed to freeze her in her tracks.

5. The target was hit in several places.

<hr>

Clauses

A clause is a word unit that contains a subject and a main verb. There are two primary types of clauses.

Independent Clauses An independent clause is complete in thought so that it can stand alone and be punctuated as a sentence. The simplest kind of independent clause consists of a noun that acts as a subject and then a verb: "I ran." Grammatically, the simplest kind of English sentence consists of only one clause, an independent one. An independent clause may have a compound subject ("She and I took a walk"), a compound verb ("We jumped and skipped through the leaves"), or a compound subject and a compound verb ("Lou and John walked the dogs and fed the cat").

Dependent Clauses A dependent, or subordinate, clause is one that can function only as a part of a sentence. It cannot stand alone and make sense. If it is punctuated separately as a sentence, it is termed a *sentence fragment*. Dependent clauses can function within sentences in a number of ways. Noun clauses can be subjects or objects. Adverb clauses function as adverbs, and adjective clauses, as adjectives. Study the examples below.

Examples

Noun clause used as subject:

That she took the job was a surprise to me.

Noun clause used as direct object:

I knew that he was going to resign.

Noun clause used as object of preposition:

Give the papers to whoever is at home.

Adverb clause:

After the storm was over, we cleared up the debris.

Adjective clause:

The fallen tree which had blocked the road had to be moved by heavy machinery.

It is important to be able to distinguish independent clauses from dependent clauses in order to understand sentence structure and to avoid sentence fragments. Dependent clauses are easily recognized by the words they begin with, either relative pronouns (*who, which, that,* and so forth) or subordinating conjunctions (*when, since, because, although,* and so forth).

EXERCISE

Label the dependent clauses in the following sentences. There may be more than one dependent clause in a sentence.

1. After the last batter had struck out, the Tigers made the long walk back through the tunnel to their locker room, which was as silent as any funeral parlor.

2. The stairs led up to a room that no one had slept in for fifteen years, and that gave Susan a feeling which she had not experienced since she was a child.

3. That she should be allowed to deliver the keynote address was an honor which Wanda could hardly comprehend.

4. Frank knew that the boys were likely to be rowdy for a time.

5. Philip was known for devoting himself to whatever task he undertook.

Identify any sentence fragments in the following passage. Then rewrite them so that they are no longer fragments.

Betty could hardly wait for Saturday night to arrive. She was so busy fantasizing about the tremendous weekend she was going to have that she completely forgot to do the ordinary things she was supposed to do on

Thursday night. Like washing clothes and writing her history paper, which had been assigned for two weeks and would count 20 percent of her grade for the entire course. Friday morning brought the first shock of realization when the other students began preparing to hand in that history paper. Suddenly she knew it. She had completely forgotten the paper. Her heart seemed to sink down into her stomach. As she strained to keep her eyes fastened to the floor so as not to encounter the penetrating eyes of Professor Looper. The second major shock of realization came about four o'clock Saturday afternoon. When she went to her closet only to find that the one blouse which matched her new skirt was not there.

SENTENCE STRATEGIES

How the writer words her sentences depends on the effect she wants those sentences to have on her reader. Consider, for example, these two sentences.

The exhausted teacher slumped into the chair at the end of the day.
Exhausted, the teacher slumped into the chair at the end of the day.

Both sentences are about the same event—the same teacher, tired after a hard day in the classroom, slumps into the same chair. But these sentences do not say exactly the same thing. Because it focuses the reader's attention on the teacher's state by placing *exhausted* first in the sentence, the second sentence is more emphatic than the first; that is, the second sentence emphasizes how tired the teacher is more than the first one does.

As a writer, your job is to create images in your reader's mind. One way to create vivid images is to structure your sentences so that each one focuses on the precise meaning you intend. Two important strategies for structuring sentences effectively are the loose sentence and the periodic sentence.

Loose Sentences

Loose sentences are also called *cumulative sentences* because of the way they are structured. In this type of sentence, the writer first gives the sentence's subject and verb and then adds details to modify, expand, or qualify the idea that the subject and verb represent. This sentence is like a train engine pulling several railroad cars; the subject and verb are followed by a string of details. It is called a loose sentence because details can be added, tacked on, until the image is as clear as the writer thinks necessary.

In this example of a loose sentence, the subject and verb are in boldface print, and the details (the modifiers) are italicized.

The writer sat at his desk, *his fingers frozen above the typewriter keys, his lips a grim, straight line, his eyes staring at the stark white sheet of paper before him.*

The effect of this sentence is to build up the image, one detail at a time, of a frustrated writer whose ideas will just not come.

We could also write the sentence placing one of the modifiers before the subject and verb—"His lips a grim, straight line, the writer sat at his desk, his fingers frozen above the typewriter keys, his eyes staring at the stark white sheet of paper before him." Even though it did not open with its subject and verb, the sentence would still be considered a loose sentence because the subject and verb appear near the beginning.

<table>
<tr><td>EXERCISE</td><td>The following are subject-verb "starters" for you to develop into loose sentences. Close your eyes for a moment and visualize the action suggested by each sentence. Add enough details to develop each sentence into a complete image. (To illustrate, we have given an example. If you wish, imitate the example's structure, but remember that you are not bound by that structure.)</td></tr>
<tr><td>Example</td><td>The old man sat by the fire.
The old man sat by the fire, cradling his coffee cup in his hands to warm them, staring at the patch of sunlight on the rough wood floor, his face a relaxed, soft smile.

The halfback turned upfield.
The cat glared down from the tree.
The baby crawled across the floor.
The protesters waved their placards.
The fans in the stadium went wild.</td></tr>
</table>

Periodic Sentences

Periodic sentences are opposite to loose sentences in their structure. In the periodic sentence, details appear at the beginning of the sentence and build up to the sentence's main idea, which is expressed by the subject and verb. A sense of suspense is at work in a periodic sentence that is not present in a loose sentence; thus, the effect of a periodic sentence is that the reader helps the writer to discover the image. With a periodic sentence, the reader participates with the writer to create the meaning because the reader has to hold in mind all the writer's images until the main idea finally appears. The following periodic sentence, with the subject and verb in boldface and the details in italics, illustrates this point.

> *Peering cautiously from behind a tent flap, her hands groping for the ax, a flashlight, the shovel—anything she could use as a weapon—***the camper sought the source of the noise.**

We could add more details to this sentence after the subject and verb. For example, we could say the camper first looked left, then right, or that her nostrils flared in fear. But we still would have a periodic sentence because the subject and verb are suspended until most of the detail has been presented. This sentence paints an image one piece at a time, saving the key element of the picture until last.

<table>
<tr><td>EXERCISE</td><td>The following are subject-verb "starters" for you to develop into periodic sentences. Close your eyes for a moment and visualize a scene based on the action in each sentence. Then add enough details to develop each sentence into a complete image. (To illustrate, we have given an example. If you wish, imitate the example's structure, but remember that you are not bound by that structure.)</td></tr>
</table>

Example

The sheriff faced the outlaw.
Standing resolutely, his feet planted firmly in the dust of Main Street, his hands hanging loose and relaxed but ready at his hips, his eyes narrowed to menacing slits, the sheriff faced the outlaw.

The pitcher released the ball.
Class began.
The bus rolled over on its side.
The principal lectured the students.
The train pulled out of the station.

Sentence Variety

One common problem in ineffective writing is the lack of sentence variety. To make their meaning clear, many writers think they need to use short sentences. But writing is a process of discovering and then revealing meaning between and among thoughts. As we said in Chapter Three, effective writing requires the writer to create a web of relationships. All too often, short sentences do not create this web for at least two reasons.

1. In creating a web of relationships, the writer needs to emphasize important ideas by putting them in independent clauses and then subordinating other ideas to those she thinks most important. When everything is written in short sentences, or independent clauses, each idea carries the same weight—the same emphasis—as all the other independent clauses around it. When everything is emphasized, nothing is emphasized.

2. Short sentences are often left unconnected; that is, the writer often fails to use sufficient transition between them to show how he thinks the sentences relate to each other.

As the following example illustrates, short sentences tend to create choppiness, so that the reader moves through the writing in fits and starts instead of moving through it smoothly.

I sit here at this keyboard. I try to think of things to say. The words are not coming very freely. I think that is probably because it is the end of a long day. It may be that I am tired. I am smack up against writer's block. Freewriting may help me break through the wall.

Each of these sentences begins the same way, with the subject at the first followed closely by the main verb and then the rest of the sentence. Obviously, the
effect is choppy, pedestrian writing, that is, writing that plods along. With only
a few changes, the paragraph will read better.

> I sit here at this keyboard trying to think of things to say, but the words
> aren't coming very freely. Probably, they aren't coming because it's the end
> of a long day, and I'm tired. Whatever the reason, I'm smack up against
> writer's block. Perhaps freewriting will help me break through the wall.

The changes between these two paragraphs are not dramatic, but the second
reads better than the first. Primarily, the web of relationships between and
among the sentences of the second are more strongly established than in the
first, with these relationships signaled by transitional words and phrases (*but,
probably, whatever the reason*) and by the sentence structure itself. Closely related
ideas are joined in the same sentence so that of the original paragraph
sentences 1, 2, and 3 become one sentence, as do sentences 4 and 5. These
combinings and transitional words and phrases slightly increase the average
length of the sentences in the revised paragraph, from 8 words per sentence to
13. Such an increase is not all that significant, because a sentence 13 words long
is not a lengthy sentence. Our point, however, is a string of short sentences that
begin the same way (for example, with the subject) tend to be choppy. And
choppiness can hinder the reader.

We need to add a disclaimer, though: In and of itself, a short sentence is
not necessarily bad; in and of itself, a long sentence is not necessarily good. Our
criticism of short sentences is not a blanket endorsement of long sentences.
Instead, our purpose in talking about sentence types and sentence variety is to
focus on your need to consider the structure and length of your sentences in
light of your purpose.

If you want your reader to get the impression of the main idea and then to
consider supporting details, use loose sentence structure. If you want your reader
to work with you to create meaning or if you want to suspend the main idea
until the end of the sentence and build up to it, use periodic sentence structure.
If you want the reader to move very quickly through a paragraph, use short
sentences that begin the same way. Look again at the passage we quoted from
Let Us Now Praise Famous Men. In that passage, Agee and Evans use a series of
sentence fragments that all begin the same way and move the reader very quickly
through the passage. The effect on the reader is that he can smell the odor being
described just as if he were entering the house Agee writes about. If you want
the reader to slow down and consider your ideas, use longer, more involved
sentences. Whatever your strategy, you should choose the appropriate sentence
structure and length to express your ideas and to move your reader through
your writing as you intend. Remember, though, that repeating the same structure again and again can put a reader off so that a lack of variety can make for
ineffective writing. How may you achieve variety in your sentences? One of the
best ways is to use a technique called sentence combining. Consider these two
sentences:

The old convertible is an interesting antique.
It has a broken windshield and a dented fender.

What is the relationship between these two sentences? How does one sentence comment on the other? Actually only a slight relationship exists between the two, signalled by *it* in the second sentence. We know only that the two sentences are about the same car. Now consider the following sentences, which combine these two sentences. How does each constitute a web of meaning about the car?

1. With its broken windshield and dented fender, the old convertible is an interesting antique.

2. Despite its broken windshield and dented fender, the old convertible is an interesting antique.

3. Because of its broken windshield and dented fender, the old convertible is an interesting antique.

4. The old convertible, its windshield broken and one fender dented, is an interesting antique.

5. The old convertible, an interesting antique, has a broken windshield and a dented fender.

6. An interesting antique, the old convertible has a broken windshield and a dented fender.

Because it allows you to choose and feature the most important ideas in your writing, sentence combining is a useful tool. The following exercise, which is divided into two parts, will give you some practice in combining sentences. In the first part, we give a sentence pattern and then ask you to combine several sentence "kernals" into a similar pattern, with these patterns increasing in complexity as you move through the exercise. In the second part, we give longer, more complex kernals, including paragraphs broken down into kernals. We ask you to combine them into meaningful sentences and paragraphs. Your job in the second part is to decide which ideas of a particular pattern you want to emphasize and then to combine the kernals so that you emphasize what you see as important.

EXERCISE   *Part 1(a) Simple Sentence Patterns*

In each of the examples a pattern sentence is given, and below it are units that can be combined to parallel the example sentence's pattern. Compose a new sentence from the units, and then create a second sentence that imitates the original pattern sentence.

Pattern 1   The gaunt, wrinkled old man tottered down the dirty, cracked streets.
The dog barked.
The dog barked at the cat.
The dog was small.

The dog was black.
The cat was Siamese.
The cat was frightened.
The cat was hungry.

Pattern 2

The small, dull-eyed child, tired and hungry, clutched her stale bread.

The locomotive approached the crowd.
The locomotive was handsome.
The locomotive was black.
The locomotive was old.
But the locomotive was well preserved.
The crowd was cheering.

Pattern 3

The dog ran past the stranger and into the barn behind the house.

The soldiers marched.
The soldiers marched out of the town.
The soldiers marched into the countryside.
The soldiers marched toward the enemy.

Pattern 4

One of my favorite teachers, a choral director, died recently.

The man ran to help the boy.
The man was large.
The man was a fireman.

Pattern 5

She moved quickly, darting through the field like a rabbit startled by a hunter.

The speaker answered slowly.
The speaker stared at the audience.
The speaker was like an animal.
The animal was frozen by fear.

Pattern 6

Pausing on the edge of the curb, he looked furtively to the left and to the right and ran deliberately into the path of the truck.

The lawyer looked over her shoulder.
The lawyer looked at the clock.
The lawyer walked to her office.
The lawyer walked hurriedly.
The lawyer worked on her cases.
The lawyer worked diligently.
The lawyer worked until midnight.

Pattern 7

Dealing with unfriendly dogs is the hardest part of a postal worker's job.

Something is a chore.
The chore belongs to John.
John walks the dog.

Pattern 8

The dying woman's skin was thin and transparent, stretched tightly over the bones of the skull.

The party was loud.
The party was boisterous.
The party was the team's.
The team was celebrating.
The party was heard distinctly.

The party was heard in the rooms.
The rooms were on the third floor.

Pattern 9

Eyes darting, nostrils sniffing the air, the deer stood frozen in the clearing.

His legs were pumping.
His lungs were gasping for air.
The cyclist seemed fixed in his determination.

Pattern 10

My grandmother told her story, her hands gesturing gently in the air.

The fire truck's siren was piercing the silence.
The fire truck rounded the corner.

Pattern 11

To finish the job was an obsession with him.

Hint: The preceding sentence would be broken into the following two parts:

Something was an obsession with him.
He finishes the job.

Something was her only goal.
The goal was in life.
She is a teacher.

Pattern 12

The announcer wanted to alert the crowd to the danger.

The police officer attempted something.
The police officer resuscitates the victim.

Pattern 13

To prepare for the championship game, the team practiced daily.

The reporter visited several neighborhoods.
The neighborhoods were ethnic.
The reporter researches the article.

Part 1(b): Complex Sentence Patterns

Follow the directions given above for simple sentence patterns.

Pattern 14

That the law is a fair one cannot be denied.

Something distressed the host.
The ambassador left the celebration early.
The celebration was gala.

Pattern 15

What you do about this problem is entirely up to you.

Hint: The preceding sentence would be broken into the following two parts.

Something is entirely up to you.
You do something about this problem.

Something is extremely insulting.
He said something to his girlfriend.

Pattern 16

Joe knew that Bill was the best person for the job.

William thought something.
The team was the best.
The team was in the league.

Pattern 17   The speech in which the department head explained her position satisfied the faculty.

The carriage delighted the children.
The carriage was gold.
The queen rode in the carriage.

Pattern 18   Feeling that he had been insulted, Mortimer sneered at the editor.

The author deleted the sentence.
The author knew something.
The author would be fired.

Pattern 19   Believing that one's work is worthwhile contributes to self-esteem.

Something is dangerous.
Someone assumes something.
Deadlines are movable.

Pattern 20   John, who dislikes both Frank and the speaker, did not attend the meeting.

Jan will not fly.
Jan is afraid of heights.
Jan is afraid of places.
The places are closed.

Pattern 21   The dog that bit the man was cowering between the garage and the house.

The alarm pierced the silence.
The silence was of the night.
The alarm awakened the citizens.
The citizens were slumbering.

Pattern 22   Although we consider the ruling unfair, we will not protest it.

George did not win the race.
George was the fastest runner.
The runner was in the race.

Pattern 23   Christmas day, when it finally comes, seems all too short.

Your job will be tiring.
Your job will involve much travel.

Pattern 24   I will go with you after I have finished my homework.

The play will begin.
The audience will be seated.

Part 2: Combined Sentence Patterns

Above we offered simple combining patterns as examples of the processes used to form longer sentences. However, these simple patterns are often combined to make much more complicated and sophisticated sentences. Below are several such combined patterns followed by sets of short sentences that you may combine into sentences imitating the example patterns.

Pattern 25   The small child who, when she awakened, found herself in a strange place cried bitterly.

Many people are now its beneficiaries.

The people complained before the law passed.
The people complained loudly.
The people complained about its dangers.

The tenor received a standing ovation.
The tenor was large.
The tenor sang.
The tenor sang after he had cleared his throat.
The tenor sang beautifully.

Pattern 26

By this time, the sun was coming up, and the child could see, by the faint light that came through the window, the outlines of the neighboring buildings.

The music was over.
The music was over now.
Mary saw the expression.
The expression was on the face.
The face was her mother's.
Mary saw the expression through the tears.
The tears welled in her eyes.

The team was practicing.
The team was practicing at three o'clock.
The coach could see the numbers.
The coach could see the numbers through the bars.
The bars were of the window.
The window was in his office.
The numbers were on the backs.
The backs were of his specialty squad.

Pattern 27

Piling up around doors and windows, rounding every angle in the landscape and making every common twig and stone a new piece of lace, the snow, which had fallen throughout the night, was finishing its magic by the time we awakened.

The students were warming themselves by the fire.
The students formed a line.
The line was crooked.
The students looked like statues.
The statues were frozen.
The students were holding cups of coffee.
The students had waited throughout the night.
The students had waited for tickets.
The grounds keeper had started the fire.

The villagers sought relief.
The relief was from the heat.
The heat was at noon.
The heat seemed almost visible.
The heat seemed almost visible in the atmosphere.
The villagers were hanging out of their windows.
The windows were in their shops.
The villagers were lounging in doorways.
The doorways were open.
The villagers were fanning themselves.

The villagers were fanning themselves with any pieces of paper.
The paper was available.
The villagers secretly enjoyed the excuse to turn away from work.

Pattern 28

John had finished the exam.
The exam was difficult.
John had checked each answer.
John had checked with care.
John slowly handed in the paper.
John slowly handed in the pencil.
Gloom clouded the face.
The face was John's.
The task awaited John.
John had to meet a stare.
John had to survive a stare.
The stare was John's father's.

Pattern 29

The clowns had completed their routine.
The routine was hilarious.
The ringmaster had chanted his announcements.
The announcements were to the crowd.
The jugglers quickly took over the ring.
The jugglers quickly took over the spotlight.
Their dexterity brought smiles to faces.
The faces were the children's.
The smiles were broad.
The afternoon had only increased the enthusiasm.
The enthusiasm was the children's.
Tte children had watched the circus.
The children had enjoyed the circus.

Below you will find two paragraphs that have been broken into simple idea units. In each case, we tell you how many sentences the original paragraph contained. Your task is to construct a unified, coherent paragraph containing all of the information in the idea units without exceeding the number of sentences in the original paragraph.

The following paragraph, from Stephanie Weickert's "Franklin Elementary School," contained seven sentences.

Franklin Elementary School awaited the beginning.
Franklin Elementary School awaited the beginning on a morning.
   The morning was chilly.
   The morning was in the fall.
The beginning was of another day.
Its frame rose.
   Its frame was ugly.
   Its frame was ancient.
Its frame rose solemnly.
Its frame rose solemnly from the ground.
Its frame met the sun.
   The sun was of the morning.
Lights shone through the windows.

The lights were from the classrooms.
The windows were dirty.
The lights illuminated the ground.
The ground was hard.
The ground was below.
The wind blew.
The wind blew through the swings.
The swings were on the playground.
The playground was empty.
The wind made the swings squeak.
The wind made the swings creak.
The swings creaked like a door.
The door was turning.
The door was turning on hinges.
The hinges were rusty.
Three trees vainly attempted something.
The trees were tall.
The trees hid the eyesore.
A fence enclosed the property.
The fence was of steel.
The property was the school's.
The fence separated the school from the rest of the neighborhood.
Surrounding Franklin were ghetto shanties.
The ghetto shanties were small.
The ghetto shanties were grim.
The ghetto shanties were filled with youngsters.
The youngsters were preparing for the day.
The day was at school.

The following, from Amy Smith's "High," originally contained eight sentences.

This pressure is a part of a society.
The society considers marijuana a safe drug.
Teens associate marijuana with drugs.
These teens are few.
Drugs are hard.
Teens associate marijuana with pimps.
Teens associate marijuana with crime.
Rather, marijuana is a part of life.
Life is normal.
Life is everyday.
The man is now your contact.
The man used to be considered evil.
The man used to be considered greedy.
The man used to be considered a pusher.
The pusher is downright demonic.
Your contact is now friendly.
Your contact is in the neighborhood.
Your contact will supply whatever whenever.
He is found no longer.

He is found exclusively.
He is found in the class.
    The class is low.
Two girls approached once.
Two girls approached while I was walking with a friend.
Two girls asked something.
Something was where to get a couple of lids.
They and my friend proceeded to carry on their business then.
Ironically, we were standing directly in front of our office.
    The office was of the high school.
    The office was central.

EXERCISE

Select any of the essays you have written in this course and examine the sentences of two or three of its paragraphs. What structure have you used most frequently (loose or periodic)? Is there any choppiness at work in these paragraphs? If so, revise them, using varied structures and sentence combining to reduce the choppiness.

Chapter Twelve

Paragraphs

In Chapter Three, "Creating Order," we described paragraphs as the structural units that combine to present the writer's perspective or point of view on his topic. We also talked about how the various paragraphs of an essay could be seen as parts of a puzzle—just as the pieces link to form the puzzle's picture, the various paragraphs of an essay join to form the essay's meaning. In the same way sentences within a given paragraph work together to form a cohesive unit of writing.

Our purpose in returning to the paragraph here is not to talk about how the writer shifts perspective from the essay level to the paragraph level to reveal meaning. Rather our intention is to talk about the detailed structure of paragraphs in terms of paragraph purpose, length, unity, and coherence.

WHAT IS A PARAGRAPH?

A paragraph is a collection or group of sentences related by subject matter. As such, its purpose or function is to develop a particular idea. In the context of an essay—the context we deal with here—a paragraph's purpose is to develop one aspect of the essay's central focus or idea, that is, to support, expand, and/or supplement that main idea. Look again at the essays by Ceci Cano (pp. 24–28), Tim Meiers (pp. 35–36), Mickey Carter (pp. 52–58), Stephanie Weikert (pp. 67–68), Arlene Yusnukis (pp. 110–112), Amy Smith (pp. 166–169), and Karen Pinckley (pp. 282–311). Each of these student writers has produced an essay that is a collection of paragraphs, and each paragraph develops some particular aspect of the essay's main idea. Also, each paragraph is tied tightly to those around it so that it links with all the rest to present the writer's complete view of the topic.

The content of a paragraph depends on the writer's purpose and on her sense of direction as she works to develop her paper's central idea. That sense of purpose or direction will determine the details she chooses to include and the arrangement of those details. Do any sentences in any of the paragraphs referred to above seem out of place? We think not, that each sentence is in its proper place and that the detail each presents is appropriate for its author's purpose.

Often, student writers ask how long a paragraph has to be, and the answer is at once simple and complex: A paragraph has to be only long enough to be complete. Ultimately, you, the writer, must decide whether a given paragraph is complete, and your decision will be based on whether the paragraph fulfills its purpose, whether it has developed what it should as fully as necessary. To make this decision, ask yourself what you want a particular paragraph to do— what is your paper's purpose? How does the paragraph in question develop that purpose? What details does or should this specific paragraph present? Are there any included details that are extraneous to the paragraph's purpose? Are there any necessary details that you have omitted or overlooked? In answering such questions, you will be considering whether a particular paragraph is complete or needs expansion.

At times it may not be easy to know when to end one paragraph and begin another, but your task will become easier if you think of a paragraph as a group of sentences related by subject matter, or content. To illustrate we return to a section from Amy Smith's essay. Below are several paragraphs from that essay printed without paragraph indentations. See whether you can decide where each paragraph begins and ends before reading past this extract.

This was a situation I found myself in all too often during my high school years. Although peer pressure was never like it is commonly illustrated on television where some ugly black-jacketed thug is ready to force the drugs he is selling at the point of a knife, it was there nevertheless. In the form of a cute date or a little out-of-the-ordinary fun at a party, the pressure was much harder to recognize, and still harder to resist. This pressure is a part of a society which considers marijuana a "safe" drug. Few teens associate marijuana with hard drugs, pimps, and crime. Rather, it is part of normal, everyday life. The man who used to be considered an evil, greedy and down-right demonic "pusher" is now your friendly neighborhood "contact" who will supply whatever, whenever. No longer is he found exclusively in the low class. Once while I was talking with a friend, two girls approached and asked where they could get a couple of lids. Then they and my friend proceeded to carry on their business. Ironically, we were standing directly in front of our high school central office. It is difficult to maintain the picture of the leering ogre-type pusher when one's friends have become "contacts." One such friend confided that he had made "a couple hundred last month, six the month before." Asked about the morality of the practice, he responded,

"... hey, it's good on-the-side money." Acceptance and familiarity with marijuana have reached an all time high. Another friend, Kevin, went with Deanna and me to The Pizza Connection, one of the best pizza places around. Two pizzas later, we left and Kevin realized that he had left his satchel of pot underneath his chair, went back and got it, and was kidded about it by one of the waiters. I overheard another user telling some girl, after she had apparently refused to toke, that he never drank booze "because it ruins your brain cells," and never smoked cigarettes because " ... they give you cancer." He went on to tell her that he smoked pot because it "is good for you." These acceptances helped make me aware of the fact that most teens accept marijuana as a fact of life, but I was not aware of the importance some people placed on marijuana until a friend asked me to imagine myself "standing there on judgment day with God pointing His finger at you and asking, 'Why didn't you smoke my marijuana? It was a gift from me to you!'"

This passage consists of five paragraphs with these opening sentences.

1. This was a situation I found myself in all too often during my high school years.

2. This pressure is a part of a society which considers marijuana a "safe" drug.

3. It is difficult to maintain the picture of the leering ogre-type pusher when one's friends have become "contacts."

4. Acceptance and familiarity with marijuana have reached an all time high.

5. These experiences helped make me aware of the fact that most teens accept marijuana as a fact of life.

What criteria did you use in dividing the passage into its paragraphs? Were you able to find where each began? You may have had some trouble separating the first two paragraphs because the first sentence of paragraph 2 repeats a key term from the last sentence of paragraph 1. But consider the content of these two paragraphs. Paragraph 1 talks in fairly general terms about peer pressure and drugs, while paragraph 2 talks specifically about the acceptance of marijuana in our society. Amy repeated that key term *pressure* to provide a bridge or transition from the first paragraph to the second.

Similarly, you may have had a little trouble in separating the second and third paragraphs, again because Amy tied the third paragraph to the second by continuing a theme—friends as pushers—that she had started in the second paragraph. But the second and third paragraphs actually differ in subject matter: The second deals with the acceptance of marijuana in our society, and the third, more specifically with the idea of friends as pushers. So the second and third paragraphs do differ in content.

This exercise should point out that a paragraph is content bound; that is, a paragraph's length and completeness are determined by the content it presents. And it should point out that the paragraphs in an essay are not separate entities in themselves but that they work together to constitute the whole of the essay.

EXERCISE Pick any essay you have written to date for this course. Identify your purpose in writing it and state that purpose in a single sentence. Then look at each paragraph in your essay. How well does each paragraph develop your stated purpose? On what do you base your judgment?

Identify the main idea of each paragraph, and state each idea in a single sentence. How well does each paragraph develop its primary idea? On what do you base your judgment?

In each paragraph, are there any details extraneous to the paragraph's purpose? Are there any necessary details you have omitted or overlooked? On what do you base your judgment?

TOPIC SENTENCES

Well-written paragraphs have a certain logic about them; that is, a well-written paragraph has a tight structure that leads the reader through the development of its content. One element of a given paragraph's logic is its topic sentence, which is the sentence in a paragraph that holds the paragraph's main idea, the idea the paragraph subsequently develops. Most often, the topic sentence carries a generalization that the paragraph goes on to develop, explain, or support. The topic sentence is like a signal to the reader that identifies what the paragraph is about. As such it directs or guides the reader through the paragraph's content. The topic sentence may also guide the writer through the paragraph and possibly guide later revision as the writer decides whether he has actually delivered what a given topic sentence has promised.

Most often, the topic sentence appears at the beginning of the paragraph, but it can actually occur anywhere in the paragraph. The topic sentence of each of the following paragraphs is italicized. After you read each paragraph, consider the questions that follow.

Example *As I have already suggested, a Quantity-Quality confusion is something most Texans have come by naturally.* The pioneer Texan could hardly help thinking of life in terms of quantities; their descendants imbibed the concept of quantity with their mother's milk, had it fed into their vocabulary, and grew up to find it complexly entangled with their sense of self. "Best" is the superlative Texans usually tack onto those things they can allow themselves to be sentimental about (i.e. the best little woman, best damn horse, best little town), while "Biggest" is reserved for a more serious category (biggest ranch, biggest fortune, biggest failure, biggest deal).*

1. What idea does the topic sentence of this paragraph carry? How well does the paragraph develop this idea? On what do you base your judgment?

---

*Larry McMurtry, "A Handful of Roses," *In a Narrow Grave: Essays on Texas* (New York: Simon and Schuster, 1968), pp. 122–123.

2. How well does this topic sentence guide you through this paragraph? On what do you base your judgment?

3. Is this topic sentence placed appropriately? On what do you base your judgment?

Example

    The tools that a writer uses to explore his subject are words. He is continually concerned with finding the words that most accurately record his impressions of the subject. *But since the words he uses will help determine these impressions, he is in a constant process of trying to equate words with concepts and attitudes.* Even at a time when he is not sure what precisely he wants to say he must understand the implications of the statements he makes so that he can see in what direction his writing is taking him. John Ciardi calls this procedure a groping for words that are intuitively recognized as right when they are discovered. In other words, the writer may not know precisely what he wants to say, but he recognizes an accurate statement of his meaning when he makes it.*

1. What idea does the topic sentence of this paragraph carry? How well does the paragraph develop this idea? On what do you base your judgment?

2. This topic sentence appears in the middle of the paragraph. What is the function of the sentences that come before this topic sentence?

3. How well does this topic sentence guide you through the paragraph? On what do you base your judgment?

4. Is this topic sentence placed appropriately? On what do you base your judgment?

Example

    You do too know her. She's wearing the panties in the department store ad on page 4 of your newspaper, and they've cropped her below the rib cage and two thirds of the way up the thighs so that you see more clunky white cotton brief than sleek chassis. She's on page 38 of your specialty store catalog, wearing the cashmere and merino suit with the Norwegian blue fox collar. She's strutting and twirling down the runway at the Apparel Mart in an Albert Nipon. She's dining at Jean-Claude with a guy who wears Giorgio Armani suits and drives a BMW 633csi. Or maybe she just got married to the lawyer who's handling your divorce. *She's the Dallas Model.*†

1. What idea does the topic sentence of this paragraph carry? How well does the paragraph develop this idea? On what do you base your judgment?

---

*James M. McCrimmon, "Writing as a Way of Knowing," in *Rhetoric and Composition: A Sourcebook for Teachers*, ed. Richard L. Graves (Rochelle Park, NJ: Hayden Book Company, Inc., 1976), p. 6.
†Michael Ennis, "The Dallas Model," *Texas Monthly*, January 1983, p. 112. Reprinted with permission from the January issue of TEXAS MONTHLY. Copyright 1983 by TEXAS MONTHLY.

2. What is the effect of this sentence appearing at the end of the paragraph? How did Ennis use it to guide him through writing the paragraph?

3. What is the function of the paragraph's first sentence? How well does it work with the paragraph's topic sentence to guide you through the paragraph?

4. Is this paragraph's topic sentence placed appropriately? On what do you base your judgment?

Not every paragraph will contain a topic sentence, but each paragraph should develop what we call a *topic idea*. A paragraph without a topic sentence must still develop some aspect of the essay's thesis, and it may do so by developing an extended example or by developing an idea from a preceding paragraph in more detail. An example is in order here. In "Politics and the English Language," George Orwell talks about defending the English language from those who misuse it. He closes one paragraph dealing with various minor misuses and ways to remedy them with this statement: "The defence of the English language implies more than this, and perhaps it is best to start by saying what it does *not* imply." Orwell then goes on to this next paragraph.

> To begin with, it has nothing to do with archaism . . . or with the setting up of a "standard English" which must never be departed from. On the contrary, it is especially concerned with the scrapping of every word or idiom which has outgrown its usefulness. It has nothing to do with correct grammar and syntax . . . or with the avoidance of Americanisms, or with having what is called a "good prose style." On the other hand it is not concerned with fake simplicity and the attempt to make written English colloquial. Nor does it even imply in every case preferring the Saxon word to the Latin one, though it does imply using the fewest and shortest words that will cover one's meaning. What is above all needed is to let the meaning choose the word, and not the other way about. . . .*

This paragraph has no topic sentence; instead, it is guided by the last sentence in the preceding paragraph—it is this sentence that our example paragraph develops.

EXERCISE   Select any of the essays you have written in this course and examine each paragraph for its topic sentence. What idea does the topic sentence imply that the paragraph will develop? How well does the paragraph develop this idea? Where does the topic sentence appear? Is it where it should be? If a given paragraph does not have a topic sentence, does it develop a topic idea expressed in a preceding paragraph? If not, should it have its own topic sentence? Why or why not? If you find problems with your topic sentences, revise individual paragraphs as your instructor directs.

---

*George Orwell, "Politics and the English Language," *"Shooting an Elephant" and Other Essays* (New York: Harcourt, Brace & World, Inc., 1950), pp. 90–91.

                                                           Paragraphs

There is a logic to the order of sentences in a well-structured paragraph in that the sentences join together, one following the next in order, to form the paragraph's meaning. In the following exercise, we have scrambled the sentences of a paragraph from a transactional essay. Your job is to reorder the sentences so that you reconstruct the original paragraph. Once you have re-created the original, answer the questions that follow.

1. What exactly a Shika was, and what it might do, had long troubled the Pentagon.

2. The American ships and planes that carried military supplies to Israel during the 1973 Arab-Israeli war did not all return empty.

3. If, as rumored, it could destroy even low-flying aircraft with ease, Shika might make Soviet armored columns nearly unstoppable.

4. Although it looked like nothing more than a small tank, Shika was in fact a radar-directed, computer-controlled anti-aircraft cannon.

5. Aboard one was a great prize of espionage—a captured Russian super-weapon called the ZSU-23-4, which was known to intelligence agents as Shika.*

Questions for Discussion

1. Is this paragraph unified and coherent? Why or why not?

2. How much trouble did you have in reforming the paragraph? What "clues" did Easterbrook provide that helped you re-create the original?

This exercise should point clearly to the necessity of each paragraph you write being unified and coherent. Easterbrook leads the reader through his paragraph by making the connections between and among his thoughts clear; there is no question about the direction of the paragraph, nor is there any question about how the various sentences relate to each other. The paragraph is unified and coherent.

Unity

A unified paragraph has a clear direction. In using this word *direction*, we intend the idea that the writer of a unified paragraph knows where she is going, and she makes it clear to the readers just where the paragraph is taking them. Her writing has a purpose that allows her to avoid sentences that should not be there and to make the relationship between the sentences in the paragraph clear. Below we offer an exercise that shows how a lack of unity can hinder the overall effect of one's writing.

---

*Gregg Easterbrook, "DIVAD," *The Atlantic Monthly*, October 1982, pp. 29–39.

The paragraph that follows was taken from a student essay dealing with E. A. Robinson's poem, "Luke Havergal."

> The speaker [of the poem] has been mentioned several times. Who or what is the voice that speaks to Luke? The speaker gives a clue to his identity in the following quotation: "Out of a grave I come to tell you this." This does not make the voice overly appealing. Most people believe that death brings with it a certain special knowledge and wisdom that cannot be attained any other way. This fact makes the voice attractive to Luke as a source of knowledge. The speaker gives another hint as to who he is. "And hell is more than half of paradise." This is the most ambiguous line in the poem, and it is open to several different readings. There is only one being who would know what hell is like and try to get Luke to commit suicide. That being is Satan. He would come out of the grave and tell Luke that hell is not so bad. Both Satan and Luke know that suicide is a sin and punished by eternity in hell. An alternate reading of that line is that hell is death or the grave. The line could be interpreted to mean that death is better than living without her, that is in "half of paradise." In this case, the speaker sounds like the dark side of Luke. If this is the case, the poet is giving us an insight into the mind of a suicidal person. This dark side was able to unbury itself from Luke's control driving his grief to tell Luke "the way that he must go." The second idea about the speaker is easier to accept.

This paragraph obviously lacks unity, with its several different ideas quite loosely connected. However, many of them could be fitted quite coherently into two paragraphs with the following topic sentences.

> In one interpretation of "Luke Havergal," the speaker is seen as a devil from Hell.
> In another interpretation of the poem, the speaker is a part of Luke himself.

Write these paragraphs and then answer the following questions.

1. How many sentences have you discarded altogether?

2. Were these sentences problematic in the original paragraph?

3. Why do you think the writer decided to include them?

Then compose a topic sentence of your own that would serve to organize some of the material in this paragraph and write that paragraph.

Coherence

Closely allied to the concept of paragraph unity is paragraph coherence. Whereas unity involves direction, coherence involves *connection*—how the various parts of the paragraph fit together. You may strengthen the coherence of your paragraphs by providing transition between the various parts, by using repetition of key words and phrases, and by using repetition of sentence structure.

Transition Perhaps the easiest way to achieve coherence is by using transitional words and phrases. However, these phrases do not always make for the most effective writing, as we illustrate in the following exercise.

The two paragraphs below were written by Stephanie Weikert, a student at Clemson University. Study the paragraphs and answer the questions that follow them.

Coach Martin's personality was another aspect that made him so unlike other coaches. He was very kindhearted. He cared for me, not only as a runner, but also as a person. Although Coach was concerned with the races I ran, it was more important to him that I was healthy mentally and physically when I was finished. There were times when I actually felt like his daughter; he was always telling me to eat the right foods and to get enough sleep at night. I could always take my problems to him, and he would listen sympathetically. Then, he would always find a way to help me solve them. He was not an unsociable monster who put himself on a pedestal above his athletes. Instead, John Martin was a friendly person that everyone liked, even the coaches of the opposing teams. He was extremely easygoing and humorous too. He was never ready to start a workout on time. However, when the training session began, he certainly could make it go quicker with his silly jokes and teasings. I found I could forget the workout was painful when I was laughing. When I heard, "Pick up the pace, Turkey! Get those scrawny legs moving!" I could run a little faster and giggle under my breath.

After I came to know Coach Martin, he seemed more like a father than a coach, someone who always told us to eat the right foods and to get enough rest, someone who could be trusted to listen to our problems sympathetically, and to help us solve them. His easygoing manner and good humor made even the harshest training session bearable. With a "Pick up the pace, Turkey!" or "Get those scrawny legs moving!" he could make me forget the pain and run a little faster with a giggle under my breath. And I could feel free to push myself, for I knew that from behind those sunglasses he was watching each of us constantly for any sign that the stress was too much. He had an uncanny ability to push us hard enough without pushing too hard.

1. One of these paragraphs is a revision of the other. Assuming that the revision is an improvement, can you tell which is which? Why is the revision a better paragraph?

2. Which paragraph makes more use of transitional words and phrases? Are these used effectively? Why or why not?

3. Can you see any connection between the mode that structures these paragraphs and the role that transition words play in them?

Repetition—Key Words and Phrases In the following paragraphs, the respective writers use repetition of key words and phrases, and we have marked it by showing how each instance of repetition works in the paragraphs. After you read these paragraphs, answer the questions that follow.

Example

```
The object of this intensive study was a plant . . . known

as the green gentian.  In recent years preliminary scientific

studies have indicated that many such plants growing in this

harsh, alpine climate may be extremely long-lived -- perhaps

60 years or more.  This knowledge is becoming increasingly

important because these fragile ecosystems, remote as they may

seem, are beginning to experience the impact of acid rain and

increasing recreational use.  With a thorough understanding of

the plant and animal life of these high-altitude zones,

scientists can help minimize damages caused by a changing

environment. *
```

Example

```
TVA is a regional development corporation owned by the people of

the United States, and ignored by most of them.  The corporation

manages a 652-mile waterway regulated by 34 dams, employs about

47,000 people, owns 1.3 million acres, has some $11.6 billion in total

total assets and conducts a variety of social and economic power

programs.  It operates the nation's largest power program, generating

electricity for almost all of Tennessee and parts of Kentucky, West

Virginia, North Carolina, Georgia, Alabama, and Mississippi.  It's

the nation's largest purchaser of coal.  It is not the largest

polluter, but it comes close.**
```

1. What is the basis of the repetition in the first paragraph? (Does this paragraph rely primarily on repetition of key words and phrases or on repetition of pronouns?) What is the basis of the repetition in the second paragraph?

2. How effectively has the author of each paragraph used repetition to achieve coherence? On what do you base your judgment?

3. Are there any revisions you would make in either paragraph? Why or why not?

---

*Boyd Norton, "Earthwatch," *Vista/USA*, Spring 1983, pp. 21–23.
**Cassandra Tate, "Ambivalent TVA Roles in Energy and Conservation," *Smithsonian*, vol. 10, #10 (January 1980), pp. 94–103.

4. Does each paragraph have a topic sentence? If so, identify it. What idea does it promise the paragraph will develop? How well is that idea developed?

5. Is each paragraph both unified and coherent? On what do you base your judgment?

Repetition—Sentence Structure In the following paragraph, the writer repeats an introductory clause to achieve coherence; he begins the sentences that provide examples to support the topic sentence in the same way. How effective is this repetition; how well does it work to provide coherence?

> As you make bread, experiment with various additives to enhance the flavor and nutritional value of each loaf. If you add honey instead of sugar as a sweetener, your bread will taste better because honey adds its own distinctive flavor as well as sweetness. If you add wheat bran, your bread will be more healthful, because the bran fiber adds the bulk necessary for proper digestion. And if you add wheat germ, your bread will be more nutritious because of the vitamins the germ holds. What you choose to add to your bread dough determines whether what you bake will be merely bread or B*R*E*A*D.

In most coherent writing, all three of these devices—transitional words and phrases, repetition of key words and phrases, and repetition of sentence structure—are used. An example is the paragraph by George Orwell that we mentioned earlier in this chapter. Repetition of key words and of sentence structure come together in Orwell's use of *it* as the subject of the first five sentences. In addition, Orwell uses these transitional words and phrases to connect his sentences: "to begin with" (sentence one), "on the contrary" (sentence two), "on the other hand" (sentence four), and "nor" (sentence five).

Coherence, then, can be created in several ways. Whatever means you choose to make your paragraphs coherent, your job is to provide enough connection between the sentences so that the reader moves smoothly through your paragraphs.

<table>
<tr><td>EXERCISE</td><td>Select any of the essays you have written to date in this course and examine each paragraph for unity and coherence. Does each paragraph follow the direction established by its topic sentence? If a particular paragraph does not contain a topic sentence, does it develop a topic idea, perhaps an idea stated in a preceding paragraph? If so, how well does it develop that idea? On what do you base your judgment?</td></tr>
</table>

Mark any transitional words and phrases you have used. Are these appropriate? Why or why not? Mark any repetition of key words and phrases. Are these appropriate? Why or why not? If you find any problems with unity and coherence, revise individual paragraphs as your instructor directs.

We have said that a paragraph's function is to develop some aspect of an essay's central idea. For nearly all paragraphs, this will hold true, but sometimes a paragraph functions not so much to develop an idea as to provide transition between major parts of an essay. In such instances, these transitional paragraphs are usually short, possibly only a sentence or two long. For example, Bill Bridges wrote an essay titled "An Analysis of 'Senator Whiffenpouf Speaks Out.'" Bill used this short paragraph to bridge the gap between two parts of his paper.

> While this distortion is relatively minor, Whiffenpouf engages in more serious abuse of language as he molds his audience's opinion. Two unfair uses of language hide the lack of substance in Whiffenpouf's message—an extended *ad hominem* attack and extensive use of emotional appeal.

While this short paragraph briefly summarizes what has come before it—an example of minor abuse of language—its primary function is to prepare the reader for what is to follow—extended discussion of two major abuses of language. So this paragraph stands as a transitional paragraph. Use such short paragraphs sparingly because they simply do not afford the space necessary to develop an idea in as much detail as you will probably need to do, and every paragraph you write cannot work as a transitional paragraph.

One reason many students write short paragraphs is that they often see them in print, primarily in newspapers and magazines. It is true that journalistic convention requires one- and two-sentence paragraphs, but unless you are writing a piece to be published in a newspaper or magazine whose format calls for narrow columns, you should not write such short paragraphs. Not all paragraphs in newspapers and magazines should actually stand as separate paragraphs except that convention demands it to enhance the appearance of the page. Journalism requires short paragraphs so that the writing does not seem so dense that it discourages the reader from reading. Below are two paragraphs from an article in *National Geographic* that would probably be only one paragraph if the essay had not been published in a magazine.

> Industrial chemists, too, are discovering unsuspected natural resources in many common herbs. From the brown berries of the wild jojoba comes a waxy oil with properties similar to the far more costly sperm whale oil prized for lubricants.
>
> One species of the *Euphorbia* genus is a weed known as the gopher plant. It yields a milky latex containing hydrocarbons that can be refined into substitutes for crude oil and gasoline.*

The second paragraph develops a topic sentence given in the first paragraph, the idea that industrial chemists are finding natural resources in common herbs.

---

*Lonnelle Aikman, "Herbs for All Seasons," *National Geographic*, 163, No. 3 (1983), 387.

Except for the conventions of journalism, there is no reason for these paragraphs to be split, especially since the second so clearly supports the topic sentence of the first.

To check the development of your paragraphs, keep these principles in mind:

1. A paragraph is a sequence of content-related sentences that develop an idea in some detail.

2. Usually a paragraph contains a topic or lead sentence. This sentence serves to guide both writer and reader through the paragraph's content. The topic sentence can occur anywhere in the paragraph, though it usually comes at the beginning.

3. In some cases, a paragraph may not have a topic sentence, developing instead a topic idea stated in a preceding paragraph. (If you find that you have written a paragraph without a topic sentence, check to be sure that the paragraph does develop some aspect of your paper's purpose, some topic idea. Be sure to identify where that topic idea is stated.)

4. Paragraphs should be unified; each should develop one particular aspect of an essay's main thesis.

5. Paragraphs should be coherent; the sentences in each should be logically connected to each other by transitional devices, by repetition of key words and phrases, and/or by repetition of sentence structure.

6. Short paragraphs (one and two sentences) are best used as transitions between major sections of a longer essay.

With the assistance of Margaret Marks

We have chosen to place concern for editing last in our text, because the writer should be concerned with editing for grammatical and mechanical correctness only in the final stages of writing. In Chapters Thirteen and Fourteen, we outline various conventions of punctuation, spelling, grammar, and usage. We do not intend these chapters to constitute a comprehensive grammar and mechanics handbook; instead, we have touched on only those grammatical and mechanical problems that trouble our students. The exercises we present are abbreviated. The best use you can make of them, and of these chapters generally, is to refer to them when you find it necessary to edit your writing as directed by your instructor.

Chapter Thirteen

Punctuation, Spelling, and Manuscript Mechanics

The mechanics of writing involve grammatical correctness and the actual appearance of the manuscript. Because mechanics are more readily codified than other aspects of writing, we outline in this chapter how you should use punctuation, how you may check your spelling, and how you may prepare the manuscript of an essay.

END PUNCTUATION

The Period

- **The period is used at the end of a statement (declarative sentence) and at the end of most commands (imperative sentences).**

Examples

John wrote to tell me of his new job.   (declarative)
School will be out in three weeks.   (declarative)
Please shut the window.   (imperative)

Periods are also used in the following contexts.

1. After abbreviations:

titles	Dr. Mr. Ms. Rev.
months	Feb. Dec.
names	R.M. Williams
states	N.M. S.C.
degrees	Ph.D. M.A. M.D.

2. In numbers, as a decimal point:

$5.98 $1,352.54

The Question Mark

?

1. The question mark is used to mark the end of a direct question (interrogative sentence).

Examples

Where are you going?
Do you know what your goals are?

2. The question mark is also used to punctuate a question that is quoted directly.

Example

"Which way do I turn?" she asked.

Note that if a quoted question comes at the end of a sentence, the question mark appears within the quotation mark, and no other end punctuation is necessary.

Example

Looking puzzled, she asked, "What am I supposed to do with all these forms?"

Note also that if quoted material appears in a question but is not itself a question, the question mark appears outside the quotation marks.

Example

Did John say, "Today we should go to New York"?

The Exclamation Mark

!

1. The exclamation mark, or point, is used to end a very emphatic (exclamatory) sentence.

Examples

I refuse to listen to this garbage!
The house is on fire!
Run for your life!

2. The exclamation mark is also sometimes used to set an interjection off from the rest of a sentence.

Examples

Ouch! Something bit me!
Help! I don't know what to do!

Punctuation, Spelling, and Manuscript Mechanics

The Comma

,

The comma is the most versatile and commonly used mark of punctuation within the sentence. It is often the most confusing mark as well. In writing, commas usually correspond with a mild pause; in speech, they correspond with some change in voice inflection. However, the ear is not always a reliable guide to the conventions of comma placement. The comma makes the structure of the sentence clear by separating elements that might otherwise be confusing to readers. The following rules and examples demonstrate how commas are used to clarify sentence elements.

1. Commas are used to separate the parts of a series, whether the series consists of words, phrases, or clauses.

Examples

Campers will need pillows, linens, towels, rain gear, hiking boots, play clothes, and a small amount of spending money.

When the orchestra begins the overture, when the curtain rises, or when the soprano steps slightly forward for a major aria, the opera has its special kind of excitement.

2. The comma is used to set off a long introductory phrase from the rest of the sentence.

Examples

Wearily carrying his knapsack in his hands rather than on his aching back, he climbed the last section of the mountain.

In the house on the hill, I saw people moving slowly as if in a dream.

3. The comma is used after an introductory yes or no.

Example

Yes, I'll go to the hospital with you.

4. The comma is used to separate an introductory adverbial clause from an independent clause.

Examples

As soon as I finish my paper, I'll join you for dinner.

If you have any questions, please call me before noon tomorrow.

If the main clause precedes the adverbial clause, no comma is necessary.

Please call me before noon tomorrow if you have any questions.

5. The comma is used before a coordinating conjunction that joins two independent clauses.

Examples

The moving van led the way, and we followed in the car.

I'll join you in Florida as soon as I can, but I have a week's worth of work to do first.

6. Commas are used to set off a nonrestrictive adjective clause.
Nonrestrictive clauses give additional but unnecessary information and must be set off by commas. A nonrestrictive clause is one that could be left out of the sentence without substantially altering it.

Examples
His father, who has run a grocery store for thirty years, retired this week.

Her remark, which was not meant to be unkind, offended Jan.

7. Commas are used to set off an appositive.

Examples
John, her husband, works for the company that designed the new engine.

They decided on a Japanese car, the only car that gets more gas mileage than their present car.

Most appositives interrupt a clause and give additional but unnecessary information. However, some appositives give information that is necessary for identification as in the following sentence.

Your daughter Dixie said to tell you she is coming this weekend.

In a situation such as this, the appositive provides information necessary for the identification of a noun, and the appositive is not set off with commas.

8. Commas are used with transitional connectives (conjunctive adverbs such as *however, therefore,* and *moreover*) when they do not help to join two independent clauses.

Examples
I disagree strongly. I plan, moreover, to speak against your proposal in the meeting. However, I wanted to tell you of my objection personally.

9. Commas are used to set off contrasting or repeated elements in a sentence.

Examples
Many students are interested only in a degree, not in an education.

Hurry, hurry, hurry! That's all I ever hear.

10. Commas are used to separate direct quotations from phrases that join them to the rest of the sentence.

Examples
After a pause he said, "I'll join you in a minute."

"Not that complaint again," she protested.

(Note that when the quotation comes first, the comma appears inside the quotation marks.)

11. Commas are used to set off interrupting constructions such as *I believe* and *you say*.

Examples
Spring, I believe, has finally come to stay.

The modern audience, according to Flannery O'Connor, presents special problems for the religious writer.

12. Commas are used to separate coordinate adjectives that separately modify a following noun.

Example
On a stark, cold, gray day the men began their search for the missing child.

There are a number of other uses for the comma as well.

1. In dates:

Example
The examination will be given on April 8, 1983.

   Punctuation, Spelling, and Manuscript Mechanics

2. In addresses and place names:

Examples

She lives at 413 South Harper Street, Lauens, South Carolina.

Steve has a job in Dubuque, Iowa.

3. After the salutation of an informal letter:

Example

Dear Mary,

4. In numbers:

Examples

55,000
150,000
275,583,439

The Semicolon

;

The semicolon is a stronger mark of punctuation than the comma. Its uses are limited and can easily be learned. The following list illustrates the uses of the semicolon.

1. The semicolon is used to join independent clauses that are not joined by a comma plus a coordinating conjunction.

Example

I'm dropping out of school this semester; I'll be back in the fall.

2. The semicolon is used to join independent clauses that are connected by a transitional connective.

Example

The content of your paper is excellent; however, you need some help with punctuation.

3. The semicolon is used to separate elements in a series when the elements already contain commas.

Example

Dr. Jackson, the president of the college; Dr. Page, the academic dean; and Jean Brown, the student body president, all support the change in rules.

The Colon

:

The colon, even stronger a mark of punctuation than the semicolon, signals a strong separation between what precedes and what follows the colon. The meaning usually carried by a colon is that of emphatic introduction to something that follows. Like the semicolon, the colon has a limited number of uses, described below.

1. The colon is used to signal a list or series that follows.

Example

In her room were all the accumulations of a typical teenager's life: the secondhand guitar, the stereo with oversized speakers, the posters of animals and movie stars, the stuffed animals, and the piles of dirty clothes.

2. The colon is used to separate a long quotation from its introduction.

Example

Describing the power of a thunderstorm through the poetic vernacular of his character Huckleberry Finn, Mark Twain writes:

It would get so dark that it looked all blue-black outside, and lovely; and the rain would thrash along by so thick that the trees off a little ways looked dim and spider-webby; and here would come a blast of wind that would bend the trees down and turn up the pale underside of the leaves. . .*

3. **The colon is used to separate independent clauses when the second clause restates, amplifies, or explains the first clause or when the second clause gives an example of what was stated in the first.**

Examples

This last statement brings up important considerations for the shaper of any argument: He must ask himself what audience he is directing the argument to and how he wishes to interact with that audience.

There is one excuse that we must not be bullied into accepting: We must not accept laziness.

4. **The colon is used to introduce appositives.**

Example

The House of Representatives faces a difficult decision: whether or not to raise state income taxes.

Other uses of the colon include the following:

1. Between the hour and minutes in time indications

Example

4:15 P.M.

2. After salutations in formal business letters

Examples

Dear Sirs:

Dear Ms. Simpson:

3. Between chapter and verse of Biblical citations

Example

John 3:16

4. Between the city of publication and publisher in bibliographical entries

Example

Belmont, California: Wadsworth Publishing Co.

The Dash

The dash usually signals an interruption in thought or a dramatic pause. Sometimes it is necessary for clarity, especially when it is used to set a series off from the rest of the sentence. (On a typewriter the dash is indicated by a double hyphen with no space in between.)

1. **The dash is used to mark the limits of a series when a nearby noun might be mistaken for a part of the series.**

Examples

The citywide conference brought together various professionals—teachers, doctors, lawyers, scientists, and artists.

---

*Mark Twain, *The Adventures of Huckleberry Finn* (New York: Holt, Rinehart and Winston, Inc., n.d.), p. 45.

Punctuation, Spelling, and Manuscript Mechanics

The citywide conference brought together various professionals—teachers, doctors, lawyers, scientists, and artists—to discuss the city's economic crisis.

2. The dash is used to set off a parenthetical independent clause that interrupts the flow of another clause.

Example

He quit his job—he had hated it anyway—in order to devote all his time to his study.

3. The dash is used to indicate interruption or hesitation in dialogue.

Example

"I don't know how—I mean, I guess it—oh, I don't know why I took the money," she confessed.

4. The dash is used for an emphatic pause before a word or phrase at the end of a sentence.

Examples

He stole the bread for only one reason—to save his child.

There was only one thing she needed now—a job.

5. The dash is used to set off a summarizing or concluding main clause.

Example

The complexities of dormitory living, the exhilaration and the temptations of new-found freedom, the demands of a new level of study—all these make the life of a freshman both exciting and frustrating.

The Parenthesis

( )

Parentheses are most commonly used to enclose material that is only loosely related to the rest of a sentence—qualifications, asides, examples, explanations, and additional but unnecessary information.

1. The parenthesis is used to introduce a qualification.

Example

That her pleasure in Indianhood and her passion for car travel might be incongruous if not mutually exclusive never occurred to Sissy (as it was to occur to Julian and Dr. Goldman).*

2. The parenthesis is used to add nonessential information.

Example

Specific words or phrases in your paper "go with" (and thus help to develop) the topic that you have chosen.

3. The parenthesis is used to enclose page numbers of in-text references in documented essays and research papers.

Example

As Mina Shaughnessy says in *Errors and Expectations,* "We cannot tell how many needless circumventions or imprecise phrasings result from the fear of misspelling, but the number is undoubtedly high" (p. 162).†

(Note: the second quotation mark comes first, then the page number in parentheses, and then the period ending the sentence.)

---

*Tom Robbins, *Even Cowgirls Get the Blues* (Boston: Houghton Mifflin Company, 1976), p. 56.
†Mina Shaughnessy, *Errors and Expectations* (New York: Oxford University Press, 1977), p. 162.

Brackets

[ ]   Brackets should be clearly distinguished from parentheses. Their uses are much more limited than those of parentheses, and most often they are used within quoted material.

1. The bracket is used to insert material not in an original text.

Example   According to X. J. Kennedy, "His [King Kong's] simian nature gives him one huge advantage over giant ants and walking vegetables in that an audience may conceivably identify with him."*

2. The bracket is used with the Latin abbreviation sic (which means thus) to indicate that a mistake in quoted material is there because it was in the original.

Example   One evaluator wrote of the course proposal, "It's [sic] goals were never made clear, so I was never sure what the students were supposed to be learning."

Quotation Marks

" "   Quotation marks are most often used to indicate direct quotation. They are also used to enclose certain kinds of titles.

1. Quotation marks are used to indicate speaking roles in a dialogue.
Study the following sample, taken from Flannery O'Connor's "A Good Man Is Hard to Find," and the generalizations that follow it.

> "Good afternoon," he said. "I see you all had you a little spill."
> "We turned over twice!" said the grandmother.
> "Oncet," he corrected. "We seen it happen. Try their car and see will it run, Hiram," he said quietly to the boy with the gray hat.
> "What you got that gun for?" John Wesley asked. "Whatcha gonna do with that gun?"
> "Lady," the man said to the children's mother, "would you mind calling them children to sit down by you? Children make me nervous. I want all you all to sit down right together there where you're at."**

From the example you can notice the following points about quotation marks.

Quotation marks always come in pairs.

A new paragraph begins every time the speaker changes.

Only what is actually spoken by one of the characters is enclosed in quotation marks.

---

*X. J. Kennedy, "Who Killed King Kong?" in *The Norton Reader* (Shorter Edition), 4th ed., ed. Arthur M. Eastman, et al. (New York: W. W. Norton & Company, Inc., 1977), p. 280.
**Flannery O'Connor, "A Good Man Is Hard to Find," in *Three By Flannery O'Connor* (New York: The New American Library, Inc., n.d.), p. 137.

A phrase such as "he said," which interrupts a sentence of direct quotation (as in the first sentence of the last paragraph), requires that the sentence contain two sets of quotation marks. The second part of the quotation in this case does not begin with a capital letter because this is not the beginning of a new sentence.

2. **Quotation marks are used to indicate a direct quotation from another writer in a documented essay or research paper.** Any sentences, clauses, phrases, or key words that are copied directly from a source must be placed within quotation marks.

Examples   Wilbur S. Howell identifies "a third great change in the theory of communication since the Renaissance" as the change of thought about "invention," which Howell defines as "the devising of subject matter for a particular speech and, by extension, the providing of content in discourse."*

Note: Use quotation marks only for quotations of four lines or fewer. For longer quoted passages, use the block quotation style, which uses a colon rather than a comma just before the quoted material and block indentation rather than quotation marks to set off the passage.

Other rhetoricians have cited the need for the reemphasis of invention. As James M. McCrimmon points out in "Toward More Rewarding Emphases in the Teaching of Composition":

What is needed in the teaching of composition at any instructional level is an emphasis on what is most important in composition. What is most important is the rhetorical sequence of invention, arrangement or organization, and style. Since both the arrangement and the style are suggested by and dependent on invention, the emphasis is most rewarding when it is concentrated in the first element of the traditional sequence.**

3. **Quotation marks are used to set off titles of short poems, essays, chapters or sections of books, articles in magazines or journals, graduate theses or dissertations, and short musical compositions.**

Examples   Robert Frost's poem "Choose Something Like a Star" has been beautifully set to music by Randall Thompson.

Hawthorne's story "The Birthmark" suggests that all human beings are flawed and that attempting to perfect human nature is dangerous and prideful.

In our chapter "Creating Order," we discuss the fact that invention and arrangement are inseparable.

Note: Titles of such works as books, plays, long poems, magazines, films, and long musical compositions are underlined. In a typed manuscript this is the equivalent of italics in a printed publication.

---

*Wilbur S. Howell, "Renaissance Rhetoric and Modern Rhetoric: A Study in Change," in *The Province of Rhetoric*, ed. Joseph Schwartz and John A. Rycenga (New York: The Ronald Press Company, 1965), p. 299.

**James M. McCrimmon, "Toward More Rewarding Emphases in the Teaching of Composition," in *Language and Teaching: Essays in Honor of W. Wilbur Hatfield*, ed. Virginia McDavid (Chicago: Chicago State College, 1969), p. 68.

Special problems that come up with quotation marks are covered by the following rules.

1. **Commas and periods always go inside the closing half of the quotation marks.**

Example "I agree with your position," she said.

2. **Question marks and exclamation marks are placed inside the quotation marks if the quotation itself is a question or exclamation.**

Example "Are you ready to eat dinner now?" she asked.
With a snort, he exclaimed, "You'd do that over my dead body!"

3. **However, these marks are placed outside the quotation marks if the whole sentence is a question or an exclamation and the quotation itself is not.**

Example Did he say, "I'll accept the job"?
No, I positively did not say, "Call me at home after midnight"!

4. **If one quoted element appears within another quoted element, use single quotation marks (') for the inner quotation.**

Example The teacher said, "Please, Mary, begin again with 'The fault, dear Brutus, is not in our stars,' and finish the speech."

Ellipsis

... **The ellipsis, which consists of three spaced periods, is used in quoted references to indicate an omission from the original source.** If the omission comes at the end of a sentence, there should be four spaced periods, the fourth being the end punctuation mark of the sentence.

Examples Speaking of varying interpretations of the Bible by Christians, Clarence Darrow says, "Yet there are some people who claim to be Christians . . . who give more credence to some portions of the book than others."*

Kurt Vonnegut is, above all else, a humanist. Perhaps Robert Scholes puts it best: "Vonnegut, in his fiction, is doing what the most serious writers do. He is helping, in Joyce's phrase, 'to create the conscience of the race.' What race? Human. . . ."**

The Apostrophe

, **The primary use of the apostrophe is in forming the possessive case of nouns and some pronouns.** Other uses of the apostrophe include the following.

1. **The apostrophe is used to indicate an omission of letters or numbers as in contractions or dates.**

---

*Darrow (1900).
**Robert Scholes, " 'Mithridates, he died old': Black Humor and Kurt Vonnegut, Jr.," *The Hollins Critic*, 3, No. 4 (1966), 1–12.

Punctuation, Spelling, and Manuscript Mechanics

Examples	hasn't	has not
	o'clock	of the clock
	don't	do not
	'83	1983

2. The apostrophe is used to form the plurals of letters, figures, or words used as words.

Examples

Please write more plainly; I can't tell the difference between your *l*'s and your *e*'s.

Your papers will be rated on a scale of 1 through 4, with 1's meaning poor and 4's meaning excellent.

Your writing style would be stronger if you would eliminate some of the vague *this*'s and *that*'s.

SPELLING

Probably no writing skill gives more trouble to the average writer than spelling. Though there are many reasons for spelling difficulties, we can isolate two primary factors. In the first place, there is no one-to-one correspondence between the sounds of the English language and the letters of the alphabet that represent those sounds. In the second place, spelling has somehow come to be the standard for literacy in our society. That is, those who cannot spell are looked on as less than adequate writers.

The English language presents particular spelling difficulties: it has undergone at least two major sound shifts, and there are nearly twice as many distinctive sounds in the language as there are letters. For these reasons writers cannot depend upon phonics alone. In order to account for all the various sounds in the language, the letters of the alphabet, particularly those representing vowel sounds, often represent several different sounds. For example, the letter *a* may be sounded as *a* in c**a**ve, as *uh* in **a**bout, as *ae* in **a**bsence, and as *aw* in **a**ll. Similarly, the sound *sh* may be represented by as many as fourteen different spellings, including *sh*ow, *s*ure, trac*ti*on, suspi*ci*on, and man*si*on.

Before the advent of the printing press and the beginning of publication as we know it today, variations in spelling were common. Apparently they were not taken as a terribly serious problem. Writers often spelled the same word and even names in two or three different ways within the space of a page or two. However, mass publication led to a desire for some agreement as to the "correct" ways to spell words. For whatever reason—perhaps it was the uniformity of the copies themselves—uniformity in spelling suddenly became desirable.

As we said above, spelling has become one of the touchstones of literacy. In fact, many educators feel that an inordinate premium is placed on the ability to spell correctly. Given the many complicated processes that a writer must master to present a coherent essay, or even a coherent paragraph, it seems wrong to label a writer as "incompetent," "illiterate," or "unintelligent" because of four or five misspellings. But in many cases, people do just that.

Why has spelling come to be so important? We can offer both negative and positive answers to this question. The most negative viewpoint probably involves the ease and certainty with which spelling errors show up. They virtually "jump off the page." Even poor spellers will often immediately notice a misspelling that they would not be guilty of. Furthermore, no real uncertainty is involved in spelling errors; any doubt about a word's spelling can be immediately resolved by referring to a desk dictionary. Upon finding misspellings, the reader can immediately "label" the writer as incompetent.

More positive reasons exist for our society's emphasis on spelling ability, though. The inability to spell probably causes many people to write less effectively than they otherwise could. As Mina Shaughnessy says in *Errors and Expectations*, "We cannot tell how many needless circumlocutions or imprecise phrasings result from the fear of misspellings, but the number is undoubtedly high."*

Just as it is hard to tell how much inexact writing results from a fear of misspelling something, it is often quite difficult to draw the line between spelling errors and other more serious communication problems. Obviously, the person who writes *recieve* for *receive* has made a simple spelling error. But other problems—sometimes mistakenly labeled spelling errors—are actually more serious communication problems. *Indignation* and *implication* have some phonological similarity, but the person guilty of writing "I don't like your 'indignation' that I did something wrong" has a very real communication problem; she does not know the difference between these two words. And what do we say about the writer whose absence was "do to a flat tire"? Does he know exactly what *due* means? Simply, then, if you care enough about your writing and the impression it leaves to devote time and effort to it, you cannot afford to ignore spelling.

We cannot offer any magic formulas for overcoming spelling errors because there are none. Obviously, you cannot memorize all the words in the language, and just as obviously, you cannot check every word of your compositions in a dictionary after you have written them. What, then, can you do? Below we offer some suggestions for improving your spelling.

Begin to pay attention to the words you encounter in your reading. In particular, note the spelling of words that are new to you. Also pay attention to the spelling of words that you know but would have difficulty spelling yourself. Below, we offer a list of things you should begin to look for as you encounter words.

1. Pay particular attention to words that sound alike but are spelled differently, called homophones. Examples include *altar, alter; base, bass; cell, sell.*

2. Pay attention to the following pairs of suffixes: *-able, -ible; -ance, -ence; -ant, -ent; -ary, -ery.* There are no rules for determining when each of these is used; you can only memorize words that take these suffixes. However, you should always keep these in mind as spellings to be sure of or to check on as you review a manuscript for misspellings.

*Shaughnessy (1977), p. 162.

    Punctuation, Spelling, and Manuscript Mechanics

3. Notice silent letters in words; these letters are vestiges of times when the word was pronounced differently. Examples are *debt, doubt, indict, know, scene, subtle.* You will often be able to clarify the origin and spelling of a word with a silent letter by pairing it with a related word that retains the letter in question in its pronunciation. For example: *muscle, muscular*; *sign, signal.*

4. Pay attention to vowels that are in unstressed positions. Most of these will be pronounced as the "colorless" sound *uh*, and sound will be no help in spelling these words. Examples are the first vowel in **a**bbreviate, **o**ccasion, and **u**ndoubtedly; the second vowel in ad**e**quately, ben**e**ficial, bull**e**tin, car** buretor, dormitory,** and gov**e**rnor; the last vowel in destruc**ti**on, illu**si**on, orchestr**a**, and persist**e**nt.

While no single set of rules will explain the spelling system of the English language, some rules can help you with the most troublesome words. You should know these rules and some of the most common exceptions to them.

1. *ie* combinations
   i comes before e except after c or when the combination is pro-nounced ey.

Examples receive, believe, weigh

Exceptions counterfeit, either, financier, foreign, forfeit, height, leisure, neither, seize, sovereign, weird.

2. plurals
   Singular nouns and third person singular verbs that end with a consonant and a y, change the y to i and add es to form the plural.

Example gally, gallies   baby, babies   cry, cries

(Note that words with a vowel immediately preceding the *y* simply add an *s* in the plural form: *boy, boys.*)

   Singular nouns that end in o form their plurals by adding es.

Example cargo, cargoes   veto, vetoes

Exceptions alto, altos   piano, pianos

   Singular nouns that end in s, ss, ch, sh, x, or z form their plurals by adding es.

Examples ash, ashes   match, matches   loss, losses   birch, birches   tax , taxes
buzz, buzzes

Exceptions fish, fish   series, series   ox, oxen

3. Suffixes added to words ending in a consonant
   Monosyllabic words: **If the suffix begins with a vowel and if the word ends in a single consonant and contains only one vowel, the end consonant is doubled.**

Examples   can, canned   ship, shipped   whip, whipped
              (two consonants)   ask, asked   part, parting
              (two vowels)   clean, cleaned   creep, creeping

Multisyllabic words: **If the suffix begins with a vowel, the word ends in a vowel-consonant cluster, and the accent is on the final syllable, the end consonant is doubled.**

Example   admit, admitted   compel, compelled   occur, occurred

4. Suffixes added to words ending in a silent *e*
   Words that end in a silent *e* drop the *e* when a suffix beginning with a vowel is added.

Examples   cycle, cycling   judge, judgment   dine, dining

Exceptions   dye, dyeing   hoe, hoeing   arrange, arrangement

Words that end in a silent *e* preceded by *c* or *g* retain the *e* when a suffix beginning with *a* or *o* is added if the sound of the consonant is soft.

Examples   advantage, advantageous   manage, manageable

5. Identical letters
   If a prefix ends with a letter that also begins the word it is being added to, both letters are kept.

Examples   dissatisfied, illogical, misspelled, override

If a suffix begins with a letter that also ends the word it is being added to, both letters are kept.

Examples   common, commonness   physical, physically

The final piece of advice in regard to your spelling is to check a dictionary whenever you are in doubt. In many cases, this will not be easy to do when you do not know how to spell a word in the first place. However, if you will keep some of the principles we discussed in mind, you may find it easier to locate words in the dictionary. Once you realize that an unstressed vowel sound may be represented by any one of the vowel letters, you have freed yourself from some preconceptions that could keep you from finding certain words. Also, as you become increasingly aware of word "families" (words that derive from the same root), you will be better able to spell words with silent letters or unstressed sounds. For example, you may not know how to spell the word represented by the sounds ăb′ ə lĭsh′ ən (abolition), but if you recognize its relation to the word *abolish*, you will know immediately to look for an *o* in the unstressed middle position. The following chart should give you a feel for the various ways that vowel sounds appearing at the beginning of words may be spelled.

      Punctuation, Spelling, and Manuscript Mechanics

Vowel/Diphthong	Sound	Example
a	ā	ate
	ĭ	any
	ə	about
e	ĕ	every, ember
	ē	eject
i	ī	hide, aisle
o	ō	okay
u	ū	use, unique
ai	ā	aim
	ī	aisle
ea	ē	each
ei	ē	cither
ey	ī	eye
oa	ō	oat
oh	ō	oh
oi	oi	noise
oy	oi	oyster
ou	ow	out
yu	ū	yule

Similarly, you will find the dictionary of more use when you become aware of the letters that represent consonant sounds. Many consonants such as *b, d, f, j, k, l, m, n, p, q, r, t, v, w, y,* and *z* have more or less one sound they represent. However, other consonants represent more than one sound, as the following chart illustrates.

Consonant	Sound	Sample Word
c	s	ceiling
	k	creep
	(silent)	scent
g	g	give
	j	Gene
h	h	hole
	(silent)	ghost
s	s	stay
	sh	sure
t	t	tall
	sh	condition
w	w	wet
	(silent)	write
x	ks	exit
	z	Xerox

Instructors have varying requirements for preparing final-draft manuscripts. For example, many require that papers be typed, while others accept handwritten manuscripts. No matter what your instructor's standards are regarding a paper's final appearance, you should recognize the value of submitting a neat, attractive paper that follows the conventions of manuscript presentation. The audience for a piece of writing (whether a composition instructor or other readers) is more likely to give the paper's content careful attention if the appearance of the paper is pleasing, not alienating.

1. **Materials.** For typed papers, use high quality white bond paper, a standard 8½ by 11 inches. To make corrections, use correction fluid or tape whenever possible. Do not strike over letters. For handwritten papers, use white paper. Avoid paper torn out of a notebook. Double space the manuscript, whether you type or write.

2. **Margins.** Leave margins of 1 to 1½ inches at the top and left of the page and margins of at least 1 inch on the right and at the bottom. Make the right margins as even as possible.

3. **Ink.** If you do not type, write with a dark blue or black ink pen, not a pencil.

4. **Titles.** Do not underline or place in quotation marks the title of your own theme. Do not use a period after your title. It is acceptable, however, to use a question mark or an exclamation mark if the title is a question or an exclamation.

5. **Handwritten corrections.** Most instructors accept infrequent handwritten corrections even on final drafts. Draw a neat, single line through a word to be omitted. If another word is to replace it or if you are correcting a spelling error, write the correct word neatly above the lined-out one. Avoid lining out only parts of words. If you have inadvertently left out a word, use a caret (∧) to show where the omitted word should go, and write the word above the caret. Use the symbols ¶ (begin new paragraph) or no ¶ (no new paragraph) to indicate that you have made an error in paragraphing.

Capitalization

Observe the following capitalization rules in editing your final draft.

1. **Capitalize the first word of every sentence or of a fragment deliberately punctuated as a sentence.**

2. **In a title, do not capitalize articles (*a, an, the*), prepositions, or conjunctions of less than five letters unless these words begin or end the title or follow a semicolon or a colon. Capitalize all other words in the title.**

3. **Capitalize proper nouns (that is, names of specific people, places, and things) and adjectives made from proper nouns.** Examples of

proper nouns are names of specific people; names of towns, cities, states, countries, continents, planets; names of geographical regions; names of monuments; days of the week; months; historical events and movements; races and nationalities; religions and their followers; the word *God* or specific references to gods; organizations, associations, government departments; names of languages and names of holidays. Treat such words as *mother, father, grandmother,* and *grandfather* as proper nouns when they are used as names but not in phrases such as "my mother." Capitalize *uncle* and *aunt* when they precede a name: Uncle Jack, Aunt Carolyn.

4. **Capitalize titles (professor, doctor, and so forth) when they precede the name of the specific person: Professor Rhame, Dr. Stewart.**

Abbreviations

Use only recognized standard abbreviations. In general, abbreviations should be avoided in papers. The following kinds are acceptable, however.

1. **Title abbreviations when they occur with names:** Dr. Smith, Mrs. Jones, James Knots, D.D.S.

2. **Abbreviations of academic degree titles. Example:** She is working on her Ph.D.

3. **Abbreviations having to do with time**—A.M., P.M.; B.C., A.D.—are acceptable only with specific times and dates.

4. **Abbreviations or acronyms for names of countries, organizations, and corporations:** USA, CBS, FBI, YWCA, NATO.

5. **Latin abbreviations used in footnotes and bibliographies and in parenthetical comments:**

    cf. (compare)
    e.g. (for example)
    et al. (and others)
    etc. (and so forth)
    i.e. (that is)
    viz. (namely)

Numbers

1. **Spell out numbers that begin sentences.** Two hundred people attended the barbecue.

2. **Spell out numbers that can be written in one or two words.** The robbers escaped with five million dollars.

3. **Generally use figures in scientific and technical writing.** Note: Consult a style manual in your field for advice on using numbers in scientific or technical writing because conventions vary from one discipline to another.

Italic type is slanted type that appears in printed material for emphasis. In typed or handwritten manuscripts, italics are indicated by underlining. Use italics (underlining) for the following.

1. Titles of books, magazines, newspapers, journals, plays, films, long poems, long musical compositions, radio and television programs, and works of art. (See under Quotation Marks (pp. 364–366) for treatment of shorter works.)

2. Names of specific ships, planes, spacecraft, and trains.

3. Foreign words and expressions.

Hyphens

The hyphen (-), a shorter horizontal mark than the dash, is used in many compound words. It is also used for dividing words at the ends of lines. The following rules govern hyphens in compounds.

1. **Hyphenate compound adjectives before a noun.**

Examples   well-dressed man, well-bred dog, heart-to-heart talk

2. **Hyphenate compounds and compound adjectives made with the following prefixes even when they do not precede the noun:** self, all, quasi, half.

Examples   self-government, all-encompassing, quasi-legal, half-done

Word Division

Whenever possible, avoid word division by planning typed or written lines carefully. When dividing a word is necessary, follow the following guidelines.

1. **Do not divide one-syllable words.**

2. **Divide words only between syllables.**

3. **Do not hyphenate after a one-letter prefix** (for example, do not hyphenate a-bout).

4. **Avoid dividing a two-letter suffix (*-ly, -al, -le,* and so on) from the rest of a word.**

5. **Divide compound words only between the elements of the compound.**

6. **Generally, hyphenate between the prefix and the root or the root and the suffix.**

Chapter Fourteen

Review of Common Problems

In this chapter, we have outlined the most common problems our students have had with grammar and usage. The section concerning grammar we have divided into problems with sentences, verbs, pronouns, and modifiers, while the section concerning usage consists of an alphabetized list of troublesome words and phrases.

GRAMMATICAL PROBLEMS

Sentences

Comma Splice A comma splice occurs when two independent clauses are joined only by a comma. Independent clauses may be correctly joined by any of the following techniques: (1) comma plus coordinating conjunction, (2) semicolon, (3) semicolon plus transitional connective, for example, *however*.

Faulty sentence	I am not the best student in my class, then again, I'm not the worst.
Corrected	I am not the best student in my class, but I'm not the worst either.
	I am not the best student in my class; then again, I'm not the worst.

Run-on Sentence A *run-on sentence* (also called a fused sentence) is two or more independent clauses presented as one sentence with no punctuation between the two clauses that run together.

Examples

I am unhappy with my math class I can't understand the material.
Fred left yesterday for the West Coast he has a job with a San Francisco company.
I tried my best I could not do my homework.

The run-on sentence may be corrected in the following ways.

1. Make the two independent clauses into two separate sentences.

Fred left yesterday for the West Coast. He has a job with a San Francisco company.

2. Join the two independent clauses with a semicolon or a comma and a coordinating conjunction to make a compound sentence.

I tried my best, but I could not do my homework.
Fred left yesterday for the West Coast; he has a job with a San Francisco company.

3. Make one clause a dependent clause.

Although I tried my best, I could not do my homework.

Sentence Fragment A sentence fragment is a part of a sentence that is punctuated as if it were a complete sentence. Correct a sentence fragment by expanding it to become a complete sentence or by joining it to another sentence to become a logical part of that sentence.

Faulty sentence

I'll help you with the painting. As soon as I finish the dishes.

Corrected

I'll help you with the painting as soon as I finish the dishes.

Faulty sentence

He quit before he had finished. Feeling that the task was impossible.

Corrected

He quit before he had finished. It seemed that the task was impossible.

Parallel Structure Faulty structures result from joining unparallel structures by coordinating conjunctions which, by definition, join grammatical units that are parallel in structure. To correct unparallel structures, make sure units joined by coordinating conjunctions are alike in grammatical structure. In other words, join words to like words, phrases to like phrases, and clauses to like clauses.

Faulty sentence

Fraternities encourage students to undertake such projects as building homecoming floats and charity work.

Corrected

Fraternities encourage students to undertake such projects as building homecoming floats and doing charity work.

Faulty sentence

Don's hobbies are diving, dancing, and to go camping.

Corrected	Don's hobbies are diving, dancing, and camping.
Faulty sentence	When we went to Colorado, we not only hiked in the Rockies but were also enjoying the urban pleasures of Denver.
Corrected	When we went to Colorado, we not only hiked in the Rockies but also enjoyed the urban pleasures of Denver.

Incomplete Construction In incomplete constructions, part of the logical structure of the sentence is left out, leading to ambiguous or awkward sentences. Such sentences are easily corrected once the missing element is identified and supplied.

| *Faulty sentence* | Teachers often take composition more seriously than their students. |
| *Corrected* | Teachers often take composition more seriously than their students do. |

Faulty Predication Faulty predication is the error that results when a subject and predicate do not go together logically.

| *Faulty sentence* | The selection of the committee was chosen by the chairperson.
 (The chairperson did not choose the selection.) |
| *Corrected* | The committee was selected by the chairperson. |

Faulty Equation Faulty equations occur when linking verbs join items that are not logically equal. This problem can often be remedied by finding a more exact verb or by making the linked elements parallel.

Faulty sentence	A sonnet is when a poem has fourteen lines. (A sonnet is not a time, which *when* implies.)
Corrected	A sonnet is a poem that has fourteen lines. A sonnet has fourteen lines.
Faulty sentence	For twenty-five years my mother's job was a professor. (The job was not a teacher.)
Corrected	For twenty-five years, my mother was a professor.

Verbs

Subject/Verb Agreement A verb must agree with its subject in person and number. Singular subjects take singular verbs. Plural subjects take plural verbs. Here is a list of common problems.

1. Indefinite pronouns like *anybody, anyone, somebody, someone, either, neither, nobody,* and *no one* take singular verbs.

| *Example* | No one *is* going. |

2. Following subjects joined by *or* or *nor*, the verb agrees with the nearer subject.

Neither Tom nor the *girls are going* to accept the gift.
Neither the girls nor *Tom is going* to accept the gift.

3. The object of the preposition is not the subject of a verb even though it may be positioned closer to the verb than the subject.

The *leaves* of the oak tree *are* covering my yard.
The *sound* of voices singing in the shower *reaches* my ears.

Note: Some subjects take their number from the objects of prepositions.

Some of the cake *is* left.
Some of the boys *are* going to be on time for the meeting.

4. Phrases like *together with* or *as well as* and the nouns that follow them do not affect the number of the noun that is subject of the sentence in which they appear.

Mary, as well as her family, *enjoys* camping.
Joe, together with the boys, *has* gone to play golf.

5. When *there* appears at the beginning of a sentence, it is not the subject, and thus the verb does not agree with it.

There *is* only one *thing* to do.
There *are* several *reasons* for his failure.

Passive Voice Voice is a grammatical term which tells whether the subject of the verb is the doer of its action or the receiver of its action. There are two voices in English: active and passive. Only transitive verbs (that is, verbs which can take a direct object) change voice. Consider the difference between these two elementary sentences:

The cat caught the mouse.
The mouse was caught by the cat.

In the first, the subject *cat* does the catching; thus the verb is in the active voice. In the second the subject is being caught; thus the verb is in the passive voice.

The passive voice is formed by a form of the verb *to be* (for example, *was, were, will be, had been*) plus the past participle of a verb (usually indicated by *-ed* or *-en*, as in *marked* or *beaten*). This voice proves troublesome for writers because it can easily create dangling modifiers, as in this sentence:

Walking down the street, the house was burglarized.

This sentence says that the house was walking down the street, because the introductory participial phrase (*walking down the street*) modifies the subject of the sentence (*house*). But houses cannot walk, so we say that the modifier dangles, that it has no clear referent in the sentence. To correct this error, shift the voice of the verb to the active and add a subject the participial phrase can modify:

Walking down the street, I saw a burglar run from the house.

The passive voice may also create another problem in that the doer of a particular sentence's action may be hidden, as in this sentence: The window was broken. Who or what broke the window? A group of children playing baseball? A vandal? A falling tree limb? Because the passive construction (*was broken*) allows the receiver of the action to serve as the sentence's subject so that the sentence has a subject and predicate and can thus stand as a complete sentence, the doer of the action need not be named in the sentence.

This is not to say that you should avoid using passive voice; instead, you should choose the voice appropriate for your purpose. Consider these sentences:

Passive   An umbrella was left in the taxi.

Active   Somebody left an umbrella in the taxi.

Here the passive voice is more logical, since the emphasis should be placed on what was left in the taxi rather than on a vague "somebody" who left it.

Passive   The "Truth in Lending" bill was labelled "a farce, the biggest consumer ripoff in the history of the state."

Active   Jill Smith, Head of Governor Johnson's Consumer Protection Committee, labelled the "Truth in Lending" bill "a farce, the biggest consumer ripoff in the history of the state."

Here we are more concerned with who did the labelling, so the active voice is more appropriate.

Tense Shift   Many beginning writers have trouble with shifting tenses for no apparent reason. You should choose an appropriate tense for your writing and stick with it unless there is a definite reason for shifting to another tense. Be especially careful of tense when writing about literature and films. Usually, the present tense is used when discussing historical facts of an author's life or when relating events in a work.

Examples   In "Ode On A Grecian Urn," Keats writes. . . .
Early in their relationship, Huckleberry Finn plays numerous tricks on Jim.
In the film *Sophie's Choice*, Meryl Streep portrays a Polish immigrant who has survived Auschwitz.
Historian Henry Steele Commanger says. . . .

Sequence of Tenses   Be sure that the tenses of verbs in dependent clauses are in logical sequence with the verbs in main clauses.

Examples

illogical   Since she has done her homework consistently, she did well on the tests.

logical   Since she had done her homework consistently, she did well on the tests.

Pronouns

Pronoun Reference **Agreement**   A pronoun reference agreement error occurs when a pronoun does not agree in number with its antecedent. This error may be corrected by changing the number of the pronoun or the antecedent. (Where possible, it is advisable to make antecedents plural to avoid awkwardness caused by the gender of singular pronouns.)

Faulty sentence   A student must study diligently if they want to succeed in college.

Corrected   Students must study diligently if they want to succeed in college.

Vague Pronoun Reference   A vague pronoun reference error occurs when the antecedent of a pronoun is not clear. Three basic problems occur from failure to make antecedents clear: (1) the pronoun has no antecedent, (2) the antecedent is ambiguous, or (3) the antecedent is vague; that is, the pronoun refers to a whole idea rather than to one word.

Faulty sentence   She had always thought about becoming a teacher because it seemed to be an enjoyable profession.

Corrected   She had always thought teaching would be an enjoyable profession.

Faulty sentence   Uncle John took Tommy to the movies because he was bored.
(Who was bored, Tommy or Uncle John?)

Corrected   Since Tommy was bored, Uncle John took him to the movies.

Faulty sentence   William had always liked camping, fishing, and other outdoor sports, which pleased his dad.
(What pleased the father, the sports or William's liking them?)

Corrected   William's fondness for camping, fishing, and other outdoor sports pleased his dad.

Pronoun Case   A pronoun case error occurs when the writer fails to understand the concepts of subjective and objective case. If a pronoun appears in a subjective case position, the subjective pronoun form must be used regardless of the colloquial acceptability of the objective form in that slot. As indicated earlier, using objective case forms in subjective slots is a major pronoun case error. However, many errors are caused by overcorrection, that is, by putting subjective forms into slots that actually require the objective form.

Faulty sentence   Me and John went to the play.

Corrected   John and I went to the play.

Faulty sentence   I don't know who you saw at the game.

Corrected   I don't know whom you saw at the game.

Faulty sentence   Between you and I, I do not trust that man.

Corrected   Between you and me, I do not trust that man.

Dangling Modifier A dangling modifier is a phrase, usually a verbal phrase, which has nothing that it can logically modify. To correct the dangling modifier, supply a word or phrase that the modifier can work with.

Faulty sentence	To succeed in today's business world, a college degree is necessary. (A college degree cannot succeed.)
Corrected	To succeed in today's business world, one needs a college degree.

Misplaced Modifier A misplaced modifier is a word, a phrase, or a clause which is placed in the sentence so that it seems to modify something that it does not or should not modify. To correct such a modifier, move it so its purpose is clear.

Faulty sentence	Climbing up the wall, I saw the spider. (Who is climbing up the wall, the speaker or the spider?)
Corrected	I saw the spider climbing up the wall.

COMMON USAGE PROBLEMS

adapt, adept, adopt These three words are easily confused. *Adapt* is a verb meaning to change for a purpose: "He adapted the text to meet the needs of his students." *Adept* is an adjective meaning competent or able: "She is adept at mountain climbing." *Adopt* is a verb meaning to claim as one's own: "They plan to adopt a child in the next year or two."

adverse, averse Both of these similar words are adjectives. *Adverse* means unfortunate, difficult, or unfavorable: "Adverse conditions in the job market affect the lives of many young people." *Averse* means not inclined to accept: "My teacher is averse to my suggestions for improving class discussions."

alumna, alumnae, alumnus, alumni These words come to English from Latin and retain their Latin endings. *Alumna—alumnae* are singular and plural forms meaning female graduate or graduates. *Alumnus* means male graduate, and its plural form is *alumni*. Increasingly, however, *alumni* is becoming accepted as a plural form meaning graduates of either sex.

amoral, immoral *Amoral* means neither moral nor immoral or not susceptible to moral judgments. *Immoral* means violating principles of what is right.

apiece, a piece *Apiece* is an adverb meaning for each. *A piece* is a noun preceded by the article *a*: "These children were given a piece of candy apiece."

as . . . as, so . . . as In formal writing *as . . . as* is preferred for positive statements and *so . . . as* for negative statements. "He is as fine a man as I have ever met." "I am not so energetic as I used to be." This distinction has largely disappeared in speech and informal writing, however.

awful, awfully *Awful* is an adjective; *awfully* is a colloquial adverb meaning *very*. The two should not be confused as in the following incorrect usage: "I'm awful glad to see you."

a, an *A* precedes nouns beginning with consonant sounds: a tree, a bush. *An* is used before nouns beginning with vowel sounds: an angel, an orange.

accept, except *Accept* means to receive what is offered or to agree to: "I accept your proposal." *Except* as a verb means to exclude: "I will except him from this requirement." As a preposition, except means excluding: "I've invited everyone except Tom."

affect, effect *Affect* is usually used as a verb meaning to change or to influence: "Your opinion will affect my decision." *Effect* is usually used as a noun meaning result: "Her criticism has no effect on me." *Effect* can also be a verb meaning to accomplish: "The student protest effected no change in the school policy."

and etc. *Etc.* is an abbreviation of the Latin words *et cetera*, which mean and so forth. As an abbreviation, etc. should be avoided in formal writing. *And etc.* should always be avoided because it is redundant.

access, excess *Access* means admittance or the ability to see or to obtain: "Do you have access to student records?" *Excess* means too much or beyond the limits of the normal: "Excess sugar can cause health problems."

advice, advise *Advice* is a noun: "I will take your advice." *Advise* is a verb: "I advise you to stay in school."

all together, altogether *All together* means all with one another, all in the same place: "It will be good to have the family all together again." *Altogether* is an adverb meaning entirely: "I am not altogether responsible for this problem."

among, between *Among* refers to more than two: "Among my many friends, she is the kindest." *Between* refers to only two: "Between the two of us, we will get the job done."

amount, number *Amount* describes the quantity of something that exists in the mass and cannot be counted: "Tomatoes require a large amount of water to grow well." *Number* indicates the quantity of things that can be counted: "A small number of people came to the game."

a lot This phrase is overworked and probably best avoided. However, if it is used, it is spelled as two words, not as *alot*.

at (used redundantly) *At* is often used to end sentences when it is not needed. Example: "Where do you buy your groceries at?" In this sentence *where* already means at what place.

ain't This word is a nonstandard contraction of am not, is not, or are not: I ain't, he ain't, they ain't. Since many people associate this word with total illiteracy, avoid it in formal writing.

alright This is a common misspelling of all right.

all ready, already *All ready* means completely ready: "We have packed and are all ready to leave." *Already* means before expected: "Is she here already?"

bad, badly *Bad* is an adjective; *badly* is an adverb. The adjective is often used when the adverb is called for as in: "He swims bad." After the verbs *feel, look,* and *seem,* the adjective *bad* should be used: "I feel bad." Not, "I feel badly."

beside, besides *Beside* means by the side of: "His wife stayed beside him the whole time he was unconscious." *Besides* means (1) "moreover," "further," and (2) "in addition to": "Besides, you don't really need to go." (3) "Besides you, John is the only other one going."

between you and I This is a common pronoun case error. Since the pronouns are the objects of the preposition *between*, the objective form, *me*, should be used: "Between you and me, I think this party is a real bore."

can't hardly This phrase is a nonstandard version of can hardly, a phrase that is close in meaning to a double negative. The *not* in *can't* negates the hardly.

capital, capitol *Capitol* refers to the buildings that house state and national governments. Consult a dictionary for the various uses of the word *capital*.

censor, censure *Censor* means to judge whether something is acceptable or, in current usage, to delete or cut out: "He had the job of censoring books for the government." "Part of this movie has been censored." *Censure* means to judge unfavorably and to rebuke: "The Congressman was censured for his statements about the national crisis."

centers on, centers around *Centers on* is preferred because *centers around*, which means focuses around, is illogical.

cite, site, sight *Cite* is a verb meaning to refer to: "Have you cited this article in your paper?" *Site* is a noun meaning location: "We explored the site of the new school." *Sight* means something seen: "I cannot bear the sight of a hungry child."

close proximity This is a redundant phrase, as proximity means closeness to.

complement, compliment Both these words can be used as nouns or verbs. *Complement* as a noun means completion: "That tie is the perfect complement to your suit." As a verb, it means to complete or go with: "That hat complements your suit beautifully." *Compliment* as a noun means a statement of praise: "My boss gave me a very nice compliment on my work today." As a verb, it means to praise: "The teacher complimented the student on her introductory paragraph."

conscience, conscientious, conscious *Conscience* is a noun meaning a sense of right and wrong: "My conscience is bothering me about my absences from class." *Conscientious* is an adjective meaning scrupulous or morally upright: "She is conscientious about her work." *Conscious* is an adjective meaning aware: "I am not conscious of any problem between us."

continual, continuous *Continual* refers to repeated action: "I am tired of the continual interruptions to my work." *Continuous* refers to actions that are never ceasing: "The continuous buzzing of the chain saw gave me a headache."

could of This phrase is the vernacular for *could have.*

counsel, council *Counsel* means advice or to advise: "Thank you for your wise counsel." *Council* means a ruling or deliberative body of people: "She is on the city council."

credible, creditable, credulous *Credible* means believable: "Your excuse is not credible." *Creditable* means worthy of credit or commendable: "You have done a creditable job on this paper." *Credulous* means gullible or easily believing: "Only a credulous person would accept your excuse."

criterion, criteria *Criterion* is singular; *criteria* is plural: One criterion, *but* several criteria.

datum, data *Datum* is the singular form; *data* is the plural form. Even though data is rapidly gaining acceptability as a singular form, to be safe, you should write "data are."

decent, descent *Decent* is an adjective meaning good, or behaving in a kind manner: "The senator is a decent human being." *Descent* is a noun meaning downward motion: "During his descent into hell, Dante was accompanied by the poet Virgil."

desert, dessert *Desert*, with the accent on the first syllable, is a noun meaning dry, sandy expanse. *Dessert* is a sweet served at the end of a meal.

desert With the accent on the second syllable, *desert* is a verb meaning to abandon: "After drilling for water for two months with no luck, Panhandle Slim deserted his homestead and moved on."

device, devise A *device* is a machine or instrument designed to perform some action: "The car contained a hidden tracking device." To *devise* is to plan or to create: "See if you can devise a way to cut the cost of tuition."

different from, different than *Different from* is generally the preferred American usage, although *different than*, from the British, is rapidly gaining acceptance because it calls for fewer words to complete a sentence: "Tom's ideas are different from those held by Mary"; "Tom's ideas are different than Mary's."

disinterested, uninterested *Disinterested* means impartial: "I will submit his argument to a disinterested party for a decision." *Uninterested* means lacking in interest: "I am uninterested in your reasons for that decision."

double negatives Some kinds of double negative statements are acceptable in educated speech and writing: "I am not unwilling to help you." Here the writer means that he is somewhat willing to help. However, two negatives cannot be used to convey a negative idea in edited American English: "I haven't done nothing wrong." Both *haven't* and *nothing* contain negative elements and thus cannot be used together in standard English if the speaker intends a negative assertion. The correct phrasing is: "I haven't done anything wrong."

elicit, illicit *Elicit* is a verb meaning to draw out or to provoke: "I am trying to elicit discussion from my students when I present controversial material." *Illicit* means illegal: "He should be jailed for his illicit activities."

emigrant, immigrant An *emigrant* is a person who leaves a country; an *immigrant* is one who comes to a country. The same distinction applies to the verbs *emigrate* and *immigrate*.

famous, notorious Both words mean well known, but *famous* has favorable connotations whereas *notorious* has unfavorable connotations: a famous war hero, *but* a notorious war criminal.

farther, further Traditionally, *farther* is used to refer to distance: "He ran farther than his brother." *Further* refers to degree: "We will discuss this problem further." *Further* can also be an adjective meaning additional: "If you need further help, I'll be in my office this afternoon."

fewer, less The distinction between fewer and less is like the distinction between number and amount. *Fewer* is used for countable objects; *less*, for uncountable substances: fewer people, *but* less water.

flunk This is a colloquial substitute for fail.

formally, formerly *Formally* means in a formal way: "The old man sat formally on the park bench, talking with the pigeons." *Formerly* means previously: "She formerly starred in two movies and a mini-series before becoming a news analyst."

good, well *Good* is an adjective; *well* is an adverb: "John feels good," "Bill plays tennis well."

hanged, hung The past participle of *hang* when it refers to a form of killing someone is *hanged*: "The murderer will be hanged at dawn." For other uses of the verb *hang*, use *hung* as the past participle and the past tense form: "We have always hung our coats on that rack beside the door." "We hung the picture over the spot where the paint was chipping."

he or she Traditionally *he* has been used generically to mean either male or female: "The student must decide how much he should study each night." Now, however, there is growing objection to this generic usage. The problem may be solved by using *he or she*: "The student must decide how much he or she should study each night." However, this addition tends to make writing wordy and awkward. Another solution is to make both subject and pronoun plural: "Students must decide how much they should study each night." Still another way of avoiding any sexist implications of the generic *he* is to use *he*'s and *she*'s in roughly equal numbers throughout a piece of writing. (This is the solution we used in this textbook.) When doing this, make sure to avoid automatic sexual stereotyping: the female telephone operator or secretary, the male lawyer or postal delivery person.

healthy, healthful Both words are adjectives, but *healthy* means in good health; *healthful*, on the other hand, means promoting good health: "Mary is healthy because she eats healthful foods."

hidden meaning This phrase is often used as a synonym for symbolic meaning, especially in analyses of literary works. The two phrases are not synonymous, however. If the writer discovers the symbolic meaning, then it is not hidden.

illicit, elicit See *elicit, illicit.*

imply, infer *Imply* means to suggest a meaning: "The advertisement implies that all users of Blimpo Detergent will be healthy, wealthy, and wise." *Infer* means to draw a conclusion: "From what you have said about the sports programs at large universities, I infer that you would want your son to play for a small school."

in, into *In* indicates location: "He was in the classroom." *Into* indicates direction: "He came into the classroom."

inside of, outside of, off of The *of* is superfluous in each of these examples: "The guests inside of the house were startled when they heard the chimney fall off." "The chimney fell off of the house."

irregardless This word is a nonstandard version of *regardless.*

is when, is where These expressions are best avoided, especially in definitions. Faulty usage: "A tragedy is when the hero has a tragic flaw in his character." Acceptable usage: "A tragedy is a play in which the hero has a tragic flaw in his character."

its, it's *Its* is the possessive case form of *it*: "Give the dog its food." *It's* is a contraction meaning *it is*: "It's like summer out today."

kind of, sort of These are colloquial expressions best avoided in formal writing.

later, latter *Later* is the opposite of earlier and refers to time: "He is later than usual today." *Latter* is the opposite of former and means the second of two: "I preferred the latter of the two movies."

lend, loan *Lend* is the preferred verb form meaning to offer temporary use of: "Please lend me the money for supper." *Loan* is the noun form of the verb: "I am arranging a loan from the bank."

less, fewer See *fewer, less*.

loose, lose *Loose* is an adjective meaning not tight: "That muffler certainly has a loose fit." *Lose* is a verb meaning to misplace: "Did you lose your mittens?"

many, much *Many* is used for countable things; *much*, for quantities of things uncountable: many rivers, *but* much water.

may be, maybe *May be* is a verb phrase suggesting possibility: "I may be there on Friday." *Maybe* is an adverb suggesting possibility: "Maybe John will do the chore for you."

moral, morale *Moral* can be a noun meaning ethical lesson, as in: "The moral of the story is clear." Or it can be an adjective meaning ethically right, as in: "He is certainly a moral person." *Morale* is a noun meaning state of mind, as in: "The morale of the team was so high that the coach felt certain of victory."

nauseated, nauseous *Nauseous* means sickening, as in: "a nauseous odor." *Nauseated* means sick to the stomach, as in: "I am nauseated." "I am nauseous" could technically be taken to mean: "I make other people sick."

nowheres This is a nonstandard form of *nowhere*.

passed, past *Passed* is the past participle of the verb to pass: "I passed all my courses." *Past* is a noun or adjective referring to time before the present: "In the past we have gone over to grandmother's on Sundays."

persecute, prosecute Both are verbs. *Persecute* means to treat wrongly and unfairly over a period of time: "The early Christians were often persecuted for their beliefs." *Prosecute* means to take legal action against: "The victim decided not to prosecute the young boy who had stolen her purse."

phenomenon, phenomena *Phenomenon* is the singular form; *phenomena* is plural: one phenomenon, *but* six phenomena.

precede, proceed *Precede* means to go before: "The Compromise of 1850 preceded the Civil War." *Proceed* means to go on with: "You may proceed with your work."

quiet, quite *Quiet* is an adjective meaning silent: "It certainly is quiet in this old house." *Quite* is an adverb meaning very: "That movie is quite good."

reason is because This phrase is redundant. A preferred phrase is: reason is that.

rise, raise *Rise* is an intransitive verb that does not take an object: "We expect that the cost of our product will rise during the next year." *Raise* is a transitive verb that takes an object: "Efforts to raise the sunken ship have failed."

real, really *Real* is an adjective meaning (1) actual or (2) true: (1) "The speaker has a real sense of timing." (2) "This is the real thing, all right." *Really* is an adverb meaning truly or actually: "It really is a good play"; "It's a really good play." Avoid the colloquial use of *real:* "I was really happy," not "I was real happy."

refer back *Refer* means to go back to, so this phrase is redundant.

rite, right *Rite* means ritual or ceremony as in sacred rite. Consult your dictionary for the various meanings of *right*.

should of *Should of* is often mistakenly used for the verb phrase *should have:* "I should have gone to town yesterday."

their, there, they're *Their* is the possessive form of the pronoun they. *They're* is a contraction meaning they are. *There* is an adverb: "They're soon going to leave their house to go over there."

theirselves This is a nonstandard form of *themselves*.

to, too, two *To* is a preposition or a part of the infinitive form of a verb: "to go, to see." *Too* means also. *Two* is the number 2: "Two children went to see a movie. Their mother went too."

try and, try to *Try and* is sometimes used colloquially to mean try to: "I'll try and come to the meeting." The preferred form would be: "I'll try to come to the meeting."

Review of Common Problems

wait on, wait for The colloquial use of *wait on* to mean wait for should be avoided. "I'll wait for the doctor," not, "I'll wait on the doctor."

who, which, that *Who* refers to people. *Which* refers to things, animals, and ideas. *That* may refer to people, animals, things, and ideas.

Review of the Parts of Speech

NOUNS

Nouns are words that name something—a person, a place, a thing, a state of being, an abstract idea or quality. In the following sentence, all the nouns are italicized.

The *scholar* sat on the *bench* thinking about *truth* and *beauty*.

The form of a noun, which indicates how the noun functions in a phrase, clause, or sentence, is labeled by the term *case*. In English, there are three cases: *subjective*, *objective*, and *possessive*. If a noun functions as the subject of a clause or sentence, it is in the subjective case; if it functions as an object, it is in the objective case; if it shows possession, it is in the possessive case.

PRONOUNS

Pronouns are words that stand for or take the place of nouns. Like nouns, they may serve as subjects and objects in phrases, clauses, and sentences, though unlike nouns pronouns do not name specific things, persons, actions, or qualities. The noun to which a pronoun refers and from which the pronoun takes its specific meaning is called the pronoun's *antecedent*. The phrase *pronoun reference* is used by grammarians to describe the relationship between a pronoun and its antecedent.

Personal Pronouns

The following list of English pronouns depicts their various forms:

	Singular			Plural		
	subjective	*objective*	*possessive*	*subjective*	*objective*	*possessive*
1st pers.	I	me	my, mine	we	us	our, ours
2nd pers.	you	you	your, yours	you	you	your, yours
3rd pers. m.	he	him	his	they	them	their, theirs
fem.	she	her	her, hers			
neuter	it	it	its			

Relative Pronouns

Subjective	*Objective*	*Possessive*
who	whom	whose
that	that	
which	which	whose

Interrogative Pronouns

Subjective	*Objective*	*Possessive*
who	whom	whose
which	which	whose
what	what	

Demonstrative Pronouns

this, that, these, those

Indefinite Pronouns

all	another	any	anybody	anyone
anything	both	each	either	everybody
everyone	everything	few	many	most
much	neither	nobody	none	no one
nothing	one	other	several	some
somebody	someone	something	such	

Reflexive (Intensive) Pronouns

	Singular	*Plural*
1st person	myself	ourselves
2nd person	yourself	yourselves
3rd person	himself	themselves
	herself	
	itself	
	oneself	

Reciprocal Pronouns

each other, one another

VERBS

Verbs have often been referred to as action words. In this simple sentence, "The child ran," for example, the verb *ran* describes the child's action. Not all verbs, however, are action words; many express a state of being, process, or condition. Verbs are classified as either transitive or intransitive. Transitive verbs may take a direct object, but intransitive verbs may not. Depending on their context, some verbs can be transitive or intransitive:

	verb direct object
Transitive:	The pitcher threw the ball.
Intransitive:	The pitcher threw as hard as he could.

ADJECTIVES

Adjectives modify nouns and pronouns. In the following sentence, the adjectives are italicized.

The *old, green* car sat on the *cracked* driveway.

In some sentences, demonstrative, indefinite, and interrogative pronouns may function as adjectives insofar as they modify nouns: "*that* coat," "*all* coats," "*which* coat." For comparison, adjectives have three forms: positive, comparative, and superlative.

Positive	Comparative	Superlative
quick	quicker	quickest
beautiful	more beautiful	most beautiful

ADVERBS

Adverbs modify verbs, adjectives, and other adverbs: "They walked *slowly* down the street." "The sunset is *perfectly* beautiful tonight." "The team played *particularly* well in its last game." Adverbs are most commonly used to express time, place, manner, negation, affirmation, or degree. Although by no means do all adverbs end in *ly*, this is a common adverb marker. Many adverbs are formed by adding *ly* to an adjective form: pretty/prettily, lawful/lawfully, probable/probably. Those adverbs identical in form with corresponding adjectives form their comparative and superlative degrees by adding *er* and *est:* far, farther, farthest. Other adverbs use *more* and *most* to show degree: more slowly, most slowly.

PREPOSITIONS

Prepositions are words that show the relationship between a noun or pronoun (the object of the preposition) and some other word in the sentence. Among the most common prepositions are these: *in, out, on, up, down, under, around, through, after, above, until, among,* and *below.*

CONJUNCTIONS

Conjunctions, like prepositions, join elements of the sentence—either words, phrases, or clauses—to each other and show relationships in the sentence. Unlike prepositions, conjunctions do not take objects. There are two kinds of conjunctions: *coordinating* (for joining equal grammatical elements) and *subordinating* (for joining a subordinate or dependent grammatical part of a sentence to a main clause). The coordinating conjunctions include *and, but, or, nor, for, yet,* and *so.* In addition to these are the correlative conjunctions that join words, phrases, or clauses: *both/and, neither/nor, either/or, not/but,* and *not only/but also.* Among the most common subordinating conjunctions, which appear at the beginning of the dependent phrase or clause they introduce, are these: *that, whether, if, when, though, although, after, while, whereas, because, since, unless,* and *in order that.*

INTERJECTIONS

Interjections are words that exist only to express strong feeling, and they have no syntactical connection with other parts of the sentences in which they appear. Sometimes they are punctuated as part of a sentence, but often they stand alone, punctuated by an exclamation point:

> *Ouch,* I cut my finger!
> *Ouch!* That limb flew in my face!

Some words such as *ouch, whew,* and *oh* exist only as interjections. But many words that are commonly other parts of speech can be used as interjections, including *great, well, gracious, goodness,* and *my.*

Revision Strategies

1. Put your writing aside for at least three or four hours before you begin revising it.

2. Write a second draft of your writing without rereading the first draft. Then compare the two drafts to find what you think is important about the topic.

3. Write at least three complete drafts (two rough drafts and one final draft) of all out-of-class assignments.

4. Identify your purpose in writing. Justify every word, sentence, and paragraph in light of that purpose.

5. Put yourself in your reader's place. Try to read from your audience's perspective, anticipating what questions your readers could ask, what information they need from you, and at what points they might agree and disagree with you.

6. When you begin revising, read the entire piece of writing without marking anything. Then reread it, this time taking notes and marking necessary changes.

7. Get an outside reader. Either have a friend read your paper or establish a reading group composed of other students in your writing class. Meet with your group to talk through your paper, before and while you write and after you have written each draft.

8. Read your writing aloud, and record your reading. Then play the recording while you read the piece of writing. Have a friend read your writing aloud to you.

9. When you reach a "stuck point" in revising, back up a paragraph or two and read from that point through the stuck point. Take notes about whatever possibilities for revision occur to you.

10. Freewrite to generate additional information or when you reach a stuck point.